Mihailo Crnobrnja, official of the former Yugoslav government and
former Yugoslavian ambassador to the European Communities,
addresses the unfolding drama in Yugoslavia and its possible resolution in the Dayton Accord. He begins by explaining the complexities of the country – both those external to the political process and
those which derive from it – and their contribution to cracks in the
political structure in the pre-Tito and Tito years. The gradually accel-
erated deterioration of the federation and the political forces that
fostered this process, particularly the politically motivated encouragement of nationalism and the absence of democracy, are chronicled
and analysed to uncover the dynamics that converted a stable, prosperous country into a Balkan powder-keg.

Crnobrnja discusses in detail the part of the drama most visible to
the world – the rapid dissolution of the country following civil war
and internationalization. He emphasizes the dichotomy between the
lack of compromise among the Yugoslav participants and the natural tendency to compromise that characterizes both the European
Communities and the processes and actions of the United Nations
and shows how important the participation of the United States has
been to achieving a peace accord.

In a synthesis of the immediate situation he draws together the
threads of the story to consider and analyse possible future scenarios and place them in a broader Balkan and European context.

MIHAILO CRNOBRNJA is former ambassador of Yugoslavia to the
European Communities. He works in Montreal as an economic and
political consultant and teaches political science at McGill University.

The Yugoslav Drama

MIHAILO CRNOBRNJA

Second Edition

McGill-Queen's University Press
Montreal & Kingston • London • Ithaca

© McGill-Queen's University Press 1996
ISBN 0-7735-1429-5

Legal deposit second quarter 1996
Bibliothèque nationale du Québec

First edition published 1994

Published simultaneously in Great Britain
by I.B. Tauris & Co Ltd

Printed in Canada on acid-free paper
Reprinted 2002

McGill-Queen's University Press acknowledges the support
of the Canada Council for the Arts for our publishing
program. We also acknowledge the financial support of the
Government of Canada through the Book Publishing
Industry Development Program (BPIDP) for our publishing
activities.

Canadian Cataloguing in Publication Data

Crnobrnja, Mihailo
    The Yugoslav drama
    2nd ed.
    Includes bibliographical references and index.
    ISBN 0-7735-1429-5
    1. Yugoslavia – Politics and government – 1945–1992.
    2. Yugoslavia – Politics and government – 1992–   .
    3. Yugoslavia – History – 1980–1992. 4. Yugoslavia –
    History – 1992–   5. Yugoslav War, 1991–   .
    I. Title.
    DR1313.C75 1996   949.702'4   C95-920926-3

Typeset in Palatino 10/12 by Caractéra inc.,
Quebec City

To my wife, Gordana, and son, Lav,
who lost a country
and
To Richard Lewis,
a friend in need

Contents

Maps   ix

Preface   xi

Preface to the Second Edition   xv

Introduction   3

PART ONE: THE STAGE

1   A Country of Diversity   15

2   Origins of the Idea and the State   35

3   Inter-War Instability   51

4   The Tito Years   65

PART TWO: THE ACTORS

5   Tito's Successors   81

6   The New Wave of Serbian Nationalism   93

7   Slovenia and Croatia: The Drive to
Independence   107

8   The Supporting Cast   115

PART THREE: THE PLOT

9   Changes in Europe   131

10   The Crisis   141

11   The War in Slovenia and Croatia   160

viii Contents

12 The War in Bosnia and Herzegovina 174

13 The European Community Steps In 189

14 A Call for Blue Helmets 205

PART FOUR: THE FINAL CURTAIN

15 Drawing the Threads Together 223

16 The Balkan Endgame 239

17 Is There a Solution? 250

18 A Chance for Peace at Last 266

Notes 285

Further Readings 295

Index 297

Maps

1   The Socialist Federative Republic of
    Yugoslavia, 1945–92   16

2   The impact of empires on the future
    Yugoslavia   18

3   The ethnic mix in Bosnia before the war;
    the division of Bosnia according to the
    Vance-Owen Plan; the division of Bosnia
    according to the Owen-Stoltenberg
    Plan   216

Preface

The unfolding of the Yugoslav Drama occurred while I was representing the country as ambassador to the European Community. I was therefore constantly faced with the need to answer, officially and unofficially, a host of questions: What went wrong? Was Yugoslavia an artificial country? How could a country with the respect Yugoslavia commanded turn into a nightmare with so much hatred and sorrow? Where does the immense hatred come from? How is it possible to have an ethnic war in Europe at the end of the twentieth century? When and how will it all end?

The questions were simple enough, the answers difficult. I found myself probing deeper and deeper, trying to find fuller yet understandable explanations both for myself and for those who asked. The results of this search gradually accumulated. The fact that I was a participant in the Peace Conference on Yugoslavia while it took place in The Hague in 1991 was an added stimulus to try to combine this political experience with my personal searching for answers.

This book is intended to arouse the curiosity of those readers who have, over the past few years, listened to bad and sad news, seen pictures of horror and destruction, wondered about the forces that brought such agony to a people. With so much exposure and coverage, it is not surprising that many think they now know the reasons for the Yugoslav drama. This book should help to transform their knowledge into understanding.

I have also tried to keep the explanation as simple as the complex phenomena that I am explaining would permit. From the very first moment that the idea to write a book crystallized in my mind, it did so in the form of a slight volume, a "weekend book" that could be read fast and would not tax the patience of the interested reader too much.

Working within such limits made the difficult issue of maintaining objectivity even more difficult, since I typically do not present to the reader different views and interpretations of events, thus letting her or him be the judge. I attempt to internalize the criteria of objectivity by not taking sides and honestly and strictly adhering to a set of guidelines, the application of which could, in my view, have headed off the drama or at least made it significantly smaller and easier to bear. The story I offer to the public is, therefore, a personal account, a personal view.

I have chosen to cast this book in four parts that would follow the logic of the title. The title was, in a way, forced upon me by events, rather than a matter of deliberate selection. I would hope that the reader will find this type of presentation not only suitable and valid but also a helpful framework for understanding the problems.

The first part of the book informs the reader about the complexities of Yugoslavia, those that are external to the political process as well as those that derive from it. This is done as concisely as possible, to prepare the stage rather than to provide an elaborate and comprehensive history. The main purpose of this part of the text is to show how this complex state was created and where the "cracks in the structure" developed in the pre-Tito and Tito years.

The second part deals with the post-Tito years. It describes and explains the gradual but ever faster deterioration of the federation, and the centrifugal political forces that fostered this process. It also deals with the gradual internalization of the crisis. The main purpose of this part is to uncover the political mechanics and dynamics of converting a respected, stable, and relatively prosperous country into a new Balkan powder-keg. The determinants of this political dynamic were the presence and pressure of nationalism and the absence of democracy.

The third part of the book deals with the final stage of the drama, the rapid dissolution of the country, the culmination of the crisis, and the civil war. In other words, it deals with the part of the drama that has been most visible in the media. This phase is also the time during which the Yugoslav drama became internationalized. Its internationalization is dealt with in greater detail, with particular emphasis on the dichotomy between the Yugoslav actors' resistance to compromise, which prevented and still prevents a solution, and the natural tendency to compromise that characterizes the procedures and actions of both the European Community and the United Nations.

The final part of the book synthesizes the situation as of the autumn of 1993. At that time the drama was far from over. As this book went to press, the war in Bosnia was still on, and all the former republics of Yugoslavia, with the probable exception of Slovenia, faced the tragic reality of more bloody and destructive warfare. The Hague Conference on Yugoslavia had not produced any visible results. The concluding chapters here draw together the threads of the previous account and discuss and analyse various scenarios for the future, primarily from the point of view of their likelihood. The potential solutions are also put into a broader Balkan and European context, since the previous analysis will, I hope, have shown the dependence of Yugoslav internal relations on outside events and politics.

I faced two kinds of problems in presenting this material in drama form. The first was the delineation of the parts, especially the need to distinguish between the "actors" and the "plot." The boundary between these two parts is very fuzzy and the demarcation I have made is admittedly rather arbitrary. My criterion was the acceleration of the process of dissolution: when it reached the point of no return is the moment when the Plot starts.

The other problem with this type of presentation, a problem that could be described as nominal rather than one of substance, is the lack of a director. Any drama on a stage needs a director. In real life one is not always available. I find it important to state this clearly because there are many in Yugoslavia who are firm believers in the conspiracy theory according to which the breakdown of the country and thus the Yugoslav drama was stage-managed by a small group of external powers or "directors" who wanted the country to be destroyed. My view is that the evolution of this particular drama had many directors, outside and inside the country. So rather than look for and uncover a grand scheme with a grand director, I have concentrated my efforts on the complex dynamics of the internal and external forces that brought about the crisis.

I owe a great debt of gratitude to people who encouraged me and helped me along the way, in particular to Richard Lewis and Daniel Gueguen, who selflessly and generously edited the English and French versions of the text. Their professional skill and their friendship are immensely appreciated. I hereby thank my father for his valuable personal insights, Rada and Zvonko Rechter for provoking the challenge of writing this book, Iraj Hoshi for reading the manuscript and providing many helpful suggestions, Tom and Irena Snyder, Gordon Smith, Madlene Feher, and Pericles Argyris for pointing out the direction of necessary search. I take this opportunity to thank two anonymous reviewers, whose valuable comments and suggestions improved the text. Dan Voudrin's masterful guidance led me through the maze of WordPerfect, and I am very grateful to him. Last but not least I must thank my wife, Gordana, and son, Lav, for their patience with me during the many hours I spent researching and writing this volume.

As is usual, I take full responsibility for the final outcome, though it would certainly not be as good without those I have mentioned. I hope that the reader will find the account interesting, frank, and unbiased, even though I readily admit that I am far from detached from the subject of my exposition – the unfolding Yugoslav drama.

Preface to the Second Edition

The second edition of a book is always a good opportunity to revise or update the story being told. *The Yugoslav Drama* is no exception. While I find little reason to revise the original text, which attempts to explain the roots and the unfolding of the drama until the time the book went to press, the fact that two years have passed, during which time significant events have taken place, makes an updating absolutely necessary.

The story as I told it in the first edition combined a chronological account with analysis, comment, and reflections on possible future scenarios. Bringing the original text up to date within the existing structure would have involved a number of interventions in several different parts of the existing text, which in turn would have caused technical problems.

I have resolved the problem by adding a new chapter, one that covers the most important events from the time at which the original text ended until the signing of the peace agreement in December of 1995. This new chapter also integrates analysis, comment, and reflections on the future. In this way I was able to preserve both the continuity of the story and the way it is told, with what I hope is minimal inconvenience for the reader.

Introduction

The Yugoslav Drama tells the story of national awakening and the victory of aggressive nationalism. It reveals how a state with a distinguished place among the nations of the world, a respectable track record on economic development, and certainly a considerable level of internal stability, came apart as a consequence of conflicting national ideologies and policies among the principal actors in the drama. It shows the circumstances and environment in which aggressive nationalism led to the dismantling of a country and a vicious and bloody civil war.

Since nationalism is the moving spirit of the drama, if not its principal actor, the first order of business is to introduce the notion of nationalism as it is used later in this book.[1]

Nationalism is an amplified expression of a national awakening and consequent national movement towards attainment of certain goals. National awakening and consequent national movements are in themselves neither bad nor destructive. Typically the goals of national movements as they were expressed during the nineteenth century covered three groups of demands, since those who took part in the movements felt deficits or inadequacies in these areas. They included, first, the development of a national culture based on the local language and its normal use in education, administration, and economic life; second, the achievement of civil rights and political self-administration, initially in the form of autonomy and ultimately of independence; and third, the creation of a complete social structure on the sole basis of the ethnic group.

Though the Yugoslav situation is neither historically nor circumstantially identical to the processes of national awakening that occurred throughout Europe during the last century, the understanding and explanation of these nationalist movements is nevertheless relevant to the Yugoslav case in two ways. Some Yugoslav nations, most notably the Slovenes, Croats and Macedonians, had not undergone the full historical trajectory of national movements before entering into the multinational state of Yugoslavia and were in some ways genuinely deficient, either in fact or in national consciousness. Secondly, the leaders of nationalist movements, unable or unwilling to formulate contemporary national programs, immediately fell back on to and drew from the ideologies and experience of the national movements of the past.

As an ideology, national awakening represents a comprehensive outlook distinguished by a deep penetration of national consciousness into every common pursuit. The characteristics that distinguish one type of national awakening and nationalism from another will answer three questions: What is the general direction of the movement? What are its specific objectives and goals? And will the movement strive to live at someone else's expense?

Nationalism derives from national consciousness, but the two are not the same. While national consciousness colours in some measure all public life, nationalism gives absolute priority to the values of the nation over all other values and interests. Nationalist ideology is a relatively modern phenomenon that emerged during the destruction of the hierarchical feudal order and is an expression of a more democratic and dynamic system of capitalism.

National awareness is typically not preoccupied with the political means of maximizing the national well-being. But nationalism is. It always seeks to change the world and usually has a vision of a new order in international relations. But not all nationalism is necessarily aggressive. Romantic nationalism rejects the idea of national aggrandizement through the imperial domination or assimilation of other nations. This benign ideology visualizes universal peace and harmony when national communities each obtain their own national state. Although benign nationalism is best suited to territories that have substantial national and ethnic mixes, the sad truth, one that is also valid for Yugoslavia, is that these are precisely the areas where aggressive nationalism has a much better base for operation.

The other, aggressive version of nationalism is the "integral" kind, insisting on the "completeness" of the nation in question. Depending on specific circumstances it can be and often is assimilationist and therefore dangerous to the integrity of neighbouring nations. Integral nationalism emerged in the second half of the nineteenth century as part of the process of liberal decline, adapting itself to the positivist spirit of the age.

The object of national movements is to promote the national ideal. The zeal of those who feel nationalistic and the needs and aspirations of those who politically ride the nationalist horse transform the normal, everyday notion and feeling of national identity into an all-encompassing and often even metaphysical drive. This is when nationalism becomes aggressive and dangerous. The risk of confrontation magnifies exponentially when "my" nation is right and all others are wrong, when the "wrongs" of the past have to be "set right" through purely national claims on ideas, borders, and territories, especially because these are situations in which there is a total disregard for other, non-nationalistic considerations.

The distinguished *International Herald Tribune* commentator Flora Lewis recounts from a relatively recent visit to Dubrovnik an encounter with a young man who conducted her, with obvious feelings of pride, about "the beautiful Croatian island of Lopud." When challenged whether it would be less beautiful if it were Serbian, his answer was: "But it is Croatian." This is typical of the irrational nationalism that is at the root of the Yugoslav drama. Needless to say, similar and even more drastic and damaging examples can be found by the thousand on all sides, not only the Croatian.

A national movement typically passes through three structural phases, according to the participants and the degree of national consciousness. In the first phase the energies of activists are above all devoted to a scholarly inquiry into the linguistic, cultural, social, and economic attributes of the nation under study. The second stage breeds a new range of activists, "the patriots," who take it upon themselves to spread the word and win over as many of their ethnic group as possible. The third stage occurs when the major part of the population comes to regard national identity as an overriding quality.

As the Yugoslav experience has shown, and as this book will try to portray, the germ of aggressive nationalism can be set in the initial phase. However, it is only latent until the "patriots" take full command and direct the campaign more in terms of opposition to others than support for anything.

In an ethnically mixed situation, as was on offer in Yugoslavia, the most dangerous aspect of national revival, one that was to lead directly to ruthless and aggressive nationalism, is the question of distinct national space. Claims to national space are based on appeals to two different criteria: ethnic homogeneity on the one hand and historic territory with "traditional borders" on the other. Needless to say, the "patriots" in what was Yugoslavia use these criteria in any way that suits their current interests, often falling into the trap of double standards to be applied to "us" and "them."

The national ideologies and policies of the new wave of national "revivalists," having nowhere else to go, went immediately to roots established more than a century ago. For them the fact that both internal and external circumstances had changed did not matter in the least.

The most deep-seated cause of the Yugoslav drama lies in the fact that although Yugoslavs have a nationality, they have never been able to form a nation. What precisely is a nation? For the purposes of the exposition that follows, the definition of the French historian Ernest Renard seems most appropriate: "A nation is a spiritual principle, grown out of a long past of common struggle and sacrifice which manifests itself in a willingness to embrace present and future solidarity."

The spirit of Yugoslavism had to coexist with, or in spite of, the spirits of the various nations forming it. Yugoslavism did not emerge as a kind of melting-pot blend of the various nationalities composing it. That is why the revival of centrifugal nationalist forces within it acted to destroy what did come together in the state of Yugoslavia. There was an insufficient history of common struggle and sacrifice; the identification with Yugoslavia was not strong enough and daily made weaker by the aggressive propaganda of the nationalist champions. Some would note that, on the contrary, there was a long past of struggle against each other. This assertion is essentially incorrect, as the later account will show. Mutual antagonism and aggression is of a relatively recent nature. However, the length and type of union that Yugoslavia represented was insufficient to cement firmly and unequivocally the willingness to embrace the present, and especially future solidarity.

Crucial to the argument that follows is the proposition that nationalism, though extremely important in its power to explain history and current events, was a necessary but not a sufficient condition for the destruction of Yugoslavia. Other ingredients that deserve mention and will figure prominently in the account that follows are the state of the political system, the international environment, economic conditions, history, tradition, and national characteristics.

The insufficiency and inadequacy of the political system go a long way in explaining why the process of national revival took the wrong turning, towards aggressive nationalism. For most of its existence Yugoslavia was ruled by some kind of totalitarian regime. Before the Second World War an absolutist non-parliamentary monarchy commonly prevailed, succeeded after the war by the quasi-parliamentary rule of the Communist Party and Tito personally. In such political circumstances nationalism had no "natural opportunity" to live itself out in a democratic, less disruptive fashion, to colour rather than dominate the issues.

An absolutist political regime hides and suppresses national questions and tensions, but this does not solve or dissolve them into the larger body of policy. As the case of Yugoslavia vividly demonstrates, the issue of nationalism was largely hidden under the carpet, along with other "problematic" phenomena, only to re-emerge at a time when the pressures had been reduced. However, it would be wrong, or at least very simplistic, to conclude decisively that Communist ideology and Communist rule have throughout the years aggravated the national question. They have done next to nothing to solve it, in spite of Stalin's famous claim and a pamphlet to this effect. But events in Yugoslavia cannot be understood properly as, simply, the product of forty years of Communist aggravation of the nationalist problem.

Communism was, however, fully responsible for the creation and existence of a political system that did not allow for democratic expression, let alone national democratic expression. The Communist political system created a gap and a deficiency in civil and human rights and freedom of political expression. Throughout Central and Eastern Europe after the collapse of Communism, and in the case of Yugoslavia after Tito left the stage, the vacuum at the top of society and within the political system was quickly filled by political opportunists who saw the possibility of very swiftly rising careers.

With the exception of the leader of Bosnian Muslims, all other nationalist leaders in Yugoslavia, and most of the national ideologues, were previously either high Communist officials or at least card-carrying members of the Communist Party. They deliberately chose to interpret the political deficits within the system as national issues rather than as deficits in human rights, civil liberties, and freedom of political expression. They did not champion the cause of democratization, with due regard for national issues; instead they championed national homogenization, unity, and solidarity against the evil conniving of "others." Their followers, which is to say the population at large, with little if any democratic experience and tradition, were easily misled in the desired direction.

The recent outburst of nationalism is therefore to a large extent a backlash, a swing of the pendulum, deriving from the fact that the political and institutional system was ill suited to dissolve issues of national renewal in the wider context of democratic policy considerations. The national issues, masterfully guided through the media by the "patriots," rapidly turned into nationalism and then into its aggressive variety, pushing the problem of the democratic deficit to the sidelines. Problems of power-sharing and decision-making, of economic competence and wealth distribution, for instance, were not dealt with adequately, even through the existing institutional structures, let alone through efforts to create new democratic structures for a lasting solution. The easiest and most expedient way to "resolve" these and other issues was to turn to nationalism. The genie was released from its bottle, soon to take full command of its masters.

The third ingredient in the current crisis, aside from aggressive nationalism and an inadequate political system, is the international environment – that is, the broader political setting in which Yugoslavia was formed, existed for over seventy years, and recently dissolved. As with most countries, and certainly every European country, the international context was and is extremely important. The territories of Yugoslavia, central in both geopolitical and strategic terms, have been of interest to large powers for centuries. It would not be an exaggeration, therefore, to say that Yugoslavia was to a considerable degree moulded by influences from without.

It would, however, be an exaggeration to say that Yugoslavia was imposed on the Yugoslavs by foreign powers with little or no understanding of the region and against the will of the people within. This argument, popular among some neo-nationalists, has several flaws in it, as this book will show. Its main use in present-day politics has been to put the blame conveniently and neatly on the foreigners, thus removing the burden of responsibility from the shoulders of the indigenous nationality and national leaders involved. Naturally, in their own eyes the nationality involved is by definition beyond reproach. The only inconvenience about this view is that, in removing the responsibility from "my" nation, it also absolves the other antagonists.

The international context has changed dramatically in the seventy years since the creation of Yugoslavia. The pressures that existed at that time, and during and after the Second World War, are there no longer. If Yugoslavia was not created by external forces alone, it certainly found one of its important reasons for staying together in the hostile environment of the Cold War. With the warming of the atmosphere after the Cold War it was thus strategically marginalized, the attention that had been focused on it for over thirty years having been removed. This lack of external pressure and attention both positive and negative allowed internal, primarily nationalistic pressures to flourish and finally to boil over.

The foreign component in the Yugoslav drama, though less important as a source of conflict, became, as the drama unfolded, increasingly important as a possible solution. As the problems deepened, foreign involvement also got deeper, so much so that today it is difficult if not impossible to see a way out without the support and services of foreign actors. But the involvement of outsiders has not been without fault and at times has added to the problems, making the situation that more complicated and difficult to solve.

The intersecting point of these three principal factors, with aggressive nationalism the dominant force, is where an explanation ought to be sought. Over and above these principal explanatory factors comes a rapidly deteriorating economy, which has prompted the "patriots" to look for quick-fix solutions to divert attention from deteriorating economic conditions and to assign blame to somebody else. Though a part of the complex problem, economic issues were not one of its causes, either in fact or in the perception of the population. The nationalist divisions were not primarily about economic injustices and deficiencies, though these were also thrown on to the stage for good measure.

National characteristics of the principal nations involved in the drama, their heritage, mythology, the pride that Serbs and Montenegrins take in their fighting tradition and capability, the disdain with which many Croats and Slovenes look upon the other nations that made up Yugoslavia, all these have some measure of explanatory power, though in the view of this author they do not qualify as primary. Neither does the history of mutual aggression. True, there have been bloody confrontations among the Serbs, Croats, Muslims, and Albanians. But we are not talking about a millennium-old history of hatred and fighting, as is sometimes claimed. Most of the fighting has occurred in the twentieth century, which fact provides for the vividness of memories.

But once nationalist and particularly aggressive nationalist goals are defined in a non-democratic setting, without the necessary positive external pressure and with negative economic internal pressure, the (ab)use of the history of fighting becomes an important reservoir for whipping up one's own national sentiments and hatred of others.

It is not easy to hold together all the elements necessary to a comprehensive study of what went wrong. But then nothing about Yugoslavia is really easy. Answers to some very important, fundamental questions can be reached only by complex analysis.

The first question, in historical order if not in actual importance, would be: Was Yugoslavia's unification flawed from the start? Then immediately comes the second: If unification was flawed the first time in 1918, why was the same mistake repeated in 1945?

Assuming that unification was not flawed but that there were some major faults in its foundations, that the reunification was again not flawed but that there were serious cracks in the structure, how was it possible for Yugoslavia to reach the level of international respectability and internal stability that it enjoyed for almost thirty years?

The next series of questions concerns the current disintegration of Yugoslavia. If the Yugoslavs could not live together, why was it necessary, or *was* it necessary to divorce in such a violent manner? Was a peaceful divorce possible? Why was it necessary to resort to arms and war in an attempt to reach a solution? That simply begs the question: What was the war about? What were the federal army, Serbs, Slovenes, Croats, and Muslims fighting for, or against? The immediate answer, of course, is that they were all fighting for their national rights. But beyond that, *was* it human rights that were denied to their respective nationalities, or was it a question of borders and territory?

We shall see later on that borders in Yugoslavia are a major issue and one of the principal causes of the current blaze of the nationalist fire. There are invisible frontiers between the republics of Yugoslavia and strong bonds transcending the visible ones. This noncorrespondence of ethnic and administrative borders made a peaceful, orderly dissolution and disentanglement almost, but not quite unimaginable.

An important question that follows immediately from the above is: If a peaceful dissolution was almost unthinkable, has there been by now enough fighting for the rival claims to be settled at the negotiating table and not by war? Have the Serbs, Croats, and Muslims had enough, or will more blood flow before reason prevails? And of course, what will be the nature of the solution? Will the visible frontiers change so that they correspond to the invisible ones, or will the nature of the bonds between people be transformed to correspond to existing frontiers? The importance of this question cannot be overemphasized. It is crucial to peace and security in the region, as well as to the future of the nations of Yugoslavia. Without a satisfactory answer to this question there is obviously no future for Yugoslavia in any form, which might be sad but not necessarily tragic. However, this will mean no lasting peace and stability, not only on the territory of ex-Yugoslavia but in the Balkans as a whole, which is a tragedy of the first magnitude.

Much is at stake. No wonder the international community stepped in to try to resolve this complex problem. But here again, a number of questions come to mind. Was there a way to stop the dissolution of Yugoslavia while the unity of the country was still the declared objective of all outside factors, both East and West? Did the foreign intervention come too late and in the wrong form, as some in Yugoslavia claim, or were the centrifugal forces too strong to stop? Was the European Community, which stepped in first, capable of handling the crisis and often simply mistaken or misguided, or was it incapable and impaired by its internal weaknesses from the outset? And the others – the Conference on Security and Co-operation in Europe (CSCE), the United Nations, the United States, Russia, NATO – they have all become involved in some manner – so far, to little avail.

The final curtain has not yet fallen on the Yugoslav drama. We are still in the thick of it. That is why the most important set of questions concerns what the future will bring. There is, of course, no crystal ball that will provide a sure and definite answer. Even if we know and understand the unfolding of the drama so far, there is no knowing with certainty how events will evolve. All we can say for sure is that the three principal factors – nationalism, political structures, and the foreign dimension – will again determine the final outcome. But what the outcome will be and how it will be achieved remains a matter of speculation and assumption.

PART ONE

The Stage

CHAPTER ONE

A Country of Diversity

Yugoslavia, the country of the South Slavs (Yug means South), was truly a country of condensed diversity. It is very difficult to find another country that has so much variety on such a relatively small territory. One expects to find complexity and diversity in countries such as China, India, or the former Union of Soviet Socialist Republics. But a country that had a territory of about 256,000 square kilometres (96,000 square miles) and just over 23 million in population?

In the "old days," when Yugoslavia was ideologically and politically in a different mould, there was a descriptive fable about it that went as follows: Yugoslavia has seven neighbours, six republics, five nations, four languages, three religions, two scripts, and one goal: to live in brotherhood and unity. The world has recently seen what has happened to the one goal. There has been very little brotherhood for quite some time, and unity was shattered in 1991. We still do not know how many states will ultimately be born out of the previously federal Yugoslavia.

But in those days the message of this little fable was: in spite of all this diversity, Yugoslavia as a country is not only possible but destined for great deeds and prosperity. It was a message of confidence indicating that the diversities had been mastered, that the centrifugal forces were in check, and that the word Jugoslavija (as it is written typically within the country) actually stood for unity.

Today we know different. To understand what happened we need to look first at the fundamental complexities of the situation. To begin with, let us look more carefully at the elements of this fable, working our way, as we have started, from bottom to top.

In Yugoslavia two different alphabets are in use. The reader of this book is, of course, familiar with the Latin alphabet in which it

Map 1
The Socialist Federative Republic of Yugoslavia, 1945–92

is written and printed. Many know about the Cyrillic alphabet, but few would know how to use it.

The origin of the Cyrillic script is not very precisely established. It is believed to have been invented in the ninth century on the territory of present-day Bulgaria or Macedonia. The principal author is also unknown, but the name implies that it was St Cyril, a renowned monk and educator of his time. It spread rapidly over the territories of the Balkans, except for Croatia and Slovenia, and eastward into Russia. Over time it underwent numerous modifications and stabilized in its current form sometime during the nineteenth century. The Cyrillic script is credited with high linguistic efficiency since there is always one and only one letter for a linguistic sound.

In Yugoslavia both scripts were in official use. In terms of usage the population of Yugoslavia was split almost exactly half and half with regard to the scripts. In school, children learned first one and then the other, depending on which was in common use in the territory where they went to school. Usually, as they grew up, they settled into the use of one, but retained a passive reading knowledge of the other. In half the Yugoslav republics Cyrillic was the official script; in two republics (Slovenia and Croatia) officialdom used the Latin alphabet, and in Bosnia and Herzegovina both were in equal use.

The difference in scripts made life a little more difficult for the average Yugoslav (but in a neutral sort of way). However, the general tendency was for the Latin script to take over gradually and spontaneously, in large part because of the openness of Yugoslavia to outside influences, most of which came from the West and in Latin script. Names of streets, many stores, even official documents in Serbia were written in the Latin script. It became the common form of writing of many intellectuals and university graduates. Problems only arose in earnest when these differences were exploited for political purposes, when the use of one script or the other was interpreted as "loyalty to the national cause" or "loyalty to the state" or, even worse, when the use of the "other script" came to be regarded as "national betrayal." The choice between scripts then offered an additional opportunity for some to politicize cultural differences.

While still at the level of two variables, it is necessary to point out one source of difference that has not been mentioned in the fable above. The territories and peoples of Yugoslavia were for a number of centuries dominated by two vastly different occupiers and cultures. The north and west of the country were under the rule of the Austro-Hungarian Empire. The east, south, and central parts of Yugoslavia were controlled by the Ottoman Empire. This could not but have a profound effect on the ethical, cultural, and economic differences of the nations that came together as Yugoslavia.

The three major religions in Yugoslavia were Greek Orthodox Christianity, Roman Catholicism, and Islam. The South Slavs, at the time of their arrival on the Balkan peninsula in the sixth and seventh centuries CE, were pagans. Eventually they took up Christianity, only to see the great schism of the Christian church, which finally occurred in 1054, go right through the middle of their territories.

The Turkish invasion and the domination of most of these territories by the Ottoman Empire brought with it the Islamic religion. The original Islamic believers were Turks who came and settled in conquered territories. But a portion of the indigenous population converted to Islam. The converts were relatively few among Orthodox Christians, even fewer among Catholics. The largest conversion to

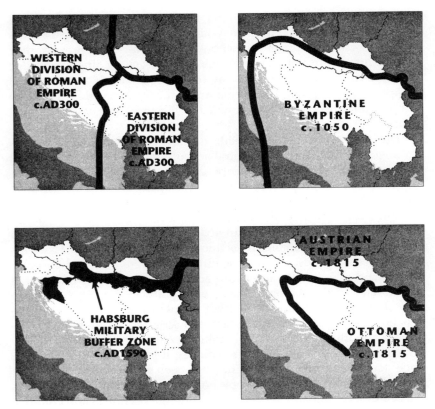

Map 2
The impact of empires on the future Yugoslavia

Islam occurred among the Bogumils, a heretical religious sect that occupied Bosnia, the central part of what was later to be Yugoslavia. Bosnia was at the crossroads between the Catholic and Orthodox churches and under the dual pressure of the powerful Byzantine state and Hungary. The weakness of their secular position made the Bogumils relatively easy prey to the conquest of Islam.

Among the peoples of former Yugoslavia the Orthodox church has the largest number of followers. In a country in which religious feelings do not generally run very deep and were even further marginalized by the forty-year rule of Communist atheism, it is generally believed that this church covers just over half the total population, being dominant in Serbia, Montenegro, and Macedonia and having large enclaves in Bosnia and Croatia. The Catholic church would then account for just over a quarter and Islam for a little less than a fifth of the total population, the rest belonging to a variety of smaller religious denominations.

Generally speaking, the farther north and west one goes in what was Yugoslavia, the more solidly the population is Catholic. Conversely, the further east and south one goes, the more solidly the population is Orthodox. The central part of the country – Bosnia and Herzegovina – is where the three religions meet and mingle, where it is not unusual to see the churches, mosques, and religious shrines of all three next to each other.

Religion was, of course, a political factor in the course of Yugoslav history. However, it would be difficult to say that it was a decisive factor, that the confrontations that occurred among the various ethnic groups on the territory of Yugoslavia were holy crusades or purely religious campaigns. In modern-day Yugoslavia, that is to say in the seventy-odd years of its existence as a state, religious tolerance was much more pronounced than confrontation. The notable exception occurred during the Second World War, when Orthodox believers were under great pressure and threat of physical extinction by the fascist Ustashi state of Croatia.

The notion that Yugoslavia had four languages is contentious. The languages that would add up to four are Serbian, Croatian, Slovenian, and Macedonian, listed here by order of magnitude of use in the former federation. Dispute arises from some of the following propositions:

The Serbian and Croatian languages are so similar (though they use different scripts) that one could speak of a Serbo-Croatian language, thus reducing the number of languages to three. In fact government policy through the educational system was to promote the idea of a single Serbo-Croatian language.

However, many Croats, more than Serbs, challenged this idea of a single language and went to great pains to identify vocabulary that would highlight the differences rather than the similarities.

Indeed, there are a number of meanings conveyed by different words in the two languages. But the level of similarity and the identical grammatical structure seem to give more weight to the contention that we are actually talking about one rather than two different and distinct languages. To put this idea into very simple terms, anyone who was to move from one linguistic area to the other would not bother "learning" the other language, any more than would an American moving to England or vice versa.

The literary language, of course, offers many more possibilities of differentiation. These differences have been exploited to predictable limits, and beyond. Although there is a grain of truth in the Croatian contention that the state, that is to say Yugoslav officialdom, exercised some pressure to "equalize" the languages, there is also truth in the statement that Croats, when they had an opportunity, bent backwards to invent or recall archaic words, with the sole purpose of stressing the difference between the two languages.

The other two Slav languages – Slovenian and Macedonian – though deriving from the same Slavic roots, are quite different from Serbo-Croatian (or Serbian and Croatian) and from each other. An educated individual from the Serbo-Croatian linguistic group could understand quite a bit of either Slovenian or Macedonian but could not really speak or write in these languages. The opposite would also hold true. The reality was and still is that the populations using Slovenian and Macedonian spoke much more Serbo-Croatian than the Serbs or Croats spoke their languages. This was a consequence of some official pressure but much more a spontaneous need to master the language in which 80 per cent of the population normally communicated.

The other possible area of dispute regarding language could arise from the fact that, besides the languages of the Yugoslav nations, one has to consider the languages of national minorities, at least the languages of the two most numerous, Albanian and Hungarian. In that case we should be talking about five languages or six, depending on whether Serbian and Croatian are counted as one or not. The Albanian language is spoken by more people than either Slovenian or Macedonian, which gave it sufficient claim to inclusion among the main languages spoken in Yugoslavia. The Hungarian language, although spoken by less than half a million people, nevertheless became a language of official use, so that all documents of the federal government were published in Hungarian also. Both Albanian and Hungarian are completely different from any of the Slav languages, and understanding or communication without translation is impossible.

And we must not forget the other minorities – Italians, Slovaks, Rumanians, Bulgarians, Turks, Roms (Gypsies), Rusines, and so on – who contribute to the complexity and richness of the Yugoslav linguistic cocktail. Minorities speaking these languages were entitled to education and cultural communication in them.

Besides making communication more difficult, the fact that so many languages existed in one country added to the cost of communication, not to mention national sensitivities and "identities." Language proved to be one of the important battlefields on which the fight for or against Yugoslavia was waged. So, if the existence of four languages was in itself not enough to add to the complexity of

the Yugoslav scene, the disputes about their number and the relationship of one language to another tended to make the linguistic
situation extremely difficult to manage.

The statement that Yugoslavia consisted of five nations was also
disputable. The Serbs, Croats, Macedonians, and Slovenes were generally treated as authentic nations. There are extremist theories that
Croats are actually Catholic Serbs, or that Serbs are Orthodox Croats,
that Slovenes are "Alpine Croats," and so on, but these are minority
views that do not belong to either the scientific or the political mainstream. But these minority views tend to gain in importance at times
of national confrontation, adding spice to the boiling nationalistic
stew.

The fifth nation is the more seriously disputed one. Montenegrins
are split between those who believe they are Serbs but living in a
different state and those who claim they are a different nation altogether. Indeed, in pursuit of this line of reasoning some have gone
so far as to claim that Montenegrins are actually not a Slav nation at
all but descendants of Illyrians.

Disputed also was the status of Muslims in Yugoslavia. The reader
is accustomed to the notion that Muslims are a religious group, that
this term does not signify nationality. Not so in Yugoslavia. The
notion of a Muslim "nation" was introduced by the constitution of
1963. Since then in Yugoslavia one could declare oneself a Muslim
national, which was written with a capital M, and also a follower of
the muslim faith, which was written with a small m. This was done
in Tito's time to preserve the ethnic tranquillity of Bosnia and Herzegovina, where the Muslims had a majority, though not an absolute
one.

Lately, the number of nations constituting Yugoslavia has been
disputed by the Albanians, who claim that they should also be
treated as a "constitutive nation of Yugoslavia," thus bolstering their
claim for Kosovo to become a republic. Their key argument is that
by their numbers (which they often inflate to make the argument
even stronger) they are larger than three of the nations that had their
own republics. The principal counter-argument usually brought
against their claim is that they cannot be a nation within Yugoslavia
since there is an Albanian national state adjacent to Yugoslavia, so
they must be satisfied with the status of a national minority, regardless of their number.

An interesting, one could say even bizarre dispute about nationalities in Yugoslavia involved the question of whether Yugoslavs
should be treated as a nationality. Yes, said those who, like the
author of this book, felt that national identification at the level of the

composite state was not only possible but for many reasons desirable. No, said those who claimed that this was an artificial suppression of authentic national feelings and/or that it "smelled" of Serbian hegemony and domination. The numbers of those who declared themselves Yugoslav nationals in various post-war censuses ranged between 3 and 6.2 per cent of the total population. This made them often more numerous than some nations of Yugoslavia and certainly a well-established "national minority" in their own state. It does seem odd that in a country called Yugoslavia those wishing to declare themselves Yugoslavs should be denied this type of national identification.

A final observation on the disputes over nationalities in Yugoslavia, indicative of the tensions and ill feelings aroused by this issue, is that according to the latest census, taken in the spring of 1991, almost half a million people were nationally "undecided."

The six republics of Yugoslavia were (in alphabetical order) Bosnia and Herzegovina, Croatia, Macedonia, Montenegro, Slovenia, and Serbia. What follows is a very brief description of each one. A deliberate attempt has been made to include only such facts as are relevant to the story.

Bosnia and Herzegovina was often called "little Yugoslavia," which underlines the diversity and complexity of this centrally located former republic. According to the provisional results of the latest census, taken in 1991, BiH (as it was usually abbreviated in Yugoslavia) had around 4,365,000 inhabitants. Of that number almost 44 per cent declared themselves Muslims, 31.5 per cent Serbs, and just over 17 per cent Croats. The rest belonged to other nationalities, including 5.5 per cent declared Yugoslavs.

But the complexity of the BiH ethnic mosaic did not stop there. One could imagine the three large ethnic groups living in relatively discrete geographic formations, perhaps similar to Switzerland. This was far from being the case in BiH. Before the latest war there were only three *opštinas*[1] that were as ethnically homogeneous as Posusje (99.5 per cent Croat) Cazin (97.5 per cent Muslim), or Drvar (97.3 per cent Serb). At that time these pure units were a rarity. Muslims held an absolute majority in 37, Serbs in 32, and Croats in 13 *opštinas*. The remaining 30 or so were without an absolute majority.

There were a number of *opštinas* like Bosanski Šamac (44.7 per cent Croat and 41.5 per cent Serb), Derventa (40 per cent Serb and 39 per cent Croat), or Doboj (40 per cent Muslim and 39 per cent Serb), with the balance coming mostly from the main remaining ethnic group.

To make matters more complicated, the majority of the Serb-dominated *opštinas* are on the western side of BiH, while this republic has a border with Serbia to the east. This, if nothing else, showed the impracticality of a division of BiH and then an annexation of Serb territories to Serbia, since there was no "natural" territorial link between Serbia and the Serbs in western BiH. But this also explains one of the reasons for the fighting that erupted.

There was yet another complication: 16 per cent of the children in BiH were from mixed marriages, more than in any other republic of Yugoslavia. This in turn shows that any and all ethnic divisions in BiH cut not only through territories but also through families.

Bosnia was an independent state in the Middle Ages. On and off it was also under Croat or Hungarian rule or a vassal state in relation to them. These episodes are worth mentioning because they laid the foundations of some present-day claims to this territory. Bosnia reached its political and territorial peak under Tvrtko I, who crowned himself king of Bosnia and Serbia in 1377. His army took part on the Serbian side in the famous battle of Kosovo in 1389.

A century later the Turks overpowered BiH, designating these territories the Bosnian *pašaluk* (region) of the Ottoman Empire. This situation prevailed for four centuries, until the San Stefano Agreement between Russia and Turkey (February 1878). Under this agreement, the Turks as the losing side had to cede autonomy to Bosnia. Only six months later the Berlin Congress revised the terms of the San Stefano Agreement, giving BiH to the Austro-Hungarian Empire as a protectorate.

Austro-Hungarian rule was very unpopular in BiH among both the Serbs and the Muslims. The Serbs fought for their religious and cultural autonomy for ten years (1896–1906), and so did the Muslims. Strained relations with the Dual Monarchy culminated in the assassination of Crown Prince Ferdinand of Austria, which in turn sparked off the First World War. Before gaining fame for daily bombardment, Sarajevo, capital of BiH, was best known for this assassination.

In the inter-war period BiH was integrated in various ways into the newly created state of Yugoslavia, but never under its original name. During the Second World War, BiH became a part of the so-called Independent State of Croatia, independent in name only as it was a puppet state of Nazi Germany and Fascist Italy. However, BiH became extremely important to another newly emerging political force in Yugoslavia. Tito's headquarters and his elite partisan troops operated from BiH for two and a half years (1942 to mid-1944), mostly because of its rugged terrain, suitable for guerrilla warfare, but also because the ethnic complexity of BiH provided for a less constraining political and military environment. This in turn had a profound effect on the position of BiH in the Yugoslav political structure after the war. The favour was returned by making BiH a full-fledged federal republic and one of the constitutive states of the new Yugoslavia.

BiH was one of the economically less developed republics of Yugoslavia. Throughout the post-war years the GNP per capita[2] in BiH stood between 70 and 80 per cent of the Yugoslav average. As such, BiH was a recipient of considerable development aid from those republics that were considered relatively more developed.

BiH is practically land-locked apart from a very narrow strip of the Adriatic coast. It was self-sufficient in energy but not in agriculture. It has potential in ferrous metals (the biggest steel mill of former Yugoslavia is located in BiH), bauxite, and forestry. A high proportion of the armaments industry was located in BiH because it was conveniently protected and a long way from the main lines of advance of potential conquerors. It has considerable unused potential for winter sports. The Winter Olympic Games of 1984 were held in and around Sarajevo.

BiH today, in a state of civil/ethnic war, is facing the pressures of its internal ethnic composition and of its more powerful neighbours (Serbia and Croatia), as well as the underlying pressure of economic underdevelopment.

Croatia was the second largest Yugoslav republic. It has featured prominently in the media lately, since the war of 1991 was fought almost exclusively on its territory.

According to the latest census Croatia has a population of 4,760,000. Of that number 78 per cent have declared themselves Croats and just over 12 per cent Serbs. In 1991 Croatia had 2.2 per cent declared Yugoslavs and just over 1 per cent Muslims. The rest are national minorities, none of which is even 1 per cent of the population (Italians, Hungarians, Czechs, Slovaks, Gypsies, etc.)

Not all Croats live in Croatia. About 110,000 Croats live in Serbia, mostly in the northern province of Vojvodina. Even more importantly, 756,000 Croats live in BiH, concentrated to a high degree in the southwest and a pocket in the northeast, but mixed with Muslims in central BiH.

The Serbs of Croatia, as a group one of the most contentious issues of the Yugoslav drama and one to which this analysis will return in detail, live in three rather different types of ethnic arrangements with the Croats. Of the 100 Croatian *opštinas*, there were a few where the

Serbs had an overwhelming majority (Donji Lapac 98 per cent; Knin 88.5 per cent; Dvor na Uni 85 per cent; Gračac 82 per cent). Altogether there were 13 *opstinas* in which the Serbs had either an absolute majority of the population or else, as in Pakrac, for example (46 per cent Serbs and 36 per cent Croats), a relative one. The second type of ethnic mix occurred in a number of *opstinas* in which the Croats had a relative majority and the Serbs a (very) significant minority. The most (in)famous such example was offered by the town of Vukovar. In this once quaint little town on the banks of the Danube, prior to the all-out fighting there were 44 per cent Croats and 37.5 per cent Serbs. Finally, almost one-third of the Serbs were, and still are, scattered in relatively small groups in a number of Croatian towns where they represent less than 10 per cent of the population.

Croatia has had a long and varied history. Trpimir, who ruled in the middle of the ninth century, is considered the first independent ruler of Croatia, which at the time did not include either Slavonia (the contemporary northern province) or Dalmatia (the coastal province). It was Tomislav in the first half of the tenth century who laid the foundations of the medieval Croatian state. The eleventh century brought expansion into some territories of Dalmatia, as well as the definitive break with Byzantium and thus also with the Orthodox church. At that time Croatia also ruled the *Neretljanska oblast*, an area that today is in BiH.

At the very beginning of the twelfth century Croatia lost its independence to the Hungarian Koloman dynasty, and from then until the First World War, Croatia was a subject of Hungarian or Austro-Hungarian rule. Two patterns emerge from this eight centuries' long period of domination by the (Austro)-Hungarian Empire that deserve special mention because they have a direct bearing on events today.

One is the constant and persistent historical attempt by the Croatian nobility, and later the Croatian intelligentsia, to attain and maintain as high a degree of autonomy as possible, even if the reality was that these territories were the sovereign domain of Hungarian kings and later Austrian emperors. In earlier centuries the autonomy of Croatia was personified by the titular head of the Croats, called the Ban. At the end of the thirteenth century the first assembly of the Croatian nobility, the Sabor, was created. This name has been preserved to the present day and is used by the contemporary parliament of Croatia.

Croatia always felt the consequences of the shifting balance of the Austro-Hungarian relationship, but at all times had as its principal goal the upgrading of its level of autonomy by siding with one against the other, or skilfully using a deadlock. Of course, over this long span of time other external influences were brought to bear on the territories of Croatia, such as Venetian, Turkish, and Napoleonic conquests, but by and large the fate of the Croatian nation and Croatian territories was determined in the Croatian-Hungarian-Austrian triangle. A high degree of autonomy resulted from this long struggle, so that Croats relied to a considerable degree on their own Sabor in making internal political decisions.

The second fact from the history of Croats and Croatia that deserves particular mention is the establishment of the Vojna Krajina, or military frontier. This was the territory that separated the Hungarian (Croatian) lands from the Ottoman Empire. It was literally a frontier. It was organized by the Habsburgs at the beginning of the sixteenth century as a separate military command, directly subject to the Austrian throne. Since the Croatian nobility and population in these regions were insufficient to form an effective defence, the Habsburg military authorities called in and settled a large number of Serbs wanting to leave occupied Turkish lands. They were given a status that made them responsible directly to the Crown and had no responsibilities or commitments towards the Croatian nobility, the Ban, or the Sabor.

The Croats never stopped attempting to regain political sovereignty over these territories, and the Serbs never for a moment accepted the idea of yielding their free and autonomous status. The perversity of the situation today is that Serbs are now settled on territories that were the heart of the medieval Croatian kingdom. Though today the Vojna Krajina is largely a barren and underdeveloped region, its symbolic and nationalistic value is far above any material or commercial considerations. (We shall very soon see this emotional attitude paralleled when we discuss Kosovo in its relation to Serbia.)

Over its long and varied history Croatia has been both smaller and larger than it is today. This has, of course, given grounds to expansionist claims to those seeking a Greater Croatia, but also to those seeking a Greater Serbia.

One perhaps somewhat premature conclusion that can be drawn at this point is that the past should not be the only criterion for determining whether one ethnic group of the South Slavs or another has a sole right to a particular territory. This is particularly true if acquisition of territory or imposition of power was achieved by force of arms or totalitarian methods, such as happened under the Fascist Croatia during the Second World War or is happening in Bosnia today.

On the economic front Croatia in contemporary Yugoslavia was a relatively well-developed republic. Its GNP per capita stood about 25 to 35 per cent above the Yugoslav average, and Croatia paid contributions into the fund for less well-developed republics. Croatia is basically self-sufficient in agriculture and had 75 per cent of Yugoslavia's production of crude oil, but it is nevertheless a net importer of energy. The manufacturing sector is broadly diversified and includes everything from food processing to shipbuilding, the latter industry having been one of the most developed of its kind in the world. The metallurgical sector is relatively less well developed since Croatia does not have the raw materials, but machine tools, clothing, chemical products, pharmaceuticals, and consumer durables are important on the list of manufactured goods. Croatia also has by far the largest part of the Adriatic coast, which is an almost unlimited source of tourist income.

Macedonia is probably most famous for Alexander the Great, but that claim to fame has nothing to do with the present inhabitants of Macedonia. The connection, as recent events have shown, actually causes considerable problems to this former Yugoslav republic.[3]

The total population of Macedonia is just over 2 million, of which 65 per cent are Macedonians, 21 per cent (over 400,000) ethnic Albanians, with a smaller percentage of Turks, Roms (Gypsies), and Serbs: 4.8, 2.7, and 2.2 per cent respectively. It could therefore be said that Macedonia is relatively free of worries about the ethnic presence of other South Slav nations. Its main ethnic concerns are with the concentration of a large and growing Albanian minority and with the Bulgarian contention that Macedonians are actually Bulgarians.

The reason for this dates back to the middle of the ninth century, when Bulgarians first succeeded in pushing Byzantium out of Macedonia. By the end of the tenth century King Samuel of Macedonia managed to establish a Macedonian state that was much larger than the present Macedonia, encompassing parts of present-day Albania, Greece, Bulgaria, Serbia, and Bosnia. This peak of the medieval Macedonian state did not last long. Only thirty years later Macedonia was retaken by Byzantium, then again by Bulgaria, and in the fourteenth century by Serbia. The most important Serbian medieval ruler, Dušan, made it his central province and crowned himself emperor in the capital of Macedonia, Skopjė.

Of all the nations that made up Yugoslavia, Macedonians were the first to fall to the Turks (in 1371) and the last to see them go (1913). But the departure of the Turks was not good news for the Macedonians. Serbia, Bulgaria, and Greece each wanted the whole or parts of Macedonia for themselves. After the Balkan Wars they managed to partition this territory into what became known as Aegean Macedonia, Vardar Macedonia, and Pirin Macedonia, controlled respectively by Greece, Serbia, and Bulgaria. Macedonia today is surrounded on all sides by not entirely friendly, and possibly hostile neighbours.

Macedonia is the poorest of all former Yugoslav republics. Its GNP per capita varied between 55 and 60 per cent of the Yugoslav average, increasing slightly over time since Macedonia was also, like BiH, a recipient of aid from the more developed republics.

Macedonians have the advantage of using one script (Cyrillic), one language (Macedonian), and of belonging to one religion (Orthodox). Lately, tensions have increased with the growth of the Albanian minority with its own language, Latin script, and predominantly Muslim religion. A further and important source of tension stems from the fact that there are Macedonians in northern Greece and also those who have declared themselves Macedonians in Bulgaria.

Montenegro was the tiniest of all former Yugoslav republics, taking up only 5.4 per cent of its area and inhabited by just over 600,000 people. Of that number 62 per cent declared themselves Montenegrins, 15 per cent Muslims, 9.5 per cent Serbs, 6.6 per cent ethnic Albanians, and 4.5 per cent Yugoslavs.

First mention of an independent medieval Slav state on this territory (then called Zeta) occurred in the eleventh century. It was independent for over a century, and then for almost two centuries it was a part of the expanding medieval state of Serbia. With the demise of the Serbian medieval state, Montenegro was alternately under the rule of Venetians and Turks, gaining considerable autonomy in the sixteenth century and total independence in the eighteenth.

The Montenegrins were and are proud of their long history of independence, being the first among the nations of Yugoslavia to achieve post-medieval freedom, even if it was a tribal and not a modern nation-state. For international recognition of this independence Montenegro had to wait until the Berlin Congress of 1878.

At that time Montenegro was ruled by Duke (later King) Nikola, who became known as the "father-in-law of Europe." One of his daughters was married to the king of Serbia; two were married to Russian grand dukes; his daughter Jelena was married to King Victor Emmanuel of Italy, and the youngest daughter was married to a Mountbatten: Prince Franz-Joseph of Battenberg. These royal connections were naturally used to full political effect.

After the First World War the Montenegrin Great Assembly voted to annex Montenegro to Serbia, so the name of this nation disappeared, as did the Petrović dynasty to which King Nikola belonged.

The Montenegrins are fiercely proud of their outstanding record on the field of battle. This small nation of rugged mountaineers spent a proportionately much longer period fighting for and securing their freedom than did any other South Slav nation. This tradition served Montenegrins well in the course of the Second World War. A disproportionately high number of them joined Tito's partisans, and an even higher proportion achieved the rank of commanding officers and generals. A significant consequence was that Montenegro became one of the constitutive federal republics in post-war Yugoslavia.

Montenegro (this Italian name corresponds to the authentic name Crna Gora, meaning Black Mountain) is a very rocky, mountainous piece of land, enhanced by a small but very beautiful stretch of coast. It is economically less well developed, its GNP per capita reaching about 80 per cent of the Yugoslav average, and thus was also a recipient of federal development aid. It is not self-sufficient in agriculture, nor does it offer a rich base of raw materials for mining and manufacturing. Tourism is rapidly becoming the most important industry.

Slovenia, "the Alpine state," is situated in the northwest corner of what was Yugoslavia. Its population, around 2 million, is ethnically the most homogeneous, more than 90 per cent Slovene.

This tribe of Slavs came into the region between the Southern Alps and the Adriatic Sea in the seventh century, but they were not generally known under the collective name Slovenes until the middle of the nineteenth century. This was mostly because the Slovenes, unlike the other South Slavs, never had a medieval national state and were for over a millennium subject to constant pressure and division by mostly German and Austrian rulers.

These divisions and consolidations of territories upon which the Slovenes lived resulted in the twentieth century in a division of the Slovene nation among three modern states: Yugoslavia, Austria, and Italy. If the Montenegrins are fiercely proud of their free and fighting spirit, the Slovenes are equally proud of sustaining and maintaining their language and culture under great Germanizing pressure.

Slovenia was by far the best-developed republic in former Yugoslavia, having a GNP per capita almost 60 per cent above the Yugoslav average. Slovenia is self-sufficient in agriculture but "imported" large quantities of agricultural raw materials from other republics for its food-processing industry. It is also self-sufficient in energy. The Slovenes have an industrial base that is the most efficient and productive among the former Yugoslav republics, and an exporting sector that accounted for a quarter of Yugoslav exports, though the population accounts for less than 10 per cent of the total. Tourism, both in winter and in summer, is an important source of national income.

The Slovenes are almost all Roman Catholic, use the same Slovenian language, and write in the Latin script.

Historically Slovenia experienced no territorial or ethnic disputes with Croatia, the only other Slav state with which she has a common border, but some are cropping up now. However, Yugoslavia was, on behalf of Slovenia, involved in disputes about the ethnic rights of Slovenes in both Italy and Austria.

Serbia is the biggest of all former Yugoslav republics both in size and in population. It was the only republic that had two autonomous provinces, Vojvodina in the north and Kosovo in the southwest, on account of the sizeable national minorities of Hungarians and Albanians living there.

According to the last census, the population of Serbia was about 9,800,000. It is made up of 65.8 per cent Serbs, 17.2 per cent Albanians, 3.5 per cent Hungarians, 3.2 per cent Yugoslavs, 2.4 per cent Muslims, 1.4 per cent Montenegrins, and 1.1 per cent Croats.

A crucial issue in both the construction and the destruction of Yugoslavia has been the fact that many Serbs live outside Serbia. The total number of people declaring themselves Serbs in 1991 was just under 8.5 million. Of that number 6.4 million live in Serbia, 1.4 million in Bosnia and Herzegovina, 580,000 in Croatia, 57,000 in Montenegro, and 44,000 in Macedonia.

The Serbian medieval state was founded by King Nemanja in the twelfth century. A significant factor for the understanding of today's events is that this medieval Serb state centred in and around Kosovo, the province that today is 90 per cent Albanian in population and, like the Krajina in Croatia, one of the sore points in ethnic disputes. However, at that time it was the seat and site of Serb spiritual and secular life. Through a number of wars with Bulgarians, Hungarians and Byzantium (but also through periodic alliances with them), the Serb state expanded to the south and east, reaching its highest point in terms of both territory and stability under the mighty Emperor Dušan. At that time the medieval state of Serbia included today's territories of Montenegro, parts of Bosnia and the Dalmatian coast, the whole of Macedonia, and a large segment of northern Greece. In the north, however, Serbia did not extend as far as its present-day borders.

Both before and after the rule of Emperor Dušan, family infighting weakened the authority of Serbian monarchs and rulers. This was especially significant after Dušan's death because the Serbian feudal rulers and lords did not act in unison to stop the conquests of the Ottoman Empire. A series of defeats at the hands of the Turks, of which the most important occurred in the Battle of Kosovo in 1389, signalled the end of the independent medieval state of Serbia. It took the Turks another sixty years to conquer all the Serbian lands, but even before the conquest was complete, the Ottoman Empire became the dominant factor in the Balkans, including Serbia.

One further word should be added on the Battle of Kosovo. Though the Serbs lost, the legend of this battle not only survived through almost five centuries of Turkish rule but became a myth and a rallying point for Serb spiritual life. Legends in verse about the exploits of the various Serb heros were carried down by word of mouth from generation to generation, especially in the eighteenth and nineteenth centuries, when a new spirit of independence and defiance of the Turks started to take shape. Therefore, the Battle of Kosovo and thus the region of Kosovo have a very high symbolic value to the Serbs.

In spite of long Turkish rule, the population of Serbia by and large did not convert to Islam. The one significant exception occurred in the territory of Sandžak (bordering on Bosnia and Montenegro), which was under the administrative rule of the Bosnian Pasha and where a considerable proportion of the population adopted Islam. But because of religious and economic pressure, quite a number of Serbs moved northward to Hungary and west to Croatia within the Austro-Hungarian Empire, thus largely explaining the scattering of this nation among all Yugoslav republics except Slovenia.

The First (unsuccessful) and the Second (successful) Serbian Insurrection, in 1804 and 1815 respectively, paved the way for Serbian autonomy in 1830, *de facto* independence in the period 1845–78, and full international recognition as a sovereign state at the Congress of Berlin in 1878. As an independent state Serbia fought three regional wars. It lost the first to Bulgaria, creating an animosity that still exists. In the First Balkan War, however, Serbia joined or possibly engineered an alliance with Bulgaria, Montenegro, and Greece, pushing out and limiting the Turks in Europe to a narrow strip of land around Istanbul. The division of territories gained from the Turks was the cause for the Second Balkan War, in which Serbia, now allied with Greece, defeated Bulgaria and divided the territory of Macedonia. Serbia got roughly what is present-day Yugoslav Macedonia, a part of the country that for a time went under the name Southern Serbia.

The Serb population living north of the Danube, in Hungary or Austria-Hungary, became nationally aroused in the nineteenth century, supporting the Serbian insurrections and taking active part in the revolutionary events of 1848. A political struggle for the autonomy of the region later to be known as Vojvodina ensued, creating in the process a political alliance with the Croats, also subjects of Austro-Hungarian rule. The Serbs of Vojvodina were also a beacon of national inspiration, instigating and helping the Serbs in Serbia proper against the last remnants of the Turkish occupation. Though there was a strong nationalist bond between the Serbs north and south of the Danube, they were not united into one state until after the First World War.

To the west Serbia was strengthening its bonds with the Serb population of Bosnia, considerably irritating Vienna in the process. The secret convention that the first Serbian king drew up with Austria in 1882, promising not to encourage Serbian nationalism in Bosnia, was dropped by King Peter I when he came to the throne of Serbia in 1903. This made life difficult for both Serbs in Serbia and the South Slavs under Austrian rule in general. Austria increased the pressure by waging a "customs war" against Serbia (1906–10) and formally annexing Bosnia in 1909. Tensions did not subside and the assassination of Archduke Ferdinand by a young Serb insurgent, member of the clandestine organization Mlada Bosna, triggered the First World War.

In summary, the history of Serbia is one of the most complex among European nations, and its relevance to the situation in Yugoslavia cannot be emphasized too strongly. Early Serbian independence (together with Montenegro) created a driving political force for the integration of the South Slavs. This was especially true among Serbs living outside the boundaries of Serbia. Its traditional ally in the Balkans was Greece and its traditional antagonist Bulgaria. Relations with Austria were strained, primarily because of the attitude of Serbia towards its brethren on Austrian territory. Relations with Albania were never easy and friendly, escalating in recent times to a high pitch over Kosovo. Serbia provoked considerable antagonism among the indigenous population by its occupation of Macedonia after the Second Balkan War.

The Serbian economy is very diversified but not very efficient or productive. The GNP per capita in Serbia was somewhat below the Yugoslav average (93–95 per cent), but Serbia was among the better-developed republics and has consistently contributed aid to the less well-developed republics. The relative levels of development within Serbia are also very different. Vojvodina in the north has a GNP per capita 30 to 35 per cent higher than the average of former Yugoslavia, while Kosovo in the southwest has a GNP per capita that hardly reached 35 per cent of that average.

Serbia is self-sufficient in agriculture and energy and was the main "exporter" of both to other republics. It has a broad manufacturing base that leaves much to be desired in efficiency and productivity. Manufacturing includes automobiles, consumer durables, electronics, furniture, clothing, pharmaceuticals, rolling stock, food processing, ferrous and non-ferrous metals, plus a large construction sector.

The diversity of languages spoken in Serbia is the greatest of all among the former Yugoslav republics, and this also created a need for the coexistence of both scripts in the two autonomous provinces. Though Orthodox Christians are an overwhelming majority, Muslims in the southwest and Catholics in the north are significant religious minorities.

After this brief survey of the six republics that constituted Yugoslavia, an even briefer survey of the seven neighbours of Yugoslavia will complete the picture.

Italy, to the west, has over the centuries been an occupying force, first as Venice and then as modern Italy. It has left a strong cultural influence, particularly along the Dalmatian coast, and has always had more than a passing interest in the other side of the Adriatic Sea. At times it has been directly hostile to the very idea of Yugoslavia.

Austria and Hungary, to the north, have separately and as the Dual Monarchy held Slovenia, Croatia, Vojvodina, and, for a brief period, BiH under their rule. This has had a strong cultural and economic impact on these regions, making them generally better developed than the regions that were under Ottoman rule, with the exception of BiH. The waning of Turkish influence in Bosnia brought into confrontation the political aspirations of Austria and Serbia, which eventually led to war in 1914. For both Austria and Hungary the creation of Yugoslavia was a fact they found difficult but at the time politically expedient to accept.

Romania borders former Yugoslavia in the east. The fact that it has not been mentioned at all until now suggests that historically there were no open questions or disputes, and the situation is similar today.

Bulgaria, bordering in the east on both Serbia and Macedonia, has had strained relations with the former mostly because of the latter. The situation today has not changed dramatically.

Greece, in the south, traditionally supported Serbia, and vice versa, against the Bulgarians, Turks, and Albanians. The question of Macedonia has been in the past, and could be in the future, a point of contention and dispute. It could again, as in the past, be a reason for new alliances and confrontations among the neighbouring countries.

Finally, with Albania, except for a brief period after the Second World War, relations have usually been very tense, partly because of the penetration of Albanian population into traditionally South Slav territories, partly because of claims for a Greater Albania reminiscent of the one that was formed as a puppet state during the latter years of the Ottoman Empire.

All these forces were brought into play in the creation of a complex entity called Yugoslavia. Some thought at the time that it was a mistake to attempt to make a cake with so many ingredients. Some think so now. The account that follows should allow the reader to decide whether the creation of Yugoslavia was a noble experiment in an inherently unstable part of Europe or an impossible task from the start.

CHAPTER TWO

Origins of the Idea
and the State

The previous chapter showed that we are dealing with old nations. All except Slovenia were also medieval states. Their territories changed in size, usually at the expense of another, neighbouring Slav tribe or state. These expansions were simple conquering exploits of strong rulers against weak neighbours. Thus, medieval Macedonia covered a territory including Serbia, Bosnia, and parts of Croatia. Croatia at its peak covered parts of Slovenia, Bosnia, and Montenegro. The zenith of Serbia brought conquests of Macedonia, Montenegro, parts of Bosnia and the Dalmatian coast, as well as half of Greece. Finally, the pinnacle of the Bosnian medieval state saw Tvrtko I crowning himself "King of the Serbs, Bosnia, Dalmatia, and the Croats."

At that time the idea of fusing, rather than conquering the South Slavs was never mentioned. But these changes of borders and national territories that occurred centuries ago left a residual effect, inspiring some of the "national champions" in the period of national awakening during the eighteenth and nineteenth centuries and the present-day national revival. With six republics there were many internal borders, and few are undisputed.

Internecine conquests of territories by South Slavs were cut short by the conquests of two external powers: the Austro-Hungarians in the north and the Turks to the south and centre. The lovingly described "golden era" of independent statehood was followed by subjection to foreign rule lasting many centuries. The two dynastic empires that, between them, split the South Slav territories were hostile to the idea of the national state, so independent statehood had to be fought for and was gained (or regained, as those concerned might say) only through fierce and bloody confrontations.

The Yugoslav idea of fostering South Slav co-operation and thus broadening resistance to foreign rule has to be understood against a background of national awakening and national ideologies that started forming during the last quarter of the eighteenth century.[1]

The tiny state of Montenegro was the first to achieve independence from the Turks, towards the end of the seventeenth century. However, it was not quick to organize itself as a modern nation-state but remained instead for almost two centuries a tribal association. The influence of Montenegro on the broader South Slav picture was therefore insignificant.

The central role in moulding relations between South Slavs was then, as it is now, played by the Serbs and the Croats. These two ethnic groups dominated the process of national awakening in territories that were to become Yugoslavia. But their contributions in terms of strength, character, and direction of national awakening were very different, and herein lies one of the keys to understanding the problems Yugoslavia faced while a country.

Serbs first took up arms in 1804 under the leadership of Karadjordje, founder of one of the two Serbian dynasties that alternated in ruling Serbia. Though this First Insurrection was unsuccessful in terms of gaining national statehood and was cruelly put down by the Turks, the strength of the national awakening could not be effaced, and very soon, in 1815, the Second Insurrection took place under the leadership of Miloš Obrenović, founder of the other alternating dynasty.

At that time the territory of Serbia was much smaller than both the medieval state and what it was to become a century later. The main objective of both uprisings was to obtain autonomy, freedom, and eventually statehood on this territory. Though the Serbs in the Austro-Hungarian empire, living just across the Danube, cheered and actively supported the Serbian uprisings, there is no evidence of an attempt by either Karadjordje or Obrenović to unite all Serbs in one state. They were wise enough to realize that this was against all the odds since it would mean taking on two powerful empires single-handedly. (Russia was sympathetic to the Serbs but had no great enthusiasm, nor would she offer material support.) In fact, Obrenović sought active support from Austria against the Turks, which also made it impossible to encourage nationalism among the Serbs under the Dual Monarchy.

Serbian national ideology was closely tied to the Orthodox church, from medieval times to the period of the national awakening. Adherence to Orthodoxy made for Serbian nationhood, thus providing a high level of national consciousness despite the scattered nature of the Serbian nation. In addition, immediately after the two Serbian uprisings, Vuk Karadžić, the famous Serbian language reformer, became a decisive force behind a new linguistic definition of Serbdom.

Karadžić correctly observed that the foundations of an autonomous Serbian principality had been laid by simple peasants. Though their vision of nationhood may have been poorly defined, the insurgents' success lifted Serbian national pride far more effectively than scores of learned treatises. After that it was less expedient for Serbian state-craft to rely on the church as the sole Serbian national institution.

Karadžić tapped this revolutionary source of energy to solidify Serbian culture thus spreading and popularizing the national awakening. He also, in a reversal of all traditional standards, broadened the definition of Serbdom to include all those who spoke the Štokavian[2] dialect, regardless of religion. The Serbian nation, according to him, was *not* exclusively Orthodox. If they spoke this common language, which according to Karadžić was a Serbian national heritage, Catholics and Muslims were also Serbs. Karadžić thus enabled a new Serbian national ideology, the purpose of which was to lay national claim to the vast majority of Catholic Croats and all Bosnian Muslims.

This task was inherited by Ilija Garašanin, who became a pivotal figure in the transformation of national ideology into national policy. He codified his ideas in a then-secret document called *Načertanije* ("Outline") in 1844. Like many of his contemporaries Garašanin believed that Serbia's national mission was to complete the task of liberation initiated by the Serbian insurrections. The frontiers of the new state had to be extended to all areas where Serbs lived. Following Karadžić's lead, he defined these frontiers to be linguistic. The responsibility of the "liberation and unification" of all Serbs into a single Great Serbian state gradually became the master principle of Serbian policy. The existence of South Slav interests other than those of the Serbs was marginalized and discounted.

The whole project was based on the conviction that the Ottomans would inevitably be pushed out of their Balkan possessions. The power succession could be resolved in one of two ways: the Habsburgs and Russia could divide the Balkans, or a new power, Serbia, would supplant the Turks. Not wanting to tackle two and possibly three powerful enemies at once, Garašanin reduced the full thrust of his doctrine and, for reasons of practicality, fixed Serbia's ambition upon Turkish patrimony, notably Bosnia and Herzegovina.

He laid the foundations of the Great Serbia policy of unification, which became axiomatic among many, especially within conservative political circles in Serbia. This same policy would survive to be conveniently revived during the latest national awakening after Tito.

Though strong, Garašanin's influence was not the only one shaping Serbian state policy and the future. An important figure was Svetozar Marković, who in his short life of thirty years (1846–75) left some important traces behind. First, he was the founder of socialism in Serbia and the most important socialist figure in the Balkans. Being modern and forward-looking, he advocated a state that would be founded on the principle of personal liberty. In that way "everybody's nationality would nevertheless be guaranteed, because civil freedoms give the right to each nationality to constitute itself as an independent group in the alliance." Second, he was an advocate of a federal Balkan state rather than a unitary one (his advocacy becoming in part a reality exactly one hundred years after his birth). Marković also coined the term Greater Serbia, (so much in vogue currently), but actually meant with it to criticize and mock Serbian expansionism. Very importantly, Marković's socialist party gave birth to the Radical Party, a key player in later events. The offspring was never able to discard totally the influence of Marković's ideas.

The national awakening in Croatia took a different course. The search for Slav integration was very old. This long and strong emphasis on seeking a broader Slav alliance was not only a result of Croatian powerlessness in the face of various forms of foreign domination but also an instinctive reaction to the fact that dispersion of Croatian lands had strengthened various Croatian regional identities, often to the detriment of a wider Croatian feeling.

As in Serbia, there was a tendency to deal with other South Slavs as a form of disguised Croats. At the beginning of the eighteenth century, for example, Pavao Vitezović, the first Croatian national ideologist, divided the entire Slav world into North and South Croatia. This particular national construction never generated a strong following. Vitezović was much more important for introducing a line of reasoning that paid very little attention to cultural, linguistic, or religious attributes of nationhood. He based his sole claim to the national revival of Croatia on historical precedent. From Vitezović to the present day, Croatian national apologists are lopsidedly historicist. They believe that the inspiration of history and the right to statehood are the most effective antidotes to both the Habsburg centralism of the old days and Serbian centralism in modern times.

Unlike the Serbs, who had their common church organization, the instruments of Croatian national integration were the Sabor (parliament) and the office of the Ban (Duke). They were both visible expressions of Croatia's history and right to statehood. But the authority of these institutions was very much diminished over time by the conquests of the Magyars and then the Habsburgs. Furthermore, the shrunken authority of these Croatian institutions encompassed only a small portion of the Croatian lands. That is why the Croats in their national revival had to rely more on self-reflective ideas. This in turn made them less firm and pointed, allowing for a broader spectrum of national ideologies.

The Croatian national revival began in the late eighteenth century in large part as a reaction to awakened Magyar (Hungarian) nationalism. In 1790 the Magyar nobility introduced Hungarian to replace Latin. The Croats tried to counter with an alternative national program. The Illyrian movement of the 1830s and 1840s constructed such a program, the linchpin of which was a common language.

In order to broaden the base of their linguistic resistance the Illyrians chose this particular name out of the conviction that the ancient Illyrians had given rise to the South Slavs. Furthermore, this was a more neutral name that could override all the regional differences so characteristic of the Croatian situation at the time.

The linguistic part of the Illyrian movement presupposed a common language that in turn would become the cornerstone in the construction of a single national culture and consciousness for all the South Slavs. They preached the politics of concession, whereby all Croats and South Slavs would give up something in order to achieve one literary language and one cultural – Illyrian – identity. But the Illyrian solutions were so heavily dependent on Croatian national and cultural traditions that they failed to attract the other South Slavs.

The Serbs were particularly cool, even hostile to the idea. The proposed linguistic structure was far removed from church Slavic; they found no use for the reformed Latin script, which was considered an obstacle to the introduction of Cyrillic, and, most importantly, they felt that the Croat reformers were attempting to diminish the Serbian national identity under the guise of the neutral Illyrian name.

The Illyrians almost completely disappeared after the harsh Germanization that followed the defeat of the 1848 revolutionary wave in Europe. A new wave of Croatian national radicals, expressing their interests in plain Croatian colours, took over. The key figure was Ante Starčević, aided by Eugen Kvaternik. Jointly they promulgated a Croatian national ideology that negated Illyrism in almost every respect.

Their revived nationalism rested on the affirmation of a right to statehood that by definition belonged to the Croatian people, as far back as their migration on to these territories. This "primary acquisition" established the eternal and natural right of Croats to the ownership of the land. Basing their claims to territory on the writings of the Byzantine historian Porphyrogenitus, Kvaternik established that Croatia extended from the Alps to the River Drina (the natural boundary between Bosnia and Serbia) and from Albania to the Danube. Starčević pushed this line even farther to the east, as far as the River Timok, which is the eastern border of Serbia with Bulgaria. Thus for Starčević the Serbs did not exist as a nation. The only two Slav nations in the Balkans were the Croats and the Bulgars.

Starčević's and especially Kvaternik's idea of the "natural frontiers of the Croatian state" would be influential in times to come, and have been thoroughly aired in the latest Croatian national revival.

At the same time that Starčević's ideology helped to arouse Croatian national sentiment, a large segment of the Croatian intelligentsia revived the South Slav idea, but now under the Yugoslav name. The principal proponent of Yugoslavism was Bishop Josip Strossmayer, who, in establishing the Yugoslav Academy of Sciences in Zagreb in 1866, created the first institution ever to bear the Yugoslav name (which it lost in 1991 under the new wave of Croatian national revival).

Strossmayer for the most part operated within the Habsburg framework, wishing to unify the South Slavs into a state within a federalized Habsburg monarchy. But his ultimate goal, about which he was much less open, was a federal South Slav state, built on the ruins of the Habsburg monarchy and embracing Serbia and Montenegro. Here, then, was for the first time a concept of joining together all South Slav nations in a federation, with the purpose of creating a broader front of opposition to the non-Slav occupiers and winning freedom. The principal reason this early concept of Yugoslavism did not work was that Strossmayer, like Starčević, stuck fast to the doctrine of the Croatian right to statehood, which in this case included all of the western Balkans. That would have meant including Bosnia at the very time that the government of Serbia, under Garašanin, was preparing the ground there for an anti-Ottoman uprising and the province's unification with Serbia.

Though it did not come to fruition, the idea of a South Slav state did not go away. It went through ups and downs over the next few decades as Serbs first attempted to win Bosnia through an uprising in 1875, then with the Austrian occupation of Bosnia and mounting tensions between Austria and Serbia. Though Serbia (with Montenegro) gained full international recognition at the Congress of Berlin in 1878, in the process it became Vienna's stalking-horse in the Balkans.

Sensing that a conflict with Vienna at that time would not be productive, Serbia reduced its foreign-policy aspirations for a while and turned its attention to the south and south east and a growing conflict with Bulgaria over territories, including Macedonia. Serbia waited for a better opportunity in Bosnia.

The expectation that Bosnia would eventually become a part of Croatia because of the "natural right to statehood," coupled with Serbia's temporary turning away from Bosnia and the worsening relations between Serbia and Austria, all helped to revive the idea of Yugoslavism, that is to say an alliance with Serbia. This was made ever more essential when the crisis of the Dual Monarchy entered an acute phase and the Croatian lands found themselves under mounting pressure from two competitive streams of imperialism.

The Austro-German policy of *Drang nach Osten* ran eastward across Croatia-Slavonia, while Hungary's drive towards the Adriatic coast and harbours led Budapest to intensify its domination over the Croats. This more than anything else triggered the formation at the beginning of the twentieth century of the first Croatian and Serbian political group: the Croato-Serbian Coalition (HSK). Very soon it won a great majority of the Sabor elections, becoming the ruling party in Croatia. The HSK upheld a form of Yugoslavism that was labelled *narodno jedinstvo Hrvata i Srba* (Croat and Serb national unity). This became the most important political idea in pre-war Croatian politics. But the ill-defined *narodno jedinstvo* gave rise to interpretation and political claims of different, even opposing tendencies.

Some Croats and almost all Serbs in the Dual Monarchy looked upon *narodno jedinstvo* as unity in action: the Croats saw it bringing an independent Croatia with the help of Serbs, and the Serbs saw it advancing the hour of Serb unification.

But for a considerable number of Croatian politicians, and especially a large segment of the intelligentsia, *narodno jedinstvo* suggested the emergence of unitarist Yugoslavism, not unity in action but unity in being. That meant an ideology that would abolish Croatia's tradition of the right to statehood in order to justify the natural right of the "Yugoslav nation" to establish a uninational Yugoslav state. Its supporters obviously interpreted the word *jedinstvo* to mean "oneness." This interpretation became dominant and preached a new ideology of Yugoslavism as unitarism. It is important to note that this ideology was of Croatian political origin because there were, and still are, different and conflicting interpretations concerning the origins of unitarism.

Thinking in terms of "oneness," it was unavoidable that the Croatian unitarists would reflect on the "comparative advantages" of the two parts of the "whole." Thus came a famous synthesis by an important Croatian unitarist: "The Croat wants to live. The Serb is ready to die ... The Croat, as an intellectual, wants to know, perceive, understand, and criticize more and more, and is as a result more contemplative, forgives more, reacts less, is more of a sceptic, almost a cynic, rather than a fanatic. He feels himself superior even when he has fallen low, because intellectualism leads to relativism and inactivity. And perhaps he is such a great moralist precisely because he has so little moral strength. The Serb is not a moralist, but he has strong morality, the morality of activism and of reacting ... the morality of atonement and revenge. His aim is not to *understand* everything but to *be able* to do more. Croatdom represents statics, Serbdom dynamics. Croatdom is the potential and Serbdom the kinetic energy of the people, Croatdom is reflection, Serbdom is action."[3]

Since contemplation, inactivity, stasis, and pure potential never brought about national dynamism, which was the need of the day, the Croats were clearly in no position to lead the struggle for the creation of the unitarist Yugoslav nation or state. Things needed to be changed, and Croats were, by their own account, insufficiently capable of accomplishing what needed to be done. It came, then, as no surprise that among Croatian unitarists the Croatian part of the Serbo-Croatian people was increasingly viewed as somehow inferior, especially after the victories of Serbia in the Balkan Wars. Nor was it surprising that the Serbian unitarists in Croatia had precious little incentive to abandon forms of expansionist Serbian national policies that still thrived among them. They simply could not match the growing Serbophilia of Croatian unitarism with a corresponding Croatophilia of their own.

The Croats were, therefore, according to the unitarists, oriented towards the "doers," since flag-burning was the high point of their rebellion against the dreaded and despised Hungarian-appointed Ban.

But it must be added that, though dominant, the unitarists were definitely not the only important force on the Croatian political scene at the time, the beginning of the twentieth century, when the idea of Yugoslav unification was on the rise. Even before unification, which occurred after the First World War, a young politician by the name of Stjepan Radić was a force to be reckoned with. After unification he became pivotal to Croatian national aspirations. Before unification Radić's main achievement was to popularize politics and bring them to the peasants, who constituted over 80 per cent of the population. Not surprisingly, his party was called the Croatian (Republican) Peasants Party. This provided the political base on which he expounded his views on the national question.

His was a curious blend of faith in the Croatian right to statehood and in *narodno jedinstvo*, but since he was convinced of the wisdom of perpetuating the Habsburg monarchy, he advocated an Austro-Slavic formula that would unite Serbs, Slovenes, and Croats, within the empire, into a federal, monarchical state. His Yugoslavism ended at the border of the empire and had nothing to do with the "doers" in Serbia or Montenegro.

The "doers" in Serbia, meanwhile, felt strong enough to mount a double challenge, expanding into territory with a Serbian population that was still under Turkish control and increasing the challenge to Austria over Bosnia, which had effectively changed rulers in 1878. Bosnia was still nominally under Turkish sovereignty, but the actual administration was in the hands of the Austrians until 1908, when Austria formally annexed Bosnia.

The Ottoman Empire, on its deathbed, could not offer much resistance, and Serbia, with its allies, was successful in throwing it almost clearly out of the Balkans. This was done during the First Balkan War of 1912–13. Later on, in 1913, Serbia was again successful in a war against Bulgaria. This expanded Serbian territory to the east and gave all of present-day Macedonia to the Serbs.

The effects were, first, a doubling of the territory of the state of Serbia and, second, boost to national pride, fighting spirit, and self-consciousness. The net effect was to bring relations with Austria to a boiling-point.

Austria was for a long time suspicious of Serbia's intentions and directly opposed to the creation of a new power in the Balkans. Serbia was not only unsettling for its great-power interests but also promoted unrest among the Serbian and other Slavic subjects of the empire. The Habsburgs were opposed not only to Serbia but to the idea of Yugoslavism.

This mutual antagonism – the Serbs defending the right of "Serbs and other brethren" in the Dual Monarchy to freedom, and the monarchy fighting for its survival – led to Austria's declaration of war after the assassination of Archduke Ferdinand. This in turn triggered the First World War.

Slovenes, the third ethnic group or "tribe" headed towards unification in one country, had no tradition of statehood to build upon. Instead they had a long tradition of cultivating their separate language. That made them similar to the Serbs in the phase of national awakening, but in contrast with the Serbs, the church played no part since all surrounding countries were also Catholic. Thus the distinction made no difference. On the contrary, it was the Catholic church that was often at odds with linguistic emancipation. After 1848 most Slovenian national programs were oriented towards attaining unification of Slovenes within a separate Habsburg unit. Right up to the war and through a good part of it the Slovenes persisted in an Austrophile orientation, which often included hostility to the Serbs. It was only towards the end of the war, when it became obvious that the old empire would not survive, that a new wave of Slovenian pragmatists, led by Anton Korošec, argued for closer co-operation with the Croats and the Serbs.

As the First World War began, the overwhelming political force on the Slav side was the Serbian program to achieve the liberation and unification of all Serbs, though there was in the background a call for Balkan or Yugoslav federalism to foster the spirit of the Yugoslav community. The governing Radicals of Nikola Pašić, a key figure in Serbia during and immediately after the war, contemplated common action with the South Slavs of the Dual Monarchy, especially after Serbia's resounding and exciting victories in the Balkan Wars of 1912–13. But the implicit, and often explicit assumption was: Serbia with its victories and established statehood was a natural and logical focal point.

The fate of Yugoslavia was determined during the First World War, and the state was created at the end of it. The principal forces that determined the path to Yugoslavia's unification as well as its characteristic features were:

- The victorious Entente powers (France, England, the United States, and Italy);
- Serbia, with its resistance and great contribution to the war effort on the Entente side;
- The Yugoslav Committee, consisting of prominent South Slav politicians in exile from the Dual Monarchy;
- Political leaders of South Slavs who remained in the Dual Monarchy.

At the beginning of the war the influence of the Entente was negative in the sense that it did not openly declare its war aims. Wanting to keep their options open, the Entente powers did not want to declare as an aim the break-up of the Habsburg Empire, hoping to be able to negotiate a separate peace with it. This was not to Serbia's liking, and if anything it increased the resolve of Serbs to fight the Dual Monarchy. But this lack of a single clear purpose regarding the Habsburg Empire confused the South Slavs within the monarchy, prolonging the political life of the tendency that thought that South Slav unity was possible in a new and restructured monarchy.

Secondly, when it became generally known that the Entente powers had secretly promised to Italy parts of Slovenia and Croatia in order to lure her into the war, the South Slavs of the monarchy, this time including the Slovenes, turned naturally to the unyielding Serbs, who were engaged in a heroic battle with the monarchy.

Thirdly, the sheer magnitude of the Serbian contribution to the war effort obliged the allies, particularly the French, to pay heed to Serbia's war aims. The weight that Serbian politicians carried with the allies was understandably much greater than anything that other Slavs from the monarchy, in exile or within it, could muster.

Fourthly, the entry of the United States into the war and the famous fourteen-point speech by President Woodrow Wilson opened the door to self-determination of nations, thus raising the hopes and efforts of the South Slavs in the direction of autonomy and independence.

Last, but certainly not least, the surprising occurrence of the October Revolution in Russia changed the planned post-war designs of the Entente powers. It became clear that the Dual Monarchy, enfeebled by the war and torn within by social unrest, nationalist movements, strikes, and the like could not deal with the impact of the October Revolution either externally or internally. The need for a stronger rather than a weaker state in the Balkans became obvious. It had to be a state that would act as an ally and a buffer against the spread of socialism and would also be capable of staving off internal unrest. This definitely shifted the balance towards the creation of one state for the South Slav nation. It also shifted the support of the allies towards the Serbian view of what this state ought to look like, principally because of Serbia's strong and conservative army.

The Serbs had had a very clear understanding, from the beginning, that the war was a gamble that would result either in Serbia's becoming a colony of Austria or in the realization of Serbian ambitions at the expense of Austria, thus making Serbia the biggest power in the Balkans. As early as September 1914 Serbia proclaimed its war aim: to create out of Serbia a powerful southwestern Slavic state; all the Serbs, all the Croats, and all the Slovenes would enter its composition.

The first year of the war went well for Serbia. Together with Montenegro the Serbs repulsed the initial Austro-Hungarian offensive, delivering the enemy a resounding defeat. This boosted the confidence of the Serbs and encouraged South Slavs from the monarchy to move a step closer to them in spirit and politics both.

However, in 1915 Austria was joined by Germany and Bulgaria in its renewed attack on Serbia. Despite great bravery, the Serbians could not hold their ground and had to retreat through hostile Albanian territory into Greece. They were down but not out. Montenegro was also occupied by the Central Powers, and its government found refuge in France.

From Greece the Serbian government organized and consolidated its military and diplomatic activity. The most important, of course, was the Serbian army, which was preserved in considerable force and fighting spirit, waiting for an opportune moment to fight its way back into Serbia and beyond.

This was the domain of diplomatic activity of Nikola Pašić, the Serbian prime minister and a very crafty politician. In his efforts he made a distinction between the Serbian territories (defined linguistically) and the demands of the new state, which would include Croats and Slovenes. There is no denying that he saw a need, political or otherwise, to foster unification with other South Slav nations. His main diplomatic effort was thus to prevent the allies from recognizing a separate state derived from Austro-Hungarian South Slavs. His main challenge in that effort came from those Croatian politicians who wanted South Slav unification but on the basis of national equality with Serbia. Pašić chose not to commit himself early on, hoping and expecting that time would work in his favour, as mostly it did.

The most prominent anti-Habsburg Croats who sought a Yugoslav state were Frane Supilo and Ante Trumbić. They put themselves at the head of Croat, Serb, and Slovene politicians who emigrated from the Dual Monarchy to Entente countries at the beginning of the war and formed the Yugoslav Committee, seeking co-operation with Serbia but on an equal footing.

They believed, somewhat naïvely for the time, that the principle of national rights and self-determination was a bargaining and negotiating chip equal to Serbian statehood and that it was equal compensation for Serbian sacrifices during the war. Seeking an agreement with Serbia, they claimed to represent the South Slavs in the Dual Monarchy. They hoped that their representation, rather than Serbia's military expansion, would lead to honourable unification. For a while they were openly critical of Serbia's expansive posture.

But the secret treaty that was signed with Italy in London tempered their criticism, exposed the vulnerability of their position based on high principle, and brought them closer to *realpolitik*. They realized that now more than ever the unity not of Yugoslavia but of Slovenes and Croats depended on Serbia's success. Therefore, a logical tactical retreat from their previous position occurred, namely a suggestion that they join with Serbia in the liberation of territories, leaving the problem of Greater Serbia for after the war and until after their lands had been secured from Austro-Hungarian domination and Italian aspirations.

If the secret London treaty pushed the Yugoslav Committee closer to the Serbs, then the outbreak of the October Revolution represented for Pašić and Serbia the elimination of a source of strong support. The loss of Russian support in turn made Pašić more flexible and conciliatory to the demands of the Yugoslav Committee.

The result was the signing of the Corfu Declaration, which brought the two parties to acceptance of a uniform course of action on unification. This agreement, signed on the Greek island of Corfu in July 1917, stated the determination of Serbs, Croats, and Slovenes to form a united and independent state that would be a "constitutional, democratic, and parliamentary monarchy headed by the [Serb] Karadjordjević dynasty." In an attempt to break from concentration on the past and historical rights, the declaration made no mention of any historical territories but rather referred to counties and other administrative units.

The Corfu Declaration was a compromise between the position of the Yugoslav Committee and that of Serbia led by Pašić. It recognized the three national names, the three flags and religions, and the two alphabets. No wonder then that this declaration was hailed as the Yugoslav Magna Carta, despite its bias and flaws.

The South Slav political leaders remaining within the Dual Monarchy went through a phase of massive anti-Serbian hysteria, caused by the assassination of Ferdinand. But they then settled into support of the Austro-Hungarian war effort, hoping to gain more autonomy and the Croatian right to statehood. The situation in Slovenia was similar. It was only a few months before the end of the war that either faced reality and found the "courage" to change its posture. The Slovenes did this first, forming in August 1918 a national council for the purpose of uniting the Yugoslav people within an independent state. The key figure was the leader of the Clerical Party, Anton Korošec.

In Croatia it took two months longer to realize the inevitable. In October 1918 in Zagreb, delegates of Croatian, Slovenian and Serbian parties that favoured an independent South Slavic state formed the National Council of the Slovenes, Croats, and Serbs, with Korošec, the Slovene, as president. But this happened only after Austria had offered an armistice, the Salonika front had been shattered by the Allies, Bulgaria had capitulated, and Serbian armies were on their way to Belgrade.

On 29 October 1918 the Croatian Sabor proclaimed "Dalmatia, Croatia, Slavonia, and Rijeka ([a coastal city] a completely independent state" and decided that this state was to enter "immediately into the new sovereign State of the Slovenes, Croats, and Serbs constituted on the territory of South Slavs that hitherto belonged to Austria-Hungary." The last decision of the Sabor was to transfer powers to the National Council, which only two days later declared its readiness to enter into a common state with Serbia and Montenegro. Thus the right to statehood, the cornerstone of Croatian legitimity, was clearly abandoned, with the Croatian political elite, middle class, and most intellectuals committing themselves to Yugoslav unitarism. The notable exception was Radić.

Only a week later the National Council sent a delegation to the Serbian supreme command, pleading for the entrance of Serbian armies to Croatia-Slavonia since they were quite unable to cope with the disorder, violence, looting, and rioting of the population after the demise of the centuries-old Austro-Hungarian Empire. The Serbian army entered Sarajevo on 6 November 1918 and Zagreb a week later.

The same day that Serbian soldiers marched, on request, into Sarajevo, there was a meeting in Geneva of all interested parties at which a formula was decided for equal participation in the transitional government. The twelve-man transitory Cabinet was to be filled with six delegates each, thus reflecting Serbian superiority on the field and the numerical majority of the South Slavs from the toppled monarchy (8 million, as compared to 4 million in Serbia). On 9 November 1918 the common state was finally agreed upon. Before formal unification the regional assembly of Vojvodina proclaimed unification with Serbia. A day later the assembly of Montenegro removed King Nikola I from the throne and proclaimed unification with Serbia. Thus Serbia entered into the unification considerably enlarged.

The actual birth of the new composite state occurred on 1 December 1918, when King Alexander proclaimed the unification of Serbia with the lands represented by the National Council. The new state was called the Kingdom of Serbs, Croats, and Slovenes. Yugoslavia, though not yet in name, was thus established.

The account in this chapter brings us closer to some conclusions regarding the initial creation of Yugoslavia.

First and foremost, Yugoslavia was created out of, and one could say in spite of, strong national ideologies and national policies. Though blended into a new state, these did not cease to exert some centrifugal force, even when the official and dominant ideology became centralist.

But it would be wrong to say that it was created against the will of the people. The people in the proper sense of the word were never asked. No one can say with certainty what the verdict would have been had a referendum on the proposition tested the will of the people. Political decision-making at that time did not take account of popular expression, and not only in Yugoslavia was this true. The people involved in politics, the unchosen representatives, clearly made the decision to unite of their own free will and without overt pressure. If there was implied pressure, especially from the big powers, that was a part of the game at the time, not entirely unlike current events.

It would perhaps be wrong and certainly exaggerated to say that unification was simply imposed in the aftermath of the war by the victorious Entente powers. True, the peace treaties left the unfinished business of frontiers, and in Yugoslavia's case this mostly meant the gift of the Dalmatian coast to Italy. But it would be against historical evidence to claim that Yugoslavia would never have existed had it not been for the pressure of the big powers at Versailles.

It is true that the new unitary state was cursed with the task of accommodating the Serbian "doers" to the Croatian political activists. The unwavering sense of purpose of the Serbian state, its uncompromising national ideology, and perhaps most importantly the enormous physical and material sacrifices during three successive wars were the defining characteristics of the one side. Politically articulated programs, not always uniform and coherent, were the property of the other. Without justifying their conduct, it is still not surprising that the Serbians felt and acted as if they had brought into the "oneness" of the new country disproportionately more than others.

A problem that was glossed over but would return to take a toll was the absence of clearly written rights, responsibilities, and obligations of the different nations creating Yugoslavia. The absence of a sound legal foundation that would define the relationship among nations allowed, or at least facilitated, the exercise of Serbian hegemony immediately after the union.

But if the separate constituent nations were not equals, this account clearly gives no support to the contention that they were enemies by definition, that the Serbs and the Croats have been perpetually fighting over the centuries. In fact there was no fighting until the First World War, and then the Croats fought as Austrian conscripts against the army of Serbia. This did leave some traumatic scars, but far from the all-pervasive enmity that is the current popular image in the West.

Serbia demonstrated a strong fighting spirit, fighting wars against Turkey, Bulgaria, and finally the Central Powers. But it must also be seen that this fighting spirit of the Serbs and their accomplishments in battle went a long way in providing substantive support for the realization of the Croatian national program.

It is true that Serbia did not want Yugoslavia as strongly as Croatia did, just as it is true that the Yugoslavia that Croatia obtained was not exactly the Yugoslavia it was looking for. The other nations, Montenegrins, Slovenes, and Macedonians, played a secondary role, if at all, at this stage.

Finally, the account shows that economic considerations, hardly ever mentioned in discussions of the creation of Yugoslavia, were obviously not in the forefront. The whole effort was conducted primarily on the basis of political and security concerns. Economic motives, to the extent that they were present in the minds of governments and enterprising individuals, played at most a secondary role.

From all the above one can conclude that the newly created country, though not artificial, did not have a very sound structure. It would have taken great wisdom and a host of favourable circumstances to put it on a solid foundation.

CHAPTER THREE

Inter-War Instability

The centrifugal forces that were present in the process of the creation of Yugoslavia[1] were obviously not sufficiently strong to forestall the rise of a single South Slav state. The credit for keeping those forces in check goes to a unique political combination comprising the ideology of unitaristic Yugoslavism, which captured the imagination of the South Slav intelligentsia in the Dual Monarchy, and the tradition of expansionist Serbian statehood. This is what the new state had in its favour. But the problems were numerous.

The new state, created on 1 December 1918, had a territory of about 248,000 square kilometres and, according to the first census, taken in 1921, a population of just over 12 million. The national structure of the population is given in Table 1.

The peoples that came together knew very little about each other. Many of them knew very little at all, since the vast majority were peasants, largely illiterate and traditionally tied to their small plots of land.

The waging of two Balkan Wars and participation in the First World War had left enormous scars on the human and material tissue of Serbia and Montenegro. Serbia alone lost 370,000 men in battle and an estimated 630,000 to other causes (widespread sickness, famine, etc.). This was a quarter of its population. The South Slavs in the Dual Monarchy did not fare much better, so that the total loss of human life of the peoples of the new state was estimated at around 1.9 million.

The economy was in disarray. Plundering and looting were widespread in those regions that had been a part of the Austro-Hungarian Empire. The debt incurred in fighting the war had to be repaid. Social tensions were high, and the threatening roar of the October Revolution could be heard in these parts as well, particularly since

Table 1

	No.	%
Serbs	4,665,851	38.83
Croats	2,856,551	23.77
Slovenes	1,024,761	8.53
Bosnian Muslims	727,650	6.05
Macedonians	585,558	4.87
Other Slavs	176,466	1.45
Germans	513,472	4.27
Hungarians	472,409	3.93
Albanians	441,740	3.68
Rumanians, Vlachs, and Cincars	229,398	1.91
Turks	168,404	1.40
Jews	64,159	0.53
Italians	12,825	0.11
Others	80,079	0.67
Total	12,017,323	100.00

Source: Ivo Banac, *The National Question in Yugoslavia: Origin, History, Politics* (Ithaca: Cornell University Press 1984), 58.

the country's northern neighbour, Hungary, was caught up in revolutionary fever.

The two parts of the integrated country brought together largely dissimilar, often diametrically opposed social infrastructures. The legal system, for example, was fragmented into several sub-units; the money used in the new state was not uniform; the postal systems were differently organized, and so on.

But perhaps most importantly, the creation of Yugoslavia brought together very different systems of government and institutions. The new state needed to work towards finding accommodations between politicians and civil servants rooted in differing state and political structures, different approaches to ethnic and national questions, different political cultures.

The Serbs brought a tradition of a centralist and unitarian state. Until the Balkan Wars this state had been nationally homogeneous with no minorities. The sensitivity of the Serbian polity to questions of national minorities was therefore understandably, if regrettably, small. But the Serbs also brought a tradition of a functioning parliamentary democracy with limited sovereign powers, and the sense of a free political spirit, gained through long struggle against an oppressive foreign power. They had attained their freedom on their own and were proud of it. The way in which they attained that freedom had a direct impact on the political structure, favouring strong, central decision-making.

The Montenegrins had an independent country but patriarchal rule, quite different from the prevailing parliamentary rule of the day. The Slovenes and the Macedonians had no experience of independent political life and no tradition of autonomous parliamentary structures. At best they brought expectations, but no political artefacts of their own.

The Croats had a lasting state tradition, old institutions, and a developed political style. It would not be wrong to say that politically they were the most sophisticated. This also caused their division into three distinct segments: those oriented towards Croatian state rights and Croatian traditions, who were typically suspicious of the Serbs; those who favoured the Yugoslav option as a unitary state but one that would be an authentic Yugoslavia, not a Greater Serbia; and finally those, mostly Serbs from Croatia and other lands under the Dual Monarchy, who favoured a strong unitary and centralist state under the clear leadership of Serbia.

International recognition had not been fully effected at the time of the formation of the first provisional government and interim parliament. The provisional government started its work in mid-December 1918 and the interim parliament three months later. France and England still had not recognized the new state, and at the Versailles Peace Conference it participated as the Kingdom of Serbia, an ally in the war. The reason for this delay lay in a political commitment to Italy, allowing it to position itself favourably on the east coast of the Adriatic Sea. It was only with the signing of the Treaty of Versailles on 28 June 1919 that the new state of Yugoslavia was fully recognized, together with a number of others. It took the Vatican another four months to grant recognition.[2]

Thus, an important point on the agenda, one that held the South Slavs together at this stage, was the attempt to secure international borders and bring into the territory of the new state as many of their Slav brethren as possible. These attempts were only marginally successful, with a large part of the Adriatic coast going to Italy, a number of Slovenes remaining in the state of Austria, and Hungary ceding less than had been demanded. This was one source of the disillusion that set in almost immediately. The new state was not even able to fulfil the aspirations of the Slovenes and Croats regarding territory and population.

Another, much more fundamental disenchantment set in as the political structures of the new state were being developed. The first

government of the new kingdom was formed twenty days after unification as a coalition Cabinet of the most prominent political figures
from Serbia and the territories covered by the Yugoslav Committee.
The king, even at this early stage, demonstrated that he would play
a strong role, bypassing the logical government leader selected by an
inter-party caucus and choosing a less influential but presumably
more pliant politician.

The formation of this first government also meant the cessation of
the functions of the National Council (in Zagreb) and the Yugoslav
Committee. The autonomy of the provincial governments still in
existence – Croatia, Slavonia and Srem (a region to the east of Slavonia), BiH, Slovenia, and Dalmatia – was drastically reduced. The
provincial governments were appointed by regent's decree[3] and
approved by the administrative decisions of the central government.
Even in this interim period a centralist state was being formed, prior
to the adoption of a constitution that was ultimately to sanction this.

The provisional parliament, or the Interim National Legislature
(INL), as it was officially called, had been envisaged in the Corfu
Declaration. It was not elected by voters but appointed by various
regional assemblies or inter-party committees (with the exception of
Macedonia and Kosovo, where 24 members were actually elected).
The 272 deputies of the INL were distributed as follows: 32 from
Slovenia, 60 from Croatia (with Rijeka and Medjumurje), 4 from Istria
(in Croatia), 12 from Dalmatia, 42 from BiH, 84 from Serbia, 24 from
Macedonia and Kosovo, and 12 from Montenegro. This distribution
roughly corresponded to the relative size of the populations and was
not contested, especially since the delegates were not elected but
appointed.

It is important to note that Stjepan Radić, already the dominant
figure in the Croatian opposition to the creation of a unitary and
centralist state, declined the two mandates that his HRSS Party was
assigned. This marked the beginning of his open political confrontation with Greater Serbian centralism.

The INL had a limited mandate, which was to establish a procedure
for the election of the Constituent Assembly and the fashioning of
that body's agenda. Over a period of a year and a half and in 137
formal sittings, the INL became an experiment in facing the central
issue that would dominate the later work of the Constituent
Assembly – the question of state centralism. The INL had no mandate
to discuss the substance of this issue, but it became the scene in
which strong and relatively successful efforts were mounted to provide the centralist forces with a better starting position in the Constituent Assembly.

In the electoral campaign for the Constituent Assembly, which raged throughout October and November 1920, political divisions principally crystallized along the lines of support or opposition to centralism, with issues from the social agenda coming in a strong second.

The elections for the Constituent Assembly were held on 28 November 1920. Out of an electorate of 2.5 million (no women voting), 1.6 million or 65 per cent cast their vote to elect 419 parliamentarians. There were 22 parties, indicating the fragmentation of the political scene. The results of the elections are presented in Table 2.

Both the centralists and their opponents hoped that the voters would bolster their respective positions. The two leading advocates of centralism (the Democratic and National Radical parties) gained a majority, each gaining a respectable number of seats. In terms of popular vote their 600,000 plus obviously outnumbered the anti-centralist vote, which stood at 534,000. But having gained only a relative majority and with almost half the electorate against them, they might have been expected to moderate their haste for a firm centralist constitution. Unfortunately this did not happen. The centralists were keen to capitalize on their victory and to use the momentum while it was still in their favour.

The Constituent Assembly was convened on 12 December 1920, and the very first preliminary sessions were already marked by intense clashes between the two centralist parties and the various opposition parties. Radić's Croat Peasant (50) and the Croat Party of Right (2) declined to participate. The first squabble occurred over the oath to the monarch, the main issue being the identity of the bearer of sovereignty. The opposition insisted on the sovereignty of parliament, while the centrists upheld the king. The latter won the first round. The second round was on the more substantive issue of what would constitute a qualified majority. The Corfu Declaration stated that the constitution could be promulgated only by a numerically qualified majority. Again, the autonomists felt that they would be protected by this clause. The centrists argued that no existing law defined a qualified majority and that the definition depended on political expediency. At the moment, they went on to argue, it was better to opt for the lowest possible numerical definition since that would provide a constitution, perhaps less than perfect, but certainly better than a long search for a possibly unworkable arrangement.

On substance, the centralist concept relegated decision-making in all state affairs to the three central powers: the king, parliament, and the government. The king, however, stood a crown above the others, which prompted a comment that the new state was "a centralist

Table 2

Party	Votes	Members of Parliament
Democratic	320,000	92
National Radical	285,000	91
Communist	200,000	59
Croatian Peasant	230,000	50
Agrarian Alliance	151,000	39
Slovenian People's	111,000	27
Yugoslav Muslim	111,000	24
Social Democrat	47,000	10
National Turks'	30,000	8
Croatian People's	38,000	7
Croatian Union	26,000	4
Republican	18,000	3
Croatian Party of Right	11,000	2
National Socialist		2
Non-party (Trumbić)		1
Liberal Party		1
Total		420

Source: Branko Petranović, *Istorija Jugoslavije 1918–1978* (Beograd: Nolit 1980), 48.

monarchy with limited parliamentarism" rather than the other way round. No national or regional autonomy was envisaged. In line with the Corfu Declaration, historical boundaries were disregarded and administrative ones advanced instead.

The opposition parties, frustrated by the unwillingness of the government to compromise, were faced with the decision to remain in parliament and be repeatedly outvoted or to boycott the sessions, hoping to deny legitimacy to the constitution in the making. Many in fact did so, and the government's constitutional proposal was adopted with a vote of 227 in favour, 93 against, all others having walked out or abstained.

The Croatian parties that walked out created the so-called Croat Block, this being one of the undesired but very important outcomes of the haste in bringing forward a centralist constitution. Even some wiser and progressive members of the National Radical Party condemned the haste with which the constitution was being adopted, a constitution that was not sensitive to ethnic issues. The words spoken in 1921 by a Serbian parliamentarian, disgusted by the failure of the government to adopt even one of the opposition's forty-plus proposals on the question of administrative authority, sound prophetic: "Because Radić, perhaps, wants a separation of Croatia and independence, you [the centralist majority] want to trample down

[Serbia's] whole previous life, you want to perform a vivisection on our people. I can tell you this: *what Radić wants is not good, but what you want cannot be good either. May we live long to see the effects."*

Incidentally, Radić at that time wanted an independent Croatia, which would join a confederated Yugoslavia. The man who spoke these words, Momčilo Ivanić, did not live long enough to see the effects, since they came seventy years later.

To rub in their victory, and in singularly bad taste, the centralists decided to proclaim the new constitution on 28 June – Vidovdan or St Vitus's Day – a day that is sacred in Serbian history. On that day the great Battle of Kosovo against the Turks was fought and lost in 1389. Over the centuries Serbian tradition and folk imagination had transformed the temporal defeat into a source of spiritual strength and victory. Perhaps not quite accidentally, Archduke Ferdinand was assassinated on the same day in 1914. And certainly by design, the new constitution of the new South Slav state was to be adopted on this very day. The associations invoked by the historical meaning of Vidovdan could not have been more unfortunate for the subsequent fate of the new charter, since a deliberate impression was created that the constitution represented the final triumph of Serbian national ideology.

One other aspect of developing centralist rule needs to be brought in at this point. The reader has probably noticed in Table 2 the strong showing of the Communist Party, which was the third largest in the Constituent Assembly. In Montenegro it carried 38 per cent of the votes, in Macedonia, Kosovo, and Sandžak 27 per cent and in both Serbia and Dalmatia about 16 per cent. This was a development that reflected social tensions and class differentiation, but to the authoritarian, centralist rule of Regent Alexander it brought considerable displeasure.

Only a few days after the elections for the Constituent Assembly a series of anti-Communist measures were introduced by the government, denying them the right to demonstrate or agitate in public or to publish newspapers. Other opposition parties looked the other way. Soon thereafter the Communist Party was banned and outlawed, and it remained in hiding until the outbreak of the Second World War. This significantly reduced its scope of operation but also helped it to develop a strong anti-centralist stance.

The issue of Communism was particularly bothersome to Regent Alexander, a former page at the Russian imperial court at St Petersburg. He was ideologically loyal to the fallen Czarists and provided protection and material support to thousands of post-Revolution Russian exiles. Moreover, he was also politically loyal to France, which saw in the conservative Yugoslav regime and in Alexander personally an important element in the Balkan *cordon sanitaire*, which was both anti-German and anti-Communist. The regimes of Yugoslavia maintained their anti-Communist stance internally and externally, thus making Yugoslavia one of the very last European countries to recognize the Soviet Union in 1940.

The Yugoslav Communist Party was, like all others, under the spell of the Communist Party of the USSR and Comintern. The Comintern's stand at that time, in favour of breaking up Yugoslavia and forming a Balkan federation, did not go down well within Yugoslavia, especially in the Communist strongholds in Serbia and Montenegro. This, coupled with its illegality, explains the relative unattractiveness to Yugoslavs of the Communist program in the inter-war years.

Meanwhile, the rift that was supposedly sealed by the proclamation of the new supreme legal charter, popularly known as the Vidovdan Constitution, made the country ever less manageable in a democratic way. The newly elected parliament could not impose itself as the legitimate and democratic body of political deliberation. It reflected the many tensions, not only ethnic ones, that shook the country. Not surprisingly, not one elected parliament managed to complete its four-year mandate. Elections were repeatedly called every two years (1921, 1923, 1925, 1927), indicating the political turmoil and instability that reigned and an inability to deal with outstanding issues, most prominently the acute national issue.

The other outward sign of political instability was the frequent change of government. During the period of the monarchy (between the two world wars) thirty-nine governments tried and failed to address outstanding issues. That is almost two governments a year!

Even more importantly, these governments were mostly formed by the king, not the parliament. In the period 1918–29 only two governments fell due to a parliamentary vote of no confidence. The rest were brought down by the king. And just as he brought down governments that commanded a parliamentary majority, he managed to keep in power those that did not have one. His authority to choose governments was further increased by his constitutional right to convene and disperse the parliament.

The political parties in and out of parliament sought to maximize their respective political programs. Sometimes this brought very strange results, as in the period 1925–27, when Radić, the most influential and important Croatian autonomist, recognized the Crown and the constitution for tactical political reasons. The political parties, like the newcomers to the democratic process they were, tried every possible combination, alliance, plot, and counterplot to change the existing order of things or to defend it.

The Croatian Peasant Party led by Radić played a knife-edge political game, boycotting the National Assembly, abstaining from deliberations or voting in it, conducting a campaign on the international scene with the principal idea of gaining the attention of foreign political circles for the plight of the Croatian people in Yugoslavia. This tactic also had as its aim to soften the centralist tendencies of the regime and induce some kind of compromise. But with their actions outside parliament, Radić and his party made it easier for their opponents to claim that this action was subversive and anti-Yugoslav.

As time passed, the parliament turned into a scene of ever-increasing political confrontation, disorder, and squabbles, culminating tragically in an incident in which two parliamentarians were shot dead and another three were wounded. One of the wounded was Radić, who died six weeks later. This tragic incident took place in mid-1928 and gave the king a pretext to dissolve parliament and proclaim absolute rule at the beginning of 1929.

With this act the king suspended the constitution and imposed a prohibition on all political parties that had a "tribal" or religious name and program. He also abolished parliament, with the proclamation that "national unity and territorial integrity" were in danger. The king believed he could accomplish the centralist aims that parliament had failed to achieve. Relying mostly on the army (a general became prime minister), civil servants, and some political leaders from Serbia and Croatia, the king went on to execute his program of *integral Yugoslavism*. This was the high point of the "oneness" of the newly emerging Yugoslav nation, but it was being accomplished in a way that could not hold.

In proclaiming absolute rule, King Alexander was far more concerned about the reaction of his own Serbs (knowing how a previous king with the same name had ended in 1903 after a dictatorial rule) than about other nationalities, including the Croats. The Croatian mainstream opposition was only mildly opposed to this new development, and the leader who took over from Radić actually welcomed it, thinking that an arrangement with the king would be easier to obtain than with the Serbian political parties.

One significant consequence of the dictatorship was the revival of separatist tendencies in Croatia and Macedonia. Though they were not yet politically important, this was the moment they made their definitive break with the concept of Yugoslavia. Ante Pavelić, later to become the notorious leader of the Ustashi state, left Yugoslavia at this time, only to come back years later as the head of the so-called Independent State of Croatia.

The king proceeded to introduce his integral Yugoslavism or national unitarism in the following way: he changed the name of the Kingdom of Serbs, Croats, and Slovenes into Yugoslavia; prohibited the use of all national flags, symbols, or heraldic insignia; abolished the division of the country according to "tribal" criteria; and introduced nine geographic rather than national administrative units, called *banovina*.[4] Thus Croatia was split into two different administrative units and Serbia into five. The only *banovina* in which the borders corresponded to the ethnic group living there was Slovenia (*Dravska banovina*).

The fact that King Alexander introduced a personal dictatorial rule did not much disturb the European powers, since all the Central and East European countries, with the notable exception of Czechoslovakia, were run by regimes that were dictatorial in nature, with strong reliance on the army.

After the initial shock and surprise, the opposition to this method of forcible Yugoslav national unification gradually started picking up. The king attempted to broaden his political support, seeking allies in the political parties of Serbia and Slovenia, but failed. He reintroduced a constitution in 1931, trying to create the impression that the decisive goal had been accomplished and that now things could go back to normal, or almost, since the new constitution did not force the re-creation of a true parliament but only a national assembly consisting of like-minded political parties. The king, according to this constitution, retained the right to act outside of it in "cases of need."

Attempting to broaden the political base of his ideology of Yugoslav unification further, the king created the Yugoslav National Party, which was anything but an independent political party, drawing its funds and political support from the government. But by 1932 the Croatian opposition had fully recovered and took a united stand, insisting on a return to 1918 and the reconstitution of the state of Yugoslavia on a more equitable basis, eliminating Serbian hegemony. Similar resolutions or statements were cropping up everywhere, including Serbia. The king did not yield until the end of his life, which was cut short in Marseilles in October 1934 by an assassin's bullet, fired by a member of a Ustashi-Macedonian terrorist group sponsored by Fascist Italy.

In 1935 new elections were called that effectively ended the monarchical dictatorship but not the attempts at a continuation of the policy of the "Martyr King." The prime minister who took over did not even bother to conceal the fact that he was creating a political coalition that would encircle and isolate the Croatian opposition and bring it to its knees. His dictatorial manner increased the resistance and opposition of the Croats, and also made many Serbs uneasy. The political tide was moving slowly but surely towards a new accommodation between the Serbs and the Croats. The government was forced to accept an agreement in 1937 that would lead to a new constitution and an equitable position for all nations in Yugoslavia. However, its entry into force was delayed with the explanation that it must wait for young King Peter II to come of age.

The winds of the Second World War were already in the air and added to the strains on the internal relations of the Yugoslav nations. Finally, on 26 August 1939, just a few days before the beginning of the war, an agreement was reached between the centralist government and the Croatian opposition.

This agreement created the *Croat banovina*, the first territorial unit within Yugoslavia that was based on the ethnic, that is, national principle. This was the first time in exactly twenty years that the national problem of Yugoslavia had been approached from a different perspective, with an eye to national diversities rather than by attempting to disguise them with unitarian policies.

The agreement provided too little and came too late. First, it was never ratified and remained more of a political symbol of good will, or a policy of expediency, never reaching the stage of a legally sanctioned document. Second, the Croatian extreme right, by that time a force to be reckoned with, was unsatisfied with the agreement since it "gave too much away" and forestalled the creation of an entirely independent Croatian state. Third, the Serbian unitarist hardliners were unhappy because this signalled the end of total Serbian domination over the affairs of Yugoslavia. So instead of settling things and bringing much-needed mutual trust and confidence, this agreement actually led to dramatic confrontations.

Negotiated from a position of mutual weakness and not from mutual strength, the agreement was, however, extremely important: it demonstrated clearly that the attempt to create a Yugoslavia without due respect for its nations and national diversities was impossible and would be counter-productive sooner or later. This development challenged simultaneously the principles of unitarism and centralism.

The virus spread fast. There were demands for the creation of an autonomous Slovenian unit, an independent BiH unit, as well as a project for an autonomous "Serb land." This would have been the beginning of a thorough internal reconstitution of Yugoslavia. It is anybody's guess how this process would have ended if the war had not intervened, destroying Yugoslavia as a state and cutting short a process of political transformation in the making.

Two more developments need to be mentioned here to complete the picture of the inter-war years. First, in 1937 the post of the general secretary of the Communist Party of Yugoslavia (CPY) was taken over by Josip Broz, better known as Tito. Having had a rich revolutionary career in Austro-Hungary, Germany, Russia, France, and Switzerland (some even claim that he was active in Spain during the Civil War), he took over a party that was somewhat disoriented. It was small but well organized. After its great initial success in the first parliamentary (and especially local) elections, then having been proclaimed illegal, the CPY went through much hardship and suffering, some of its own making, some under the extremist directives of Moscow and the Comintern. The number of party members and supporters fell drastically, but those who remained were hardened revolutionaries who had gone through thick and thin at the hands of a regime that kept it outlawed. The CPY was also truly Yugoslav, meaning that it had well organized if small units all over the country. These were not the token representations that some other parties also had in various part of the country but lean and active organizations with a revolutionary purpose.

The other development that should be mentioned is the evolution of the foreign policy of Yugoslavia. Coming out of the First World War, the new state leaned heavily on France, both because of traditional ties but also because of the joint effort during the war. The principal antagonist of Yugoslavia among the victorious powers of the First World War was Italy. That remained the case almost without exception throughout the inter-war period.

With Hitler's rise in Germany, the political power structure in Europe started to change, and with it Yugoslav foreign policy. Though not openly pro-German or pro-Nazi, Yugoslav foreign policy was changing in ways that took account of the new realities in Europe. Especially disturbing for King Alexander was the Franco-Soviet rapprochement, which he opposed. Ties and links with the Third Reich were gradually increased, augmenting imperceptibly the dependence of Yugoslavia on Germany. A feeble attempt at maintaining "neutrality" was made, immediately after Munich, just at a time when Britain was recovering an interest in the Balkans, and specifically Yugoslavia. But one neighbouring country after another – Italy, Austria, Hungary, Romania, Bulgaria, Albania – became a part of or an ally of the new German power, thus making it increasingly difficult to resist the lures and pressures of the Third Reich.

By 1941 France, having already capitulated to Germany, was no longer in a position to help. Britain, incapable of organizing a strong Balkan front against the Nazi onslaught, was nevertheless quite capable through its intelligence network of organizing a putsch in Yugoslavia. The pro-German government, which had signed a pact with the German-Italian Axis, was overthrown in March 1941 and a pro-British officer clique and the young King Peter II (who was still a minor) were brought in. They tried in vain to convince Hitler that their position was not anti-German, even though they were known not to be pro-German. Only ten days later Germany attacked Yugoslavia and overpowered it within a week. Thus was the demise of the "First Yugoslavia," which was partitioned among Germany, Italy, Hungary, and Bulgaria, with two puppet regimes being formed in Serbia and Croatia. The latter became notorious for the atrocities it committed against minorities within its borders.

Another small but significant point is worth mentioning. On the eve of the invasion German foreign minister Joachim von Ribbentrop offered Croatia secession from Yugoslavia and independent statehood. Vlatko Maček, who at the time, besides being a deputy prime minister of the central government, led the HSS Party and was the undisputed leader of mainstream Croatian politics, declined, choosing to stay with Yugoslavia. It was the Ustashi, protected and financed in Italy, who came into Yugoslavia with the occupying forces to "create" (or rather be given) an independent state of Croatia.

Trying to recapitulate the most important features of the inter-war period, the following general observations seem appropriate.

First, the new country, created on the ruins of two fallen empires, did not have much to build on in terms of a political system or a political structure that would be sensitive to its complexities. On the contrary, neither the Ottoman nor the Dual Empire had models of statecraft that would favour the development of a pluralistic political culture, much less a flexible one. That is why the inbuilt but nevertheless genuine pluralism of Yugoslavia, and its diversity of cultures, barely stood a chance of being properly accommodated.

Secondly, after unification, the fact that national individuality was denied to each of the South Slav nations, a position inherent in the precepts of unitarist Yugoslavism, greatly facilitated the establishment of centralism as a form of state organization. It appealed to the Serbs to have a state to which they aspired, but it left a big crack in the foundations of this new state.

Thirdly, the thesis of "national unity" and its ideological underpinning – integral Yugoslavism – could not withstand the reality of a multinational state. What Yugoslavia needed after unification was a consolidation of the state and the recognition of differences within it. That would have made the state stronger, not weaker. This did not happen until 1939, when the *Croat banovina* was formed. Then it was too late to matter, although an important lesson could be, and possibly was drawn from this lack of sensitivity towards national aspirations.

Fourthly, the policy of the state was doubly wrong. Not only did it not take account of differing political needs and diverse identities, but in insisting on putting everything into one unitarist "supranational" mould, Crown and government merely irritated sensitivites and helped to complete the process of national identification, even where this had been in only an embryonic stage.

Fifthly, in spite of the gross mistakes of the Yugoslav centralist government and the Crown in dealing with the complexity of the country they were to govern, the objections to and animosity felt for central authority did not reach a point at which the unsatisfied would seek a solution outside of Yugoslavia. Only a few days before the war came to Yugoslavia, when it was quite clear that the survival of the country was almost impossible, the Croatian mainstream political forces *rejected* an offer by the Germans to create an independent state.

Lastly, the previous point, plus the fact that the various nations of Yugoslavia nurtured numerous links to each other even when there were serious divisions, leads to a tentative conclusion that even an ill-conceived Yugoslavia had some *raison d'être*. We can only speculate on the fate of this country had mature and modern statesmanship been applied from the outset.

CHAPTER FOUR

The Tito Years

By being drawn into the Second World War, Yugoslavia was destroyed as a state. A large part of Slovenia and a part of Serbia (in the northern province of Vojvodina) were annexed to the Reich. The rest of Slovenia, together with the Dalmatian coast and Montenegro, went to Italy as an occupying force. Macedonia was given to Bulgaria as a reward for taking part in the war on the German side. Kosovo was annexed to "Greater Albania," which was already under Italian rule. Hungary also "corrected" its borders at the expense of Yugoslavia. Serbia had a puppet and collaborative regime under General Nedić. Bosnia and Herzegovina were given to the new puppet Independent State of Croatia, which was ruled by the fascist Ustashi. The fact that a significant part of Croatia went to Italy could not have pleased the new regime under Ante Pavelić, but there was little he could do against his mentors.

His attention was oriented towards making a racially pure, Catholic state in Croatia. The objective, somewhat crudely but not incorrectly stated, was to convert one-third of Orthodox Serbs into Catholics, to expel another third to Serbia, and to exterminate the rest. For this action he had the implicit support of the Vatican and specifically the head of the Croatian Catholic church. Pavelić started passing anti-Serb and anti-Jewish laws less than a month after coming to power. During the summer of 1941 a campaign of terror, mass arrests, detention, deportation, and extermination began in earnest. The atrocities committed in the Independent State of Croatia, primarily against Serbs but against other minorities also, left an enduring mark on the national relations of Serbs and Croats and go a long way towards explaining more recent events in Croatia.

The estimate of Serbs killed in Croatia vary greatly. Franjo Tudjman, the current president of Croatia, also a historian, claims the figure is "a few tens of thousands." The Serbs, by contrast, believe the number to be close to a million. According to the *Encyclopedia of the Holocaust* an estimated 600,000 people were killed in Croatia, of which close to 25,000 were Jews.

But in the minds of people the bestiality of these mass murders is perhaps even more important than the number killed. Without attempting to offer a full explanation for the recent round of bestialities and atrocities, and certainly not to excuse them as "an eye for an eye" or "tit for tat," one can see that we are not talking about a new phenomenon but a repetition of an awful period in Serb-Croat relations.

The Serbs organized their own nationalist group, called the Chetniks, under the leadership of General Draža Mihailović. They were active in Serbia, Montenegro, parts of Bosnia, and on Serb territories in Croatia, the latter in very small numbers. Bosnia, being a part of Croatia and as mixed as it was, became fertile ground for nationalist clashes between the Ustashi and Muslims, on the one hand, and the Chetniks on the other.

The Chetniks organized guerrilla units in the summer of 1941 and declared their intention to fight against the occupying German and Italian forces. Initially they joined with the partisans, but after only six months of strained co-operation they split with them, eventually becoming bitter enemies. They had completely different long-term aims and therefore different tactics to pursue them.

The Chetniks were involved in a waiting game, waiting for the "right moment" to strike against the Germans. In the meantime they played a significant role in the perpetuation and intensification of national discord in Yugoslavia, since they were prepared to resort to ethnic, nationalist terror to advance exclusively Serbian interests.

The big difference between the Chetniks and the Ustashi was that the former were relatively isolated guerrilla units, especially in territories where they mixed with other ethnic groups, while the latter had a state organization. Thus the scale of murder, plunder, and "ethnic cleansing" performed by the latter far outstripped the evil deeds of the former.

The only truly Yugoslav fighting force that emerged in 1941 were the partisans led by Tito. Tito took over the Communist Party of Yugoslavia (CPY) in 1937. At the time it was an insignificant factor on the Yugoslav political scene, small and outlawed. But it was well organized and spread throughout Yugoslavia. The CPY was somewhat disoriented by the German-Soviet Pact and for a while even took part in anti-war activities. But after October 1940 and its fifth conference, the party started preparing for imminent war.

The fifth party conference was even more important for the fact that it laid the foundations of "an all-Yugoslav struggle," based on the principle of federal unity within the party. At this historic meeting, which took place just outside Zagreb, representatives from Slovenia, Croatia, Serbia, BiH, Dalmatia, Montenegro, Macedonia, Vojvodina, and even the district committee of Kosovo were present.

The decision to organize an armed uprising was made in July 1941, just after the German attack on the Soviet Union. From a relatively minor guerrilla force of about 11,000 in 1941, the partisans grew into an army of 700,000 by the end of the war.

Tito's strategy was two-pronged. The foreign-policy element of it was to become a recognized member of the anti-Fascist coalition. In order to do this he had to engage in armed combat against the Germans and Italians, which he did, thus parting with the tactics of the Chetniks. Some critics today will say that the partisans paid too heavy a price for this recognition and that Mihailović was correct in stating that a small country cannot liberate itself in a continental war but has to wait for a decisive breakthrough of its more powerful allies. But Tito felt that recognition would not be forthcoming otherwise (except from Stalin, of course, which was not enough). Other critics say that in fact Tito was not fighting the Germans and Italians at all, especially not after 1943, but rather was involved in fighting his civil war against the Ustashi and Chetniks. It is certainly true that the partisans fought them as well. But according to German and Italian sources, his fighting spirit and fighting units did effectively engage at certain times up to thirty Nazi and Italian divisions on the territory of Yugoslavia. And it is an undisputed fact that his armies marched over the Italian border into Trieste, which certainly could not have been accomplished without fighting.

This substantial engagement of German-Italian forces finally shifted the support of the British, and with them the Americans, away from Mihailović.[1] At that time (1943) the southern european front was in preparation, and the active support of strong fighting units was sought to minimize the human and other costs of opening a new front. Another advantage for Tito was the fact that he had units all over Yugoslavia. Mihailović had nothing comparable, since his Chetniks operated only in Serbia, BiH, and Montenegro.

The other prong in Tito's strategy was to come out of the war as a winning political (and not only military) force, thus dictating the political agenda in post-war Yugoslavia. In this respect he carried out an authentic socialist revolution at the same time as he fought an anti-fascist war. Though his partisans, except at the very outset of the war, were not all Communists, the Communists held key posts in the movement and decisively determined the political profile of the war effort. Together with the patriotic slogan of fighting against the invading enemy came the battle cry for a better and more just future for the people and nations of Yugoslavia.

Tito managed, for the first time in their history, to bring together in significant numbers all Yugoslav nations in a fight for a common cause. But this put the partisans at odds with the Croatian nationalist Ustashi and the Serbian nationalist Chetniks. Tito, himself a Croat, had a following of Croats in the partisans. In the beginning they were mostly from Dalmatia, a part of Croatia that was under Italian rule. The Croats there fought under the patriotic slogan of liberating the country. The number of Croats from the Independent State of Croatia in partisan units was proportionately much smaller until after the fall of Stalingrad and the collapse of the African front. They then started joining in larger numbers.

The majority of Tito's fighting force was made up of Serbs.[2] It was in Serbia that he started the armed uprising, but after a heavy offensive by the Germans he moved into the rugged mountains of BiH. The Slovenes, faced with rapid assimilation, took to the woods and were, after initial hesitation in 1941, also prominent in the partisan resistance movement. So, to a smaller extent, were the Muslims of BiH, and later during the war the Macedonians. The only ethnic group that did not offer significant support to the partisan effort was the Albanians of Kosovo. Until the very end of the war only a symbolic number of Albanians joined the partisans.

In November 1943, during a later-much-celebrated meeting of the Council of the Anti-Fascist Alliance of Yugoslavia, the foundations for the post-war Yugoslavia were set. It was to be a federal state made up of six republics. The basic arrangements made at this council meeting were sanctioned by the parliament of the new state called Democratic Federal Yugoslavia in November 1945, and a new constitution was passed in January 1946. The partisans, having emerged victorious as part of the anti-fascist alliance and in the civil war against Chetniks and Ustashi, set the political agenda very much along the ideological lines of the force that led them – the Communist Party. At the end of the war and immediately after it, they also involved themselves in the brutal liquidation of political and military opponents in war.

The first post-war elections, which were overwhelmingly won by the Communist-led National Front, were manipulated by the CPY and rigged in their favour – unnecessarily so, since the popularity of Tito and the partisans would have easily led them to a comfortable victory even in an honest election. But it was in the nature of Communism to be as all-embracing as possible, to pretend to have more support than was real. Thus a shadow was cast over the legitimacy, if not the legality, of the new Communist regime led by Tito.

Tito came out of the war an immensely popular figure inside and well respected outside Yugoslavia. Mindful of the mistakes made during the inter-war years, he set out to build a structure that would be more stable and durable.

The first obstacle to stability was inter-ethnic strife. This was at one and the same time a matter of principle in a multinational state and a concrete problem in the aftermath of a war that brought many mutual confrontations. Tito therefore advanced the slogan of "brotherhood and unity," which was to remain the political credo of the years he spent in power. He was thus fully aware that there would be no Yugoslavia without the constituent parts looking towards rather than away from each other. He also realized that there was no point in striving toward "oneness," as had King Alexander, so his unity was a unity in action of ethnic groups, not a symbiosis into an artificial supranational "nationality," so much so that those feeling and identifying themselves as Yugoslav nationals were mildly discouraged from it. The emphasis was on "brotherhood," which is to say equality and mutual respect of nations.

This was no easy task. Relations between different nationalities just emerging from a civil war, particularly between the Serbs and Croats, were tense. The victims of the Ustashi regime demanded retribution. The Croats, while collectively carrying the guilt of having tolerated, and in many cases collaborated with, such a dreadful regime, felt that they were being indiscriminately persecuted. Tito chose a path different from Germany's, where the post-war period witnessed years of intense discussion and public debate about "collective guilt." He closed this chapter of history rather abruptly. He and the CPY thought that by encouraging the population to look to national reconciliation, wounds would be healed. Manifestations of national discord and mistrust were discouraged in an attempt to wipe the slate clean. For a long time it looked as if this approach would succeed. Today we know different.

The second lesson learned from the previous Yugoslav experience was to be anti-centralist. That created a bizarre situation. Yugoslavia was formed as a federation of equal states, the smallest having a population of less than half a million and the largest more than seven million. They were assumed to be so united in their purpose that the question of officially determining boundaries and fixing them by law never really occurred to the new authorities. It was felt that they were only administrative anyway. But this gave rise to mutually exclusive interpretations and claims the moment the political power that determined them was no longer present to arbitrate.

But the peculiarity of the situation does not end there. Though nominally a federation, Yugoslavia almost to the very end had a central non-state source of power: the CPY. Thus it became possible during the height of the post-Tito crisis to have diametrically opposed views on the question of the level of centralization, and both with "valid arguments." Those who looked at the state structure said that Yugoslavia was not federal – that is, centralized – enough, while those who looked at the power structure thought that it was too centralized.

The third lesson of the inter-war years concerned the position of the Serbs in Yugoslavia. Since previous experience showed that the Serbs, the most numerous and widespread ethnic group, tended to dominate the political agenda, Tito's idea was somehow to cut them down to size as a group, thus making them more equal against the reality of their majority. The most convenient vehicle for this project was the existence of Hungarian and Albanian national minorities on Serbian soil, which provided the necessary pretext to form autonomous provinces. Similar arrangements for the Italian minority in Croatia and the Serbian population of the same republic were discarded, as that would, in Tito's judgment, have seriously weakened the main countervailing power within Yugoslavia. This architecture "solved" the problem at the time, as would have been the case with any other solution suggested or offered by Tito, but it came back to haunt Yugoslavs after his death.

Tito's popularity, and therefore his hold on power, increased even more at home and abroad after his defiance of Stalin and the mighty USSR in 1948. It would not be entirely true to say that he broke from Stalin (though that is the most usual interpretation) but rather that he stood his ground when Stalin excommunicated him from the Communist camp. It is easy to say today, as some do with hindsight, that Tito was safe in the knowledge that the West would not let Yugoslavia fall to Stalin. However, there is no denying that he took a big gamble at the time. There were no Soviet troops in Yugoslavia, as there were in countries liberated by the Red Army. This is yet further testimony to the fact that the partisans did most of the liberation of Yugoslavia themselves. But Tito was fully aware that there was a greater danger for him from within Yugoslavia, from those who thought that "the Great USSR and Stalin were the mother and father of Socialism." A "differentiation" in Communist ranks ensued, with all those not in favour of Yugoslavia's independence on state matters being treated very harshly.

There has been considerable recent criticism both inside and out-side of Yugoslavia of the way Tito manhandled the pro-Stalin oppo-sition in the period 1948–51. The criticism certainly holds true on humanitarian and democratic grounds, for numerous punishments were unwarranted and extremely severe. However, the West at that time, though not fully cognizant of every sordid detail, was never-theless well aware of what was going on. But Tito's internal unde-mocratic and often brutal confrontation with his opposition met with complete silence, since, for the West, his confrontation with Stalin meant that one sheep had been drawn out of the Communist flock, or at least that Stalin faced a serious irritant.

Since the Serbs and the Montenegrins were the most numerous "orthodox" Communists, no wonder they suffered the heaviest toll. Oddly enough, the minister of the Interior and in charge of this purge was a Serb himself.

After the schism with Stalin the so-called Yugoslav model started to emerge. Although without a formal education, Tito was a masterful, one could say born politician and statesman. He realized the impor-tance of political dynamics, so he kept coming up with ideas, or endorsing them, that prolonged the political power of the CPY and his own personal authority. The fact that these ideas were historically untested did not disturb him; it was the dynamic he was after.

Tito presided over a series of economic and political changes that distanced the country more and more from its initial Communist model. Though he sought change and endorsed it, he was not an advocate of change that would disturb the dominant role of the CPY. In fact, when it came to touching his source of power, Tito became quite ruthless and extremely harsh but still a much softer version of his "ideological brethren" in other Communist-dominated countries. The first to feel this was Milovan Djilas, with his early attempt in 1954 to modernize the country politically and eliminate the absolute hold on power of the CPY. A lone voice on the Central Committee, he had no power to swing the course of events in another direction. Djilas, a proud, stubborn, and intelligent person, did not yield but kept on fighting for his ideals. Tito promptly jailed him twice for "anti-state propaganda." Djilas, at the time of his expulsion from the CPY a member of the innermost circle around Tito (he carried a CPY membership card with No. 3 on it), became the best-known dissident not only from Yugoslavia but from the entire Communist-dominated world.

Yugoslavia became the first country to introduce the self-manage-ment economic system. This system was nominally initiated in 1950 but was actually instituted by means of a series of economic reforms from 1950 to 1965. These reforms changed the way economic decisions were made and also shifted the locus of decision-making power. Central planning was gradually abandoned, and independent decision-making by autonomous enterprises, with worker councils having an important say, was encouraged. Prices were less and less administered and more and more set by a peculiar form of market economics – peculiar because there was a tendency to develop markets for goods and services but not for labour and capital, which was still considered a heresy for a socialist country.

Ownership gradually shifted from state to social, which meant that there was no firm titular owner for enterprise or property. The national means of production, except land,[3] thus became "everybody's and nobody's" at the same time, with the workers being entrusted to use them responsibly for national, collective, and individual benefit.

Partially because of the post-revolutionary fever, partially because of a low starting base, partially owing to the substantial foreign aid that started pouring in after 1951, and certainly in some measure because of the initial stimulative effects of this new economic system, in the 1950s and early 1960s the Yugoslav economy grew at a pace that was among the fastest internationally, comparing well with Japan. Communism was very often about growth rates and about "overtaking the capitalists in their standard of living." While the Yugoslav standard of living never really came close to that of the average Western European, it nevertheless increased considerably and visibly over that of the other Communist-led countries. In the late fifties the consumer was no longer viewed as a simple statistic but as a bearer of real needs to be satisfied. This had two important political consequences. It maintained, even increased the level of popular satisfaction, and thus internal stability, at the same time increasing pride in relative accomplishments, convincing most Yugoslavs that theirs was a way that paid dividends.

But there was an inherent weakness in the whole structure. If the other Communist states stand rightly accused of having disregarded the consumer for the sake of developing a heavy industrial base, the Yugoslav economic model tended to be superficial and often involved in change for change's sake rather than for fundamental change in micro- or macro- economic relations.

The pride and sense of accomplishment was bolstered even more by the parallel development of an independent foreign policy. In the fifties the Cold War was raging and dividing Europe. A precarious balance kept Yugoslavia in a relatively sheltered position, but this was not an environment for an "activist" like Tito to create a more prominent foreign policy. Regarding the two main powers Tito ploughed a course "in between," remaining ideologically closer to the Communist East while drawing materially and financially closer to the capitalist West.

But Tito was not going to have Yugoslavia follow the neutrality of Sweden or Austria. He therefore focused Yugoslav foreign policy on arenas largely outside of Europe, aligning himself with numerous countries that had just attained their independence or were still fighting for it. In the late fifties the policy of "non-alignment" was conceived, and the first conference of non-aligned countries (twenty-five attended) took place in Belgrade in 1961. Throughout the sixties and seventies Tito was seen as a champion of non-alignment, increasing his popularity at home as well as in countries like Egypt, India, and Algeria. And he gained the respect, if not always the approval and admiration, of the big powers. It was Tito's foreign policy, more than any other factor, that allowed Yugoslavia to attain an international presence way out of proportion to its size, population, or economic power.

The political system also underwent changes, in the direction of more authentic federalism. After closely following the Soviet centralized-state model in the early years, Yugoslavia catered increasingly to the interests and aspirations of its constituent parts, but always with the understanding that the CPY and Tito were the constant and imbedded trouble-solvers, should things go too far. The constitutional amendments of 1953, and subsequently the new constitution of 1963, introduced an arrangement between the republics and the centre that was truly federal in substance. This had the inevitable effect of federalizing the party, though that development was not intended, nor was it as obvious at the time as it later became.

The zenith of the post-war development of Yugoslavia came with the reforms of 1965. Noticing signs of strain in the revolutionary spirit that had carried post-war development, while at the same time continuing the logic and path of gradual liberalization, Tito and the CPY introduced what were for that period very modern, market-oriented economic reforms, with the declared idea of gradually introducing a full-fledged market economy. This had to include the liberalization of foreign trade and foreign investment[4] and movement towards a convertible currency. At the same time, borders were completely opened, thus allowing redundant workers to seek employment abroad. This had the dual effect of reducing tension at home and bringing in desperately needed hard currency in the form of workers' remittances.

After a confrontation with conservative forces within the party in 1966, it seemed that nothing could or would stop Yugoslavia from moving rapidly towards modern economic and political organization, away from Communism and towards some kind of social democracy. It turned out, only a few years later, that the same political forces that had set this process in train were to stop it. A series of unrelated events brought about this reversal.

First, in 1968, following an all-European wave of student revolt, students in Yugoslavia, primarily in Belgrade and Zagreb, came out with social and political demands that were not conducive (to say the least) to the continuation of liberal, market-oriented reform. It can only be speculated whether this initial setback to reform would have occurred had Rudi Dutschke and Daniel Cohn-Bendit not fired the imaginations of young left-wing Europeans.

Secondly, as a result of the genuine federalization brought about by the constitution of 1963, coupled with the settling of inter-republic trade and investment accounts on economic rather than administrative terms, a result of the 1965 economic reforms, there was a drive for greater, primarily economic independence in Croatia. When the initial response to this novel development in Titoist Yugoslavia proved somewhat soft, the hard-core Croatian nationalists joined in, seeing an opportunity to revive the "Croatian question." Though they were not numerous, and certainly not in the mainstream of the Croatian opposition to Tito and Belgrade, they provoked the now fully alert centre to crack down with as much force as if all the opposition had been hard-line Croatian separatists.

Thirdly, in Serbia, and to a somewhat lesser extent in Slovenia, again as a result of the reforms of 1965, a new type of political coalition was being forged. It included successful business leaders as well as liberal-minded and forward-looking party officials. These were not the party zealots nor the conservative apparatchiks. They took the idea of carrying out economic reform very seriously, fully aware of the political consequences. They were willing to see through the reshaping of decision-making and the shifting of the locus of power away from the party and towards the economy, and eventually towards the citizen, realizing full well that this would undermine the formal basis of their power. But since they were the agents of the change they sought, they were well-motivated, thinking that this change in itself would keep them in a position of influence.

Tito, who until that moment had lived on change and political dynamism, perhaps tired, and certainly fearing that this could spell the end of the leading role of the CPY, backed away. He correctly perceived this development as far more dangerous for the party and his power structure than either the student revolts or Croatian nationalism, since both of the latter could be localized. The liberalization of economic, political, and social life, together with the liberalization of the media, would, by contrast, have a tendency to snowball and spread beyond control. So, in 1972, he declared the intentions of the Serbian and Slovenian liberals "anti-revolutionary," against the interests of the working class, capitalistic, and so on.

The added convenience for Tito was that the previous year he had emerged from a confrontation with the Croats, so this new battle against the Serbs and Slovenes could not be viewed as simple confrontation on national lines. On the contrary, on the surface it looked as if he were defending the true socialist faith and the interests of the working class from both nationalist and bourgeois elements that endangered it.

Another event that favoured Tito was the invasion of Czechoslovakia in 1968. With the so-called Brezhnev Doctrine of "limited sovereignty," the external threat to Yugoslavia again loomed large, causing Yugoslavs to rally round Tito and the CPY as the only viable leadership with a proven track record against the Soviets. Thus all tendencies that were contrary to the official Tito and party line were easily branded unpatriotic and therefore dangerous.

So that the reader can better understand the political quagmire of those days, it must be pointed out that the instrumental figures in knocking out the Croatian leadership were other prominent leaders from Croatia (admittedly a number of them Serbs), and in the confrontation with Serbian and Slovenian liberals the key players were "loyal" party Serbs and a Slovene, Edvard Kardelj, who was a key adviser to Tito from the war days to his death a year before Tito's.

Kardelj masterminded the institutional framework and ideology that was to rise from the rubble after the various purges. In 1974 Yugoslavia passed a new constitution for which he had drawn the blueprints. The main idea was to rationalize the abolition of the economic reforms by characterizing them as too centrifugal and to reassert the primacy of social(ist) authority as embodied in the "guiding role of the party" and the priority of collective interests over those of the individual economic units. In order to avoid making this plainly obvious, no immediate reversal of policy was effected. Rather an elaborate scheme, involving various institutions of "associated labour," "social compacts," and "self-managed communities of interest" were invented to foster "the harmony of negotiation over the anarchy of the market."[5] Gradually this arrangement was dubbed "contractual economics" and was trumpeted as far superior to either central planning or market economics.

The system was chaotic, to say the least. The transaction costs of its functioning were immense, the incentive for productivity and efficiency practically nil. Instead of increasing the decision-making power of the workers, which it was supposed to do, contractual economics increased the importance of the arbiters, the state and the party, marginalizing the position of both workers and managers.

With the system already deteriorating, the economy was unable to adjust to the first oil shock of 1974. Being rigid and unresponsive to cost signals, the economy took a tumble in real terms, while both the investment and consumer sectors had an artificial boost from the heavy foreign debt that Yugoslavia incurred at the time. Petrodollars were cheap, and Yugoslavia borrowed and spent lavishly, with little regard for efficiency of investment and returns on them.

The new constitution brought in largely confederal institutional arrangements among republics. Every unit, including the two autonomous provinces (Kosovo and Vojvodina), had a veto power, since all decisions had to be made by consensus. The institution of the Federal Presidency (one representative from each republic and province) was invented with the idea of easing in the transition to a post-Tito era, since he was already eighty-two.

The last years of Tito's rule were wasted in muddling through the new economic and political arrangements, with the cohesive power of the CPY and Tito himself rapidly eroding. The economy was already spiralling down, and Tito's popularity was considerably if not even totally shaken. Tito died on 3 May 1980, the last of the Allied commanders of the Second World War to leave the scene.

Recent criticism notwithstanding,[6] the Tito years are generally regarded as years of ascendance, prosperity, stability, and respectability for Yugoslavia. The national question, except for a few isolated instances, did not raise its ugly head. The situation in that respect was definitely different from the inter-war years. The average Yugoslav saw his standard of living, quality of life, and life expectancy rise considerably. The system, though in permanent change, generated expectations but also a sense of confidence in a better tomorrow. Most Yugoslavs were proud to say who they were when they were outside the country. There was a widespread feeling of freedom, even if this was not shared by every citizen. A British observer once stated that she had "never been in a country with so much freedom and so little democracy," a very telling statement.

All this was to a considerable extent the result of Tito's leadership, and beyond this statement lies the fact that his leadership, though authoritarian, was not brutal, especially when compared to other non-democratic regimes both East and West. Though he relied mostly on the Communist Party, he was not insensitive to other interests and political realities. He was a keen power player, but his power derived always more from his popularity than from the brute force that he also used at times. Therefore, it would seem appropriate to conclude that Tito was just as much a product of Yugoslavia as he was the moving force behind its re-creation. He brought and held Yugoslavia together.

The purges that he carried out, among opponents ranging from the pro-Stalinists to the Serbian and Slovenian liberals, were founded on political and ideological rather than ethnic or national premises of power. Though these purges caused a nationalist backlash after his departure, nationalist factors were not important to his calculations.

Tito was a very charismatic leader, and he used his charisma to utmost advantage. Though he was helped in the portrayal of himself as "the leader" by a vast propaganda machine, it was not an artificial creation but rather an amplification of a potential that was genuine. He was not very good with words – his public speeches were often incoherent – but people understood his messages.

He came out of the Second World War as the undisputed national hero and commander of a strong army that had always been loyal to him to the end. The army, it would develop, had the most trouble in adjusting to the post-Tito world.

Tito was not an ideologue but rather a pragmatist, though he was entirely capable of grasping the broader, strategic, even global picture and maximizing his position and the position of Yugoslavia in it. The CPY was the medium that brought him to power, and he had a strong grip on it throughout his years of leadership, never facing serious opposition from within, let alone from outside the party.

Tito was not a democrat at heart; he was always suspicious of both the intrinsic virtues of democracy and its validity as a system of political organization. He had little patience with differing views, let alone with a system that would institutionalize them. All his flair for experimentation and political dynamism was to stop at a line that would preserve, and hopefully solidify, his hold on power under difficult circumstances.

He conducted a risky but highly effective foreign policy. He liked to hold the initiative rather than take situations for granted. Relations with all neighbouring countries except Albania were good throughout his years in office and in some cases excellent. The biased "equidistance" that he maintained between the two major powers was something for which he became famous, as was the fact that he provided political leadership for more than a third of humankind through the non-aligned movement.

In retrospect, it could perhaps be said that his greatest virtues, from which Yugoslavia benefited, were his determination to remain independent and his political courage, combined with a flair for experimentation. He also correctly perceived the national problem in Yugoslavia but chose a less than satisfactory way of dealing with it. His greatest drawback, which also became the drawback of Yugoslavia, was his inability to carry his political dynamism and experimentation beyond merely breaking out of the Leninist mould. The political monopoly of the CPY, to which Tito was committed until his dying day, prevented the country's logical continuation along the path of economic and political liberalization on which it had set out several decades before.

The golden opportunity was lost in the late 1960s and early 1970s, an opportunity that would, in all likelihood, have prevented the tragic confrontations that occurred twenty years later. Yugoslavia stood on the brink of full democratization and total economic overhaul. Tito and the CPY hard-liners took the country back into the "soft Leninist mould" of which they were so proud.

PART TWO

The Actors

CHAPTER FIVE

Tito's Successors

With the passing of Tito the stage was set for the Yugoslav drama, although his political ghost lingered for another decade, haunting Yugoslavs like the ghost of Hamlet's father. Tito's death had left the country in a double shock: emotional, which did not last long, and political, which lasted too long. Tito did not die suddenly. He was in hospital for four months, the daily state of his health starting every news bulletin. Although the nation, or rather nations, of Yugoslavia were well prepared for the inevitable, there was sorrow, grief, and tears during the days of mourning.[1]

Tito's funeral brought together the biggest assembly of world statesmen and dignitaries ever known for such an occasion. Yugoslavs were proud of the friendship and concern expressed by almost all, and certainly the most important countries of the world. At the funeral one could see Brezhnev sitting next to Hua Guofeng (China), and United States Vice-President Walter Mondale practically rubbing shoulders with Yasser Arafat of the Palestine Liberation Organization. Tito was buried in a modest marble tomb, inscribed simply JOSIP BROZ – TITO 1892–1980. Much to everybody's surprise (and much speculation as well), there was no engraving of a red star, the symbol of Communism, for which he had fought almost his entire life. His burial place was, according to his wishes, in the garden of the residence he lived in throughout the post-war period. The burial place, popularly known as the "Flower House," became the object of massive pilgrimage. In the first four years after Tito's death his tomb was visited by over 11 million people, or half the population of Yugoslavia.

The collective Federal Presidency, until then a symbolic body since Tito was the president, immediately began to function as the representative of Yugoslavian sovereignty and the supreme commander of its armed forces, the Yugoslav People's Army (JNA). The first president of the Presidency was a Macedonian who held the post for only twelve days. The regular rotation within the Presidency took place as it always did on 16 May, bringing in a representative of another republic according to a scheme that had been established well in advance.

Among other things, this orderly succession gave the impression of smooth continuity. By far the most important political task that the largely anonymous men who collectively took over from Tito set for themselves was to create the impression that nothing had changed. This political objective was converted into a popular slogan: "After Tito – Tito". Every effort was made to portray the situation as being fully under control. And it was, not so much because of the institutions and mechanisms that had been set up during Tito's life but because of a political inertia that set in, the Presidency still riding on the crest of Tito's popularity. The population was constantly reminded that the country had suffered "a great loss" but would continue living and functioning normally.

The political void that was left with Tito's departure was deliberately glossed over. In part this was done to preserve public opinion about the viability and stability of the country. Nobody wanted to rock the boat. The new leadership wanted to be able to invoke the undisputed authority of Tito and his chosen path in the face of expected and anticipated difficulties. Though these difficulties did not appear immediately in the open (except for an incident soon to be described), the political leadership was aware of potential problems, the dangerous economic and political undercurrents and the possibility of having to face them. They chose to hide behind Tito's authority and "greatness" rather than to tackle them with their own very limited capacities. Needless to say, the new leadership did not shift from the Leninist mould of Communist Party political monopoly. There was no attempt to solve problems, as they gradually surfaced, by reverting to the reformist path of the late sixties, or to resolve or dissolve them through democratic burden-sharing.

The lone incident occurred within a year after Tito's death. In the spring of 1981 there was a major student riot in the autonomous region of Kosovo. Kosovo had already been a scene of violent confrontations in 1966 and 1968, but these incidents had been hushed up. The rebellion of 1981, however, was televised and widely publicized. It took the form of student demonstrations over social conditions at the university but was inspired and manoeuvred by the Albanian nationalist movement, which was clearly testing the strength or weakness of post-Tito Yugoslavia. This outburst, which left eleven dead, was condemned by the whole country and even by the vast majority of the Albanian leadership of Kosovo.

Except for this incident, life in Yugoslavia – political, economic, and ethnic – continued in a pattern of inertia. However, problems were slowly and cumulatively bubbling under this inertia. A slow and persistent degradation set in. The leadership was too weak and still too much in the shadow of Tito to be able to tackle fundamental problems. With the possible exception of Yugoslav foreign policy, all other segments of political and economic life were under increasing strain and becoming less and less manageable. Even foreign policy, which can be credited with the disproportionate stature of Yugoslavia in world affairs, gradually lost touch with changing global and European realities. However, this was the last element of the Titoist strategy to surrender to mounting internal problems.

The first to pass the critical threshold, signalling a need for corrective action, was the economic system and economic performance. The "contractual economic system" institutionalized by the constitution of 1974 after the abortive market-oriented reform kept producing weaker and weaker results and ever clearer signs of malfunctioning. By 1980 foreign debt had reached $18 billion, and the trade deficit that year alone was about $3.5 billion. The growth rate, once the pride of Yugoslav politicians and citizens alike, plummeted towards zero. Unemployment was increasing, and inflation was starting to creep up slowly. Except for the "invisibles" in the balance of payments, there was hardly a favourable economic indicator. The economy was strangled in a "self-management" bureaucratic grip that was sapping its life-blood.

The patient was kept alive by external borrowing and by inflated consumption and investment. The first indication that something was fundamentally wrong came with the need to service foreign debt. The weakened economy was incapable of repaying the debt, and the leadership was finally stung into action rather than simply presiding over a downhill slide.

A need for change became politically evident, even acute, for the first time since Tito's death. Also, for the first time the leadership was faced with the prospect of backtracking on the intrinsic and pervasive worth of the "socialist self-management system" without having anyone to hold responsible for it. A mistake had to be corrected, and there was no experience of correcting mistakes. Leninist ideology, still very strong, would not allow for this, since economic and social problems were always explained away as stemming from external factors (class enemies and the like) rather than from the bad design of those in power.

Only three years after Tito's death Yugoslavia's economic situation went rapidly from bad to worse. Rationing had to be introduced for petrol, electricity, and some food items (sugar and flour). That had not happened since the early fifties. Rationing, a result of malfunctioning systems of distribution, was commonplace in almost all socialist countries, most prominently in the USSR and Romania. But Yugoslavs were very proud of the fact that they had always had ample supplies of all, even luxury products. In spite of the clarity of this signal, the official line was that the word *crisis* was far too strong and politically disturbing.

The crisis, which showed all the signs of further deterioration, was unfortunately interpreted by the leadership as needing only minor stabilization efforts on a course that was otherwise correct. In 1983 the Presidency of Yugoslavia formed a high-powered commission headed by its then president Sergej Kreigher (a Slovene). The fact that it was headed by the president and that it was made up of eminent politicians and experts from all the republics and autonomous provinces suggested that the Kreigher Commission meant business.

The commission worked for almost two years, tinkering with almost every aspect of the economic system, from trade and market liberalization to regional aid and development. The end result was very disappointing. The commission obviously could not muster the political clout needed for a more radical reform of the economic system. The main criticism levelled at the work of the commission was that its diagnosis and the therapy it prescribed were at odds. While the analysis of the situation clearly described a crisis, without actually saying so, the policy prescriptions were vague, far too mild, and often contradictory. There was no political courage or willingness to advocate a stronger dose of economic reform.

A large number of modifications were suggested to increase the power of the market, to liberalize trade, and to make the redistributive mechanisms more efficient, but the essential structure of the "contractual economy" remained virtually intact, as did the sacrosanct notion of social ownership.

Within the commission there was a split between the conservative, orthodox "self-managers" and the more reform- and market-oriented politicians and experts. Of course, the split was not a drastic one, since all of the participants, including most of the invited experts, originally shared the same Communist Party–monopoly mentality. But there was a difference between those who thought that economic laws could be shaped into any mode the party thought expedient (conservatives) and those who believed it to be politically opportune to recognize the importance and essential independence of the functioning of economic laws (liberals). It is worth noting that Slobodan Milošević, then the president of the largest bank in Yugoslavia and an aspiring Serbian politician, was a very vocal representative of the reformist, liberal group. He portrayed himself as an advocate of more rather than less change, with more reliance on market-economy signals than on sheer political will.

Parallel with the deliberations of the Kreigher Commission but not independent of it, an external effort was mounted to relieve Yugoslavia of the heavy debt burden that was coming due in the mideighties. With trade and the balance of payments deteriorating rapidly, Yugoslavia was approaching a desperate situation. Internally, the crisis had already been manifest in the tightening and rationing of consumption as well as in the administrative control of investments. This latter measure was viewed as potentially dangerous, with possible negative effects both inside and outside the country. A group of nations, headed by the United States and involving fourteen industrialized nations plus Kuwait, formed an informal club that was called the "Friends of Yugoslavia." The main purpose of this club was to ease external financial constraints in an attempt to create a better environment for the economic reform that was thought to be in progress.

These countries, accounting for over 85 per cent of Yugoslavia's foreign debt, reprogrammed the government component of it and provided a political justification for the commercial banks to refinance the commercial component of the debt. The understanding was that Yugoslavia should use this political and financial credit to consolidate the situation at home, but primarily through market-oriented reforms.

There was no externally imposed design for these reforms, nor was there a definition of an "acceptable minimum" that would justify the financial aid. Neither were there any political conditions imposed other than the understanding that the aid should foster market-oriented reforms. This is in stark contrast to the conditionality of Western aid to the ex-socialist countries after the fall of the Berlin Wall.

The aid did not stop there. Besides rolling over the repayment on existing debt, there was also fresh money, primarily in the form of International Monetary Fund and World Bank loans, as well as guarantees on export financing. This was the last occasion on which the West participated in an organized and orchestrated manner in shoring up the faltering Yugoslav economy, investing in the maintenance of the stability of Yugoslavia. The danger was not conceived of at the time as a possible breakdown of the country along national, ethnic lines but as a possible economic and social collapse with grave political and strategic consequences. The Cold War was still on, and the strategic significance of an independent and stable Yugoslavia carried a price that the West was still willing to pay.

The way Yugoslavia used, or more accurately misused, this opportunity left a mark on the future relations of the country with its main financial and economic partners in Europe and the United States. The economic breathing-space provided by the financial injections was hardly used to restructure or in any other way to seriously modernize the economy. The economic slide was not stopped, not even moderated. Most of the fresh financial sources were used to cover up the extremely high cost of labour and the inefficiency and lack of productivity of Yugoslav enterprises. This had the dual effect of keeping political and social peace, at least temporarily, and at the same time creating the illusion that the consumer-led sector was reviving the economy. It was not, nor could it. Yugoslavia's problems were not those of a cyclical downturn but of major systemic and structural maladjustment.

Having burned their fingers with Yugoslavia on the occasion of the stabilization program, the West would understandably be reluctant and cautious in its assistance on the next occasion, when a true and deeper reform would be taking place. There would be little confidence on the side of creditors that it could or would be carried through. So the cost of an unsuccessful stabilization program would be payed in full only several years later.

Even the meagre recommendations for reform that the Kreigher Commission produced were not acted upon. Political hard-liners considered them too risky. The argument was that the economic reforms had been conceived in an abstract political context and did not take account of the political realities in Yugoslavia, most notably of the existing political system. If economic reforms were to be carried through, prior adjustments and modifications in the political system were needed to allow and facilitate future economic changes. Therefore, a new commission was formed, this time with a mandate to reflect on the state of the political system, the need for its modification, the political changes necessary to the constitution of 1974, and the coupling of economic and political reforms.

The Vrhovec Commission, headed by Josip Vrhovec (a Croat), worked for almost two years (1985–86), with disastrous results. The previous Kreigher Commission had not closed the floodgates, but had at least made an attempt to stem the flow. Its successor opened the gates even wider. First it destroyed even the small positive bridge-head that the previous economic commission had established. Instead of modifying the political system to allow for economic reform, it criticized the economic commission indirectly by saying that its recommendations were incompatible with a "true socialist self-management system."

The Vrhovec Commission studiously avoided the question of democratizing the political structure. Multi-party, free democratic elections were barely mentioned, almost in a footnote. The recommendations dwelt on "democratizing" the federation from the point of view of rights of federal units, leaving aside altogether the question of democratic political representation both within these units and in the federation. And here conflicting interests appeared, demonstrating that nobody was happy with the existing federation but that nobody was willing to change it into a democratic structure that would correspond to the interests of citizens.

As a consequence of the political momentum of the post-Tito era, gradually but unavoidably shifting from the federation toward the republics, enormous effort and considerable time were spent exacerbating existing differences and creating new ones. The constitution, which was a hybrid between a federal and a confederal arrangement, offered ample room for centrifugal forces to work gradually towards the extreme interpretations of the word and spirit of the constitution and thus eventually to its negation.

That constitution also allowed, even created, a feeling of mistrust and suspicion, since it allowed for everyone to maximize his own interests at the expense of others' rather than harmonizing interests for the benefit of everyone. It was a constitution of consensus, which is not characteristic of a federal arrangement. But the other side of the consensus coin is the veto power that each and every unit can use in order to stop the others. The combination of all-pervasive suspicion and the ability to use the veto led to a total decision-making blockade, including a blockade of decisions that could have changed the system.

With its total mishandling of the structure of political problems, the Vrhovec Commission opened the Pandora's box of national rather than citizen-oriented political change. The impulse to change would very soon become dominated by strong national-bureaucratic aspirations within the country as a whole.

On top of the political problems of changing the strategic course of Yugoslav society, the political leaders of the republics, gaining strength by the day, were faced with the reality of a deteriorating economic situation. Rather than blaming systemic causes for poor economic performance, because that would have involved self-criticism as well, the popular line became that others were to blame.

Slovenia and Croatia complained about the aid they were channelling toward the less-developed republics, which was draining them of resources, and the less-developed republics reciprocated by complaining about the terms of trade, which favoured the developed regions, claiming that the developed republics got more back through trade than they gave in terms of investment.

This debate about the sharing of a shrinking cake was not the central issue in the growing confrontations. The reader might find this surprising, but it becomes understandable if one keeps in mind that the object of the exercise was not to modernize the country (as had been the case with the previous and authentic reforms of 1965) but to readjust the system in a way that would ensure the bureaucracy's hold on power. In such a situation it is always easier and politically more expedient to look for blame elsewhere, to charge others for economic suffering.

The two failed attempts at reform in Yugoslavia, one economic, the other political, took up almost four years (1983–86), without any positive result worth mentioning. On the contrary. Titoism was gradually fading away, and with it the political glue that could have held the country together through essential changes. Though lip-service was still paid to Tito, it was obvious that his political shadow was becoming smaller and smaller. Yugoslavia could no longer be viewed nor guided according to the Titoist model. Something quite different had to be done.

Two options were available.

One was the transformation of Yugoslavia into a market-oriented pluralistic democracy, aware of and attentive to its multinational structure. This would have led to political organization primarily on the basis of human and citizens' rather than national rights, which in turn was a necessary condition for the country's conversion into a modern, democratic state capable of gradually *dissolving* rather than abruptly *resolving* the national question. This would have meant breaking away from Titoism in terms of the party and other monopoly and monolithic structures, allowing for a plurality of interests and political parties representing them. The political leadership that succeeded Tito, unlike the Serbian liberals of the sixties or the Hungarian Communist leadership in the late eighties, was incapable of heading in that direction.

Of course, in Yugoslavia the danger always loomed large that the plurality of interests would correspond to the plurality of nations, thus casting the nations, and not citizens, as the bearers of political interests. However, with the liberalization of the economic and political structure this nationalist twist would not have had an exclusive and overriding significance; it would have been one among many possible points of political differentiation, not the only one.

This option unfortunately came to life rather late, at the very end of the decade. The last try at solving the mounting economic and political problems of Yugoslavia on an all-Yugoslav platform was made by Prime Minister Ante Marković, who took office in March of 1989.[2] By then economic, social, and ethnic decay had progressed to a significant level. Pessimists felt that the point of no return had already been reached and changes in Yugoslavia were impossible because Yugoslavia had become ungovernable. However, the popular feeling and the expectations of the majority of politicians still did not offer significant support to the pessimist view.

The time wasted in the post-Tito era had allowed for an accumulation of grievances, some valid and many self-made, increasing suspicion, and mutual accusations among the leaders of various republics. Marković's strategy was to consolidate the immediate economic situation in order to create confidence and a platform for deeper and fundamental changes. He was aware that he was fighting heavy odds and that the only way he could consolidate his federal power was by delivering economic results that would reduce the relative attractiveness of nationalistic policies. Since no one else was seriously concerned with economic issues, he saw a chance to gain the initiative.

His reform was radical and thorough by any standards. Though in his acceptance speech he talked about "modernizing socialism," it very soon became evident that his reforms were chipping away at the very foundations of the old socialist structure, aimed at overhauling the system and providing a rational barrier to rapidly expanding nationalism. The idea was to bring economics to centre stage, thus relegating national considerations to a secondary role. The reforms that Yugoslavia undertook at the end of 1989 were the first very radical reforms in the ex-socialist countries and established a broad pattern that was to be repeated, albeit with a great deal more success, in other Central European countries.

The linchpin of the reforms was the pegging of the value of the national currency, the dinar, to the German mark (at a rate of 7:1) and making the currency freely convertible for the first time since the Second World War. This was a clear sign that the stability of the currency and of the monetary authority was paramount to every other change. Marković also liberalized imports, thus increasing supplies, broadening the assortment of goods in the shops, and creating a more competitive situation on the domestic market, forcing inefficient Yugoslav producers to shape up or close shop. A plan for large-scale privatization was set in place that would, over a period of five to seven years, have radically transformed the ownership structure. Self-management was significantly reduced, though not entirely abolished. But instead of an all-encompassing and all-pervasive system in economic affairs, this plan was largely relegated to the function of consultancy within enterprises. The banking system, which had been that only by name in the previous "contractual" economy, regained its basic banking functions and responsibilities. The budget and other social expenditures were trimmed. Monetary policy was drastically tightened.

After a short period of administrative control, prices were largely allowed to form freely, in spite of the fact that the annual inflation rate had reached over 2,500 per cent. Surprisingly, in a very short period of time the inflation rate came down to a level of 60 per cent on an annual basis. During the late spring and summer months of 1990 price increases were virtually nil, even though there were hardly any price controls.

The biggest problem lay in determining wage rates. Since there was no free labour market and the economy was not yet completely privatized, the setting of wage rates, and associated derived incomes, presented a big problem. This point deserves mentioning because, apart from the financing of the JNA, this ultimately turned out to be the major weakness that thwarted Marković and his reform attempts.

The other previously mentioned alternative open to the post-Tito leadership was to challenge and change the second pillar of Titoism: his concept of "brotherhood and unity." This would have meant abandoning his attempt at even-handed national policy, his concern for not opening the national wounds of the past and healing them by shifting attention to the common factors rather than differences. This alternative path would have highlighted the national interest as *the* most important one, but at the same time it would have retained from Titoism the concept of monolithism, except that now the base for monolithism would not have been the traditional Communist class and social issues but rather the national issue and national homogenization.

The discussion about the changes in the political system opened the possibility for Communist leaders in the republics and autonomous provinces to begin to differentiate their political positions. If there was one real difference that they could count on, though it had lain dormant for decades, it was the national difference. Increasingly politicians from the federal units based their political and social power on national programs and national identification. This had two important effects: on the one hand it stirred up not only national but nationalistic sentiments and passions in the various republics; on the other it increased the disputes and confrontations within the Yugoslav federation.

This in turn had the effect of transforming the CPY into a more or less loose coalition of six national Communist parties with equally bankrupt political programs. But as long as the CPY existed as the continuation of the political force that had once held Yugoslavia together, there was a chance, a small one but still a chance, of reversing the trend. With the break-up of the CPY this road of peculiar but possible transformation was effectively closed. In effect, the CPY did not break up into a hard-line and a soft-line (social-democratic) wing but into six almost equally nationalistic fractions of one party.[3]

In the post-Tito period Yugoslavia was for too long a time politically and economically adrift. The strength of the previous system, at least on the surface, was sufficient to prevent a radical confrontation with the negative reality of the situation. The one-party system was not seriously challenged until it was too late. The working class was by and large very timid and non-militant. At the same time, workers in Poland were openly and militantly cracking open the foundations of the socialist system.

Yugoslavia's had been an authentic socialist revolution that started from the grass-roots level and secured immense popularity for its leader – Tito. The fact that the system had been built from within, and not imposed from without, gave legitimacy to the system Tito created and others inherited. By and large the system was liked by the majority of the population. Or, if this sounds too strong a statement, it was not disliked sufficiently to keep the leadership constantly on its toes, as was the case with other Communist regimes in Eastern Europe. It existed with the more or less open support of the citizens much more than it relied on the army and the police.

There was still too much self-satisfaction and insufficient motive or pressure to change. The weeding out of intellectual opposition within the CPY left it with a bunch of self-aggrandizing apparatchiks incapable of great vision and sophisticated political strategy. Yugoslavia was living off old glory and the dying flame of Titoism. To quote Jacques Delors: "No integration can be successful without a true institutional dynamic." This certainly held true for Yugoslavia.

A golden opportunity of doing away with a system that had no functional future was missed because positive institutional changes were not promoted but deliberately avoided.

In the process of drifting, the main nations of Yugoslavia were increasingly brought into a position to reject the federation – at least in the form in which it existed – because it allegedly or actually did not measure up to their very different and often mutually exclusive needs and interests. The size and inefficiency of the federal bureaucracy did not help: it was gargantuan, with an oversized army that stuck to outdated doctrines, with an inefficient mechanism of resource transfer, and so on. This situation allowed for a chorus of criticism, strengthening the position of the republics.

The interests of the nations at the time of the major split were represented by very small groups of Communist Party bureaucrats in the republics and provinces. These were not democratically elected leaders with a broad popular mandate. Even Milošević, who was immensely popular in Serbia, did not obtain his mandate through a democratic procedure but through a Communist Party power struggle.

A democratic society is based on the confidence of its citizens in the functioning of the rules. A revolutionary movement is based on the mutual confidence of revolutionary fighters. Since Yugoslavia was not a democratic country and had long since lost its revolutionary spirit, there was neither a set of rules nor a bunch of revolutionary cronies who could inspire and hold the confidence needed for deep change. Mistrust and lack of confidence set in, allowing the Machiavellian scheming of the various republican leaders to gain the upper hand.

At a superficial level the crisis can be explained by the incompetence of the leadership, which over a decade had demonstrated its inability to solve problems. On the contrary, it was capable only of creating new ones. But this, of course, begs the question of why or how such a thing was possible. So we have to look to a more fundamental level for an explanation of the crisis. This is to be found in the crisis of the political system, which brought to the surface incompetent leaders and by design brought them into a conflicting rather than a co-operative situation.

Yugoslavia did away with itself because it was unable to generate the internal momentum for democratic change at the right time. This offered an opportunity for the momentum to shift to national interests, which the national leaders did not hesitate to seize. They *chose* to dwell on differences, to expand them and exaggerate them, rather than to look for ways to strengthen the shaking common structure by building on similarities.

CHAPTER SIX

The New Wave of Serbian Nationalism

The ethnic, national dimension of the Yugoslav crisis did not come fully into the open until 1987. By then the economy was already in crisis and the political system practically incapacitated, with power rapidly shifting from the federation to the republics.

Prior to that shift, in 1981, occurred the student uprising in Kosovo, which was quickly subdued by a joint effort of all Yugoslav nations, including the Albanian leadership of Kosovo. Although this incident can hardly be said to have marked the beginning of ethnic and national tensions, it was a foretaste of possible problems to come, had the leadership been more mindful of the potential dangers in national conflicts.

It was Kosovo that again started the rapid deterioration of national relations in Yugoslavia. Ironically, it would be the fate of the Albanian population of Kosovo and the political attitudes of others towards it that would ultimately be the cause of a deep conflict among the South Slavs. The issue of Kosovo triggered a new wave of Serbian assertiveness, which in turn provoked reactions from other nationalities.

What was at stake? The province of Kosovo is by far the poorest part of Yugoslavia, with a poorly developed industrial structure,[1] the highest rate of population growth in Europe, and, except for large deposits of low-grade coal, hardly any development potential worth a major confrontation. When the trouble started, the population mix was 83 per cent Albanian and 15 per cent Serb and Montenegrin. Albanian nationalists were applying overt and covert pressure on the Serbs and Montenegrins to move out of Kosovo, with the purpose of making it ever more ethnically homogeneous.

But the real political problem lay in the fact that Kosovo and Vojvodina, though nominally parts of Serbia, had such a high level of autonomy that they were equal to the republics in everything but name. Thus Serbia, according to the provisions of the 1974 constitution, had within her borders two political entities that, for all practical purposes, had political equality and full representation in the federal bodies. This considerably weakened the position of Serbia both within its own boundaries and in negotiations at the federal level. Such an arrangement was the consequence of the intent "to cut Serbia down to size," to prevent a possible resurgence of hegemonism and Serbian domination on the basis of its size.

Internally, Serbia faced problems because the two autonomous provinces were basically not integrated into the Serbian legal and judicial system. For example, laws approved in Serbia had to be confirmed in provincial parliaments, while legislation passed in the latter did not go to the Serbian parliament for approval. In the judicial system, the court of appeal beyond the Supreme Court of Kosovo (or Vojvodina) was not the Supreme Court of Serbia but that of the federation. Thus a situation was created in which the provinces could block Serbia's passage of laws for the entire territory but Serbia could not block its own autonomous provinces on their territory, though they were nominally a part of the republic.

On the federal level Serbia faced the problem that these two provinces, like all the republics, had a power of veto over any possible constitutional changes. In order to change the existing constitution, all had to agree. But since the objects of change were, as far as Serbia was concerned, to redress this balance and gain a fully equal constitutional status with the other republics, the possible losers, Kosovo and Vojvodina, were strongly opposed, with Slovenia and Croatia largely backing their position.

In the mid-eighties Serbia tried to change this situation by argument, both within the republic, in endless discussions with the provincial leadership, and at the federal level, again in endless discussions in and out of the Vrhovec Commission, but to no avail. The leadership of Serbia at the time was reluctant to move on this issue in a more decisive or assertive way. Most of the other federal units enjoyed the exercise of their power of veto in the weak political structure and were quite unwilling to compromise. It is difficult to say what lay behind this inflexibility: petty concerns, bureaucratic inertia in maintaining entrenched positions with total disregard for political realities, or perhaps a deliberate attempt to irk and irritate Serbia. The most likely explanation would probably include all three.

Very indicative of what was actually going on is the relationship that existed between Serbia and Vojvodina. The political leadership of Vojvodina was made up largely of Serbs. The Hungarians, who as a national minority had actually provided the pretext for the autonomy of this region, had a token presence in the leadership and were not very vocal in the conflict between Serbian and Vojvodinian leaders. Thus it was largely that one Serbian party bureaucracy was fighting another for control. This clearly indicates that the predominant nature of the struggles going on was that of a quest for bureaucratic power and did not derive from authentic national or ethnic strife.

It would be wrong, however, to conclude that only an internal power struggle for control of turf was at stake. There were legitimate national grievances and problems of national relations that were genuine. These were understandable in a complex country like Yugoslavia. But these authentic national grievances were *processed* through a self-asserting elite, that is to say the Communist Party bureaucratic structure, which was ill suited to compromise and convergence. On the contrary, the party autocrats in the republics and provinces saw this as an opportunity to amplify and maximize politically those characteristics that would in turn solidify particular interests and positions. It can safely be said, however, that at the time few if any of the participants in this dangerous political game felt they were taking part in a deliberate plot or the beginning of a grand scheme to break up Yugoslavia.

The total lack of political will and political wisdom to accommodate Serbia's complaints, often entirely justified, irritated many in Serbia, thus feeding nationalist sentiment. It would be very difficult, indeed impossible, considering the political situation created by the 1974 constitution, to say that the Serbs had no reason whatsoever to assert their national stance, to try to reconstitute the Serbian state by reducing the autonomy of the two provinces in order to attain a position analogous to that of the other republics of Yugoslavia. The level of autonomy that the two provinces had *was* excessive and unparalleled in any country of the world that has to face the political issue of national minorities.

The autonomous provinces were "constitutive parts of the federation," which meant that they were represented as equals in all federal state and political structures. They did not have equal numerical representation in the parliament and other bodies where there was more than one representative. Since the principle of national (and minority) consensus was in force, this was totally insignificant, since just one regional representative could exercise veto power. Moreover, unlike in most countries, minority leaders rose to prominence and the highest offices in political life precisely because they were minority representatives. It was automatic. Furthermore, the autonomous provinces had full cultural and educational autonomy, extending from elementary school to universities and academies of science.

It is true that the human rights of national minorities were not sufficiently protected, and their status left much to be desired. But this was true of the rights of the citizens of Serbia proper as well, and of all other republics. It was not a specific attribute of the situation in the provinces.

Thus, the main thrust of Serbian political assertiveness was for Serbia to become a republic as any other. There was no mention whatsoever of Serbs in Croatia or those in BiH who would become the centre of the wars to follow. At that time the Serbs in BiH were well protected by a carefully designed trilateral formula of representation, which was not disturbed until the first free, multi-party elections were held in BiH.

In Croatia, it is true, the position of Serbs was contradictory. On the one hand, in terms of political and institutional representation Serbs were if anything overrepresented in many significant walks of life: in politics, the media, the police, the army. The backlash against this imbalance was later to become a part of the problem. None the less, the Serbs' relatively larger representation can be explained, if not justified. They had been more loyal to the system during its formative stage. We have seen that Serbs from Croatia constituted proportionately a much larger segment of the partisan fighting force, so they came out of the Second World War with a legitimate claim on important posts in the party, army, and police structure of the new Communist regime. Throughout the post-war period there were a proportionately larger number of Serbs in the Communist Party, with the result that, other things being equal, they were more likely to obtain positions of influence and importance. Finally, after the first and relatively mild national-revival movement in Croatia, which Tito suppressed, the Serbs gained relatively more important positions because Croats were reprimanded for the nationalistic uprising. This brought major changes in the leadership of many institutions of Croatian life, particularly the media and the police.

At the same time, there was a subtle but persistent reduction of the cultural autonomy of Serbs in Croatia, which was reflected in a gradual closure of Serbian cultural societies, the publishing house Prosvjeta, and so on. This meant that Serbs as an ethnic group fared less well, even though Serbs in the nomenclatura were disproportionately represented.

For the time being, however, Serbian assertiveness was limited to Serbia and its internal relations with the two autonomous provinces. It was a political struggle that did not rely on the awakening of the Serbian national spirit. But changing the balance within Serbia would, of course, have redressed the balance of power among republics at the federal level. This was what the others, primarily Slovenia and Croatia, were mostly afraid of and why they took sides with the autonomous provinces. Rather than accommodate legitimate and justified Serbian grievances, they sought to preserve the old Titoist structure, pulling the tiger by the tail.

The new wave of national awakening in Serbia went through the typical stages that historians have established for national integration, especially appropriate to small and frequently dominated European nations.

The first stage occurs when a group of "awakened" intellectuals start studying the language, culture, history, and economic position of a subjugated people. This initial stage came to fruition in Serbia through a group of nationally minded members of the Serbian Academy of Sciences and Arts. In 1986 they wrote a "Memorandum on the Position of Serbia in Yugoslavia."

In a second stage the scholars' ideas are accepted and then transmitted by a group of "patriots." They are the carriers and political transmitters of national ideologies, who take it upon themselves to convey national thought to the wider population. In Serbia this task was performed by Slobodan Milošević and those who followed him in the autumn of 1987 when he confronted the previous leader.

Finally, the national movement reaches its apogee among the general population. In Serbia this happened through the phase of so-called national homogenization. From the end of 1987 to the end of 1989 this populist campaign for Serbian unity brought millions on to the streets of almost all the larger towns in Serbia and made Milošević a living Serbian national hero. Despite his relative youth (forty-five), he became the father-figure of Serbia and, later on, as the ambition spread, of all Serbs throughout Yugoslavia.

The Memorandum of the Serbian Academy was a cocktail of critical views on the failure to transform the economic and political system of Yugoslavia on the one hand and deeply expressed and emotional views on the position of the Serbian nation in the federation on the other. Though it came from the Academy of Sciences, it was not written as a scientific document but rather as a platform or pamphlet for political action.

In its preamble this document stated that the Serbian nation faced a fateful moment because it found itself in an ambiguous, difficult, and immensely hostile situation. It claimed that the two developed republics – Slovenia and Croatia – had accomplished their national programs largely because they had control of the federal leadership, while the Serbian nation, in spite of its disproportionately large sacrifices, had not been able to do the same.

The document pursued a long discussion on the evolution of the Yugoslav economic and political system, which, it stated, deliberately left Serbia economically underdeveloped. The authors considered the reason to be in CPY's adherence to the old Comintern[2] dogma that Serbia was an economic oppressor in the inter-war period and so ought to pay in some way in the post-war period. But the authors pointed out that Serbia was also politically underprivileged, since the Serbs were the only Yugoslav nation without a right to form their own state.

The Memorandum called for a redrawing of the federal constitution on the following basic principles:

a *The sovereignty of the people*: While criticizing the monopoly of the CP elite, the document favoured a classless society, but made no mention of parliamentary, multi-party democracy.
b *Self-determination of nations*: In substance the suggestion was that Serbs should be in an equal position as a nation, which they were not, throughout Yugoslavia.
c *Human rights*: The document presented a valid critique of the situation on the basis of the United Nations Universal Declaration on Human Rights.
d *Rationality*: While it included a plea for a more centralized federal structure on grounds of efficiency and economic decision-making, the Memorandum made no mention, for example, of the market as an efficient and rational economic mechanism.

In opening the discussion on the position of Serbia and the Serbian people in Yugoslavia, the document stated, correctly, that many of the hardships that the Serbian people felt derived from problems common to all Yugoslav nations. But the authors considered that the Serbian nation laboured under the weight of additional hardships.

The Memorandum pointed to the economic hardships resulting from terms of trade that had been unfavourable to Serbia throughout the post-war period; it noted as well that Serbia had had to pay into the federal development fund though it lagged economically. Slovenia and Croatia were politically and economically dominant, having taken the initiative in all economic and political changes, while Serbia had been reduced to the role of a passive recipient. In the process of gradual disintegration that had set in throughout Yugoslavia, by far the worst hit had been the Serbs. This process, the Memorandum said, was oriented towards the total destruction of unity of the Serbian nation.

Just before the Memorandum was written, the new five-year plan (1986–90) had been agreed upon. The Memorandum was very critical of the Serbian leadership, which, after long debate and much horse-trading, had accepted a compromise and agreed to pay contributions to the fund for less-developed republics – this in spite of the fact that Serbia was indeed lagging in its economic development. The Memorandum labelled this outcome "the capitulation of Serbian representatives" who were "unprepared for the historical task" forced upon them by the complicated constellation of relations in Yugoslavia.

The Memorandum mentions in this context for the first time a cliché that was later to become very popular: the "anti-Serbian coalition." This coalition was said to have included all the other federal units,[3] since, on the question of redistribution of income through the development fund, the four recipients (BiH, Kosovo, Macedonia, and Montenegro) easily found common ground with the three developed regions (Slovenia, Croatia, Vojvodina). The net recipients feared that, if Serbia were excluded from contributions, they would receive less, and the donors feared that they would have to contribute more.

The Memorandum drew the conclusion that the economic relationships of other federal units with Serbia showed that the policy of revanchism had not decreased over time. On the contrary, fed by its own success, revanchism had flourished and ultimately led to genocide. Here the Memorandum threw in another catchy cliché, stating that the beacon of such a revanchist policy was "A weak Serbia makes for a strong Yugoslavia." This phrase was also much exploited in the latter two stages of the reawakening in Serbian national assertiveness.

But that was not all. According to the Memorandum, the Serbian nation, which after long and bloody battles and after losing 2.5 million of its nationals in multiple wars, having through them fully consolidated its own state, had found itself in a situation where an ordinary commission of party bureaucrats (the reference being to those who wrote the constitution of 1974) could determine that after thirty years of post-war reconstruction the Serbs were to be the only nation without a state of its own, certainly not one that would include all Serbs. That led to yet a third popular cliché: "Serbia – winner in wars, loser in peace."

But the strongest words were reserved for the situation in Kosovo. The exodus of Serbs from Kosovo was described as spectacular testimony to Serbia's historic defeat. The events of 1981 were called "a declaration of *total war*" (emphasis mine), and the Memorandum suggested, as the only logical reaction, a determined defence of the Serbian people and Serbian territory. The destiny of Kosovo was seen as vitally important to the whole Serbian nation.

The Memorandum then described the position of Serbs in Croatia. Together with statements on the economic and cultural position of Serbs in Croatia, which were factual, it offered assessments that were inflammatory: "The integrity of the Serbian *nation* in Yugoslavia is *the* crucial issue of its existence," or "the solution of the *national* question of the Serbs in Croatia is the most important political question of the day" (emphasis mine).

The Memorandum did not offer its own fully developed solution of nationalist contention by looking backwards into history. It maintained that the Serbs had been made to feel guilty for the inter-war years by the Communist regime. This feeling of guilt had been forced upon them and therefore had to be removed since it had largely contributed to the depressive state of the Serbian population. The biggest problem that the Memorandum repeatedly emphasized was that the Serbian nation did not have a state of its own.

Today the wording of the Memorandum would be considered extremely mild, since nationalism has escalated many times over. But at the time it came as a great shock, in Serbia as well as in other federal units.

How the Memorandum of the Serbian Academy of Sciences and Arts became a fuse to the contemporary nationalist explosion is a bizarre story. It was "leaked" to the press by an enterprising journalist. The academy reacted immediately, stating that this was only an initial draft by a group of academicians, that it was not a document of the academy, and that the way it had surfaced in public was illegitimate and unethical.

The Serbian political leadership promptly attacked the substance of the Memorandum, partially to appease the political leadership of other republics, partially because the Memorandum was critical of them. It has been noted that Milošević was by far the most muted in this chorus of criticism, though he was at the time president of the Communist Party of Serbia and as such the keeper of the faith. In retrospect, it seems very likely that he saw an opportunity to capitalize on this radical line of thought but felt himself still too weak to do anything since he was only freshly installed in the presidency. Relying mostly on the recommendations of the Memorandum, however, Milošević saw his chance a little less than a year later. He made a successful grab for power, performing a typical Communist *coup d'état*.

Milošević used the year at the top to secure his grip on the Communist Party apparatus, to take full control of the media, and gradually to make public his new strategy, denying that it had anything to do with the Memorandum. Two public statements he made during 1987 established him as a leader who was ready and willing to jump on the nationalist horse. First, in a rally near Belgrade he proclaimed that "Serbia will either be united or there will be no Serbia." At the same time that he called for the administrative unity of Serbia, to be achieved by the reduction of the autonomy of the two provinces, he pleaded for the political unity of Serbs to be accomplished by rallying around Serbian national sentiment.

Soon after, Milošević visited Kosovo, ostensibly to learn on the spot about the plight of the Serbs and Montenegrins there. In a rally of thousands of Serbs the predominantly Albanian police used force, and Milošević intervened by saying: "Nobody is going to beat these people." These seven words made a difference. He did not say that nobody would beat *the* people but that nobody would beat the Serbs. He took a national stand, committing himself to a radical line of action but also demonstrating courage in a difficult and potentially dangerous situation. That was something his predecessors had lacked, something Serbs held in high esteem and longed for in their leadership. Thus he became the real if not yet the nominal leader of the "patriots."

Milošević gained full and undisputed control in Serbia after a plenary session of the Central Committee of the Communist Party of Serbia in October 1987. His pretext for taking power avoided the national issue, for Milošević was unsure of the strength of support for his nationalist line, nor did he want to be divisive when he was advocating national unity. He chose instead a minor incident, involving the Belgrade Communist Party organization,[4] to have the previous Serbian leader, and his opponent, disqualified on grounds of ideological deviation and usurpation of power. Since the main accusation was bureaucratic behaviour and abuse of power, the whole effort, later to be turned into the third, and mass stage of national revival, eventually became known as the "Anti-bureaucratic Revolution."

Although he mentioned Serbian-Albanian relations in Kosovo, Milošević did not emphasize them, and attitudes towards the other republics were not discussed at all. Milošević won an overwhelming majority in the show of hands at this plenary, thus forcing the previous leader to resign his post as president of Serbia. Though "patriotism" was not the central issue, "patriots" had won a clear and decisive victory, rallying around Milošević, who had made his "patriotism" known.

Everything was now set for the third stage, the gathering of popular support for a confrontation with the two political leaderships in the autonomous provinces. The central issue was the need to reform the state of Serbia (as recommended by the Memorandum), so that instead of having three heads, it would have only one. The emotional underpinning for the campaign was provided by the precarious position of the Serbs and Montenegrins in Kosovo. Every incident was promptly recorded and in a number of cases exaggerated.

The Serbs of Kosovo became pivotal in the new national awakening. Having found strong support in Milošević, they now moved towards more radical national claims. During 1988 a large number of "rallies for truth" were organized all over Serbia. The common theme in all of them was that other Serbs outside Kosovo should know the "truth" about the predicament of the Serbian minority there. Of course, the accompanying political line was that they were *not* a minority since Kosovo was a part of Serbia and the Serbs should rightfully consider themselves members of the majority population. It was the Albanians who had to realize that *they* were a minority, even though they were the most populous ethnic group in Kosovo.

The plight of the Serbs in Kosovo was real and cannot be denied. However, it was skilfully overdramatized and deliberately, through mass rallies and the press, emotionally presented to the rest of Serbia as a matter of the utmost national priority, as described in the Memorandum. Questions of human and civil rights were deliberately and solely projected as national rights.

The mass rallies escalated in their tone and demands. Towns organizing the rallies felt morally and nationally obliged to outdo their predecessors, proving themselves to be "more patriotic" and thus gaining favour from the new "patriotic leadership." These rallies were, in principle, very well organized. There was no delinquent behaviour, and the people turned out by the hundreds of thousands.

The fever of national sentiment was spreading fast. The depressive state of the Serbian nation (as diagnosed by the Memorandum) was rapidly turning into a sense of purposeful national behaviour, escalating by the day, increasing national, moral, and therefore political support for Milošević, who became the first personality to eclipse Tito. Though Tito was officially still held in high esteem and his pictures were perforce hung in all the right places, Milošević's pictures far outnumbered those of his great predecessor, decorating homes, trucks, buses, and private shops like Orthodox icons. Even the stage managers of the campaign were surprised and failed to produce sufficient numbers of official photographs, so adoring followers improvised by tearing off cover pages of colour magazines with the grim-looking, baby-faced leader.

During 1988 the full iconography of the new "patriotic" leader had emerged. In part it was spurred by the controlled media and propaganda. But the overwhelming contribution to Milošević's popularity came from the "nationally awakened" sentiments of the Serbian population. This, of course, strengthened manyfold the political position of Milošević, rapidly crippling that of the provincial opposition.

Parallel with the mass rallies, political discussions on changes to the Serbian constitution continued. Of course, the position of the Serbian negotiators were now much tougher. More often than not it was reduced to a "take it or leave it" proposition. After the "Anti-bureaucratic Revolution" the position of president of the Constitutional Commission went to Borisav Jović. This man rightly deserved the nickname he acquired at this time, "Absolutely Unacceptable," because of his totally inflexible negotiating position.

Jović was the tactical master-mind for the implementation of the strategy of Serbian national awakening designed by the academy. He will return to the stage of this drama later, when the Serbian national question invades the Yugoslav scene, as the tactical genius. The international audience will remember him as the Yugoslav president who would not yield his post at the time of regular rotation to Stipe Mesić, a Croat.

Milošević himself firmly believed Jović's contention that the problem would be solved by a show of determination. If Serbs were to show strength *and* national unity, their arguments would be greatly enhanced. The opposition would have to yield either out of respect or because they were frightened. To Milošević and Jović it really did not matter which was the case.

A key element of Serbian tactics was to topple the leadership of Vojvodina first, thus completely isolating the Albanian leadership of Kosovo. This was thought to be easier because in Vojvodina, which was predominantly Serbian, the question was simply one of demonstrating to the population that they were led by a corrupt leadership that had no heart and understanding for the plight of Serbs in Kosovo.

It worked. Under pressure of a number of mass rallies the leadership of Vojvodina "voluntarily" resigned and was promptly replaced by one loyal to the Serbian cause, thus solidifying the Serbian position and completely isolating the Albanians of Kosovo – isolating them in Serbia, that is, because by now even stronger support for the Albanian position was coming from the Slovenes and, to a lesser extent, from the Croats.

With Vojvodina in his pocket, Milošević could turn his full attention to Kosovo. The situation on the ground there was very much in his favour. He knew that he could not muster the kind of support among the Albanian population that he was able to generate in Vojvodina, so his tactics in Kosovo were dependent on Albanian reaction to this new Serbian drive. The reaction was predictable in that the Albanians organized rallies of their own in support of their leadership and the existing autonomy of Kosovo.

Since the Albanians could not and, more likely, did not want to focus only on the constitutional issue at hand, extremist Albanian demands like "Kosovo – Republic" arose in sufficiently significant numbers for Milošević to step in with the police and army. His explanation was that he was defending the integrity of Yugoslavia from secession-minded Albanians. Their alleged objective, he claimed, to create a republic of Kosovo within Yugoslavia, was obviously only a first step that would make it easier to break away at a later stage.

A strike of Albanian miners, who stayed two thousand metres underground for several days for political purposes, gave Milošević the pretext to arrest and detain the principal Albanian leader, Azem Vlassi. Soon after, the Albanian-dominated provincial assembly voted in favour of the constitutional amendments proposed by Serbia under circumstances about which one can only speculate but which undoubtedly involved considerable pressure.

Thus the new Serbian constitution, limiting the autonomy of the provinces and making Serbia an "equal" republic in Yugoslavia, was promulgated in March 1989. This move introduced a new problem. Serbia was now "more equal" than others. True, Serbia was no longer blocked by her own autonomous provinces, but the provinces had not been removed as decision-makers at the federal level because the federal constitution had not been changed. So Serbia now had three votes in the Federal Presidency and three delegations in parliament, which voted in unison. Serbia also had a nationally inspired momentum, a homogeneity, and an activist sense of purpose that was still absent in other republics. However, this purpose, and the accompanying activism, would soon appear in the other republics as well, partially as a result of their respective national sentiments, which were still dormant, but largely as a pure reflex to what was going on in Serbia.

The other, eventually much more disturbing after-effect of the Serbian awakening was the fact that Serbian nationalism could not be contained within the borders of Serbia. Since there were Serbs living in BiH and Croatia, and a number of Montenegrins felt themselves to be Serbs, the nationalistic wave swept clear across republican borders, firing up the imagination of Serbs in other republics, whose enthusiasms again were defined and directed by the Memorandum agenda.

The first to feel this development was the republic of Montenegro. Soon after the fall of the provincial governments in Serbia, the Montenegrin government fell, having tried unsuccessfully to draw its population away from the strong pro-Serbian sentiment in their midst. Rallies "for truth" in support of the Montenegrins and Serbs of Kosovo, plus two relatively violent confrontations, brought in a new leadership much more sympathetic to the Milošević line. The effect on Montenegro itself was not that significant, but the balance of power in federal institutions shifted dramatically. Instead of an "anti-Serbian coalition" commanding seven votes against Serbia, the balance was now four against four, with the momentum on the Serbian side. As will be seen later, this had a strong effect on the thinking and actions of other republics.

Milošević had at least three good opportunities to reflect on his accomplishments and try to rein in the nationalistic horse before it started taking him places he initially perhaps did not want to go. The first such opportunity offered itself at the "rally to end all rallies of truth," which was held in Belgrade in the autumn of 1988 and drew over a million people. It was the biggest gathering ever held in Yugoslavia. Instead of speaking positively about the need for change and offering a chance for a negotiated solution, now from a position of considerable strength, Milošević chose to speak about the dangers that Serbia faced and about the enemies who surrounded her. Thus the pressure in the Yugoslav cooker was increased instead of being reduced, just as Serbia was about to achieve its goal.

The second opportunity was in Kosovo, where it all began. To mark the six hundredth anniversary of the Battle of Kosovo, more than a million people gathered again in June 1989, after the new Serbian constitution had already been adopted. They heard Milošević say that this land was sacred to Serbia, that it was now again Serbian and would remain so for all time. No mention at all was made of the Albanians who made up the overwhelming majority of the population, and no mention of the need to work out a *modus vivendi* between the people who populated Kosovo. Milošević seemed incapable of extending a hand that was different from the fist that had brought "justice for Serbia" on a wave of rampant and eventually uncontrollable nationalism.

The third opportunity to move away from nationalism and look for a non-nationalistic solution within Yugoslavia was missed when, after regaining Kosovo and Vojvodina, Serbia did not offer in the course of the constitutional debate to have only one representative at the federal level. Hiding behind a technical formulation that this could only come about as a result of the constitutional debate, the offer was never made, and all the others were made more suspicious and afraid of Serbian intentions.

All things considered, Serbia was not wrong to bid to redress the awkward political structure left by the 1974 constitution. Neither was she alone in triggering the events that would ensue. There was a total lack of democratic structure, a shortage of wisdom, and no desire to seek actively an acceptable solution. Milošević filled this political void by feeding the Serbian population with nationalism. The feeling was latent if dormant, but a Communist political bureaucracy woke it up to serve its own political ends.

Communist ideology had as an article of faith the belief that every nationalism is dangerous but the nationalism of the largest nation is the most dangerous. Since all leaderships in Yugoslavia at that time were strictly Communist, and since they all had learned this item of faith by heart, chances are that the non-Serbian leaderships were wagering that Serbian Communists would never *dare* to draw on nationalism as a means of solving their grievances.

The Serbian leadership, however, pulled out this powerful weapon thinking that it could be well aimed and controlled. They did not foresee the possibility that it would ultimately backfire and shoot them in the foot after having damaged all of Yugoslavia. The belief that nationalism was controllable, coupled with the belief that others, confronted with Serbian nationalism, would take fright and concede ground rather than rely on nationalisms of their own, proved to be fatally wrong, not only for Yugoslavia but for Serbia as well. What started out as a cure for national depression led the Serbian nation into a much deeper depression than the one it had when the nation-alist adventure started – many would say a deeper one than at any time in the proud history of the Serbs.

Taking a firm stand eventually led to taking an ever more aggres-sive stand. The "solving" of the Serbian problem was starting to shake Yugoslavia, even if that had not been the prime objective. Serbia had opened Pandora's box. The problems were let loose in larger numbers than could be solved or managed.

CHAPTER SEVEN

Slovenia and Croatia:
The Drive to Independence

Serbian nationalism was disruptive to the delicate Yugoslav balance because of its centralizing assertiveness. The Serbs felt a desire to dominate the political agenda for a number of reasons: because they were the most populous and most dispersed in this composite country; because they felt they had given most for the creation of Yugoslavia; because they also thought that the long period of suppression of Serbia ought now to be succeeded by a period that would "right the wrongs" of the Tito era. They therefore sought aggressively to redress the balance of power within Yugoslavia in their favour.

Croatian and Slovenian nationalism contributed to the dissolution of Yugoslavia in quite the opposite way. The essence of their nationalism was not *towards* Yugoslavia but *away* from it. This is not to say that from the very outset they adopted an explicit strategy of abandoning Yugoslavia or, as the official Serbian version would have it, of destroying Yugoslavia. But they clearly wanted to have less of it, to reduce the number of bonds tying them to the other nationalities, especially the Serbs.

While Serbian nationalists saw Yugoslavia as a more centralized state with a more Serbian dimension and content, Slovenian and Croatian nationalists saw the reshaping of Yugoslavia as a process of further decentralization and reduction of federal authority. The issue was largely the position of Serbia in Yugoslavia. "Weak Serbia – Strong Yugoslavia" was quite unacceptable to Serbia. "Strong Serbia – Strong Yugoslavia" aroused the suspicions of Slovenes and Croats because it suggested that the strength of Yugoslavia would derive from the strength of the biggest federal unit, thus reducing others to a subordinate and inferior role.

In this early stage of the confrontation, building up to the crisis that would break out in earnest in 1990, the Slovenes took the lead in redefining the structure of Yugoslavia. In closed discussions in the Vrhovec Commission but also through open and public political action, they set out on a course to weaken the political structure of Yugoslavia.

Slovenia was, rightly or wrongly, always considered by the other nationalities to be the republic that was least enthusiastic about the concept of Yugoslavia. It was often spoken of as "a country within a country," as evidence for which others cited its homogeneity and its far greater hermetic closure.

Dobrica Ćosić, the Serbian writer and nationalist ideologue, relates that Edvard Kardelj, Tito's principal ideologue and a Slovene, told him in the mid-fifties that Yugoslavia was a temporary construction and a transitory phenomenon. Kardelj, the creator of many Communist utopias in Yugoslavia, was also known for his pre-war pamphlet on the "Slovenian National Question," where he argued the case for a Slovenian national state. It could be that Kardelj, in the incident related by Ćosić, was indeed looking towards a Slovenian national state. But with his Communist ideology in the background, it could also be that he was speaking of Yugoslavia as a transitory phenomenon in the context of historical materialism, that is to say, on the historical path to broader international communities. In any case, Kardelj's views, expressed in the fifties, were not necessarily indicative of an existing undercurrent in Slovenian politics that would have had as an ultimate strategic objective the abandoning of Yugoslavia. The Slovenes needed Yugoslavia while it was an arrangement from which they benefited. Within that arrangement they persistently pushed towards greater independence through more decentralization, always suspicious of more centralization and the possibility of a resurgence of Serbian hegemony.

The Slovenes opened a fresh debate on centralization and decentralization in the mid-eighties, more than five years after Tito's death. The closed debate within the Vrhovec Commission was already under way, and the position of the Slovenians was expressed through press reports. They felt that the time was right to take the debate out of the closed confines of the commission and into the broader public political arena.

Predictably, the debate started on a cultural issue. At that time there was an attempt to create a core curriculum in primary and secondary education, which had been decentralized in Yugoslavia since the mid-sixties.[1] It was thought that the core curriculum would make the educational systems in the republics more compatible. It was also thought that this would provide for broader knowledge and more mutual understanding, since the idea was to include a selection of various national literatures in this "core." All the republics agreed to the idea except the Slovenes, who found it to be unacceptable. They argued that this amounted to unnecessary centralization and was an encroachment on national identity and individuality. So the idea of creating a minimum, homogeneous educational syllabus for all schools in Yugoslavia failed.

Whereas the failure of this attempt can be seen as a lack of will to integrate, the next moves were directed squarely at loosening the existing structure of Yugoslavia. The Slovenes took a hard look at the realities of post-Tito Yugoslavia and concluded that these amounted to no more than the image or ghost of Tito on the one hand and the army, the JNA, on the other. These were the only bonds still holding federalism together. In order to obtain more independence, these two last remaining elements of cohesion had to be loosened, and the Slovenes set their minds to performing this task.

The first to be challenged was the image of Tito. They did not strike directly at him, nor was the political leadership of Slovenia directly involved. The unravelling of the myth was more roundabout and subtle. Since the Second World War and the creation of Tito's Yugoslavia a traditional "youth relay" had taken place every year. It symbolized the unity of the youth of Yugoslavia. The relay would be organized to pass through all the Yugoslav republics, and the baton, hollow inside and with a message to Tito, would be carried by hundreds of thousands of young runners. The relay was organized so that the running would end on 25 May, Tito's birthday, in a grand spectacle at the JNA sports stadium, always in the presence of Tito. That day was also officially proclaimed Youth Day.

This tradition, continued even after Tito's death, symbolized probably more than anything else the continuity of Tito's Yugoslavia. It was therefore the logical choice for the Slovenes to strike at if Tito's charisma was to be reduced. In 1986 the youth organization of Slovenia declared that they would no longer participate in the relay, that the whole concept was outdated and made no sense since the principal reason for the relay – Tito – no longer existed.

One could hardly argue with either of these contentions. The concept was indeed outdated, and Tito had been dead for six years. However, the broader implication of this move was of such importance that the Slovenes must have been aware that it was not only the baton and the relay that they were challenging with this unilateral decision. Officially, the party bosses of Slovenia stayed aloof from the decision of their youth organization, but it was no secret that they actually endorsed such a challenge.

In retrospect, as in the case of the strong language of the Memorandum of the Serbian Academy, the whole incident looks very naïve and insignificant. But at the time it occurred – at just about the same time as the Memorandum – its symbolic meaning was enormous. It was seen as a direct attack on Tito and on Yugoslavia as he had left it. The Slovenes were completely isolated on this issue. Not even the Croats supported them.

The fact that their decision stood shows that the centralizing forces in Yugoslavia had been significantly reduced and that the Communist Party of Yugoslavia, nominally the guardian of unity, was no longer in a position to act or react strongly and decisively. This reality more than anything else was what the Slovenes were actually seeking to test and, if possible, even to reinforce.

Having accomplished this important break with the heritage of Tito, the Slovenes consolidated it even further by proposing a national reconciliation between the winners and the losers of the Second World War. An important characteristic of Tito's Yugoslavia had been that all nations had their heroes – the Communists and those who followed them – on the one hand, and their villains – those who had openly collaborated with the occupying Nazi and Fascist forces or those who openly opposed the Communists on the other. The dividing lines cut across lines of national unity because they followed ideological and political considerations.

In Tito's time it would have been unimaginable for the Communists of, say, Slovenia to feel closer to their wartime enemies, even though they were Slovenes, than they would towards Serbian or Croatian Communists. The Slovenes were the first to break with this type of identification, substituting national for political and/or ideological loyalties. They accomplished this quietly, without arousing the others much, even before the Serbs had finished their national integration. The Slovenian method of nationally integrating the population, which meant further reducing ties with Yugoslavia, was much less robust and spectacular than the Serbian mass rallies, but it was perhaps even more effective in its own way.

Next on the agenda was the destruction of the myth of the JNA. This was a tougher task to accomplish since the JNA was alive and well and constituted a respectable fighting force. The Slovenes were perfectly aware that they could not tackle it head on, not only because the JNA was too strong but more importantly because the Slovenian population did not resent the JNA enough to support such an attack. Many Slovenes remembered that it was the JNA that had brought back to Slovenia from Italy almost a third of their territory at the end of the Second World War, a fact not easy to counter in an open attack on the JNA.

The perception of the army had first to change in the eyes of Slovenes so that the confrontation could be carried a step further.

The nationalist leadership therefore used the same tactic that had produced such good results in the destruction of the Tito myth. Again it was the Slovenian youth organization that launched the attack through its newspapers and journals. And again the central issue in the anti-JNA campaign was not the constitutional position of the JNA nor the cost and large budgetary contributions needed to finance it. That type of criticism came later.

The tactics were centred on the notion that the JNA was not only alive and well but too much so. The press carried reports on the extravagant expenses incurred by the army in fulfilling the whims of the minister of defence and other generals. These reports were largely true, so the JNA was not at all convincing when it tried to label this attack a smear campaign. Besides securing the backing of its own population, this tussle with the JNA had the important purpose of testing how corrupt and vulnerable the army had become after many years of easy living and a highly privileged position in Yugoslav society. The Slovenes were lucky, and satisfied, that they had obtained a positive response on both counts.

In all this it is hard to see an overt or covert desire to leave or to break up Yugoslavia. The Slovenes maintained their stance that the purpose of their criticisms was not to leave but to have more freedom and autonomy to conduct their own affairs. Even after the break-up of Yugoslavia their explanations of their behaviour leading up to the crisis and open confrontation emphasized the desire to combine the benefits of Yugoslavia with the attainment of a more decentralized structure.

There was no denying, even on their part, that Slovenia benefited economically from the existence of Yugoslavia. Their main economic argument, tabled much later in the process of gradual disintegration, that Slovenia's financial contributions to the federal government (and the JNA) as well as the less-developed republics were too large, is only one side of the story. This one-sided focus on what Slovenia had to contribute to the budget and the federal development fund totally disregards the considerable benefits to Slovenia of the existence of Yugoslavia. Slovenian businessmen rarely argued that they were unduly taxed by the federation. That argument was made mostly by the politicians and especially the opposition that won the first free multi-party elections.

As the most developed of all the Yugoslav republics, specializing in industrial manufactured products, Slovenia benefited considerably by the terms of internal trade, exchanging its high-value-added manufactured products for the raw materials and other inputs from other republics. Over and above this, the Yugoslav customs union protected Slovenia's manufactured products with a much higher tariff than the one applied for energy and raw-material imports. This amplified the economic advantage of the Slovenes.

The contributions that the Slovenes made to the federal budget and to the fund for less-developed republics were relatively small compared to the gains of the common market. The complaints about financing the federal budget were much more political in nature than economic or financial; they were designed to undermine further the centralized authority of the federal government. As for the payments into the development fund, the standard, and very valid complaint of the Slovenes was about how the money was spent rather than the overall amount.

The development fund was run in such a way that the recipients decided how to use the money. Much of it was wasted on prestigious projects or conspicuous consumption.[2] The Slovenes insisted on having more of a say in how the money was spent. In effect, they were arguing the rational notion of dealing with development aid as a joint venture rather than a blank cheque. Their republic's contributions to the development fund were, however, emphatically *not* the issue that made Slovenia leave Yugoslavia.

The issue that definitely made it both possible and in their minds necessary for Slovenians to break away from Yugoslavia was that of Serbian nationalism. The more the Serbs pressed for control of Yugoslavia, the easier it was for Slovenia to muster internal and external support for quitting the arrangement it found unacceptable. In a way, Serbian nationalism pushed the Slovenes out of Yugoslavia more than they withdrew of their own accord.

But the Slovenes contributed their fair share in escalating the confrontation leading, ultimately, to a short but violent "war of independence." They openly and actively backed the Albanian leadership of Kosovo. During the miners' strike staged in support of a drive for the independence of Kosovo from Serbia, the leadership of Slovenia proclaimed that "the miners at Stari Trg[3] were defending the concept of Yugoslavia." By this they obviously meant that the only way in which they could conceive and accept Yugoslavia as a functional entity was as it had been defined by the constitution of 1974. That meant that Serbia should be saddled with autonomous provinces that were also constitutive parts of the federation.

The Slovenian Communist leadership claimed that very early on, almost immediately after the historic plenary of the Communist Party in Serbia in which Milošević gained power, they had realized that they were now dealing with a force with which a compromise was virtually impossible. But to be on the safe side, they adopted an attitude that made any kind of compromise even less possible.

The culmination occurred in the autumn of 1989, when the Serbs of Kosovo, with the full knowledge and backing of Milošević, decided that it would be a good idea to hold a "rally for truth" in Ljubljana, the capital of Slovenia. In the weeks between the announcement and the day the rally was supposed to be held, the tension escalated exponentially, with the media on both sides attacking and defending heatedly the two respective positions. The Slovenes felt nationally homogenized enough to threaten that the rally participants would be physically prevented from entering Slovenia, though this was still one country – Yugoslavia – and freedom of movement was constitutionally guaranteed. The rally never took place, but the damage to relations between the two republics was irreparable.

While this confrontation between the Serbs and Slovenes was taking place, the other republics tried to soothe the inflamed spirits. The federal government of Prime Minister Marković tried to offer formulae that would allow a compromise, while others were sympathetic to the Slovenian challenge to Serbia but mindful of the possible adverse consequences of an outright and total confrontation. Their position, therefore, was unassuming, almost reticent.

This was especially true of the Croats. Unassuming they were at the time, but their sympathies on the future of the Yugoslav federation drew them closer to the Slovenes than to the Serbs. The Croats still nurtured keen memories of how their first wave of national revival had been treated in the late sixties and early seventies. Therefore, they felt it to be wiser, and safer, not to take the lead in debates about the future constitutional reorganization of Yugoslavia. They silently followed the Slovenes as they spearheaded the drive for loosening the ties of federal Yugoslavia.

The position of Croatia in the heated confrontation between the Slovenes and the Serbs was so muted that it got a political label: "the Croatian silence." As long as the Croats were silent, the cookie could crumble either way. There was no denying that in their silence they were leaning towards and supportive of the Slovenian position. The Slovenes knew that and constantly maintained pressure on the Croats to come out openly on their side. The Serbs regarded their silence as a sign of Croatian weakness and confusion, and felt that their pressure could swing the Croats, if not to their view, at least into accepting realities.

Thirdly, the Croatian Communist leadership, proud of their silence and regarding themselves as power brokers, at the time sincerely thought that a deal with the Serbs was possible. They were led in this belief by Stipe Šuvar, a Yugoslav-oriented Croat and for a while the president of the CPY, who aspired to be a new, albeit lesser Tito. To fulfil this ambition he needed a formula that would not pit the Serbs against the Croats. The idea was to offer the Serbs in Croatia greater autonomy and in return to obtain greater autonomy for the Croatian state *within* Yugoslavia.

The problem was that this aspiration stood in the way of Milošević, who thought that *he* could inherit the image of Tito, in fact one that would be bigger than the original. While the Communists were still in power in Croatia, a deal, deflecting the later bloody confrontation, was still possible. But the Serbs, led by Milošević, remembering that the Croats had followed the Slovenes in not accepting a deal to revise the constitution of 1974 and accommodate Serbian grievances, decided to play for all or nothing, brushing away overtures by the Croats. The Serbs would not, and at this stage of national euphoria probably could not forget that Croats were backing the Albanians while the struggle for Serbian statehood was being fought.

Meanwhile, as Croatian Communist officialdom was trying to formulate a relatively moderate stance, on its home ground it was rapidly losing its monopoly on political representation. Franjo Tudjman made extremely good use of the official Croatian silence to develop and orchestrate a new, nationalist Croatian view as a solution to Serbian nationalist pressure. He led a strong and vocal Croatian national alliance to victory in the first multi-party elections in the republic, more than compensating for the silence of his Communist predecessors.

In the years of inertia after Tito's death the escalation of centrifugal forces, propelled by the Slovenes and, to a lesser extent, by the Croats, was gradual, but had a tendency to accelerate. On the surface it was not comparable to the violent eruption of Serbian nationalism, but as far as the fate of Yugoslavia was concerned, it was almost as crippling. Of course, the eruption of Serbian nationalism reinforced and further fuelled the tendency to redefine Yugoslavia according to a lower and lower common denominator. But the tendency was there to begin with, and its practical political manifestations contributed to the sudden upsurge of Serbian nationalism. There is, therefore, an element of truth on both sides of the mutual accusations over who destroyed Yugoslavia.

CHAPTER EIGHT

The Supporting Cast

The previous three chapters have described the principal actors on the Yugoslav scene: Tito's successors – the inert, inept, and gradually fading federal bureaucracy, and the assertive Serbs – trying to fill the substance of the federation with a new concept, more centralized and reflecting the specific Serbian position in Yugoslavia; the centrifugal drive of Slovenia and Croatia, trying to diminish the authority of the federation as much as possible for its own sake, but also to stave off the Serbian centripetal push. These were undoubtedly the principal forces that determined the fate of Yugoslavia.

But they were not the only ones. The other three republics onstage before the crisis occurred did not play a significant role. Montenegro fell into step with Serbia, while BiH and Macedonia were trying to define and defend a middle ground. Thus a situation of 2 + 2 + 2 was created, and this situation would prevail for quite some time, right up to the moment when the arithmetic of alliance was abandoned altogether.

An important supporting cast that deserves "honourable" mention in the Yugoslav drama consists of the intelligentsia, the media, the army, and, of course, as was always the case with Yugoslavia, the guests in the cast – the foreign actors. This chapter will describe their role in bringing about the crisis in and eventual dissolution of Yugoslavia.

THE INTELLIGENTSIA

In the Yugoslav crisis this segment of the elite played an unbecoming and uncharacteristic role. The intelligentsia are typically credited with liberalism, open-mindedness, a feeling for democratic values.

Above all, the intelligentsia are normally supposed to be swayed by the strength of arguments, not the argument of strength.

None of these exceptional values was present in the Yugoslav intelligentsia as the crisis approached. There were, of course, a few notable exceptions, but the bulk of the intellectuals rallied to serve their national flags and national leaders. Whereas in developed democratic societies, right-wing nationalistic movements hardly ever manage to attract into their ranks intellectuals of repute and recognition, in Yugoslavia it was the other way around. Intellectuals played the role of chief ideologues for the nationalist movements and the spreading of mutual hatred.

The undisputed spiritual leader of the Serbian nationalist movement at the time was Dobrica Ćosić.[1] He is a well-known Serbian writer with a long list of widely acclaimed books to his credit. His views were instrumental in creating the Memorandum of the Serbian Academy of Sciences and Arts. Milošević warmed up to those views, and eventually to the man himself. Ćosić's popularity rose, bringing him in 1992 to the position of president of the left-over Yugoslav federation. That was when Milošević had him brought down, for reasons we shall discuss later.

In turning the attention of Serbian politics to the moments of Serbian greatness in the past and co-opting Serbia's "glorious history" as a basis for the nationalist movement, Ćosić adumbrated a political strategy that was essentially anti-historical, in that it went back into history and stayed there. The realities of the present day were seen only in the negative form of "repression for Serbs." This national ideology was quite incapable of providing answers to the challenges of the present. That is why it returned, in spirit and often in content, to the Garašanin days, more than a century back. Ćosić, and a large segment of the humanities section of the Serbian Academy of Science, nourished and expanded the *mythical* component of a self-conscious Serbian population, converting it in the process into the prime mover from which everything is derived and explained, and from which present-day policy is formulated.

The Serbian intelligentsia, or at least the part that made itself heard and visible, thus turned out to be narrow-minded, provincial, even primitive. Incapable of fathoming and constructively shaping the realities of the present day into a coherent strategy that would take as its corner-stone the democratic traditions of citizenship, the majority of the Serbian intelligentsia followed Ćosić in resurrecting an irrational Messiah syndrome based on cults of yesteryear.

The Serbian intelligentsia were not the only elite to cater to and enhance the nationalistic attitudes that translated into aggressive national policies. To a greater or lesser extent that happened in all the nations of Yugoslavia. The others were not "blessed" in having such a domineering father-figure as Ćosić in Serbia, but the most influential segments of the intelligentsia in Slovenia, Croatia, and later on in BiH and Macedonia also contributed mightily to the formulation and execution of nationalistic policies.

Even during the Tito and immediate post-Tito years the national-istic streak in the Slovenian intelligentsia was typically stronger than in other parts of the country. This is understandable since Slovenian national identity had throughout the centuries centred on the ques-tion of Slovenian language and culture. Therefore, the intelligentsia involved in the humanities were always a step ahead of the others in promoting the authenticity, individuality, and separateness of the Slovenian nation. But mainstream Slovenian politics did not yield to this call of the sirens until other nationalistic strategies, primarily the Serbian, came into play.

In Croatia the intelligentsia, like the political elite, were rather muted for a long time, mostly as a consequence of having once burned their fingers in the mass nationalist movement of the late 1960s, and hedged against the risk of sticking their national ideology and political necks out too far. But whatever they lost in terms of an early start they more than made up for in terms of force and content once Croatian nationalism picked up momentum. Again, it was the intelligentsia that led the way in ideology, arguments, and a platform for an aggressive policy stance.

The make-up and behaviour of the Yugoslav intelligentsia, there-fore, were not typical of democratic societies where divisions are centred on basic principles of human organization. The Yugoslav intelligentsia were split along national and national-political bound-aries. A partial but plausible explanation of their motives is that the intelligentsia were in a perverse and certainly unintelligent way taking revenge for the decades of anti-intellectualism that had pre-vailed while the Communist Party was in full power. In thoroughly destroying the remnants of the Communist ideological structure and the long-dominant perspective of the "class struggle," the Yugoslav intelligentsia by and large proved incapable of shifting towards dem-ocratic and pluralistic lines of distinction. Instead they chose the model that was closest to hand and easiest to formulate and argue – the ideology of nationalism.

The intelligentsia thus played a very important supportive role in the spiritual preparation of their own nation for a confrontation with the Others. The word confrontation is used here, as it was by the nationalistic intelligentsia at the time, for all forms of conflict and encounter, including confrontation with arms. The nationalistically exclusive and mutually aggressive ideologies were served up to the respective political leaderships, escalating over time from claims about the righteousness of one's own nation to denunciations of the debauchery and wickedness of the Other.

There were, of course, exceptions. In all the republics there were intellectuals who warned of the imminent crisis to which the abuse of nationalist sentiments would lead. There were attempts to form Yugoslav intellectual forums, to rise above the tide of nationalism, to steer a course towards the pressing issues and away from nationalistic narrow-mindedness. But these were drops in the ocean. The nationalist virus had caused a widespread intellectual epidemic.

THE MEDIA

For a considerable period of time the media in Yugoslavia were considered to be by far the best or, at least, the least bad in any of the socialist countries. After Tito's death and in the mid-1980s freedom of expression increased, and party or state control of the media were reduced even further. One would have thought, therefore, that the media would represent a moderating force and influence, using their increased independence to point the way towards a generally more free, transparent, and democratic society.

That did not happen. The media turned into villains, encouraging the worst in political life even though they had only a supporting role at the outset. The control of the media, of course, was not a new phenomenon in Yugoslavia. Though relatively free and informative, the media were nevertheless one-directional. The breadth and scope allowed to journalists and commentators was much broader than in other socialist countries, but the tendency was to praise the chosen direction and the political forces carrying it out, reserving criticism for those inside or outside who thought differently. The novelty was the new political direction towards nationalism and the readiness, even eagerness with which the media accepted this new role, allowing themselves to be instrumentalized in the nationalistic war of words that ultimately led to the war with guns.

It was Milošević again who demonstrated the usefulness of control and direction of the media towards nationalist goals. He effectively took control of the main Serbian newspapers and television while still Communist Party boss of the city of Belgrade. The media played an important role in the overthrow of his predecessor and an even more important one in expounding the new national awareness and nationalist political program he promoted.

If Milošević was the first to use the media in this way, he was certainly not the only one. At the same time there was in Slovenia a birth of national feeling and sentiment expressed mainly in the youth and professional journals. These were, however, marginal expressions of nationalist feeling, and mainstream Slovenian politicians had a hard time defining their position vis-à-vis this new phenomenon. It was only a few years later that the Slovenian press and television would join fully in the media war that preceded the ethnic war and escalated even further during the actual fighting. Eventually all the principal antagonists, from the Serbs and the army to Croats and Slovenes, joined in the terrible propaganda warfare in which the first and most important victim was the truth.

The scenario was relatively simple and blatantly devilish. The point was to emphasize as strongly as possible the distinction between *us* and *them*. By definition, *we* were good and *they* were bad. With respect to the media this meant that our media always tell the truth, the whole truth, and nothing but the truth, while their media always lie. So the truth that is believed in our media is one that portrays them as Satans, warmongers, national chauvinists, and generally people and a *nation* that one should hate for what they are doing to us. Our truth is a genuine and justified criticism of their hatred, while they, in attacking and condemning our truth, actually show how much they detest truth.

This glorification of one's own position and satanization of the other led to an unprecedented sowing of hatred and the escalation from confrontation to conflict and eventually a full-scale war. The media were used to exaggerate or even fabricate bad news concerning the other side, mostly, perhaps exclusively with the purpose of firing up nationalist feelings of hatred. At one point during the crisis and the ethnic war it became almost impossible to say whether the unity of Yugoslavia was more threatened by events or by media interpretation of events.

The other side was by definition the Dark Side. This logic was mutually reinforcing. If one considered the possibility that his own media might be biased and tried therefore to look at the truth from the other side, one was faced with the same tone and attitude but from the other side. Hearing and reading what the other side had to offer as its own truth, one could hardly resist the tempting call of one's own nationalism.

Front-page headlines, normally never exceeding an inch in height, suddenly tripled when reporting on what was done to "us" by "them." "Serbs subjected to fascist genocide" reported the Milošević-controlled daily *Ekspres Politika* as early as 1990. "JNA amassing troops for an attack" reported the Slovenian daily *Delo* in February 1991, completely fabricating the substance of the article.

But perhaps the most bizarre incident involving the media occurred at the beginning of the Croatian-Serbian/JNA war when, in August 1991, both sides got hold of independent television footage showing dead bodies being loaded on to a wagon. On Croatian television these bodies were reported as those of "Croat heros who fell in the struggle for Croatian independence." On Serbian television the bodies were recognized as "innocent civilians butchered by the hated Croat Ustashi."

In all fairness one must mention the exceptions to this general trend. There were a number of gallant, if futile, undertakings to bring to the Yugoslav public an unbiased view of events, one that would not take sides and, perhaps even more importantly, would not promote nationalism. The two most outstanding attempts were made by the federal newspaper *Borba* and the new reform-minded television station called YUTEL. In Slovenia and Croatia *Borba* was labelled a Belgrade (which is to say Serbian) mouthpiece, and about fifty of its sales outlets were ransacked, mostly in Croatia. In Serbia *Borba* was viewed as distinctly "anti-Serb" and was faced with a number of problems threatening its survival, such as printing strikes orchestrated by the Serbian government.

YUTEL, the Yugoslav television network that was to bring an objective and unbiased view to the citizens of Yugoslavia, had a hard time establishing itself. When it finally started broadcasting from Sarajevo,[2] YUTEL was picked up by other republics' television networks only after their respective programs had gone off the air, in the late hours of the night or early hours of the morning. Even these extremely unfavourable viewing hours attracted enough of an audience to make all the national leaders extremely hostile to it. Eventually, one by one, they took YUTEL off the air.

In the last two years before the splitting of Yugoslavia a number of independent magazines appeared in all the republics. Their editorial policy was honest and objective, their tone low-key and factual rather than high-pitched and inflammatory. Their appearance, though extremely encouraging, is still a long way from creating the sort of context in which the average citizen (of any republic) might be informed fairly, honestly, and without national prejudice.

Thus the media bear a heavy responsibility for the rapid deterioration of the situation and, with it, the disintegration of the country. Theirs was an important and sadly effective supporting role in this drama.

THE ARMY

The JNA,[3] as it was called, is the supporting actor with probably the most bizarre and least well-understood role in the Yugoslav drama. This once-proud army ended up disliked by all sides, weak, demoralized, and confused, a perverse sort of ending for an army that had a strong fighting tradition and a sound reputation. The JNA was formed on the tradition of the victorious partisans towards the end of the Second World War. It numbered well over half a million at the time and was one of the strongest fighting forces in Europe. It remained large and strong throughout the post-war period, mostly because of the Soviet threat, which was present on and off. Tito never fully trusted the Soviets and always thought it prudent to have a strong defence.

In fact, it was the perceived Soviet threat after the Warsaw Pact invasion of Czechoslovakia that made Tito instal a supplementary component of the armed forces – the territorial defence. This element of the armed forces was under the command of the republics and formed the embryo of the nationalist armies that would eventually turn and fight the JNA.

The JNA was, right up to the crisis and the outbreak of war, fiercely Titoist and devoted to the preservation of the sovereignty and territorial integrity of Yugoslavia. It was visibly present in the political life of Yugoslavia, notably the CPY, the Socialist Alliance, the Federal Presidency, and parliament. As the crisis developed and war approached, the JNA took it upon itself to flex its political muscle, trying to influence events by deterrence rather than by force. As there appeared to be less and less of Yugoslavia, the JNA tried to fill the void by maintaining the integrity of Yugoslavia. However, it resisted throughout the temptation to take over and show decisively who was the only remaining "integrative force" in Yugoslavia.

As in all other Communist-dominated countries, the army was loyal to the party and accepted Communism as its official ideology. Though the JNA did not play a particularly active part in political life, it was a valuable ally to keep in one's corner, and politics were ever-present in army life. The army was too slow in adapting to the new, multi-party political reality. It was therefore caught in a situation in which it found it extremely difficult to deny bias and partiality towards one side in the emerging conflict. The side it would eventually support was naturally the one that did not attack the values the JNA held in high esteem, particularly the unity and integrity of Yugoslavia.

Much has been said and written about the ethnic mix of the JNA. Serbs were understandably the most numerous, as they were in the total population of Yugoslavia. They were also more numerous in the officer corps for traditional rather than political reasons. The predominance of Serbs, as well as of Montenegrins, can be explained by the esteem in which an officer's career had long been held in these parts of Yugoslavia, as opposed to the lack of esteem, even disdain for the uniform, that was characteristic of some other republics. Before the outbreak of the war neither the general behaviour of the JNA nor the behaviour of the officer corps could have been considered antagonistic towards any particular nationality in Yugoslavia.

The army was very energetically pro-Yugoslav. Yugoslavia had provided its *raison d'être*, had always been generous, perhaps even too generous, providing for the production and purchase of expensive hardware that not many armies of the world could boast. The officer corps led a relatively privileged life by Yugoslav standards and had every reason to support the idea of a JNA serving a unified and integrated Yugoslavia. Tito used to point out that the JNA was one of the true melting-pots in which the sense and feeling of Yugoslavism was created. This feeling lingered on in the JNA long after his death.

At the inception of the Yugoslav crisis the JNA influenced events primarily through others' *perception* of its position rather than through its own political or military action. This balance shifted dramatically during the war, however, and the JNA moved from its supporting role to that of a key player.

During the build-up to the crisis, the Slovenes and the Croats tended to perceive the JNA as a possible opponent, though at the time it was neither anti-Slovene nor anti-Croat.[4] Their attitude was such because they were politically interested in weakening what they considered to be an overcentralized Yugoslav structure. They also felt, rightly, that the JNA was likely to defend this structure because, through defending Yugoslavia, it would be defending its own existence. The Serbs and Montenegrins, by contrast, perceived the JNA as a "natural ally" because of their common aim of securing a more united, stronger, and more centralized Yugoslavia. It was thus a community of interests that brought Serbia and the JNA closer rather than the fact that it was a Serbian/Montenegrin-dominated army.

It must be emphasized that the behaviour of the JNA was *very unusual* by the standards that normally apply to the role of national armies in crisis situations, particularly in countries with underdeveloped democratic institutions. This unusual behaviour can best be explained by the fact that the army had traditionally viewed itself as an executive organ of a political bureaucracy and found it hard to rid itself of this pattern of thinking. The disintegration of the Yugoslav political bureaucracy that the JNA served caused considerable confusion within army ranks. The ensuing separation of republics from the federation then provoked many to switch their allegiance – or to "desert," depending on the side from which this was observed – with a resulting massive outflow of officers and men from the JNA to the new republican and nationalist armies.

The army was politically and militarily unprepared for an attack from within. Its doctrine, strategy, and tactics were geared to defence from a foreign (most likely Warsaw Pact) attack. The fact that Yugoslavia was attacked by itself, that the "enemy" was within the borders of Yugoslavia, forced the JNA to improvise and wade through the political quagmire without a clear strategic or tactical view of its own role. This is the only logical way in which the gross blunders it committed in an undeclared war can be explained.

Its political presence and strength was misused, both inside and outside the army, its military might often abused. The JNA, as we shall see, in insisting rigidly and unyieldingly on controlling the means by which Yugoslavia was held together, was largely instrumental in provoking the mistrust of Slovenia and Croatia. Its political clumsiness was in turn skilfully exploited by these republics in their quest for independence. Yet the JNA did not throw its lot in with Serbia and Montenegro until almost the very end. In its supporting role the JNA was primarily in favour of preserving Yugoslavia. As the political substance and content of the old Titoist federation slipped away and as Serbian views of what Yugoslavia ought to be gradually filled the emptying shell, the JNA was drawn into support of the Serbian view and thus, finally, of Serbian politics. In the final analysis, somebody *had* to finance its existence: the Slovenes and Croats resisted such support; the Serbs gave it.

The behaviour of the JNA exposed many problems inherent in its role and nature that have all led to the collapse of its image and fighting ability. The most important factor was its loyalty to the disappearing structure of Titoist Yugoslavia. By sticking to this commitment the JNA could hardly avoid taking sides as the crisis deepened. The lack of a clear strategic objective made it vulnerable to political manipulation from without its ranks and the disruption of the chain of command from within. Its "stop and go" tactics, in proclamations as well as in action, raised the question of its determination and competence. This again had the effect of antagonizing and polarizing the nationalist fevers that the JNA was supposed to suppress.

The JNA was rendered powerless, without actually suffering defeat in battle, by participating in the wrong war – an ethnic war – and by being drawn into the nationalist tensions that were tearing Yugoslavia apart. It found itself involved in tasks that it was not used to, performing political arbitrage among hostile nationalities, some of which were also increasingly suspicious of its motives and role. These suspicions eventually turned to hostilities, and the JNA responded in kind, contributing largely to the bloody nature of the war that followed.

THE FOREIGN ACTORS

Foreign influence has always been of considerable importance in determining the fate of Yugoslavia. It was never one of those countries in which the big powers of Europe and the world could take only a passing interest.

At the end of the First World War the victorious powers were deeply involved in the creation of the Kingdom of the Serbs, Croats, and Slovenes, and continued through the inter-war period to exert political pressure on the Serbs as well as the Slovenes and Croats. During and after the Second World War, when the new Titoist Yugoslavia was being created, it was caught between the two superpowers of East and West.[5] This in turn helped Yugoslavia to maintain an independent foreign policy. The Cold War made Yugoslavia strategically significant to both East and West, and Tito knew very well how to capitalize on this fact.

After Tito's death both East and West helped to maintain the unity and preserve the stability of Yugoslavia. The West was, of course, much more involved financially and commercially, pouring billions of dollars into a series of largely unsuccessful attempts to reform and restructure a rapidly deteriorating economy. But the Soviet Union, perhaps under the influence of the Helsinki Agreement on security arrangements in Europe, also had no desire, nor did it make any moves, to destabilize the country.

The Yugoslav nations were, for the first time, very much on their own in determining their faith, with no external power or powers trying to impose their will. The crisis that set in and the war that followed were not caused by foreign forces. They were a result of pressures from within and were therefore, in the first instance, strictly of domestic origin.

If anything, during the build-up of the crisis interested foreigners tried to play a constructive role, insisting on the unity of the country and urging a peaceful and democratic settlement of outstanding disputes. In trying to be helpful the outsiders were often in a position to suggest where the problems lay, but few if any within the country would listen. At one time the idea was floated to send to Yugoslavia a "council of wise men," clearly indicating that wisdom was the deficient ingredient on the Yugoslav political scene.

The exception to this general assessment was the behaviour of some neighbouring countries. Seeing Yugoslavia tumbling into a deep internal crisis was too much of a temptation for some of them, and they could not resist attempting to intervene. This was particularly true of supposedly neutral Austria, which made a point of interfering as much as possible, as did Albania and Hungary, which considered this to be a unique opportunity to put pressure on Serbia.

Once the crisis broke, and especially during the ethnic wars, foreign involvement once more became extremely important. Yugoslavia became the centre of Western European attention even though, as a country, it was on the margins of Western European development. Like the JNA, and partially because of it, the foreign actors gradually moved from a supporting to a lead role during the evolution of the Yugoslav drama.

In the same manner as the army, the foreign actors influenced events – more than they realized – through the way their supposed role was perceived by the Yugoslav parties. This perception derived partly from the false belief that Yugoslavia was as important as it had been during the Cold War and under Tito. But instead of the unity within the country that had been taken for granted, the sad reality now was that it was gradually but surely falling apart. From there it took only one step of the imagination to conclude that some major power or powers were scheming to break up and destroy Yugoslavia.

Conspiracy theories fall on extremely fertile ground in a region like the Balkans. The taste for conspiracies has been called the malaise of the region and has always been exploited to the full. Though such a theory can be challenged, it is extremely difficult to refute partial and individual assertions by its adherents. When faced with an individual statement by a conspiracy-theory zealot, a rational person runs the risk of appearing naïve or uninformed, especially if the conspiracy theory comes from such authoritative sources as academies of science, the leadership of political parties, or individual political leaders who have a considerable following.

The other reason for the popularity of conspiracy theories lies in old Stalinist notions about the duplicity of democracy and the conviction that real power is always hidden behind the scene. Proponents of such notions find it hard to believe that there is no "capitalist politburo" that is scheming behind the backs of elected officials – presidents, prime ministers, ministers of foreign affairs, and so on. These front men are either foolish enough to believe what they are saying or are paid to say something they do not believe, something that would throw a smokescreen before the eyes of the poor victims, while the truly powerful go about their destructive endeavours in the background.

The past history of Yugoslavia and the behaviour of some foreign actors during the crisis and the war offer some justification for such a scenario. But it is one thing to scheme for the sake of maximizing interests in a situation that is going from bad to worse, quite another to set the whole disruptive sequence in action. The theory loses even more credibility when one looks at the supposed conspirators, who often include such unlikely allies as the Vatican and the Comintern.

The spread of these theories, however, performed an important function in mobilizing nationalist sentiment, in convincing many that the "enemy" was being helped by dark and conservative forces from the outside, and, most of all, in shifting the responsibility for the tragic and bloody consequences of confrontation on to somebody else.

Today the foreign actors are drawn deep into the Yugoslav drama, more than they initially expected and perhaps more than they ever wanted. The United Nations is present in force, and the expectation is that the number of troops will have to increase. The European Community has been engaged in trying to find a political solution for over two years. In the process, Yugoslavia fell apart and the European Community was severely jolted by internal divisions over the issue of Yugoslavia. The United States entered at a later stage and, with frequent about-turns and no decisive stand, has lost much of the credibility that it gained in the Gulf War. The foreign actors are very much in command, or would like to think that they are. They are certainly in a position to influence events, provided that a strategic consensus emerges. At this stage the foreign influences have shifted from a supporting to a leading role.

But they were drawn into the drama with considerable reluctance. One can hardly escape the feeling that the overriding objective of the foreigners was and still is to contain and minimize involvement rather than to find a solution. It is difficult to argue that foreigners wanted to *impose* a solution against the will of the Yugoslav nations. Indeed, at every step of engagement diplomatic circles have stated clearly that their aim is to help the Yugoslav parties reach their own solutions.

Which is not to say that everything outsiders have done has *helped* to bring about a solution. None the less, a distinction must be made between deliberate attempts to make things worse (as imagined by conspiracy theories) and the more banal reality of human error (and not just a few), committed while searching for lasting solutions.

The responsibility for breaking Yugoslavia apart rests with Yugoslavs alone. Had they desired to maintain peace, introduce democracy, and preserve the unity of their country, it is difficult to see how any power in Europe or elsewhere could have taken it away from them.

We have seen that, as Yugoslavia gradually disappeared, the JNA shifted towards the Serb/Montenegrin political position, losing its direction in a country that had ceased to exist in all but name. For those foreign actors who persisted in believing in the unity of Yugoslavia even longer than the JNA, after its disappearance in substance a return to *realpolitik* and some basic principles of international security seemed in order. It was no longer a question of preserving a country but of securing peace and an orderly transition to a post-Yugoslav stage. This approach was far from ideal, and the new *realpolitik* as it would be applied to Yugoslavia would turn out to be a reflection of the emerging new realities and *realpolitik* within post–Cold War Europe, leaving a number of European countries uneasy, if not unhappy.

PART THREE

The Plot

CHAPTER NINE

Changes in Europe

As the Yugoslav crisis deepened, the whole of Europe was undergoing epochal changes. Something had happened to interrupt customary patterns of political behaviour and security concerns. The end of the Cold War had a profound effect on the whole of Europe, including the Yugoslav republics.

The sudden demise of Soviet-led Communism, the collapse of the Soviet Union as a country and the Warsaw Pact as its military arm, had opened an era of hope and new possibilities for political and economic relations between all the nations of Europe. But these events had also ushered in a time of much confusion and bewilderment, leading to fundamental political and security reappraisals. The old equilibrium of fear and suspicion so characteristic of the Cold War was gone. A new one had not set in automatically to take its place. The old order was undesirable and frightening, but it was predictable. There had been a perverse sense of security deriving from the balance of power and fear.

The new order, if it could be called an order, offered great potential because it appeared to present a fundamental commonality of interests and goals. The ideological propositions were now almost unanimously assented to, and there was no cause for confrontation on those grounds.

But this order in the making also brought about potential dangers on both sides of the now defunct Iron Curtain. These had to do primarily with expectations, or more precisely with the disillusionment that typically sets in when expectations are not fulfilled. The societies of the East expected, and still expect, the West to embrace them like long-lost brethren and to provide all necessary financial aid and security. This has not been forthcoming at anywhere near the expected levels, nor is it likely to be.

The message of the West to the people of the East, set out through the principles of aid conditionality, was that if they would just become more democratic and more market-oriented, then the West would be morally bound to help them. But this moral bond proved difficult to sell to the population in the West itself. Pressing economic problems at home made Western politicians shy away from large-scale economic transfers to the East. It was and still is very difficult to convince people in the East that the reasons for aid that is less than expected are domestic economic problems. Easterners believe that the West is rich, rich enough to solve *all* problems, but that it is selfish and restrictive with its money.

The West expected the East, now that it had been freed of its Communist shackles, to reorganize its economic and political structures and, without looking back, to build a brave new world modelled after the successful Western experience. This did not and is not likely to happen at anywhere near the expected and necessary speed to fill the void left by Communism. The institutions and structures, the habits and propensities, the dead weight and inertia of the old system are too large an obstacle to be removed very rapidly.

The people of the East thought, wrongly, that they would enjoy the benefits of a market-oriented economy the moment they declared their intention to create one, and that they could somehow forego the efforts that people in the West have made over generations to reach the standard of living that they enjoy today. The lack of effort in the East makes people in the West think of them as lazy and selfish, trying to improve their lot by simple monetary transfers from the West. Nowhere is this more clearly evident than in united Germany. The situation three years after unification is still a long way away from what both sides expected to attain.

Yet another element providing for increasing rather than decreasing difficulties in defining and creating the new order in Europe came with the diffusion of focus that occurred on both sides. The line of engagement was no longer simply drawn and therefore clearly focused. The much broader span of mutual engagement brought with it a recognition of complexities and incompatibilities, highlighting many divisions in Europe, including the ethnic and the national.

The Cold War had, through its brutal reality, held security interests in very sharp focus in the West, dictating the creation of NATO as an effective defence alliance and securing American military presence on European soil. The end of the Cold War brought about a relaxation of the discipline of common Western interests, making the profile of security considerations less clear.

With the end of the Cold War, and especially with the formal ending of the Warsaw Pact, there were arguments that NATO had lost its *raison d'être* because the adversary had simply disappeared. NATO is going through a continuous redefinition of its position and role. The concept of the "European Pillar" was floated, and the idea of a European Defensive Alliance (primarily through the Western European Union) gained in prominence. European rapid-deployment forces are being discussed, and the embryo of a future European defence force has been formed in the shape of Franco-German units.

NATO has basically withstood all attempts at drastic change with two simple propositions. First, it is a defensive alliance, and the fact that an expansionist adversary of long standing is there no longer does not mean that there is nothing to defend. This view is coupled with the proposition that the dangers of all-out war may have been reduced but the number of uncertainties has actually increased – danger has changed its name. In that context, the disintegration of Yugoslavia provided fresh fodder for military and political talk within the alliance.

It remains a fact that in the aftermath of the Cold War, Western European citizens, and certainly aspiring Western European politicians, are less certain of which element of security they rely on first and foremost in the event of a crisis. In the present and the immediate future there is no alternative to NATO. But in the longer run Western Europeans are hoping, or at least were hoping at the time Yugoslavia fell apart, to come together in a common defence system, just as they had for decades in the European Economic Community for their economic interests.

It is also true that the United States is a slowly fading presence on the European scene. This is an inevitable result of the "push and pull" effects that were felt after the end of the Cold War. The "push" effect was provided by those Europeans who wished to "take European affairs into European hands." The "pull" effect was provided by Americans themselves, in the form of strong sentiments to "bring the boys home" now that the danger of the Cold War had ended. Americans are turning inwards and towards the Pacific Rim, and are as a consequence less interested in Europe. The situation in Yugoslavia, probably more than any other, epitomizes this tug of war between the allies and the hot potato of responsibility and leadership that they try to pass to each other.

The gradual withdrawal of the United States, combined with the impressive performance of the European Community since the mid-1980s, has made the Community the pillar of prosperity and stability in Europe and a strong generator of integrative forces.[1] The magnetic force of the Community has lured such wealthy countries as the EFTA group, and with the fall of the Iron Curtain, most if not all the ex-socialist states have looked immediately to the Community for help, guidance, and membership.

But the European Community, with all its impressive accomplishments during the period of Euro-optimism, has a much less clear view of its strategic interests in the new situation. At the same time, the loss of the discipline imposed by Cold War security concerns has caused some of the internal bonds within the Community to be relaxed. The call for greater unity within the Community was initiated at a different time, a time when further European integration was deemed vital for the long-run security interests of Europe. But the Community had no ready response faced with the reaction to its own success, namely that others would naturally wish to join or at least come as close to the Community as possible.

This was best seen in the discussions of "deepening versus broadening" that took place in the early 1990s. The issue: Should the Community consolidate and increase its mutual bonds first, before letting new members in, or should it let in new members first and then redefine its internal structures? This discussion has taken up a great deal of time and effort in the Community and has had considerable side-effects on the Eastern Europeans who anxiously await the results.

The debate was initially held with a view to the aspirations of countries that had not gone through the same process of change as those of Central and Eastern Europe. But the fact that these countries also made it clear that they saw their future in integrating with the European Community focused the debate even more sharply on one fundamental issue: Was the European Community strong enough to absorb new members without loss of standards, integrity, and security, or was a strengthening of its institutions required before new members could be admitted?

This debate also made the foreign- and economic-policy stance of the European Community towards the ex-socialist countries, including the then existing Yugoslavia, less than perfectly clear. Though they were an issue in the debate, these countries felt sidelined, their pressing problems somewhat marginalized. The Community offered a number of token programs, improvising along the way as things developed but without a sense of clear direction or purpose.

One of the most dramatic and far-reaching changes in Europe has been the rise of Germany as a powerhouse both within the European

Community and in the broader European context. The end of the Cold War, nowhere more welcome than in Germany, has reintegrated the country and has offered it new opportunities it was eager to seize. The "economic giant and political dwarf," as Germany was cynically described during the 1970s and 1980s, has suddenly turned into the most powerful, influential, and assertive force in Europe. She has taken the lead (in Maastricht) in defining the ingredients of a new and strengthened European Community, while at the same time taking the most active role economically and politically in the ex-socialist countries. Thus Germany is effectively trying to perform a bridging operation, securing its central position and status in Europe.

The new foreign policy and aspirations of Germany have been variously described and assessed. At one extreme there are warnings that this is "the Fourth Reich in the making" and that German assertiveness could soon turn into domination, making Europe a part of German interests rather than Germany a fully integrated member of a European community. Others welcome the political and economic responsibility that such a powerful country is willing to shoulder and its desire to join more fully and genuinely into the community. The proponents of this view are not bothered whether this newly integrated force would be called a "German Europe" or a "European Germany" as long as it was truly strong and adhered to the basic principles of Western democracy.

But one particular aspect of newly found German assertiveness deserves special mention: the German attitude towards the East and in particular the Balkans. Accusing the Germans of being overly assertive in this region is to accuse them of pushing their way into a quagmire. Neither is it easy territory to control, nor are immediate gains to be had by any country from increasing its presence in these chaotic, depressed, and needy regions. Other countries have had and still have the same opportunity to be involved but have not seized it, generally preferring the comfort of detached policy recommendations. Perhaps there is a certain jealousy of Germany, which has developed since the fall of Communism, regarding its influence and success in Eastern and Central Europe.

German assertiveness in the ex-socialist countries is not always helpful and constructive. The case of Yugoslavia, as we shall see, offers a good example of poor German judgment. But Germany shows an interest and desire to influence the course of events in these countries, an interest that is typically much more limited, even absent among other Western European powers. No wonder, then, that the decisions of the others were swayed by German foreign policy. Again, it is a question of less than clear focus and insufficiently defined interests among Western, primarily Community countries, towards the "Other Europe."

On the Eastern European side, Communism had provided a compass pointing in a single, albeit erroneous direction. In doing so, it was unwavering and authoritative. Though the general direction now seems clear in most of the countries of the East, the pointing needle is wobbly and increasingly influenced by the magnetic field of nationalism. Some of the nations that have just shed the strait-jacket of Communism have also without hesitation accepted another mind-boggling ideology – nationalism. Instead of focusing on the problems of the present day and the challenges of the next century, some of them have followed Yugoslavia in looking at the unsettled scores and ideological values of the nineteenth century.

In almost all aspects of their relations, and certainly in the most important ones – economic, political, and security – the East and West of Europe have had to redefine and renegotiate old structures and create new ones. This process is still under way and will take some time. But in the meantime the massive disequilibrium that exists between the prosperous and stable West on the one hand and the impoverished, needy, and inherently unstable East on the other threatens to give rise to a new set of problems, unknown at the time of the Iron Curtain. Not since the end of the Second World War has Europe reached a turning-point so clearly fraught with dangers and yet so tantalizingly rich in promise.

The one institution that is a carry-over from the Cold War days and is also in need of radical transformation is the Conference on Security and Co-operation in Europe (CSCE). The CSCE had an extremely important influence on the devolution of socialist countries while security was still maintained by the balance of power between NATO and the Warsaw Pact. The Trojan horse of the Helsinki Agreement creating the CSCE was the so-called third basket of human rights, which provided for greater access to information in the East and legitimate leverage for criticism by the West. The CSCE meeting at Vienna in January 1989 enhanced the mechanisms for challenging the lack of human rights in Eastern Europe. These instruments wielded considerable influence in bringing about the end of Communism.

Today, in the aftermath of the Cold War, the CSCE is obliged to juggle three balls of its own creation: the principle of self-determination, the sanctity of borders, and the upholding of human rights. It seems incapable of this feat. It performed well when two of the balls could scarcely be launched – namely, the self-determination of nations as a high principle towards which few aspired, and the unchangeability of borders secured by a military deadlock. The new crisis situations, like the one in Yugoslavia, generally pit these high principles against one another, and the CSCE has neither the means for finding a solution nor an enforcement mechanism to control explosive situations. It is not an overstatement to say that the CSCE is running into considerable problems in crisis management now that it is expected to perform on its own. The creation of a crisis-prevention centre as part of the CSCE has proved to be singularly ineffective, in particular but not exclusively in the Yugoslav crisis.

Again, the best and most convincing demonstration of change has been provided by the unification of Germany. Germany was the most tragic victim of the Cold War, even if it did provoke the situation by starting the Second World War. But the country was obviously artificially divided, and nothing could be done to overcome that division without risking a nuclear confrontation. With *perestroika* in Soviet foreign policy, Germany was free to unite. A frontier was changed, but with the full consent of all parties concerned. The people of the former German Democratic Republic were allowed to express their right to self-determination and reunite with the rest of the country, again with no one objecting. In fact, everybody applauded the new reality, which allowed a national wrong to be corrected.

But the ease with which Germans changed European borders and exercised their right to self-determination was later to be abused by the same nation in the case of Yugoslavia, in an entirely different context and under vastly different circumstances. Though many, both inside and outside of Yugoslavia, were opposed, Germany held out its own example as the prime justification for a policy that contributed to the further and violent partitioning of the country, rather than the reverse.

In discussing the impact of these changes in Europe on the Yugoslav drama, the first observation that comes to mind is that the drama took place in an environment quite different from the one in which Yugoslavia had prospered, successfully maintaining a balance between East and West.

With the ending of the Cold War the geo-strategic significance and political importance of Yugoslavia diminished. Instead of being one of the key points in the supposed "grey area" of Europe, where NATO and the Warsaw Pact nations had a tacit agreement to leave things as they were, it now became just one of the trouble-spots on the European map. Since it was not under attack by a Cold War adversary but was rather under the destructive assault of its own people, the

West was very slow in formulating a response, both because of insufficient interest and because of a lack of precedent.

Though this strategic shift occured in reality, it was very late in affecting the minds and political reasoning of most Yugoslav-oriented politicians within the country.[2] They maintained that Yugoslavia was extremely important and that the interested foreign players would come to intervene diplomatically and politically. The corollary was that those players (the EC, UN, CSCE, NATO, and/or the United States) would intervene on their side, in support of their view and arguments about the future and unity of Yugoslavia. But in correctly reading the posture of foreign powers towards Yugoslavia, the nationalists in Serbia, Croatia, and Slovenia did a much, much better job than the federalists.

Just before the war broke out in Yugoslavia, there occurred the American-led resolution of the Gulf Crisis, culminating in the "Desert Storm" offensive. These two crises do not offer grounds for adequate comparison in any way but one: the demonstration of will and capacity to act when a vital interest is at stake. The fact that the "enemy" in Yugoslavia was much less well-defined at the time was thought to be a secondary, not a primary issue.

In the Gulf Crisis the United States, perceiving a strategic threat to the control of oil and oil prices, reacted firmly to secure its interests, which were shared by the West in general. The Soviet Union went along with this policy to demonstrate the new climate of mutual understanding and shared principles of international conduct. The strategic interest of the United States in the Balkans generally, and Yugoslavia in particular, was at that time already too small for the Americans to try to engineer anything comparable to resolve the Yugoslav crisis. By the time it exploded with full force, the United States and Europe had already agreed that European affairs would be handled by Europeans, with the background support of the United States.

NATO, it was determined, was not going to get involved outside its defensively defined perimeters. In any event, Yugoslavia in the past had never seriously figured in NATO thinking except for the scenario that saw Soviet troops passing through Yugoslav territory in an attack on Italy. According to senior NATO officials, contingency plans for NATO involvement in Yugoslavia were never made.

The Western European Union had a name and a structure but no military mechanisms, certainly none that would involve crisis management in a third country. As the Yugoslav crisis intensified, talk about using the WEU rapid-deployment forces started, but nothing came of it.

The CSCE, though important as a political structure, proved to be quite incompetent in crisis management. The mechanism of crisis management was only then being set up and could not be expected to make an immediate contribution. In fact, Yugoslavia proved to be a test case that showed up weakness in its design.

That left, of course, the European Community as the strongest economic and an emerging political power in Europe, and, therefore, the regional organization best suited to exercise a calming political presence. The role of the European Community is discussed in a later chapter, but it must be said that the main aim the Community set for itself, to seek and find a political solution in an environment of peaceful negotiations, has so far failed miserably. The environment not being peaceful, a solution is nowhere in sight.

Furthermore, Community involvement came to be largely influenced, one could say dominated by Germany. Not only did the reunited Germany present a formidable and dominant political force, but the *way* it was reunited (change of borders with self-determination of the German people) became a German recipe for a situation that was fundamentally different. The unfolding drama has proved the Germans wrong, but at the time the Community was too interested in appeasing Germany to offer much resistance to a forceful Hans-Dietrich Genscher, the German minister of foreign affairs.

The inability of the European Community to cope effectively with some of the key elements of the crisis, notably the maintenance of a workable cease-fire, which would provide the necessary precondition for political discussion and settlement, ultimately brought the United Nations, for the first time ever, to intervene on the European mainland – a clear indication of European impotence in the face of a major crisis. But the UN, fresh from victory in Kuwait, found itself more and more involved in the Yugoslav drama and yet never any closer to a solution.

One further connection between the Yugoslav drama and the changes in Europe needs to be clarified, and that is the relation of events in Yugoslavia to the so-called Velvet Revolutions, which, except in the case of Rumania, brought down in a peaceful and non-violent manner the Communist regimes in almost all socialist countries.

The Berlin Wall, and with it the Iron Curtain, came down in the autumn of 1989. Within one year all the Central European countries had repudiated their Communist governments and turned towards the West, primarily the European Community, for economic help and guidance. The exceptions to this trend were Poland, whose Solidarity movement pioneered the upheavals contributing to the change in the Soviet attitude towards its satellites, and Albania, which was two years behind other countries in converting from Communist Party domination.

It is remarkable that Yugoslavia was not caught up in this peaceful revolutionary upheaval, which transformed the autocratic, dictatorial systems of the Central and Eastern European countries into multiparty, market-oriented, westward-looking democracies. Yugoslavia was different for two reasons. First, the roots of the socialist/Communist ideology were much deeper in Yugoslavia, and it was therefore stronger there than in any of the other ex-socialist countries except the Soviet Union. Yugoslavia, after all, had carried out an authentic, grass-roots socialist revolution during the Second World War. The doctrine of socialism/Communism was not imposed from outside, rolling in together with Soviet tanks, but nourished from within.

The Titoist brand of socialism, especially after the split with the Soviet Union, was not felt to be alien but rather an authentic, distinguishing feature of Yugoslav society. At the same time, Yugoslavia was extremely open to foreign, primarily Western economic and cultural influence, so the gap between the Western and domestic standard of living was far smaller than it was in other Communist countries. This made the sort of confrontation that occurred in Poland, Hungary, or Czechoslovakia almost impossible at the time that the Velvet Revolutions shook Central Europe. Yugoslavs travelled abroad in large numbers, and even though the status of human rights was often compromised within the country, they had access to information from abroad and spoke freely, often critically. The socialism of Yugoslavia was destined to fade away much more slowly than in the countries where it was an imported ideology.

Second, the dissolution of the old Yugoslav political structure actually preceded the Velvet Revolutions. Two years before the fall of the Berlin Wall marked the end of the old Cold War equilibrium of fear, Milošević and the Serb nationalists marked the end of the national-political equilibrium in Yugoslavia, substituting national flags, slogans, and policies for those of class unity and solidarity. By the time of the Velvet Revolutions the peoples and nations of Yugoslavia were so immersed in their respective national awakenings that the alienation from Communism, and from civil rather than national rights, came only as an afterthought.

The democratic winds sweeping across Europe did have an effect on Yugoslavia, but unfortunately they came too late and were secondary to the tide of national awakenings. It is unfortunate that the nationalistic gales in Yugoslavia had, and still have, an effect on events in the rest of Europe. It now appears that the nationalist virus that hit Yugoslavia first is more contagious and widespread than seemed possible when the Yugoslav crisis first hit the headlines.

CHAPTER TEN

The Crisis

Given the dominant tendencies in the key republics and the international environment in a state of post–Cold War flux, the stage was set for the crisis that eventually led to war. There was a last-ditch effort to save the unity of Yugoslavia, led by Prime Minister Ante Marković. At the time he had the full support of the significant foreign players: the European Community, the United States, the International Monetary Fund, the International Bank for Reconstruction and Development, and others. But the hour was late, and this last show of strength still proved a poor match for the combined disintegrative forces of the Serbs, Croats, and Slovenes.

Having completed the unification of Serbia and obtained the support of the new leadership of Montenegro, Milošević now set his eyes on Yugoslavia. The odds had changed considerably in his favour. Whereas his predecessor as leader of Serbia, Ivan Stambolić, often faced a situation of one to seven in deliberations on federal matters, Milošević already had a balance of four to four and the momentum on his side.

At the rally in Gazimestan in the summer of 1989 he threw away a major opportunity to reign in the nationalistic horse and extend a hand of compromise and co-operation. Seated on the podium as honorary guests, listening to Milošević's speech, loaded with Serbian pride and patriotism, were the entire Presidency of Yugoslavia, headed by Janez Drnovšek (a Slovene), the whole government, headed by Ante Marković (a Croat), the top brass of the army, and a majority of the diplomatic corps.[1] They listened, and many applauded.

Milošević took this to be a sign of their weakness, since he was sure that it could not be a sign of outright approval. The Croatian leadership was still silent, as were the leaderships of Macedonia and BiH. Thus open confrontation would take the shape of a feud between Slovenia and Serbia, the former resisting the spread of the wave of Serbian nationalism with a nationalistic wave of its own. The net loser was, of course, Yugoslavia.

The Serbs continued with their "rallies for truth," insisting that all Yugoslav republics hear about the terror and genocide to which the Serbs of Kosovo were subjected. Rallies were organized in BiH and in the Serb communities of Croatia, and an attempt was made to organize a truth rally in Slovenia. Seeing that other leaderships were showing signs of weakness, Milošević once again applied the bully and scare tactics first designed by Borisav Jović to get the Albanians of Kosovo in line. The calculation was that this would soon add BiH to the list of republics ready to follow Serbia into a new type of federation.[2]

But things in BiH did not evolve as expected. The "rallies for truth" organized in the Serb communities there did not yield the desired destabilization and retreat of the BiH leadership. By and large the leaders of the Bosnian Serbs were still not ready to disturb the centuries-old tranquillity of coexistence with the Muslims and the Croats.

In Croatia these rallies had an impact in the solidly Serb Kninska Krajina,[3] fermenting nationalist feeling among the population there, but on the broader political scene in Croatia there was no visible impact. The Croatian (Communist) leadership of the time still maintained that a deal with Serbia was possible. The offer was more autonomy for the Serbs, without declaring an autonomous province of the Serb regions, in exchange for less pressure and more independence for Croatia from the centre, which was thought to be controlled by Serbia. So there was no immediate confrontation. But neither was there submission to the Serbian view of restructuring the federation.

The attempt to organize a rally in Ljubljana, capital of Slovenia, led to the most visible and tense confrontation up to that moment. The rally was to take place at the beginning of December 1989, and Serbs were preparing to go there by special trains and buses. Tens of thousands of nationally agitated Serbs were ready and eager to challenge the Slovenian contention that "Yugoslavia was being defended by the Albanians of Kosovo," an unnecessary and irritating slogan launched by the Slovenian leadership while the "battle for Serbia" was still on. In the event, the Serbs did not go because the Slovenes said they would stop them forcibly at the border. But Serbia retaliated with a political proclamation, asking the Serbian business community and population to stop buying Slovenian goods. So it happened that Serbs were the very first to introduce the concept of economic sanctions into the Yugoslav drama.

All this was happening in parallel with the Velvet Revolutions in Central and Eastern Europe during the autumn of 1989. Since these revolutions raised the valid question of the legitimacy of leaderships, Milošević decided to secure his hold on Serbia by having early presidential elections, in December 1989. No opposition parties were as yet legal, so the farce of multiple choice was conducted by having four of his close political allies and advisers, all from the Communist Party of Serbia, appear as the "opposition" candidates. Needless to say, Milošević won handsomely, gaining ten times more votes than the next contender.

Although the Albanian population of Kosovo boycotted *en masse* this "democratic expression of choice," Milošević and those who followed him were convinced that this was a clear and legitimate mandate. Still, the elections were one of the biggest mistakes Milošević made. The results showed that he was *popular*, which was beyond doubt. But they also showed that he was not interested in democratic ways of gaining and holding power. He could have secured a much better political position in Yugoslavia, and certainly in the international community, had he, by facing a genuine opposition, been the one to champion the shift to a multi-party democratic political structure. The irony is that he was much better poised for this than either his Slovenian or his Croatian Communist Party counterpart, as later events will show.[4] But he chose to cling to the Communist Party method of grabbing and holding power, partially out of conviction but basically because he judged this to be a more effective method for securing the desired result.

The congress of the CPY was approaching. Serbs and Montenegrins were demanding that it be held as an "extraordinary congress" and as soon as possible, rather than at the previously set time (summer of 1990) following a regular four-year pattern. Milošević, still thinking that he could count on the political strength of the CPY to press others into submission, actually wanted to gain control of the vital functions of the federation by gaining control of the CPY, long the real political power behind federal structures.

But the CPY was already only a shadow of what it had been. The political inertia of Yugoslavia during the 1980s had at the same time considerably reduced the party's role and created deep cracks within it. It was still nominally tied to the principle of "democratic centralism," but in fact it was already largely confederalized. Prior to the congress of the federal party, the congresses of the parties of the individual republics were held, producing platforms and mandates for their delegates to the central party congress, which made it extremely difficult to reach compromises there.

The central issue was, as was expected, the transformation of the party itself. While Milošević insisted on the maintenance of "democratic centralism," which meant maintaining his own power to outvote and pressurize the in-party opposition, the Slovenes insisted on a looser arrangement in which the CPY would be a loose alliance of national CPs. Both were unyielding. Milošević himself took a very active role in the proceedings, twisting the arms of the uncommitted and putting considerable pressure on the Slovenes. But the latter would not budge. They finally walked out,[5] leaving the rest of the Yugo-Communists to adjourn with the face-saving formula that they would reconvene again after a platform acceptable to all had been renegotiated. They never did, and the CPY today is a small, marginal party of hard-line Communist die-hards, including Milošević's wife, Mirjana Marković.

Thus ended a political entity that had had a profound influence on the very life and existence of Yugoslavia for so many years. For Yugoslavia the era of Communism was definitely over. Most unfortunately, it was not to be succeeded by a democratic, civil political structure but by nationalism, whose potency as a political medium had already been demonstrated in Serbia.

The first free multi-party elections, which were held in Slovenia (April 1990) and Croatia (May 1990), demonstrated the appeal of nationalist arguments. As was the case in almost all ex-Communist countries, scores of new parties took part in these elections.[6] The winners were those parties and individuals whose platforms pivotted on the importance of national emancipation. Of course, the corollary was the unhappiness and injustice of that nation's position in Yugoslavia. The previous Serbian national revival provided the recipe for success. Unity and homogenization along national lines produced a significant, if dangerous, political power. The nationalism of the Serbs both incited and seemed to require a "defensive" nationalism of the other nationalities in Yugoslavia.

In Slovenia, Milan Kučan, the ex-Communist who had challenged Milošević and led the drive towards Slovenian independence, became the first democratically elected president of that republic. However, in parliament the centre-right coalition called DEMOS won the majority of seats. In any Western democracy this would have induced a political crisis or, at least, an extremely tense political situation. Not so in Slovenia. Members of both the left and the right of the political spectrum were Slovenian first and socialist, Christian-democrat, liberal, or anything else later. They had a common cause: the Slovenian national interest. At that point it was defined as maximum independence and sovereignty for Slovenia, with a possible confederal arrangement for Yugoslavia.

In Croatia the right-wing nationalist coalition called Hrvatska Demokratska Zajednica (Croatian Democratic Alliance) won an absolute majority of seats in Sabor, and its leader, Franjo Tudjman, became the first elected president of Croatia. The key slogans of his election campaign were "a thousand years of uninterrupted Croatian statehood" and "the thousand-year-long dream of independence." This was at one and the same time a reminder of the time elapsed to fulfil the dream and a revival of the traditional belief in Croatia's right to statehood.

Tudjman and HDZ lost no time in consolidating their victory in the most provocative way possible: by making sure that Croatia would constitutionally become a state of Croats. So eager were they to please the nationalist sentiment of Croats that they disregarded the existence of over 600,000 now nationally very conscious Serbs in Croatia. Croatian nationalism, like that of the Serbs and the Slovenes, tended to take lightly the rights and grievances of other nations and nationalities, concentrating with exaggerated attention on the rights of Croats.

The more moderate parties in the Croatian Sabor and the handful of Serb representatives were easily outvoted. The debate on the constitutional amendments was very heated, at moments even physically violent. In the end the Serbs walked out of the Sabor, deepening the political division and mistrust among the ethnic communities in Croatia.

Tudjman took a similarly arrogant attitude towards the republic of Serbia and Milošević personally. While his predecessors had considered that a deal with Milošević was possible, Tudjman thought at first that a deal with Milošević was unnecessary because he would not last long enough to deliver. Completely forgetting that Milošević was a nationalist first and a Communist later, Tudjman, and his HDZ with him, firmly believed that Milošević's days were numbered and that he would fall just as all Communist leaders in Eastern Europe had before him. Therefore, not only did Tudjman nourish Croatian nationalism; he openly advocated anti-Serbianism under the pretence of confronting Serbian Communist and autocratic behaviour with Croatian democracy.

So all three important nationalisms in Yugoslavia were now in full swing. The Macedonians, in their first elections (autumn 1990), elected a moderate leadership in spite of a strong showing of the extremist and nationalist vMRO party. In BiH the elections (autumn 1990) produced a coalition government of all three national parties (Muslim, Serb, and Croat) headed by Alija Izetbegović, the leader of the Muslims. The leadership of BiH, together with the Macedonians, tried in vain to exercise a moderating influence on the powerful nationalisms and the inevitable confrontation of the Serbs, Croats, and Slovenes.

Since the CPY structure had collapsed, the political confrontation shifted to the federal parliament and inter-republican informal and unconstitutional channels. The Yugoslav parliament was, from the first (Slovenian) elections to the very end of Yugoslavia, a very curious set-up. It had two houses: the upper, federal house, in which an equal number of members were elected directly from the republics and provinces, and the lower House of Republics and Provinces, in which an equal number of delegates were appointed by republican and provincial parliaments.

As elections were held in various republics and as various republican parliaments were constituted, they immediately changed their appointed representatives in the lower house. These were now representatives of various parties, but there were no party caucuses, only national ones. At the same time the upper house remained intact, consisting of elected (Communist) representatives, relics from the previous, one-party era. Predictably, this made the functioning of the federal parliament, normally the supreme expression of a democracy, very difficult.

One of the issues that arose as the crisis built up was whether to change parliament first and then bring in a new constitution or to change the constitution and then elect a new parliament. The Serbs were in favour of the first, insisting also that the new parliament should form the federal chamber (by direct vote) according to the principle of one person, one vote. They expected that their numerical superiority would be adequately represented in the parliament. Their demand was quite legitimate and based on a proven democratic principle.

The Slovenes, backed by the Croats, opposed the idea of electing the parliament first. In fact, they opposed the idea of elections for a two-house parliament. Knowing quite well that in a truly democratic setting it would be difficult to deny the principle of one person, one vote in the lower chamber, they opted for a parliament that would be *without* a lower chamber. It would consist only of appointed delegates from the republics (and provinces?), and decisions could only be made by consensus.

The main issue, of course, was the character of the new Yugoslavia. There was general agreement that the old one had to be modified but no agreement on what shape it should take. Since there was no ready-made recipe, the outcome was to be decided by a political process of negotiation. For negotiations one needs a powerful position, but in this instance the power of the positions relied heavily on nationalism, which in turn proved to be non-negotiable.

The Serbs, backed by the Montenegrins, wanted a "modern, efficient, and functional federation." Serbia vigorously supported this concept both for historical reasons (contending that it had brought the most into both pre-war and post-war Yugoslavia) and because significant parts of the Serb nation lived in other republics.

Croatia and Slovenia favoured a confederation, since both republics were convinced that this was the only way for them to acquire national sovereignty and full statehood. They also felt that a federal state would perpetuate "Serbian hegemony" and were highly suspicious of the adjectives "modern, efficient, and functional," since Serbia was hardly the one to contribute, with its existing leadership, to attaining such qualities.

The Macedonians and BiH leaned strategically towards the federal option. Without the backing of the Yugoslav state Macedonia would be much more open to its three other, hostile neighbours. For BiH the existence of Yugoslavia was a life-or-death question, since if Yugoslavia were to disintegrate, it was very doubtful that this republic could survive on its own with such an ethnic mix.

At the same time, the latter two republics also felt an uneasy respect for the current Serbian nationalism. They tried to formulate a position that would have the ingredients of a federation but would not be associated with the Serbian national position. Therefore, independently and later jointly, they struck a "middle ground" between the two extreme positions, trying to provide a bridge and ground for compromise. This was seen by the others as weakness, and both sides tried to woo them into their respective camps. The Serbs thought that pressure would get them BiH and then Macedonia. The Slovenes and the Croats kept pointing out the element of pressure from the Serbs, feeling that this was the best way gradually to move these two republics towards the confederal option.

The whole discussion of the form of the future state was conducted in an upside-down manner. Form was put before substance. Arrangements, actually names with empty shells, were preferred or rejected before the interests of republics regarding joint functions had been established. The Serbs, tactically led in these discussions by Bora

Jović, claimed that a discussion on the substance of the future state would be possible only after all the participants first clearly expressed their desire to remain in a common state! So, according to him, the political will was paramount, not the interests of the populations to perform a certain set of state functions together – as if the political will were independent of or somehow superior to those realities it was to express.

The suggestion, made by the "neutral" Izetbegović, that Serbia define the minimum of common state functions it would find acceptable, and that Slovenia and Croatia define the maximum above which they would consider any new function unacceptable, was flatly rejected by both sides. Guided by nationalism, both sides were unyielding and uncompromising, making their differences greater by the day and the solution that more difficult to reach.

The situation was further exacerbated by the war of the media, which instigated and deepened divisions and conflicts. The cultural dimension reserved for information, once truly unified, gradually became partitioned and segregated. The media stopped at nothing to spread false accusations and even barefaced lies, which had the effect of gradually but surely increasing distrust and even hatred between members of different nationalities. In all this, of course, the media were merely following the tactless, provocative, and inflammatory statements of many political leaders and high officials in the nationally minded republics.

And where was the federal government of Ante Marković? Marković had received his mandate from the old Communist leadership of Yugoslavia and the republics. In office since spring 1989, he had tried to steer a course clear of all nationalisms, to introduce a set of economic and political reforms that would transform the frail Yugoslav shell into a modern, functional, and efficient state. He personally picked his Cabinet, in which the key posts (defence, foreign affairs, finance, development) were held by Yugoslav-oriented Croats, as he was himself. This tight-knit group managed to function extremely well under very difficult conditions and produced a reform package that was loudly applauded in the West and international financial institutions as being bold, consistent, and effective.

His first year in power was spent consolidating what could be consolidated after the failed reforms of his predecessor and in view of the escalating nationalism. He became an instant hit with the public at large by removing previously imposed controls on the hard-currency savings of citizens, which were sizable. Instead of producing a run of hurried withdrawals, this measure actually boosted the hard-currency reserves, and boosted even more the prestige and ratings of the prime minister. Increasingly, throughout the year he gradually built up his position and became, as witnessed by numerous polls in all the republics, the most popular Yugoslav political figure.

In December 1989 Marković managed to push through the federal parliament a tough anti-inflationary package. At the time inflation was running at over 60 per cent a month; it dropped to virtually zero by midsummer 1990. This success consolidated Marković's position even more.

When the CPY congress ended in disarray in January 1990, Marković was largely considered the principal beneficiary of such an outcome. He believed as much himself, seeing his Cabinet as the only policy-forming body in the federation. No wonder he stated, with a broad smile, at the end of the CPY congress: "The end of CPY is not the end of Yugoslavia." He saw and felt considerable difficulties on the road ahead but failed to assess adequately the size of the nationalist obstacle that lay in the way of transforming Yugoslavia into a civil instead of a nationalist-ridden society.

Marković also made an attempt to free the exchange of information in Yugoslavia by creating a federal television network – YUTEL – and taking over *Borba*, the only all-Yugoslav daily newspaper. But the circulation of *Borba* only briefly surpassed 100,000 copies, and YUTEL was allocated late and odd hours by republican television authorities, prevented from ever offering unbiased news and analysis in prime time.

As these reforms were taking shape inside the country, a concentrated effort was made to connect Yugoslavia to the integrative processes that were under way in Europe, particularly by attempting to form closer ties with the European Community. As early as November 1989 the foreign minister of Yugoslavia, Budimir Lončar, requested the opening of exploratory talks, with a view to negotiating an association agreement with the Community. In February 1990 the federal parliament adopted the European Declaration, making the integration of Yugoslavia into Europe of prime strategic interest and the corner-stone of Yugoslav foreign policy and diplomacy. In May 1990 the president of the Federal Presidency, Dr Janez Drnovšek, made an eloquent and passionate plea for the acceptance of Yugoslavia into the Council of Europe and, through that, into the ongoing integration of Europe.

The logic was simple. Centrifugal domestic forces could only be checked by integrative forces, which would slow down and moderate nationalistic aspirations and policies. The prospect of closer ties with the Community and the West in general, something *all* the leaders of the individual republics declared was desirable, and the resulting commercial, financial, and technical assistance were promises that Marković was to play as his strongest cards in the months to come.

Unfortunately, other than applause and strong verbal support, he got little real help from the West. Marković was particularly impressed by the strong verbal support of the American administration. Convinced that the West, led by the United States and the European Community, would support his reforms in more than just words, he bluffed in the domestic card game. When the other players, Serbia first, called his bluff, it then transpired that the international backing for his reform program was only verbal and heavily conditional. This considerably reduced his credibility and with it made the prospect of a unifying platform for Yugoslavia more remote.

The main elements of his reform package, other than the anti-inflationary program (pegging the Yugoslav dinar to the German mark, putting a lid on wage increases, and reducing government expenditure), were movement towards trade liberalization, full convertibility of the dinar, privatization, making the economy more efficient and productive, creating the capital and labour markets that had not previously existed in Yugoslavia, overhauling the banking sector, and promoting small- and medium-sized enterprises.

It was a bold and ambitious program even without the difficulties provided by rampant nationalism. With the spectre of nationalism expanding even further, threatening violent conflicts, Marković needed all the support he could get. He was caught in the cross-fire of two different domestic criticisms. He, like Milošević, advocated a modern and efficient federation with a pluralistic, democratic structure and privatization in the economy. Thus he was open to criticism from Slovenes and Croats for being too centralist and therefore pro-Serb. The Serbs, by contrast, criticized him primarily for his speed and methods of implementing the process of liberalization and orientation towards the market, claiming that the reforms were anti-Serb because they made the Serbian economy suffer most. The Serbian leadership was also less than keen on introducing the multi-party democracy that was an important ingredient of the Marković reforms. They were the last to hold elections for their new, multi-party parliament, in December 1990.

In the summer of 1990, when his anti-inflationary program had yielded spectacular results, Marković formed his own all-Yugoslav Reform Party, expecting to consolidate even further his position on the turbulent Yugoslav political scene. That turned out to be a big mistake. First, he was criticized from all quarters for "abusing" his prime ministership in forming a political party. Leadership should work the other way around, it was argued. Secondly, Slovenia and Croatia had already held elections, so Marković's party could not gain a legal foothold in these republics until the next round of elections. Thirdly, Serbs, who had not yet held their elections, were highly suspicious of Marković for wanting to participate in their republican elections while foregoing an opportunity to do so in Slovenia and Croatia. Marković's Reform Party had a significant showing in Macedonia (winning the seat of president of the parliament) and a modest showing in BiH. These were also the republics most sympathetic to his view of the future of Yugoslavia. He failed in his attempt to close the gap between Slovenia/Croatia and Serbia. This failure left him weaker and much more at the mercy of local nationalisms, which were by now expanding at full throttle.

The main arena of nationalist confrontation was by now Croatia. Having been silent for a couple of years, including during the nationalistic confrontations of Serbs and Slovenes, Croatian nationalists had a lot of catching up to do, so they intensified their efforts. The Serbs in Croatia, already infected by the spread of Serbian nationalism, responded in kind.

Tudjman declared that there was Croatian state continuity, which included the infamous Ustashi Independent State of Croatia. This immediately intensified the fears of Serbs in Croatia that the policy of this new state would also be a continuation of the old fascist policy, namely genocide against the Serbs. This fear grew even stronger when the new Croatian leadership lost no time in wiping out the symbols of "socialist Croatia" and restoring all the symbols (flag, coat of arms, and so on) of the state that had been responsible for mass murders of Serbs, Jews, Gypsies, and, of course, "unyielding Croats" during the Second World War.

Croatomania escalated from day to day, as its counterpart had two years before in Serbia, much too often stepping over the boundaries of national pride into the realm of national chauvinism, even a return to fascism. For example, it was and is extremely difficult to explain to Serbs and others who suffered Ustashi brutalities during the Second World War the name change of an elementary school in Zagreb. It had been named after a school principal killed by the Ustashi, along with a class of schoolchildren. The new Croatian regime named it after an ill-famed Ustashi minister who made an agreement with Hitler to send Jews from Croatia to Auschwitz!

Wiping out the symbols and experience of forty-plus years of socialism was not enough. They had to be replaced by Croatian nationalism, even when this meant accommodating the Ustashi past.

The Serbs in Kninska Krajina responded violently. During the summer of 1990 they proclaimed self-rule and self-policing. They threw up log barricades on the main railway line connecting Zagreb with Split, the major city of Dalmatia, thus disrupting the flow of goods and people, many of them tourists. The Serbs of Croatia were also quick to organize a militia and later paramilitary units. These well-trained and -organized units became popularly known among Serbs as Kninjas, a play on the name of the capital of Krajina – Knin – and the ferocious oriental fighters the ninjas.

The Croatian government felt too weak to tackle this uprising against Croatization immediately. Knowing that the federal army would never participate in the Croatization of the Serbian parts of Croatia, Tudjman decided in the summer of 1990 to start forming his own paramilitary units, a risky step that put him on a collision course with the JNA.

The relationship of the new, non-Communist governments of Slovenia and Croatia with the JNA was uneasy, filled with mutual contempt, from the very beginning. As soon as elections brought in new governments in these two republics, the JNA ordered that all arms of the territorial defence be taken into the depots of the JNA. The Croats were caught by surprise, and most of their arms (mainly rifles and light infantry armament) were taken from their republican control and put under the control of the federal army. The Slovenes were better organized, having also better intelligence in the general staff, and they managed to keep under their control a much larger portion of the arms, which then served as a nucleus for the clandestine formation of Slovenian national defence units.

For a full year before the war broke out in Slovenia there existed a top secret plan to form a Slovenian army. It says much about the slack attitude of the federal army that it did not know or, if it knew, did not care about the formation of a parallel army on the territory of Yugoslavia.

The Croats had to start arming themselves almost from scratch. Considerable quantities of mostly light arms came into Croatia, financed by radical and relatively wealthy Croatian nationalist emigrants from Canada, Australia, the United States, and Germany. The federal authorities, particularly the JNA, knew about this development but decided to wait for an appropriate time to reveal its knowledge of the clandestine flow of arms across the Austrian and Hungarian borders.

The JNA was mistrustful of the new regimes on both ideological and patriotic grounds. The new Croatian and Slovenian regimes had no sympathy for Titoism and socialism, and they were toying dangerously with the unity, sovereignty, and territorial integrity of Yugoslavia. For their part, the newly elected regimes in Slovenia and Croatia were highly suspicious of an army that still had as an ideological platform the defence of socialism and the integrity of the *Socialist* Federal Republic of Yugoslavia, though by that time two important republics had done away with socialism and two others were clearly on their way to doing so.

There were mutual accusations, provocations, and statements of mistrust on both sides, the JNA and Slovenia/Croatia, but there was no open confrontation until the break-out of the war in Slovenia. In fact the JNA served as a neutral buffer for over six months between the Serbs and the Croats, who were gradually building up their mutual hatred to a point of shooting at each other.

In autumn 1990 the republics, after realizing that Marković actually had no carrot, and he certainly had no stick, that would channel events in Yugoslavia, openly and blatantly abandoned the agreed-upon course of reform. Government expenditures rose in all republics; the process of privatization was stopped, cancelled, or delayed, with social property[7] being nationalized equally vigorously in the "socialist" Serbia and the "Western-oriented and capitalist" Croatia and Slovenia. Incomes, which were also supposed to be controlled, grew exponentially, thus wrecking the second of the three anchors that held the anti-inflationary boat. Foreign reserves were depleted rapidly, forcing the government to carry out two consecutive devaluations, abolishing thereby the third and last anchor. The reform program was all but finished.

The final blow was delivered in January 1991, when it became known that Serbia had broken monetary discipline, dipping into the federal monetary reserve system to the tune of 1.8 billion dollars. This was done presumably to meet income, pension, and other personal expenditures in Serbia in November and December, two crucial months prior to the elections. The accusation, of course, was that the Serbian leadership had "bought" the votes of the electorate. Their defence, true if rather feeble, was that everybody in Yugoslavia was doing the same thing and that the only mistake Serbia had made was to try to make it legal by voting (secretly) on a special bill in the Serbian parliament!

The news of the Serbian penetration into the monetary system visibly shook the position of the Serbian leadership, putting it on the defensive even among its own citizens. But then the JNA saved the day by making public tapes allegedly proving that Croatia was being armed and had developed plans to kill army officers and to deal brutally with its Serbian population. The Serbs were infuriated; the Croats claimed that the tapes were rigged. The whole discussion and confrontation moved away from the monetary system.

There is little doubt that the tapes were authentic; later events proved them to be so. Few at the time questioned the legality of such use of secret filming. But the major unanswered question concerned the timing of their presentation. The tapes were made in October 1990 but were made public only in mid-January 1991, immediately after the revelation that Serbia had penetrated the federal monetary system. By moving the focus of attention to the clandestine arming of Croatia, the JNA had taken the heat off the leadership of Serbia.

Discussions of the future shape of Yugoslavia were also getting nowhere. The Slovenes, and after them the Croats, spoke ever more openly and with an increasing sense of urgency of the need to separate and perhaps, after separation, to form a much looser confederation of sovereign states. The Serbs would have none of this, saying that the constitution had to be changed first. It is interesting to note that the Yugoslav constitution was sufficiently imprecise to allow both sides to read and interpret it in the way that suited them best. The Slovenes and Croats pointed out that the constitution of 1974 mentioned the right of secession. The Serbs pointed out that, while this was true, the mechanism had not been specified and the republics that wanted to leave could not just walk out with total disregard for the union that had been jointly formed.

Both sides were right in their own way, and the solution would have lain in convergence and compromise. But each side stuck stubbornly to its own view and policy, constantly adding new "arguments" to prove the absolute right it defended and the absolute wrong of the other side. The Slovenes finally took a radical step in organizing a plebiscite on the independence of their republic. In December 1990 the Slovenian parliament published a declaration of independence, which stated that, if a solution were not reached in six months, Slovenia would unilaterally proclaim its independence. Only a month and a half later, disregarding its own timetable, Slovenia suspended all federal laws on its territory. Croatia followed suit the next day.

As of the beginning of 1991, the year in which war eventually broke out, the reforms of Prime Minister Marković were for all practical purposes dead. Though there was still strong verbal support from the outside, the coalition within Yugoslavia, bringing *together* Serbia and Slovenia, prevented an execution of the reforms. Marković then concentrated his efforts on trying to organize an orderly economic transition to a post-federal state of affairs and to broker a peaceful solution to the political problems at hand. His political position was further weakened by a row with the JNA leadership. The federal prime minister and his Cabinet lost their domestic importance by the day.

The Federal Presidency, split and in confusion, could not perform the necessary task of soliciting unity. The most sensitive function it performed was that of supreme command of the armed forces. Since 15 May 1990 the Presidency had been led by Bora Jović, the instigator of aggressive Serbian tactics. He managed to discredit this federal institution by constantly insisting on the theme of "law and order," but based his leadership on force or the threat of force rather than insisting on political agreement to abide by the laws or to change them.

Jović and the Presidency were quite right in pointing out the immense danger that lay in the constant creation and arming of different militias and paramilitary units. But the medium he chose for his warnings, threats that he would deploy the JNA, alienated everyone except the Serbs. Even the minister of defence, General Veljko Kadijević, was reluctant to follow the risky and threatening tactics of Jović.

Jović insisted regularly on using the JNA to disarm paramilitary and militia formations. One of these occasions led to a bizarre incident. He was outvoted in the Presidency on the use of the JNA and promptly resigned. Milošević immediately declared publicly that Serbia would not honour decisions made by the Federal Presidency without a Serbian representative on it. The situation was temporarily "saved" when the Serbian parliament "requested" Jović to resume his position, which he did two days later. The episode is indicative of the irresponsibility with which decisions were made, of the light weight of the Federal Presidency, and of the fact that power had now shifted completely to the republics.

The only possible way out was to seek a political settlement that would then remove the need for various armed units. Since the Federal Presidency was incapable of providing a meaningful solution, an attempt was made to find one in a series of meetings of republican leaders. Six were held, one in each republic, but no formula was found. Most of these meetings were taken up with the idea of an all-Yugoslav referendum that would test the feelings and interests of the population.

In the event, the referendum took place only in Croatia. Instead of soliciting a unified show of popular feeling, the referendum was held first and separately in the territory populated by Serbs, decisively showing that Kninska Krajina wanted to remain in a federal Yugoslavia, and then in the rest of Croatia, decisively showing that Croats wanted an independent and sovereign state, possibly tied confederally to other Yugoslav states. Both sides claimed this to be a major victory. But these referenda only showed how wide the breach between Croats and Serbs in Croatia was. The Slovenes did not hold their referendum, claiming that the plebiscite held in December of the previous year defined the Slovenian position clearly. The referendum did not take place in Serbia either, Milošević arguing that the position of the Serbian population was clearly in favour of a unified Yugoslavia.

The divisive and war-mongering rhetoric, and deeds, increased on all sides.

The Slovenes: All we are interested in is leaving Yugoslavia and making an arrangement with the others on how to go about this. Slovenia stopped sending recruits to the JNA and formed its own regular army.

The Serbs: Every nationality has the right to leave Yugoslavia but no one has the right to drag along those wishing to remain in it, because all Serbs wish to live in one country. Serbia will use all means available to help those Serbs who want to preserve the unity of Yugoslavia.

The Croats: Croatia, as a sovereign and independent state, belongs to the Croats, who will defend it to the last man. Croatia created its own regular army on 28 May 1991, the mayor of Zagreb sending a dramatic message to Tudjman that he could count on two hundred thousand volunteers from this city alone.

The JNA: All means shall be used to uphold the constitution and territorial integrity of Yugoslavia. The state of general readiness of the JNA was lifted to pre-combat level. After an incident in Split, Croatia, on 6 May in which a soldier was killed, the JNA announced that it would use live ammunition to defend itself.

The threat of force, soon to be followed by the use of it, entered the Yugoslav political drama in 1991. Tudjman and the Croats orchestrated a media campaign about the imminent threat to the "young Croatian democracy" and the need to defend it with arms. His army, which was almost exclusively Croatian and predominantly from his own HDZ party, grew rapidly in size if not in heavy arms.

The Serbs were also preparing to fight. The Serb paramilitary units in Croatia, supported by volunteers from Serbia, increased their state of readiness. In Serbia itself Milošević, in a confidential meeting with the presidents of all Serbian opštinas, according to the transcript said that "Serbs might not be good at the workplace but they certainly know how to fight." This was leaked to the press, but Milošević, no matter how embarrassing such an aggressive statement might have been, made no public disclaimer and offered no explanation.

Though the hot points of the Yugoslav drama were then in Slovenia, which wanted to leave, and in Croatia with the eruption of the conflict between Serbs and Croats, the first use of military force actually occurred in Serbia itself. On 9 March 1991 the opposition staged a large demonstration in Belgrade, basically demanding more access to the media. Saying that there was a danger that the gathering of over a hundred thousand demonstrators would turn into uncontrollable riots, Bora Jović, with full support from the Serbian leadership, ordered the tanks on to the streets of Belgrade. At the same time, the main opposition leader was arrested – within the Serbian parliament building! Several clashes occurred between the police and the demonstrators, a young protester and a policeman losing their lives. But ultimately the Serbian leadership were the big losers, since Serbia lost the last fig-leaf covering its intention to use force if necessary to attain its national political objectives. If Milošević was ready to use tanks against those among the Serbs who disagreed with him, what could others expect?

The first violent ethnic confrontation occurred on 2 March 1991 in the little town of Pakrac in western Slavonia,[8] when the Croatian ministry of the interior decided to change the predominantly Serb personnel of the police station in this town of seven thousand. The Serbs protested and violence broke out. The JNA stepped in and prevented greater bloodshed. But in the last day of the same month another confrontation between Croatian policemen and Serb paramilitary forces occurred, this time in the national park of Plitvice. The result: two dead and twenty injured. The JNA again stepped in as a buffer.

By now the fever was spreading all over Croatia – that is to say, in all areas where Serbs and Croats either lived together or touched each other's territory. Only a few days after Plitvice barricades were erected all around Vukovar, a town that was to become a symbol of insane destruction. On 2 May 1991 the Croat militia raided the Serb village of Borovo selo but met unexpectedly strong resistance. There were seventeen dead militiamen and about twenty dead civilians.

After the events in Borovo selo mutual killings became an everyday occurrence, so that, by the time full-fledged war broke out in Croatia, there were already about four hundred dead on both sides.

Parallel to the violence in the field, there were political attempts to reach some kind of a solution. Milošević and Tudjman met twice secretly; they met three times with Izetbegović, the Bosnian leader, a little less secretly, and all the presidents of the republics met in full view of the public and press. But none of this brought a political solution any closer. The main national leaders of Yugoslavia had obviously decided that confrontation and not negotiation would solve their respective national problems. Therefore they engaged in the semblance of negotiations only to pacify international public opinion and to be able to proclaim to their own nations, "We tried but the others are unyielding and insist on terms that are unacceptable to us."

By the end of May 1991 the country was in total disarray. Bora Jović prevented the normal and orderly succession of Stipe Mesić (a Croat) to the post of president of the Presidency. Jović's argument: it is nonsensical to elect to this high office a man who openly declares that Yugoslavia must fall apart. Indeed, Mesić did walk triumphantly into the Croatian Sabor six months later declaring, to the exuberant cheers of Croatian nationalists, "I have accomplished my mission – Yugoslavia is no more!" But at the time of his election to the post of president, and in view of Jović's own constant insistence on "law and order," his attempt to block Mesić meant that legal structures and procedures could be (ab)used in any way that suited one's political purpose.

This obstruction, although the office was largely a symbolic post, infuriated the Croats, Slovenes, and to a somewhat lesser extent the international community. Mesić needed five out of eight votes but the Serbian block of four was solid and prevented his election. It eventually took an all-night session of the Presidency, with the presence and the pressure of the European Community "troika," to elect Mesić into office.

There were also last-minute efforts among high-ranking delegations from the West to try to stop the disassembly of Yugoslavia and to preserve some peace and unity of purpose. At the end of May 1991 Jacques Delors, the president of the EC Commission, and Jacques Santer of Luxembourg, then the presiding prime minister of the Community, visited Yugoslavia and in discussions with federal and republican leaders offered, in effect, economic and financial aid if there were a peaceful and political settlement to the crisis.

Three weeks after the Europeans, the American secretary of state, James Baker, also came to Yugoslavia with a last-minute plea to Slovenia and Croatia not to take unilateral steps towards secession, and a plea to all to support the reforms and the government of Ante Marković. He left Yugoslavia three days before the proclamations of independence by Slovenia and Croatia, having heard their solemn assurances that they would refrain from unilateral acts that would aggravate the crisis.

Obviously, it was too late to change anything. Both the Serbs and the Croats at this point wanted war, the Serbs to gain territory and the Croats to gain recognition. Slovenia figured that the best and easiest way out was to stick to its chosen strategy and timetable and hope that it would gain independence at minimal cost, which it did. There was absolutely no desire for compromise or for earnest negotiations on any side. The logic of confrontation and maximization of particular rather than common interest had by now set in too deeply and passed the point of no return. War was imminent.

CHAPTER ELEVEN

The War in Slovenia and Croatia

The war that broke out as a final consequence of the escalation of the crisis is by far the most tragic event in the Yugoslav drama. The senseless loss of human lives and the massive destruction have left and will leave a deep scar on all the peoples of Yugoslavia.

The character of the war fought in Yugoslavia defies easy description. All the media and many politicians have called the bloody fighting in Yugoslavia a civil war. Actually it was and is not the type of confrontation best described as a civil war. It has no resemblance to the civil wars fought in Spain or the United States, for example. The ethnic rather than the civil components were and are predominant in the Yugoslav case. Yet it started of as some kind of a "civil" war in the sense that it was an internal confrontation of the people of one country. Later on, with the general recognition of Slovenia, Croatia, and BiH, the war became potentially international. For a while the JNA fought in BiH. Any renewal of an all-out war between the Serbs and Croats would now also fall into a classic war between states.

But again, in BiH the confrontation among three ethnic communities within a state that has been internationally recognized prevents it from being treated as a genuine international conflict. The irony is that nobody ever bothered to *declare* war on anybody else in Yugoslavia.

For the strongest military component in this war, the JNA, it was a peculiarly constrained affair. Except when it indiscriminately pounded a few cities, the JNA did not exercise its full power in the conflict. A full explanation of this odd self-restraint has yet to be provided. But if the JNA largely acted with a measure of restraint (which is not to say that it acted with justification at all times), the most nationalistically frenzied units of the various ethnic militia waged an all-out war of hatred and revenge, committing atrocities hard to believe possible in our times. These nationalist extremists, eager and willing to see a trail of blood behind them, left a strong imprint on the course of events and on the swelling of mutual hatred. They also contributed disproportionately to the image that the outside world has of the conflicts.

Slovenia and Croatia proclaimed their independence and sovereignty on 25 June 1991, suspending the constitution of Yugoslavia and federal legislation on their territories. This bold and reckless move by the two republics can be taken as the date the war started. The previous skirmishes, which were numerous in Croatia and had already claimed a few hundred dead, could hardly be viewed as a war, not because of their magnitude but because the confrontation was not open, direct, and pointed. The declaration of independence of the two republics provided for this laying of cards on the table and the massive, open, and violent confrontations that were soon to follow.

The confrontation in Slovenia came first chronologically, though its dimensions and character could hardly qualify it to be considered a civil war. The Slovenes were in a hurry to demonstrate that they were serious. In the very heated atmosphere generated by the political and media build-up to the historic meeting of the republican assembly that proclaimed independence,[1] the centrifugal force was hardly stoppable. Slovenian state agencies undertook to enforce their decision the very next day. This they did by taking over control of their borders, removing border posts marked SFR Jugoslavia and replacing them with those marked Republika Slovenija. Thus, in addition to the unilateral cessation of federal turnover tax payments and the collection of customs that were legally federal, they now enacted yet another unilateral decision: changing the borders of Yugoslavia.

The Slovenes, proclaiming their full right to self-determination, were however very careful not to fall into the category of *secession*, which they knew to be internationally unpopular. They described their move to independence as "disassociating" themselves from Yugoslavia, using a term unknown in international law.

Federal authorities responded to this challenge by proclaiming the Slovenian acts illegal and charging that in the Republic of Slovenia some federal functions, notably customs services and air traffic control, had been forcibly taken over. At the same time the federal parliament declined to recognize either the internal or the international legitimacy of the Slovenian assembly's decision to secede unilaterally.

The rashness of the Slovenes was matched by similar rashness among the federal authorities. The taking over of borders by the Slovenian militia, territorial defence, and customs officers was deemed sufficient grounds to order the JNA to move out of their barracks and towards the frontiers. The order came from the ministry of defence, which had no legal authority to move the troops since it was the Presidency of Yugoslavia, at that time still without a president, that was the supreme commander of the armed forces and had sole authority to issue orders in such situations.

The whole affair was organized as military support to federal police and customs personnel, who were to take their rightful places on the borders of Yugoslavia. Initially, only about 2,000 members of the JNA were engaged to make sure that some 400 policemen and 270 customs officials would reach their destinations.[2] The ill-conceived military move was immediately seized upon by the Slovenes. They offered strong resistance with their territorial defence units, politically organized the withdrawal of their representatives from the Presidency and the Executive Council of Yugoslavia, and most importantly directed a massive propaganda campaign presenting themselves as victims of brutal JNA aggression. Pictures of tanks being used to remove makeshift barricades, turning cars and even buses into shredded metal, were seen all over the world. Public opinion, especially in Western Europe, immediately sided with the underdog. The propaganda battle, which was probably more fierce than the confrontation on the barricades, won the Slovenes their first major point.

The downing of a JNA helicopter by the Slovenian territorial defence irritated the army into stepping up the use of military hardware. Eventually fighter planes were deployed, though they could in no way secure the installation of the police and customs officers at the border posts. The army also tried to knock out television and radio relays to prevent the propaganda campaign, which was building up anti-army hysteria in Slovenia. It did not succeed either in knocking out the targets or in reversing Slovenian opinions of the JNA.

The Slovenian withdrawal of their political representatives from the federation underlined their disapproval of the actions taken by the federal government on their territory. They managed, again with skilful propaganda activity, to shift the public gaze and focus it on events *after* the declaration of independence, thus hiding their own responsibility for events that took place before the declaration and preceded the outbreak of fighting – another important point scored by the Slovenes.

The Slovenian territorial defence put up fierce resistance to the movement of JNA columns. There were a number of small battles fought mostly around border posts, but also in villages and towns on the way to them. Ljubljana, the capital, was never attacked, though the air-raid sirens were used excessively, again with the purpose of securing and deepening the anti-JNA and anti-Yugoslav sentiment of the frightened population.

A short-lived agreement on ceasing hostilities was negotiated two days after the fighting started, but it was breached immediately. The definite end of armed hostilities was reached on 3 July 1991, after the JNA undertook "more resolute action by the air force" and the Slovenian leadership requested the truce and a cease-fire.

The Slovenian war for independence, as they like to call it, lasted exactly a week. The rest of Yugoslavia was unable to muster any meaningful response. The Presidency as supreme commander was inoperative and could not order a full-fledged war against a secessionist state, even though there was a conviction among some members that this was the only way to solve the crisis. The JNA itself was disoriented by the fact that it was fighting an enemy from within – that is to say, its own people, who were supposed to be living in "brotherhood and unity." The Executive Council, which approved the first order to secure the border posts, backed away, realizing too late that force would not solve anything. The Slovenes stood fast and scored yet another point.

The outcome of this senseless confrontation, which one side called a war for independence and the other dubbed the "restoration of constitutional order," was about sixty dead and perhaps five hundred wounded. But Slovenia had managed to sever its ties with Yugoslavia. With a three-to-nothing score against an incompetent, confused, and disoriented adversary, the rest of the way to full independence was like rolling downhill.

Soon after the cease-fire the Presidency of Yugoslavia, which was in the meantime reconstituted under considerable external pressure, announced the withdrawal of the JNA from Slovenia. Saving its face, and that of the army, the Presidency declared that this decision did not prejudge the question of the territorial integrity of Yugoslavia.

Slovenia accepted the foreign mediation that followed, which was supposed to include supervision of a cease-fire, with the arrogance of a victor that had triumphed over "one of the strongest fighting forces" in Europe and brought it to its knees. In the interim, during which the Brioni Agreement, brokered by the European Community, was to restore the *status quo ante* the declaration of independence, the Slovenes did little if anything to comply with the provisions of the agreement, prompting the Dutch, as presiding country of the EC, to lodge a formal complaint. But by then attention had turned elsewhere, and the Slovenes used the lack of attention paid them to the utmost.

Three months later Slovenia again unilaterally judged that it had complied with all the provisions of the cease-fire agreement and was now a fully independent state. To demonstrate this, Slovenia introduced its own currency – the tolar. In just another three months, Slovenia was recognized by the European Community, soon followed by most other Western countries.

The Slovenes violated the federal constitution in both the preparation and the execution of their independence. Federal authorities violated the same constitution by their illegitimate use of force. Both sides felt free to defy it because the constitution, through the numerous violations of all in Yugoslavia, had already become a nominal, non-enforceable document.

It was a terrible mistake to try to keep Slovenia in Yugoslavia by force, though there might have been some normative grounds for this in a strict, but unrealistic, reading of the constitution. Several conditions made such a decision extremely unwise.

First, the use of force agitated the Slovenes, intensifying their desire to separate from a federation that was willing to use force against them. Second, the use of force, and the use of propaganda to make this force seem even more terrible and destructive, caused European public opinion to shift decisively to the Slovenian side.

Third, the use of military force to retake the border crossings overshadowed their forcible and unilateral seizure by the Slovenes. The police, customs officers, and the JNA did not resist the Slovenian takeover. But when the federation "struck back," it encountered resistance, and this resistance led to fighting. Thus the Slovenes managed to refocus attention, away from their illegal takeover of the boundaries of Yugoslavia and on to the attempt at forcible dislocation of Slovenes from posts they ought not to have occupied in the first place.

Furthermore, the Slovenian episode agitated war-mongering sentiments in Serbia, raising fighting spirit to a higher pitch. The fact that "Slovenia was lost" meant that other places, settled by Serbs, must be held with greater determination. At the same time, the half-hearted use of force in Slovenia had a ripple effect in Croatia, further encouraging confrontation there.

Finally, the use of force where there is no precise strategy nor a definite decision to stick to it never pays a dividend, even when there is a good (instead of a flimsy) legal pretext for it.

Croatia, which declared its independence on the same day as Slovenia, took a somewhat different course. Initially it was much less aggressive towards the federal authorities and the question of control of borders and customs. During the Slovenian crisis, even though there had already been many skirmishes on their territory, with more than a hundred dead, the Croats did not join their neighbours and tactical allies in an immediate all-out confrontation.

The most likely explanation for such conduct is to be found in a combination of a number of factors. First, during the Slovenian crisis Croatia still was not fully committed to unequivocal independence and did not therefore want to slam the door completely shut, as the Slovenes did. Secondly, the Croats were also feeling and testing the pulse of the federation (and Serbia) and closely watching the reaction of the international community, particularly the attitude of, and possible encouragement from, Germany. Thirdly, the Croats did not yet consider themselves to be militarily ready for a radical confrontation, even if they had the most radical plans in mind (and the first point above would suggest that radicalism was still only one of their options, not the only one). Fourthly, the Croats wanted to see how the confrontation in Slovenia would go before committing themselves to a definite line of action. And finally, Croatia was stuck with the difficult problem of Serbs in Croatia, a problem the Slovenes never had to consider.

But the fact that Croatia did not challenge the federation as immediately and as directly as had the Slovenes does not mean that they were not set on achieving as many attributes of independence as possible. On the contrary, the Croatian Sabor was in permanent session, consolidating statehood at a very quick pace indeed, passing hundreds of laws and by-laws in a matter of a few weeks, severing legal links with the federation, and creating its own legal structure. This led to two forms of conflict provocation: the hasty attempt to force Serbs in Croatia to accept the new political realities and the new Croatian legal system, which excluded them as a nation or national minority; and the creation of an independent and strong army to defend and, where necessary (as in the regions inhabited by Serbs), enforce independence, but with the parallel presence of the JNA on Croatian territory.

The day after the Croatian Sabor declared independence there was violence only forty kilometres southeast of Zagreb, the Croatian capital. In an area that had suffered greatly from the atrocities of the Ustashi regime during the notorious Independent State of Croatia, a clash between the Croatian National Guard (ZNG), the new symbol of Croatian independence and statehood, and the local Serb militia left four dead and fourteen wounded. It was two weeks before the next serious skirmish was reported, in Ilok, the easternmost town of Croatia, and yet again about two weeks before the next and, to that point, most serious confrontation occurred. It also occurred in eastern Slavonia, very near Vukovar, and involved the Croatian armed forces and the local Serb militia. Twelve people were killed.

On that very day the leaders of the federation and all the republics of Yugoslavia were meeting in Ohrid, Macedonia, trying to find a peaceful solution for Croatia and prevent a further escalation of confrontation. The meeting came to an abrupt end when President Tudjman of Croatia suddenly and dramatically left the meeting with the explanation that events in Croatia required his immediate presence in Zagreb. The last opportunity to prevent further escalation and avoid an all-out war was thereby lost.

Three days later the first of many direct battles between the ZNG and JNA took place. Significantly, it was in the vicinity of Vukovar, a town that was to become a symbol of the Serb-Croat ethnic war. The immediate cause was that the Croatian government had disbanded the local assembly in Vukovar and appointed its own representative to govern the area. While the town of Vukovar had a Croat majority, the area of the Vukovar *opština*, which was brought under the governorship of a Zagreb-appointed bureaucrat, was more evenly matched, with a slight Serb majority. This provoked the Serbs into rejecting the Zagreb decision and the Croats to try to enforce it with their militia.

On this occasion the JNA for the first time sided openly with the Serb "freedom fighters." From then on, that was to be the case most of the time. The Croats, who, as we have seen, did not accept the neutrality of the JNA even when it was indeed a neutral peacemaker, jumped on this opportunity and started an all out anti-JNA campaign.

This direct and open confrontation between Croats and the JNA increased the pace of preparation for the undeclared "dirty" war that was to escalate over the next five months. Tudjman demanded that the JNA abandon their buffer function and return to the barracks. By the beginning of August a general mobilization was announced in Croatia, and it was carried out three weeks later. Croatia declared that it would fight for independence.

The JNA responded by saying it took orders only from the Presidency of Yugoslavia and not from Tudjman, that it was constitutionally obliged to protect the integrity of the country and to preserve peace when it was endangered. All army units in Croatia were put on highest alert and ordered to shoot back if shot at. And the shooting started in earnest in August 1991. It took four and a half months of bitter fighting and destruction before Cyrus Vance and the United Nations negotiated a precarious cease-fire, fourteen previous attempts failing miserably.

Tudjman saw, correctly, that the JNA would not defend the Croatian constitution and the territorial integrity of Croatia, which was challenged by the Serbs in Croatia. The Croatian leadership was also fully aware that it did not have a force to match on the battlefield the combined forces of the JNA, Serb territorial defence units in Croatia, the local irregulars and militia, and the irregular volunteers coming from Serbia. Although Croats were arming themselves illegally (because first the EC and then the UN embargo on exports of armament had already come into effect) and benefiting from the decision of a number of Croat JNA commanders to change sides in favour of Croatia and bring arms with them, including tanks and heavy artillery, they still could not hope to achieve a clear victory on the ground – this in spite of the fact that they were conducting a defensive action, which typically requires fewer forces and resources than an offensive one. Therefore, their strategic aim was not a military but a political and diplomatic victory. Croatia's only hope was to have the (temporary?) loss of territory compensated for by the gain of recognition, by making the most of the other side's aggression, and by gaining sympathy as the defender and underdog.

The previous "war" in Slovenia had exposed a number of JNA weaknesses that the Croats hoped to capitalize on. These included the lack of a clear strategy and the demonstrated lack of determination to follow in full force the official doctrine of preserving the "sovereignty and territorial integrity" of Yugoslavia, as envisaged by the Yugoslav constitution. The Croats could also count on a number of officers wishing to change sides.

Nevertheless the Croatian leadership felt that they could not accomplish their goals while the JNA was *in* Croatia and saw no way to expel them politically or militarily on their own. So the best bet was to provoke the JNA into the type of action that would lead to international condemnation, thus securing sympathy and support for the Croatian cause. Germany was already preparing to orchestrate full media support for Croatia if the JNA were drawn deeper into the conflict.

Croatia decided to provoke the JNA by blockading barracks and cutting off communal supplies to them. This was the big gamble: to draw the JNA across the invisible line between the acceptable and the unacceptable, to draw it into offensive action. That would be the way to gain political, material, and even military support from the outside. The lesson from Slovenia suggested that. But, unlike the Slovenian campaign, the confrontation in Croatia was neither short-lived nor conclusive. Croatia did gain independence in the process, but the price paid and the inconclusive result cast considerable doubt on the success of the gamble.

The position of the JNA was much less clear and much more stop and go. That is the only way one can describe its confused, hap-hazard, and erratic performance during the Croatian campaign. It demonstrated unnecessary strength where it was not called for and unbelievable weakness where determination was required if its own objectives were to be accomplished. The destruction and devastation it caused did not correspond to any known tactical considerations.

The JNA had been drawn into the confrontations six months earlier and had tried to stay away from taking sides on the ground, though it was well known where it stood politically. Until it was allowed to be drawn into the fighting, it received commendations from the West, most notably from the American state department,[3] as a force for peace and stability in Yugoslavia.

But the JNA was very pro-Yugoslav, and the new leadership of Croatia was not. Since the latter insisted on demonstrating to the Serbs in Croatia who was boss, often not choosing carefully the means to prove their point, the JNA was faced with a difficult choice: pull out and let the Croats handle the situation through a rough imposition of the "Croatian legal state," or try to disarm all paramilitary and irregular units on both sides, making the inevitable confrontation between Serbs and Croats softer and less bloody. It did neither, but insisted on being a buffer. By sitting on the fence the JNA effectively defended the Serbs and thus, even if it had not been their initial intention, became involved on their side.

The possibility cannot be ruled out that the JNA actually waited for such an opportunity, jumping eagerly at the chance to attain and maximize its own goals. One of them was to show determination and strength after the humiliation in Slovenia. Another was to secure militarily the perimeters of a potential Greater Serbia, which is to say all lands inhabited by Serbs.

General Veljko Kadijević, minister of defence, and General Blagoje Adžić, the chief of staff, increasingly disqualified Croats from the army on ideological and political grounds, claiming that they were fascist and genocidal towards the Serbs.[4] The generals thus proclaimed the goals of war to be politically circumscribed, with traditional war doctrine, especially in strategy, being of little use. As political goals changed, so did the conduct of the army, until it was reduced finally to a force that was fighting its own war, for its own survival, outside any political control.

The JNA was losing a state, and fast. That meant danger for the JNA as an institution. Not only were the barracks and JNA personnel in danger in Croatia, but more and more of the republics were refusing recruitment of fresh contingents into the JNA, at the same time suspending its financing. Serbia and Montenegro were the only republics to "honour" their financial commitments, and it was logical that the link between the JNA and Serbia, strong to begin with, was to grow ever stronger.

Serbia thus *de facto* took political responsibility for the actions of the JNA, its military force on the ground. Though Milošević insisted repeatedly that Serbia itself was not at war, that the federation was simply fighting to retain the boundaries and legal order of Yugoslavia, the fact that the JNA became exclusively Serb/Montenegrin and was ultimately fighting to accomplish Serbian political objectives could not be camouflaged by this fig-leaf. It was the young men of Serbia who were being killed and the population of Serbia that financed, mostly through rampant inflation, the political objectives of Milošević and the military objectives of the JNA.

The Serbs in Croatia, after being subjected to a systematic campaign of Croatomania, in which they lost the right to use their alphabet, lost jobs, were harassed by Croatian ultra-nationalists, saw their houses blown up, and so on, organized strong militia and paramilitary forces that took an active part in the war in Croatia. At the same time, thousands of ultra-nationalist desperados were infiltrating Croatia (and later Bosnia) from Serbia to incite the Serb population against the Croats, inasmuch as that was still necessary.

It was these ultra-nationalist and undisciplined, often drunken hordes of Serbs and Croats who committed most of the atrocities that shocked the civilized world. Slaughter, mutilation of bodies, torture, killing of young and old, men and women, were among the bestialities performed by men who were quite often psychopaths or professional murderers. Their number was not large but their imprint on the war was.

On both sides paramilitary units were formed that proudly took up the iconography of their notorious predecessors. Men with long untidy beards, untidy clothes, fur caps, cartridge belts crossed over the shoulder (all traditional symbols of Chetniks) were formed into units that bore names of Serbian heros from the Battle of Kosovo. On the Croatian side, black-shirted neo-Ustashi units were formed, shamelessly bearing the same names and symbols as those used during the Second World War.

But a new breed of fighters also emerged in this nationalistic turmoil. Appropriately labelled "the technicians of violence," these were common thugs, small-time hoods, criminals, and profiteers.

With a nationalistic motive, or often without one, they set out to maximize personal gain in a disorderly situation. They would loot, plunder, rape, and kill mercilessly when not involved in fighting along with the regular units. Their objective – profit. Their usefulness to the nationalist leaders obviously lay in the fact that they ruthlessly intimidated the "other side," thus making ethnic cleansing easier.

Among the most notorious war-lords, commanding a clean-shaven, well-dressed, and well-armed unit of "Tigers," was Željko Ražnjatović, better known as Arkan. A criminal sought by Interpol, he suddenly emerged in the wake of the Serbian-Croatian war as a leader of fighting men and an entrepreneur involved in gun-running, illegal foreign exchange, and later sanction-busting. He conducted bloody operations in eastern Slavonia and Bosnia, killing Croats and Muslims alike. His exploits were selectively reported in Serbia, the gruesome details omitted, the only impression remaining that of a fearless fighter. He became a Serbian hero and today sits in the parliament of Serbia as one of its more active and prominent members.

A leading example of a similar thug turned nationalist fighter turned politician on the Croatian side was Branimir Glavaš, commander of the "Glavaš Unit." This unit gained fame by ethnically cleansing Serb villages in the vicinity of the front-line town of Osijek. However, Glavaš did not hesitate to murder Croat policemen who maintained good relations with Serbs or just happened to step in his way. Today he is the mayor of Osijek.

These vicious murders were seized upon by both sides in unprecedented media campaigns against their opposite numbers. The horrors were duly reported in gruesome detail by the television stations so that all, including children, might see and learn how low, disgusting, and barbarous the enemy was and that he deserved no sympathy. Hate and the desire for revenge grew exponentially after every screening of such ultra-vicious and debasing war conduct.

Though this horrendous behaviour of combatants on both sides provided for chilling accounts of the war, the major destruction of both lives and property was actually carried out by regular troops on both sides. It is unnecessary to enumerate all the battles that took place over the four and a half months of fighting. To get an overview of the undeclared but bloody war in Croatia it should be enough to review some of the crucial battles and turning-points.

Chronologically, most of the early skirmishes took place around Krajina and in the central part of Croatia just south of Zagreb. This is the area most densely populated by Serbs. The Croatian government made the mistake of trying to tackle the issue of the Serb population in Croatia by grabbing the bull by the horns. Since this area was almost solidly Serb, the fighting that took place was basically to secure, or deny, the Serb perimeter.

The fighting then spread to Slavonia, the region between Belgrade and Zagreb, inhabited by a mixture of Croats and Serbs (plus other minorities). Here the objective was to solidify the ethnic hold over towns and villages. Since a number had sizable minorities from the other side, fighting was inevitable, as was the attempt to "ethnically cleanse"[5] the territory.

For example, in one major sweep the Croats expelled Serbs from twenty-seven villages in western Slavonia, forcing thousands of refugees to drift into Bosnia. The Serbs forcibly expelled thousands of Croats from towns and villages in eastern Slavonia. At this stage both sides instinctively applied "ethnic engineering," lured by tactical rather than strategic considerations. This was not the type of ethnic cleansing to be pursued later in BiH. If they had not left on their own, scared by the fighting, members of one or the other ethnic group were forced to leave by intimidation, swelling the number of refugees to well over half a million.

Two major battles marked important turning-points in the war in Croatia – the battle for Vukovar and the siege of Dubrovnik, both under assault by the JNA. In the case of Vukovar, it took the JNA over three months to win the city for the Serb side. In the process thousands were killed, tens of thousands left homeless, and hardly a building left intact. The Croats, who at that time had little heavy weaponry, used sniper fire and mortars to provoke the JNA into indiscriminate and heavy pounding of the city. Serb volunteers from Serbia proper lent a hand, as did the local Serb territorial defence. But it was the JNA that wreaked most of the destruction with its heavy weaponry and aircraft bombardment.

The battle for Vukovar became a media event, both in and out of Yugoslavia. There were a number of attempts to organize humanitarian aid, relief, or the evacuation of children, the sick, and the wounded. These efforts were obstructed by both sides but did capture the attention of the media. Vukovar became a symbol for both sides – for Croats a symbol of the defence of independence and territorial integrity; for Serbs and the JNA a symbol of Serbian determination to help and promote the cause of Serbs in Croatia. The JNA used almost all the fire-power it had to take this town of fifty thousand.

Both sides promoted their fallen martyrs, and both sides declared victory. The Serbs, with the JNA, won control of the town, or what was left of it.[6] But the battle for Vukovar went a long way towards swinging international opinion in Croatia's favour. In losing the town, Croatia came much closer to winning independence.

But first the JNA opened its so-called southern front, and with it the siege of Dubrovnik. If the siege and destruction of Vukovar had some military and political explanation, though very short of a justification, the army onslaught on Dubrovnik was unequivocally senseless. Dubrovnik had never had a majority of Serbs to be "rescued" by the JNA, nor was it of any strategic military value. For two previous decades it had been without a garrison, completely demilitarized. But when the Croats blockaded the JNA barracks all over Croatia, the JNA responded by blockading all the major ports in Croatia, among them Dubrovnik.

Nobody has yet offered a fully convincing explanation of why the siege and bombardment of Dubrovnik occurred. The most likely explanations suggest that the JNA wanted an important bargaining chip to force the Croats to lift the blockades around its barracks in Croatia. Another explanation would have the Montenegrins holding Dubrovnik ransom for Croatian recognition of the Prevlaka peninsula, about forty kilometres south of Dubrovnik and at the entrance to a strategically vital Montenegrin fiord, as Montenegrin rather than Croatian territory.

If the siege of Dubrovnik was bad from a publicity point of view, the shelling of the old city, often referred to as the "Pearl of the Adriatic," was disastrous. The whole world turned against the JNA as a force without scruples. Even those who had a measure of understanding, if not outright support, for the Serb/JNA position in the conflict could not withhold condemnation of such barbaric acts as the shelling of an ancient cultural and historic treasure protected by UNESCO.

No matter if the destruction of the old town was relatively restricted, or that Croats amplified the picture of destruction by burning old tires to generate thick black clouds of smoke coming from the old walls. The *idea* of holding Dubrovnik hostage and inflicting even the smallest damage on it was unacceptable to public opinion throughout Europe and beyond. After that the JNA lost any credibility as an "honest" participant in a "dirty" war and was soon to gain the label of the dirtiest of them all.

But the army continued to support the Serbs in securing and consolidating contested territories. By the end of the year over 30 per cent of Croatian territory was under Serb paramilitary or JNA control. This occurred at about the time the recognition of Croatia, under strong pressure from Germany, became imminent. At that point both sides lost their overriding motive to continue the fighting and a cease-fire could finally hold. The previous fourteen cease-fires had fallen on deaf ears, since both (or all three) sides in the fighting had still had goals to accomplish. The personal efforts of major statesmen such as Mitterrand, Gorbachev, and Bush, who either summoned Tudjman and Milošević for talks or else sent personal letters to them, had also previously had no impact on the course of the fighting.

On 3 January 1992 a final cease-fire was signed, and this one allowed events, at least temporarily, to move away from direct and violent conflict. For a full year the cease-fire basically held, fighting erupting only as local skirmishes. The attention of both Serbs and Croats was focused on Bosnia over the next eighteen months. Ways and means were sought, developed, and implemented to destabilize the precarious Bosnian state structure and to gain territory for Serbs and Croats in Bosnia.

But in January 1993 the world was reminded again that the Serbian-Croatian dispute over territory and sovereignty had not been laid to rest. The Croats mounted a one-week offensive, taking over an airport, some territory, and the strategically vital Maslenica Gorge, which, when bridged, connects Dalmatia to the rest of Croatia.

Six months later, after protracted negotiations with the Serbs in Croatia, Tudjman ceremoniously opened the new Maslenica pontoon bridge. The agreement involved returning some territory to the Serbs in exchange for their allowing the airport and bridge to be opened. Since the Croats did not retreat to the lines insisted upon by the Serbs, the latter promptly bombarded with artillery shells the one-week-old pontoon bridge.

As this book goes to press the two sides are looking at each other through gun barrels and across the negotiating table, and future events, as we shall see in the final part of this book, could still take any direction.

CHAPTER TWELVE

The War in
Bosnia and Herzegovina

For a time it looked as if war in Bosnia could, miraculously, be avoided. While the war raged in neighbouring Croatia and the roar of cannon there could be heard in Bosnia, internal pressure had not yet increased to the point where fighting was imminent. Most of the population of Bosnia, as well as people elsewhere, were hoping that the tragedy would avoid this region, often referred to as "an ethnic scrambled egg" or "Yugoslavia in little." The fact that Bosnian Serbs, Croats, and Muslims had lived together for centuries without warring with each other[1] gave hope that they might be spared the conflict created by the dissolution of Yugoslavia. Some, a little more cynically, expected the unique balance of terror to prevent the scale from tipping in any particular direction.

But pressures from without as well as those within, plus two bad judgments by the West – not sending observers when requested and recognizing BiH – were too much for the fragile balance to hold, and all hell broke loose. Bosnia and Herzegovina proved too vulnerable and the peace too fragile for the onslaught of aggressive nationalism.

The government of BiH, chosen in autumn 1990 in the republic's first free elections, was, understandably, a national coalition government. All three major national parties were represented in the parliament (headed by a Serb, Momčilo Krajišnik), the Presidency (headed by the Muslim Alija Izetbegović), and the Executive Council (headed by a Croat, Jure Pelivan). The constitution of BiH specifically required consensus on all matters dealing with the strategic issues of state sovereignty, independence, and inter-ethnic relations.

In June 1991, just before the secession of Croatia and Slovenia, Izetbegović, together with the leader of Macedonia, offered a compromise platform for organizing relations between the republics of

Yugoslavia. Izetbegović was sincere in presenting this offer because he saw it as the best chance of keeping his own republic intact. If Yugoslavia stayed together, so would BiH. If Yugoslavia fell apart, the pressures on BiH would increase manyfold. The three communities in BiH were still living in relative harmony, and the offer was made on behalf of all citizens of BiH. As if to prove the point, a spontaneous demonstration of over fifty thousand Muslims, Serbs, and Croats took place in Sarajevo in support of the unity of Yugoslavia and thus of BiH.

But ominous winds were already blowing. Tudjman declared, in a July interview with the *Times* of London, that an important ingredient in the solution of the Yugoslav crisis would be the division of BiH along ethnic lines.[2] In less than a year after this interview Tudjman had repeated the idea of partitioning of BiH no fewer than a dozen times. So much for the Croatian strategic interest in BiH.

Milošević was even more ambitious. He wanted to keep the whole of BiH in the federation so that he would have a natural geographic link with the Serbs in Croatia. "If BiH does not stay in Yugoslavia, you will have war on your hands," was his message from Belgrade. In August 1991 Milošević launched the so-called Belgrade initiative, which was to assemble representatives of all those who wished to remain in a unified Yugoslavia. The expectation was that the Bosnian Muslims would attend, on the assumption that the Muslims always side with the stronger side; it was obvious, to the Serbs at least, that in their confrontation with the Croats, they were stronger.

What the Serbs failed to see was that they were not only taking on the Croats but all those who would support Croatia if it were attacked, or who simply objected to the Serbian use of force in pushing through their claims, no matter how justified they might be. The Croatian position would thus be considerably strengthened. Izetbegović saw this and tried to stay on the sidelines, proclaiming neutrality and declaring that the war in Croatia had nothing to do with BiH.

But he was also proved wrong because the war in Croatia did have a strong bearing on the situation in BiH. The flow of Serb refugees into BiH, resulting from Croatian ethnic cleansing of mixed territories, increased the level of Serbian irritation about the position of Serbs in Yugoslavia, and thus also in BiH. Furthermore, JNA units that had left Slovenia and then Croatia had moved largely into BiH, providing the Serbs with a mighty weapon with which to articulate their irritation. Finally, the war in Croatia was about splitting Yugoslavia, and it was naïve to expect that BiH, which in many ways resembled Yugoslavia as a whole, could avoid the ugly virus. Also, it stood in the middle of the warring sides and could hardly remain untouched.

The Serbs tried, for a short time, to split the ranks of the Muslims by pronouncing a "historic agreement" with the second largest but still very tiny Muslim National Party (the Bosniaks). When this failed, they returned to more aggressive forms of intimidation of the Muslim relative majority in BiH.

One way of doing this was to deny the republic's authority over the territories in which Serbs were a majority. Like mushrooms after rain, throughout the fall of 1991 so-called Serb autonomous provinces kept appearing all over BiH, denying the republic's authority and legal system and proclaiming allegiance to the Yugoslav federation. Altogether, seven such territories were proclaimed.

A dramatic session of the Bosnian parliament occurred in October 1991, immediately after the definitive withdrawal of Slovenia and Croatia from Yugoslavia. When Izetbegović proposed a declaration of sovereignty, as a way (he thought) of avoiding war but also of preserving his majority position in BiH, the Serb members were violently opposed, denouncing it as an attempt at secession of BiH from Yugoslavia. The fact that the parliament of BiH voted, with only two votes against, to remain *in* Yugoslavia was insufficient guarantee for the Bosnian Serbs, coached by Milošević, and they immediately proceeded to destroy further the political structure of BiH. A smear campaign about the true intentions of the Muslims, who were alleged to be aiming to create an Islamic fundamentalist state, was also orchestrated.

When Izetbegović saw that the three-way coalition was breaking up, and fast, he called both the European Community and the UN to send in observers and peacekeeping forces. But the political readiness to get involved in peacekeeping was still evolving at a painfully slow pace, and the UN troops did not come to BiH for almost a year.

The Serbs proceeded to constitute their own parliament in BiH, holding the first session in November and provoking a further escalation of tensions by holding a referendum asking the Serbs of BiH if they wanted to remain in Yugoslavia. A predictable majority responded that they did. When recognition of BiH as an independent state became a possibility in December, the parliament of Serbs announced that a Serb republic of BiH would be created on the same day BiH was recognized, if this happened. Needless to say, the Serbs of BiH had nothing to do with the application for recognition of Bosnia that Izetbegović submitted to the European Community.

The Bosnian Serbs wanted to stay in a rump Yugoslavia. The Muslims and Croats feared that they would become underlings in what would actually be a Serb-dominated country. The Croats of Bosnia were also playing a more subtle game. Initially their objective was to declare BiH's independence from Yugoslavia, just as the state of Croatia had six months earlier. This they could accomplish only together with the Muslims. Once removed from Yugoslavia, they were going to remove themselves from BiH also and annex themselves to Croatia. Confronted with a request for recognition from Bosnian Muslims and Croats, the EC asked for a referendum. The result was again predictable. Muslims and Croats voted in favour. Serbs boycotted the referendum, saying that their own previous referendum had clearly shown that the Serbs of BiH wanted to stay in Yugoslavia.

A last-minute attempt to reach an accord among the ethnic groups was brokered by the EC Conference on Yugoslavia. The three ethnic groups initialled an agreement according to which BiH would be "composed of three constituent units, based on national principles and taking into account economic, geographic, and other criteria." The territory of each unit was to be "based on the national absolute or relative majority." This agreement, though reducing the central government's level of unitary control, nevertheless meant that no one nationality could dominate the others, nor would the majority of the ethnically mixed population feel a minority in their own country or home territory.

But this rational solution, the maximum attainable under the circumstances, actually provoked all three sides into additional action. The recognition of BiH irritated the local Serbs since mutual relations within the republic had not previously been settled. On the other side, it gave the Muslim majority a feeling of superiority far beyond what was reasonable.

In this context the Muslims, led by Alija Izetbegović and with the support of the few remaining unitary-minded Serb and Croat politicians, decided to use all means to have the international community put pressure on the Serbs and the JNA and, if need be, to fight them. They calculated that they had little to gain by accepting the conference proposal and much more by getting the Serbs and the JNA into an aggressive mode. They knew well that it would not take much to set the Serbs and the JNA off and were banking on the international community's response to Serb and JNA aggression.

The Serbs overtly and the Croats just a little less so wanted to consolidate territory that would be theirs, especially territories with relative majorities, and to expand beyond those to settle certain strategic interests. The Muslims, having had second thoughts, decided that they would try for a unitary BiH with the help of the EC and United States, which had by then recognized their independence.

That configuration set the pattern of what was to come. The Bosnian Serbs and Croats fought first to secure their territories and then to expand them. The Muslims, aware that their military position was weak, fought to secure international support and, if possible, military intervention on their side.

The fighting broke out in earnest only after the referendum and the failed accord on new constitutional arrangements in BiH. This was at the end of March 1992, a week before the European Community and the United States granted BiH "preventive" recognition, as they called it. Soon after, armed and masked Serb militia threw up barricades in Sarajevo, and there were several casualties to sniper fire. It is noteworthy that the initial fighting was done with masks and hoods covering faces. The fighters did not wish to be recognized because, after leaving the barricades, they would still need to integrate into the mixed community. As war progressed, masks began to fall off, in more ways than one.

The war in BiH went through several distinctly recognizable stages. It was variously labelled a "civil," "tribal," "ethnic," and "religious" war, and a "war of aggression." It was undoubtedly all of the above. Fundamentally, like all the conflicts in the former Yugoslavia, it was a result of aggressive and uncompromising political abuse of national feelings. But above all it was a dirty and gruesome affair of unspeakable brutality. The main strategy of the paramilitary formations of each of the three groups was mass expulsion, popularly known as "ethnic cleansing," of the other two groups.

Therefore, the common thread in all phases of war was, tragically, the immense suffering of the innocent civilian population. In less than a year and a half the war had claimed more than 150,000 lives, an equal number of missing, and about two million refugees. The horrors of slaughter, raping, looting, beating, detainment in camps, and sheer intimidation bypassed very few families. The level of destruction was also vast and relatively constant throughout the war, although the immediate political and military objectives changed in three different phases.

In the first phase, lasting until May 1992, the main objective of the BiH government was to get the regular JNA units, at this time almost solidly Serb and Montenegrin, out of BiH. The Serbs in BiH had very few and only light arms at this initial stage, and their fighting fist was the JNA.

Though Izetbegović had said in February 1992 that the Bosnians would not make the mistake of blockading JNA barracks but would rather build "golden bridges" for the army to leave, this sweet talk achieved nothing, and he saw as the only alternative a repetition of the strategy that had earlier yielded results in both Slovenia and Croatia. He was, of course, aware that the result would be costly in terms of human lives, but that seemed to him an acceptable price to pay for sovereignty.

In this initial phase the Croats also engaged the JNA in the small pocket of land they inhabited in the north of BiH and in Herzegovina, particularly around the city of Mostar. This was a direct continuation of the fighting between Serbs and Croats that had stopped some months ago in Croatia but was now continued in BiH. History repeated itself. Small, provocative moves by the Croats were answered by the JNA with predictable ferocity, which immediately made them the bully and the aggressor.

A good example of this dynamic is offered by the case of the first bombardment of Mostar in April 1992. During the initial, relatively light fighting initiated by the Croats, two pilots switched sides from the JNA to Croat units. The Croats claimed that they had defected. The JNA commander, General Perišić, claimed that they had been kidnapped. He threatened to bombard the town of Mostar with heavy artillery if the airmen were not returned. Since they did not reappear by the given deadline, Perišić ordered indiscriminate bombardment of Mostar, destroying mostly civilian targets. Today, General Perišić is the commander-in-chief of the Yugoslav army in recognition of his "fearless exploits and brilliant military conduct during the wars in Croatia and BiH."

Not to be outdone by the Croats, nor to yield to the Muslims, who had betrayed their expectations, Serb irregulars from BiH, with the help of paramilitary units from Serbia, organized offensives in territories bordering Serbia that were heavily populated by Muslims. Arkan and his "Tigers" as well as the radical Chetnik formations of "Duke Šešelj" made a sweep through the region, looting and expelling the Muslim population by threat, intimidation, and massacre.

The Croats did much the same but on a smaller scale and, at this stage, only in regions where the contest was between Croats and Serbs, avoiding direct confrontation with Muslims. Soon Muslim paramilitary units and local bands entered into this "bloody orgy" of ethnic cleansing, retaliating in kind against the innocent Serb civilian population.

Thus an alliance came into being, one that pitted the Muslims and the Croats against a "common enemy" – the Serbs. Tudjman and

Izetbegović signed a formal defence treaty and for a while even had a joint military command. The overriding objective of the alliance at this stage was to prevent BiH from staying in Yugoslavia and to expel the JNA from the Bosnian territory.

This in turn increased the propaganda efforts as well as the fighting spirit of the Serbs, who pointed out that the same type of alliance, with BiH as part of the Independent State of Croatia during the Second World War, had cost Serbs several hundred thousand lives. The Serb population of BiH before the current war was not in fact threatened by genocide at the hands of the Muslims, but most started to believe this to be possible once the Muslims joined hands with the Croats.

The Serbs, aside from the most aggressive stance, also had the much more powerful weapons. The JNA, by now made up only of Serbs and Montenegrins, lent its hand to the Serbs of BiH, using rockets, tanks, heavy artillery, and planes to accomplish Serb objectives. But the JNA had reasons of its own for wanting to stay in BiH or, alternatively, for wanting to keep BiH in Yugoslavia. A large proportion of army supplies, from soldiers' boots to helicopters and fighter planes, were produced in BiH, and the JNA did not want to leave those facilites in the hands of its "enemy."

When the JNA finally left BiH in May 1992, it dismantled and removed to Serbia the production facilities it deemed useful, destroying everything it could not move or thought to be of lesser value. The best-known and most expensive act of this episode was the deliberate destruction of an airport built into a mountain in western BiH, estimated variously to have cost between $1.2 and $2.5 billion US.

The fighting in this first phase was heavy, though the two sides were obviously mismatched in terms of arms. The Muslims and Croats engaged the JNA even when they were outgunned and outnumbered, in the hope of involving the international community on their side, since this was a case of a foreign army's aggression against a sovereign state. The JNA did not ignore these provocations. It hit back with almost all it had.

By June 1992 the withdrawal of the JNA from BiH was complete. This meant only that there were no longer officers and conscripts born outside of BiH now fighting in it. Nationals of Serbia and Montenegro were withdrawn, as well as some armaments and technical or production facilities. The bulk of the weaponry – tanks, helicopters, airplanes, heavy artillery, etc. – was handed over to the Bosnian Serbs. A number of JNA officers, born in BiH, remained as the new officer corps of the Bosnian Serb army, most notably General Ratko Mladić, who had gained fame for his fearless and ruthless conduct in the previous war in Krajina. He became the commanding officer of the new army.

General Mladić masterminded and engineered the siege and strangulation of Sarajevo, started in this first phase of the war and carried on throughout later developments. He was reported to have ordered his gunners to "drive them crazy" and "burn it all."

In the second phase of the war, which set in after the JNA withdrew from Bosnian territory, Serbs mostly fought with Muslims and, to a lesser extent, with Croats. The process of "ethnic cleansing" was fully under way, with Muslims and Croats forced off Serb territories, Serbs forced off Muslim and Croat lands, and some repositioning as well between Croats and Muslims. Their alliance, in spite of strain, occasional fighting and some mutual "ethnic cleansing," was still very much alive in this second phase. It was during this second phase that the Serbs conquered most of the territory still under their control, expanding that area from about 55 per cent before the war to around 70 per cent.

Most of the gains made at this time occurred in the north and east of BiH. Some "corrections" were also made in the west, but without much fighting, while in the south the Serbs actually ceded territory to the Croats in Herzegovina.

The Serbs had as their strategic goal to secure a land link from Serbia proper to the western part of Bosnia, also known as Bosanska Krajina, where the Serbs were a clear majority. The Serbs in the west were cut off by the central part of BiH, in which a predominantly Muslim-Croat ethnic mix prevailed. So their strategy was to open up and ethnically cleanse an east-west corridor through northern Bosnia, between the town of Tuzla and the River Sava, a natural boundary between BiH and Croatia. No wonder this area went through some of the heaviest fighting reported during the war. This was also one of the few areas in which Croat and Muslim forces jointly fought the Serbs. In October 1992 the Serbs mounted a decisive offensive, broke the stalemate, and secured a narrow corridor between the eastern and western parts of BiH.

In the east of BiH, a territory heavily populated by Muslims, the objective was to enlarge Serb holdings, squeezing Muslims into a few pockets that would then fall to the Serbs because they would be unsustainable as independent Muslim units. Thus we witnessed offensives on Goražde, Žepa, Srebrnica, small towns that swelled to five or six times their normal size with the inflow of refugees from surrounding areas cleansed by the Serbs. The tactic was similar to that applied at Sarajevo: encircle and intimidate into submission by cutting off vital supplies.

This phase of the war is also known in the West for the horrifying pictures of detention camps, reports of torture, rape, and killing of Muslims by advancing Serbs. Territories previously held by the Serbs, mostly in western Bosnia, were systematically cleared of Muslims and Croats. Though Croats and Muslims engaged in similar atrocities against the Serb population on their respective territories, during this second phase the Serbs were singled out for international condemnation. They were seen as the destroyers of the independence of BiH, a country that the West had blessed only a few months before. The premature decision of the West was still not questioned at this time. The Serbs had also exerted more force and brutality, and conquered a larger territory. All this made their "exploits" more visible to the Western media, who set out to report only on Serb brutality in the first place.

The international condemnation of the Serbs during this second phase of the war, together with the sanctions imposed on Serbia and Montenegro, if anything only hardened the resolve of Serbs like Karadjić, the "head of state" of the Bosnian Serbs, and Mladić, the commanding general in the field. They claimed that their cause was unjustly presented and their use of force unfairly reported. Their followers, by now convinced that an international conspiracy against the Serbs must be in the works, stood solidly behind the leadership. Why were the Croats allowed self-determination and the Serbs not? Why was only Muslim and Croat maltreatment at the hands of Serbs reported and the reverse not? This could only be understood as deliberate "genocide against the Serbs." To the Serb population of BiH the principle of unchangeable borders, which was at the root of the original demands of Croatia and BiH for recognition, and also at the root of the fighting, meant very little. To them the maintenance of the delicate security balance in Europe, which was the motive behind this principle, meant next to nothing.

Only by understanding this point is it possible to comprehend the stubborn persistence of Bosnian Serbs in the face of many threats. Couple it with the fact that most of the threats were either empty or irrelevant (like the imposition of a no-fly zone) and that the Serbs had superior gun-power, and we get closer to a fuller understanding of how and why they gained what they did in BiH. As early as 26 June 1992 the Serbs were faced with a UN ultimatum: Stop shelling Sarajevo and put away all heavy guns under UN control or face military action. But the guns kept on blazing and systematically destroying Sarajevo. The likelihood of outside military action today is only slightly greater than it was when this first threat was made. The Serbs have taken Western dithering as evidence that they can pursue the policy of ethnic cleansing without fear of punishment. Furthermore, if the Serbs, who were under constant threat and pressure from the outside world, could do it, so could the Croats and the Muslims, who were not in the spotlight. And they did. Civilians on all sides paid the heaviest price of this war.

The Croats went after their piece of BiH with much less bombast, gradually but surely wiping out all symbols of the BiH state from territories under their control, even while they were still joined with the Muslims in an anti-Serb alliance. The full scale of their dismantling of BiH became known only at the outset of the third phase of the war: when they started openly fighting their allies the Muslims. This occurred in the spring of 1993, when it became obvious that the West was resigned to a partitioning of BiH.

Fighting between Muslims and Croats broke out in central Bosnia, where there were conflicts over the priority of claims to territory, and over the city of Mostar, which the Croats wanted as the capital of their state called Herzeg-Bosna. The Muslims, by now squeezed down to about 10 per cent of the former territory of BiH, undertook offensive actions in order to regain ground at the expense of the Croats. A strange thing occurred: Croats fleeing Muslims took shelter behind Serb lines, and the Serbs escorted them to safety in their own region!

A old/new alliance came out into the open, an alliance between Serbs and Croats intent on partitioning BiH. They had had a common interest in BiH from day one, but they had first to sort out their line of separation. Since by this time their separation in BiH was complete, they now ganged up politically, though not militarily, against the Muslims. The Muslims pressed the Croats in an offensive in central Bosnia. The Croats reciprocated with the strangulation of Mostar. The story of Sarajevo repeated itself, albeit on a smaller scale and with the Croats now in the culprit seat.

This beautiful Oriental town was first fought over by the Serbs and Croats, though Muslims made up the majority of the population. It sustained heavy destruction in this first phase. After the Serbs withdrew there was relative but uneasy peace until the new wave of Croat bombardment, designed to oust the Muslims or terrify them into submission. More destruction and more civilian suffering followed. The same stories, previously reviling the Serb conquerors, now depicted Croat behaviour as identical. They told of the starvation and beating of prisoners, killing, intimidation, ethnic cleansing. The

Croats in turn reported gruesome stories of Muslim behaviour in central Bosnia.

The Serbs, in the meantime, mainly watched the other two, while keeping pressure on Sarajevo and consolidating the vital corridor in the north. They were basking in the feel of victory, not only against the Croats and Muslims on the ground but against the pressure of the international community at the negotiating table. For them the only question remaining at the time this book goes to press is whether BiH will be split three ways or two, with or without the Muslims. And this open question will prolong the third phase until some kind of resolution is reached.

But the prolongation of conflict became early on a favourite tactic of the Muslims, especially once the Serbs were close to accomplishing their objectives and appeared more ready to negotiate. Spurred on by the conflicting signals that the West, and primarily the United States, was sending, the Muslims kept alive the hope that intervention on their behalf might materialize. Their favourite tactic was to continue the fighting but make it appear that Serbs were responsible for it. Given the vain, single-minded, and belligerent behaviour of the Serbs, this was not difficult to accomplish. But almost every time a lull in the fighting occurred, the Muslims made sure that this would not lead to a loss of interest by the West.

While desperately trying to convert the attention of the West into military action, or at least a lifting of the arms embargo, the Muslims were inexorably losing ground to both Serbs and Croats. If some territory conquered by the Serbs and the Croats is not returned to the Muslims and a sizable Muslim political unit created, the Muslims will be a people without a homeland, much like the Palestinians. The tragedy and the irony of the situation is that the Muslims of BiH could become homeless people just as the Palestinians stand a good chance of gaining a political unit for self-rule.

A curious aspect of the war in BiH is that most of it was fought using guerrilla or partisan methods of warfare. As opposed to the war in Croatia, there was very little of a front line. Except for the siege of cities, most notably Sarajevo and Mostar, enemy units were rarely in constant engagement. Given the topography and ethnic composition of BiH, most of the fighting occurred between small units acting in familiar areas, creating numerous "fronts" of varying duration. This aspect of the war had a significant bearing, though it was not decisive, on the reluctance of the West to deploy military forces. It suggested that intervention would require a great number of troops as peace-keepers, something the international community was not ready to provide.

The war in Bosnia is perhaps best known for the siege and destruction of Sarajevo and the untold suffering of the remaining population. Estimated at the beginning of bombardment to be between three and four hundred thousand, the citizens of Sarajevo were brought to the verge of starvation and collapse of all civilized life. The Serb siege and bombardment of Sarajevo, which lies in a valley and is thus exposed to artillery on the hills around it, had three objectives.

Initially, the objective was to secure the withdrawal of JNA units from barracks in Sarajevo, which were surrounded and blockaded by Muslim forces. As the BiH government held the JNA hostage for wider political objectives, Sarajevo became a hostage for the release of the troops.

After the JNA was able to withdraw, the heavy bombardment was meant to intimidate the Muslim population within and elsewhere into submitting to the Serb proposal to partition BiH ethnically. The more the Muslims rejected the idea of partition on cantonal lines, the heavier the bombardment was. It is this desire to frighten and intimidate that explains the indiscriminate shelling of apartment houses, offices, even hospitals, squares and streets, gatherings of people, the snipers who shot at anything that moved, including children.

Initially, the Serb leadership was not interested in holding on to Sarajevo, or a part of it, because Banja Luka in the west of BiH was proclaimed the capital of the Republika Srpska (as the new state was called). As it became increasingly clear that Banja Luka was not the right choice (too far from Serbia, and Serbs from Sarajevo and the eastern and southeastern parts of BiH did not approve), the fighting in Sarajevo gained an additional objective: to create an "ethnically pure" part of the city that would enable its division into two communities and allow Serbs to proclaim their part as capital, much as the East Germans did in East Berlin. The Serbs have publicly suggested that Sarajevo be divided like Beirut or Berlin.

That they could contemplate such a division shows how little in touch the Bosnian Serbs were with the political principles governing present-day Europe. While Europe and the world were rejoicing in the fall of the Berlin Wall, the Serbs of Bosnia saw as their best future the erection of a wall and the ethnic division of a community. They wanted to have the capital of the Serb Republic of Bosnia in Sarajevo, but not in a Sarajevo where Muslims were a majority. For a Serb Sarajevo to come into existence, street fighting, even in apartment houses, was necessary.

By far the worst in the arsenal of Serb brutalities was the total blockade of Sarajevo, which brought the whole city to the brink of collapse. That this would also victimize at least thirty thousand Serbs inside the city did not stop the radical national extremists, who were determined, if necessary, to starve the whole city to death.

This tactic backfired in some ways. The whole world community, including the Russians (traditional allies of the Serbs), stood together in condemning the Serb action. The starvation and bombardment of Sarajevo galvanized international support for the Bosnian Muslim leadership, making the Serb objective that much more difficult to accomplish. Relief flights and land convoys were sent into Sarajevo, and the Serbs had no choice but to stand back and allow them to pass. Cynics would say that Serb conduct in and around Sarajevo made the attainment of their objectives more messy.

However, the fact that Bosnian Serbs now stand to benefit from Western resignation to and recognition of their conquests (as well as those of the Croats) shows that they probably read and understood the post–Cold War security void in Europe better than did the powers supposedly in charge of maintaining this security.

This war will also be remembered for the entry into contemporary discourse of the expression "ethnic cleansing," as first Serbs and then others close on their heels systematically laid waste to the homes of their rivals. Ethnic cleansing, and the ways and means of accomplishing it, gave this war an imprint of cruelty, brutality, and inhumanity believed impossible at the end of the twentieth century. In spite of the many exaggerations about the numbers of killed, tortured, and raped, those victimized were tragically numerous, many of them women, elderly, and children, segments of the population that a "civilized" war would spare.

Who gave the order to proceed with such brutality and bestiality in sweeping the territories of other ethnic groups? Thus far we know only that such orders were carried out by the men on the ground, mostly by paramilitary and irregular units. From how elevated a level these orders emanated is difficult to tell. But the entire chain of command, up to and including the principal leaders – Milošević, Tudjman and Izetbegović – bears heavy responsibility for not putting an end to these gruesome methods of "cleansing" and for not publicly denouncing them.

As this book goes to press[3] the war continues and no political solution is in sight. This should come as no surprise. Even if a solution is reached on some kind of partitioning of BiH, it must be understood that the whole conflict and the carnage in BiH are only a sideshow in the main Serb-Croat conflict. Until some solution to that conflict is reached, peace in BiH is unfortunately not very likely. The war in BiH, more than the war in Croatia, has become the focus of international attention. From the original decision to grant "preventive" recognition to this ethnically mixed state up to the present, all international organizations and political forums have expressed concern and a desire to contribute to a settlement of the conflict. But this concern has had little real effect on the ground.

The fact that the Islamic world is also involved makes the West even more interested in finding a political solution. But what *would be* a solution in Bosnia? The lack of genuine knowledge of the place and its people has hampered the efforts of the international community, contributing often to an increase rather than a decrease in the desire of the three ethnic communities to solve problems with guns and not with negotiations.

The ferocity, barbarism, and zest for fighting in BiH has been well documented in the media. At great personal risk and at the cost of some lives, reporters from various battlefields, besieged cities, and ravaged hamlets have brought out horror stories on video and in print. However, the complexity of the situation has led to the spread of a number of oft-repeated errors by reporters who have flown in with a mission to cover a war story with little or no background preparation.

One of the most often repeated errors, especially in the first year of the war, was that the Serbs were fighting the Bosnians. There *are* no "Bosnians" except Muslims, Croats, *and* Serbs living in BiH. At the beginning of the campaign one could say that this meant Serbs from Serbia proper or the JNA, but the backbone of the fighting force in BiH on the Serb side was always constituted by Serbs from Bosnia, including those fighting in the uniforms of the JNA. The number of Serbs and Croats who supported the Muslim-led government of Alija Izetbegović soon became so small and symbolic that calling all of them collectively Bosnians, as if nothing had changed between the ethnic communities, was a gross inaccuracy.

Secondly, the media often reported that the Serbs had won almost 70 per cent of the territory of BiH. There was no mention of the fact that in times of peace the Serbs populated well over 50 per cent of the territory, choosing to reside in less well-populated areas, in contrast to the Muslims, who were typically concentrated in towns and cities. The Serb territories were always proportionately larger than their numbers in the population. Of the Muslims, the opposite was the case. Thus, the Serb gain was not from 0 to 70 per cent, as many reports would imply, but was rather a matter of much more limited territorial expansion to meet strategic goals, mostly concerning the corridor and territories in the east of BiH.

Thirdly, the Muslims were the clear victims of this ferocious campaign by the Serbs and a less openly vicious one by the Croats. But after a time they deliberately chose to continue fighting, even to the point of provoking incidents systematically. They succumbed to the logic of "the worse it is, the better," in the hope that the world community would step in on their side. Therefore, it was the Muslims who kept saying that they would not take part in the EC-sponsored peace conference until the fighting stopped, at the same time making sure that the fighting continued.

Fourthly, Croat territories were defended, consolidated, and expanded with the help of regular troops from Croatia, just as the Serbs had help from Serbia proper. This for a long time went largely unnoticed by the media and the public at large.[4]

All the above is not meant to minimize the responsibility of the Serbs. Theirs is by far the greatest, especially since they "transformed" most of the ex-Yugoslav army into the army of the Serb Republic of Bosnia, making the match in armaments brutally unequal. But if a way is to be found to stop the war, it does make sense to point out that *all* sides had an interest in continuing it. Putting the blame on only one side, no matter how unacceptable its conduct, has not brought a solution any closer.

And the international community? We shall see in the next chapters the evolution of their engagement in what was Yugoslavia. Suffice it to mention here that it became deeply involved in the tragedy of BiH in a political and humanitarian way. While the second intervention deserves undivided praise, the political engagement has left a lot to be desired. By violating the principle of the three constituent nations in BiH, the international community has itself unwittingly become a fourth constituent part of that tragic place. It is now difficult to see a solution to the problems of BiH without the participation of the UN as the country's arbiter, with, if necessary, enough police and military force to ensure compliance with agreements – in effect, a UN protectorate. If the fourth constituent participant pulls out or is inactive, the fighting in BiH will probably end only with the political liquidation of the Muslim component.

CHAPTER THIRTEEN

The European Community Steps In

The European Community was promoted to a leading role in the Yugoslav drama when the crisis was at its peak and the war was just around the corner. A flurry of Community activity can be traced back to the visit of Jacques Delors and Jacques Santer to Yugoslavia on 29 and 30 May 1991. The federal government of Ante Marković pinned great hope on this visit, as did the governments of BiH and Macedonia. The European Community also felt that high-level mediation was not only necessary but potentially worthwhile. But by then the three principal national leaders, Milošević, Tudjman, and Milan Kučan, were only interested in impressing on Community officials the importance of their respective national problems and programs.[1]

Since that visit the involvement of the European Community has increased in numerous ways, from sending "troikas"[2] and observers or organizing a peace conference to humanitarian aid and military involvement in protecting the aid effort. In the first year of its involvement, before the lead role finally went to the United Nations, there was hardly a dossier on the agenda of the EC Foreign Affairs Council, save the Maastricht agreements, that took up as much of its time. The Community has tried the carrot and the stick, mediation and taking sides, arbitration and sanctions. Except for military intervention, it is difficult to think of a policy instrument the Community has not tried over the years of its involvement. But all of that has produced few results, certainly less than the Community and the rest of the world expected, much less than those desiring peace in Yugoslavia hoped for.

Why did the European Community become so deeply involved in the Yugoslav drama? At the time the Community stepped in, virtually all observers considered it a logical choice and the best-placed mediator to solve this complex problem.[3] It was not only a question of others, primarily the Americans, opting out; there was rather a general acceptance of the Community's claim to be the most interested and effective mediator. The Americans were happy to let the Europeans handle this hot potato for themselves.

On the supply side – which is to say the Community side – of mediation, the most important reasons for involvement seemed to be three.

First, the experience of the Gulf War clearly established the United States as the only remaining power in the world capable of crisis management. The Community acknowledged this fact but not without remorse, especially among some of its bigger and more important members. The Community was largely confused at the time of the Gulf crisis and, as a consequence, was marginalized in solving it. The Community now sought an opportunity to redress the image it had projected during the Gulf War.

Secondly, two EC intergovernmental conferences – on economic and monetary union and on political union – were in full swing, and two important treaties were being negotiated. The Conference on Political Union obviously looked on Yugoslavia as a challenge and an opportunity to demonstrate the Community's ability to design and carry out common foreign and, more ambitiously, a common security policy. This, as we shall see, had a profound influence on the attitude of the Community towards the crisis it was dealing with.

And thirdly, the Yugoslav crisis was taking place on European soil and after the end of the Cold War. The Community felt responsible for handling a crisis taking place on its doorstep, all the more so since, during the forty years of the Cold War and over thirty years of its own existence, the Community collectively and as individual countries had played a minor role in foreign relations with the Eastern block. Perhaps because Yugoslavia was never fully on the other side and the Community had had very good relations with it for a long time, the task to be performed seemed easier. "This is the hour of Europe," proclaimed the ministerial "troika" just before boarding the plane to be deposited into the Yugoslav quagmire.

On the demand, or Yugoslav side of mediation, again all parties involved thought that the European Community was the natural choice. The fact that the Community comprised twelve countries and constituted a sort of a United Nations in miniature appeared to offer a guarantee of its neutrality. It seemed at the time that the various countries of the Community, with their specific interests, would keep each other in check.

The government of Prime Minister Marković thought that the Community would *fully* back their economic and political reforms. Their expectation was, therefore, that deeper political involvement through mediation would be accompanied by the necessary financial support for the government's program. The same hope was shared by the leadership of BiH and Macedonia.

Serbia and Milošević liked the sound of the Community's early declarations that "a united and democratic Yugoslavia stands the best chance to integrate itself into the new Europe." This they took to mean that the EC would uphold the unity of the country and would therefore implicitly help the Serbs.

The Slovenes and the Croats did not much like the reference to the unity of Yugoslavia, but they were also keen for European mediation. They knew that with the European Community they stood a much better chance against the Serbs than on their own. Perhaps even more significantly, they had been actively encouraged by powerful political forces within the Community, most notably in Germany, to maintain their drive towards independence. In order to allow these forces to work for them and their desired goal it was necessary to support and not to oppose the Community.

All sides in Yugoslavia agreed genuinely that the future of the country, together or separately, was to be sought in closer ties with the Community. The political leaders of the Community also knew and felt this, judging the Yugoslav leaders to be sincere in their declared intention to seek closer ties with the Community, membership in the Council of Europe, and so on. But they failed to see that this in itself was not sufficient bait for more constructive and conciliatory conduct on the part of the various nationalist leaders. The logic of rational choice was deflected through thick layers of nationalism, producing unforeseen and undesired responses and results.

The Community felt that it could handle the situation partly on the strength of its long-lasting relationship with Yugoslavia. Relations had been established as early as 1967, Yugoslavia preceding by more than twenty years all other socialist countries in its recognition of the Community. Over the next two decades the Community became by far the largest trading partner of Yugoslavia, with almost 60 per cent of trade going to or coming from the Community. Trade relations were complemented by financial protocols, scientific co-operation, and in the last few years of the 1980s by an established political dialogue that elevated Yugoslavia to full-fledged political partnership with the Community. All these maturing ties encouraged feeling in the Community that it had a strong presence in and influence on

Yugoslavia, and help to explain the readiness, even eagerness of the Europeans to step into the crisis.

As far as the Yugoslavs were concerned, particularly the federal government, the operative assumption of foreign policy was that the internal crisis would be solved by pressing on with the orientation towards Europe begun in November 1989. Soon after, the federal parliament voted unanimously for a European Declaration, which made European integration and the EC in particular a strategic foreign policy interest of Yugoslavia.

However, the corollary was heightened expectations of even more open markets and financial aid to enable the reform process to take off without too many political and economic upheavals. These never materialized except as promises, conditional on political changes in Yugoslavia. But the Yugoslav government expected the Community to step in with economic aid first, so that it *could* change the political situation. Inevitably, in the context of this stand-off, the aid that came was itself slowly conditioned by other, unexpected kinds of political change.

The mutual expectations of the federal government and the EC were never fulfilled; time passed, and nationalism on the ground reached boiling-point. The situation deteriorated rapidly, making any kind of solution more difficult. The break-neck speed with which the Yugoslav crisis developed was in stark contrast to the Community's snail-paced, cumbersome crawl in making decisions. The Community was always at least one step behind events, reacting rather than acting.

The question of its speed and agility in decision-making soon became the least of the EC's problems. The Community felt a need to act; it knew that it must do something to demonstrate its political credibility as a powerful entity and the chief architect of a new Europe. But it was less than clear and determined about the *goals* to be accomplished and almost totally innocent about the *means* required to accomplish them.

The initial position of the Community, to uphold the unity of and democratic transformations in Yugoslavia, was officially proclaimed as policy in November 1989, when Yugoslavia applied for associate status in the EC, and survived until July 1991, after the Croatian and Slovenian secessions and the armed intervention of the JNA in Slovenia.

This goal of the Community was torpedoed by the Slovenes and the Croats with their proclamations of independence and sovereignty. The Community did not reward them with recognition immediately.

At the time it was more concerned about the use of force in the attempt to restore the territorial integrity of Yugoslavia.

The Community dispatched two "troikas" in rapid succession immediately after the conflict in Slovenia had started; their purpose was to establish the framework for a peaceful resolution of the conflict *within* a Yugoslav federation. It was agreed that this would require the army's withdrawal to its barracks, the suspension of the declarations of independence of Slovenia and Croatia, and the election of Stipe Mesić (a Croat) to the post of president of the Presidency. Only the last and least important of these three conditions was fulfilled.

This engaging work on the ground, with the presidency of the EC for the first time in its history passing from one country to another (midnight 30 June) while in session, meeting with its Yugoslav counterpart in an effort to pacify the war-mongering Yugoslavs, was soon followed by a meeting of the Foreign Affairs Council. In its declaration the council chose to stress that "it is on the people of Yugoslavia to decide their future," to express "firm opposition to the use of force," and to "note that in Yugoslavia all parties concerned accept the reality that a new situation has arisen."[4] For the first time there was no mention of the "unity and integrity of Yugoslavia." Furthermore, punitive measures were introduced: an arms embargo and the suspension of the financial protocols.

Obviously, the use of force in Slovenia by the JNA had shaken the determination of the Community to insist on the unity of Yugoslavia. Continued insistence might have sounded as if the Community were willing to preserve the unity of Yugoslavia at all costs, including overlooking bloodshed. Thus the Community substituted the goal of seeking a political solution acceptable to all and offered its own good offices as a neutral and influential mediator. Initially this meant stepping in between the warring sides but not offering political mediation on matters of substance.

This led to the Community's brokerage of the so-called Brioni Agreement, according to which a cease-fire would come into effect, the army would withdraw to barracks and eventually leave Slovenia, while the Slovenes (and the Croats) would resume the *status quo ante* their unilateral proclamations of independence. The Community also decided to send in monitors, under the auspices of the Conference on Security and Co-operation in Europe, to oversee the disengagement of the JNA and the Slovenes as well as general compliance with other provisions of the Brioni Agreement. The situation in Slovenia, though still volatile, seemed under control, especially after the Federal Presidency decided to withdraw all JNA troops from Slovenia.

But tensions in Croatia were mounting, the skirmishes becoming more frequent and the conflict ever more violent. The Community still thought, or hoped, that with a little pressure a political solution could be found without political mediation. However, at that moment Tudjman chose to make an "informal" visit to Bonn and came away encouraged to step up the level of confrontation with the JNA. Five days after his visit to Bonn he walked out of the meeting of the Federal Presidency with the leaders of all the republics, who were making their last attempt to reach a political settlement. Thus he prevented the acceptance of a compromise formula that all others, including Stipe Mesić (the Croat president of the Federal Presidency), accepted. That was the end to self-propelled attempts to find any compromise formula.

The Community, "dismayed at the increasing violence in Croatia" but also increasingly dismayed at its own inability to stop the violence at an early stage, now had to take one step further and offer a political framework for mediation. During August 1991 it established the following political principles: any change of internal and *international* borders by force was unacceptable; any solution should guarantee the rights of peoples and minorities in all the republics; and the Community would *never* accept a policy of *fait accompli*. On 7 September 1991 the Community convened the Conference on Yugoslavia in the Peace Palace at The Hague. Its political involvement was now complete.

The Hague conference, chaired by Lord Carrington,[5] officially set out "to adopt arrangements to ensure peaceful accommodation of the conflicting aspirations of the Yugoslav peoples." It reiterated the principles the ministers had already made known, adding but one: full account would be taken of all legitimate concerns and legitimate aspirations. At the same time an arbitration commission of five eminent European jurists was established.

Almost immediately, the optimism and high hopes of the opening ceremony were jolted by the extremely tough and uncompromising opening speeches of Tudjman and Milošević. Tudjman accused Serbia of waging a dirty war against Croatia, and Milošević, who spoke later, countered by accusing the "totalitarian and chauvinistic regime of Croatia" of intimidating the Serbs in Croatia. Later events would show that their predictions, rather than the optimistic expectations of others, were to come true. From a bad start, the Hague Conference rapidly deteriorated over the coming months, showing how badly out of tune it was with events on the ground.

The conference proceeded at a leisurely pace. Plenary meetings were few and far apart, considering the increasing drama in the collapsing federation. Lord Carrington travelled to Yugoslavia several times and consulted with various factions in bilateral meetings, but he clearly demonstrated his preference for closed-door, "tête-à-tête" meetings rather than full conferences. In these bilateral meetings he was feeling out the positions and various interests of participants, trying to find common ground, which he would then deliver to the plenary meetings for comment and possible agreement. The plenary sessions he saw as a means of verifying his personal and individual efforts. Often, these were only matters of procedure rather than substance.

The plenaries never lasted more than two hours, and there was hardly ever any debate in them. Lord Carrington would not have that, much to the astonishment of the Yugoslav participants. All of them, except the president of BiH, had been seasoned Communist Party officials in the past, quite accustomed to long, tiresome, and gruelling sessions that would, with great effort and considerable time, produce platforms and statements indicating political agreement. The elegant conference format that Carrington pursued was wasted on the Yugoslav participants and certainly did not help in finding a solution.

Lord Carrington also tried his hand at arranging several cease-fire agreements in order to secure a more peaceful atmosphere for the continuation of the conference. He met with the entire Presidency (the nominal supreme commander of the JNA), with General Veljko Kadijević, Tudjman, and Milošević jointly and separately. All of them solemnly proclaimed, even signed, their intent to honour cease-fires. But no sooner had the ink dried than the fighting resumed, sometimes initiated by the Croats, sometimes by the JNA, and sometimes by the Serbs.

Carrington later complained in an interview that none of his interlocutors was sincere and honest with him. He had taken their word that they would abide by an agreement, only to find out that he was not dealing with a "league of English gentlemen." This was a mistake that Carrington's successor, David Owen, again a British lord, would not repeat.

It was obvious that the fighting would not stop, because *all* sides felt that they were still gaining something from it. Most of the breaches of the cease-fire were made by the Croats because their strategic interest, at that point, was international recognition, which seemed far more difficult to achieve if the fighting stopped. The JNA and the Serbs, however, as the far better-armed and -trained fighting force, perpetrated most of the destruction, a great deal of it absolutely senseless and militarily unnecessary. This played right into the hands of the Croats.

The Community, tired of its inability to influence events in the desired direction, and particularly by the excessive use of force by the JNA and Serb irregulars, decided to move from mediation and offering good services to a more assertive position. It now offered a political framework for a solution, making quite clear what a lack of acceptance would lead to.

The Community announced that in the future it would take selective and restrictive action against "those parties continuing to flout the desire of the other Yugoslav parties as well as the international community for a successful outcome of the Conference on Yugoslavia." This announcement was followed by the threat of termination of the co-operation agreement with Yugoslavia and its "renewal with those parties that are contributing to the peace process."

But the question left unanswered was: What *would be* a successful outcome of the conference? Carrington and the majority of countries felt very strongly that, whatever the outcome, an *overall* solution to the Yugoslav problem was required. No satisfactory arrangement could be found by dealing piecemeal with individual republics. In this spirit the Community offered through the conference the following principles as a basis for new relations between the republics:

- sovereign and independent republics, with an international personality for those wishing it;
- a free association of the republics, with an international personality;
- comprehensive arrangements, including supervisory mechanisms for the protection of human rights and special status for certain groups and areas;
- European involvement where appropriate; and
- in the *framework of a general settlement*, the recognition of the independence, within existing borders, unless otherwise agreed, of those republics wishing it.

Five republics accepted this framework, but Milošević rejected it. Theatrically he proclaimed that Serbia could not agree "to an abolition of Yugoslavia by a stroke of a pen" or to the assumption "that Yugoslavia no longer exists." This he claimed in deliberate defiance of the fact that Yugoslavia had already been destroyed by strokes of the pen in the Slovenian and Croatian parliaments and by the sword of the JNA, which Milošević fully supported.

Carrington tried, at the next session of the conference, to integrate the Serbian objection by including a further principle: a common state of equal republics could be created for those republics wishing to remain a common state. Tudjman was strongly opposed to this amendment, and the other leaders had various but milder objections, the strongest being that the new principle was "confusing." So it was dropped, and the Serbs were annoyed. In the meantime, and under considerable pressure, the Montenegrins rejoined the Serbian position. The die was then cast: Serbia and Montenegro would go on insisting on the continuity of Yugoslavia; the others would seek independence and separation from it.

With this the conference came to a dead end, and the attempt to mediate a peaceful political solution, acceptable to all, that would also respect the above principles came to naught. Incidentally, this session of the conference was the last to have representatives of federal bodies attending. At the next session, in December, only leaders of republics participated. In effect the Conference on Yugoslavia, on the insistence of Lord Carrington, "killed" Yugoslavia *before* the results of the Arbitration Commission, which was to offer a legal opinion on the succession of state, were known.

But events in and around Yugoslavia were never actually determined by the conference. The escalation of fighting on the ground on the one hand, and German assertiveness in the final lap to Maastricht on the other, determined the future position of the Community.

The brutal destruction of Vukovar and the bombardment of Dubrovnik had the effect of generating considerable public pressure within the Community to act. So the Community responded once more by changing its immediate goal. Now it was to pressure Serbia and the JNA to stop the fighting. Though the Croats were fighting almost as hard in order to sway international public opinion in their direction as underdogs, there was, on German insistence, no call nor pressure on them to stop deliberate provocations.

The Community also decided to impose punitive measures on those who did not co-operate and to restore privileged relations with those who did. With this decision the Community could no longer claim neutrality. It took sides. It took the side of those (Croatia and Slovenia) who *unilaterally* changed the existing *international* borders of Yugoslavia, thereby accepting a *fait accompli* even though one of its fundamental principles at the beginning had been never to do so.

But, it was argued, there was little else the Community could do. The conference was achieving little, and the war was continuing. So in taking its next step the Community chose what it thought to be the lesser of two evils. It certainly could not accept the use of military force for political ends. Therefore it could not insist on the "unity" of Yugoslavia if that unity was maintained by brute force.

The recognition of Croatia and Slovenia, which effectively occurred during December 1991 though it was nominally proclaimed in mid-January 1992, came in stark contrast to the statement, made only five weeks before, that the Community "remains firmly committed to a comprehensive political arrangement" and that the "prospect of recognition of independence can *only* be envisaged in the framework of an overall settlement." The recognition came, but the overall settlement was nowhere in sight even eighteen months after recognition.

German pressure for the recognition of Croatia and Slovenia had been building since the summer of 1991 and came to a peak in mid-December when, just prior to the Maastricht summit of EC heads of state, Germany succeeded in persuading its Community partners to agree to piecemeal recognition. The others agreed, a number of them with considerable reticence, because nobody wanted to cross the Germans just before the Maastricht summit. The Community, and those in favour of non-recognition, were running out of viable alternatives.

Nobody argued the case against recognition with such political force, even arm-twisting, as the Germans argued for it. Without speculating on other motives for such strong German pressure, it must be observed that the argument the Germans themselves like to advance as most important is certainly invalid in the case of Yugoslavia. The Germans are fond of saying that their support for the self-determination of Slovenia and Croatia derives from the benefits they gained themselves by exercising self-determination and reuniting their divided country.

Neither the analogy nor the policy prescription applied in the case of Yugoslavia. For one thing, Yugoslavia was not an arbitrarily or artificially created unity (as was the case with German division), nor was its federation imposed by force, as was the division of Germany during the Cold War. Secondly, the self-determination of the East Germans was not opposed by anyone, while the self-determination of Slovenia and Croatia was opposed by all the other Yugoslav republics and by the United States and other great powers.

Whereas self-determination in Germany contributed to peace and stability in Europe, self-determination without an overall agreement on Yugoslavia could not and therefore did not yield the same result.

The argument, often put forward, that recognition of Croatia and Slovenia stopped the war is dubious on many counts. First, the war in Slovenia had stopped long before recognition. The war in the rest of Yugoslavia did not. The example of BiH clearly shows that recognition undoubtedly escalated, even if it did not initiate, the confrontations in that republic. As for Croatia, if it is indeed true that recognition stopped the fighting, then it is also true that the Croats were mostly interested in prolonging the fighting to gain it. Yet the Serbs were held solely responsible.

The search for Germany's motives should be directed towards their domestic political and strategic foreign policy interests. But whatever their real motives were, the chosen arguments for their action were, and are, extremely weak.

The position of the Community within the conference was weakened after recognition of the independence of Slovenia and Croatia. The most powerful political weapon the conference had – granting or withholding recognition – was lost. With the prospect of recognition attractive to Croats and the threat of it compelling to Serbs, some leverage could be had. Recognition had to be *potential*. Once granted, it became useless. No wonder Lord Carrington was privately furious. He stayed on as the EC mediator for another six months and, after resigning, was replaced by Lord Owen in July 1992.

After abandoning the idea of holding Yugoslavia together, and then abandoning the idea of negotiating a political settlement acceptable to all, the Community now offered a platform for settlement on a take-it-or-leave-it basis, promising recognition to those accepting and further sanctions to those who did not. Prior to this, the Arbitration Commission of the Hague Conference had proclaimed that Yugoslavia was "in a process" of dissolution. This was a clear *political* statement, as international law does not deal with processes but with states. It was interpreted by those wishing Yugoslavia dead to mean that it no longer existed. Those wishing its continuation or desiring to inherit its name insisted that the dissolution was a consequence of secession and that what remained of Yugoslavia should inherit its rights and obligations. The seeds of further legal, political, and economic wrangling were thus sown.

The Community invited all Yugoslav republics to apply for recognition subject to certain conditions and acceptance of guidelines that the Community had previously established for the recognition of new states in Eastern Europe and the Soviet Union.

Four of them – Slovenia, Croatia, BiH, and Macedonia – responded by the deadline, while Serbia and Montenegro did not. These two republics wanted to carry on the continuity of Yugoslavia. They also pointed out that they had been recognized by the Berlin Congress in 1878, and they felt it to be "shameful" to apply for recognition of sovereignty for a second time. The applications were forwarded to the Arbitration Commission, which ruled that Slovenia was a clear case for recognition; Macedonia, with minor modifications of the constitution, was also a clear case; the commission warned that Croatia left much to be desired in terms of protection of human rights; and BiH should hold a referendum to determine whether the majority of the population sought independence or not.

The ruling of the commission was very controversial. In three of the four states it created new problems rather than sorting out old ones. The Germans would not accept that Croatia was unrecognizable. They had already publicly recognized it! Hastily a letter of intent was solicited from Tudjman in which he solemnly pledged to amend the constitution in a way that would protect the human rights of Serbs in Croatia. This letter was apparently sufficient for the Germans to pressure the Community into recognizing Croatia. The substance of Tudjman's letter of intent never materialized.

The Greeks objected to the recognition of Macedonia under that name, arguing that the use of this ancient Greek name opened possibilities for irredentism in northern Greece or territorial claims by the new republic of Macedonia.[6] In repeated attempts, and much to the frustration of almost all other members, the Community was unable to overcome the Greek objection internally. Finally, the issue was passed on to the UN, where Greece has no veto power.

But the most controversial and tragic consequence of the Arbitration Commission's ruling, one that the Community fully accepted, only to regret it later, was the call for a referendum in BiH, to be followed by recognition in the event that a majority sought it. It was clear that the referendum would not solve anything since it would only show how different ethnic communities felt about independence and sovereignty, which by then was already well known.

It was naïve to think that a citizens' referendum, with a majority voting in favour, would solve the problem. If this had been a possibility, why did the Community not make the same kind of prescription for Yugoslavia as a whole? Why was there no pressure nor recommendation to hold a referendum in Yugoslavia to establish what the *citizens* of Yugoslavia, and not ethnic groups, thought about self-determination?

Secondly, this proposal was contrary to the constitution of BiH, which specifically states that all matters of general importance, such as sovereignty and independence, must be agreed upon by a consensus of the three ethnic groups in the republic. The Community totally disregarded this important provision, making things worse.

Thirdly, it was against all odds to expect that BiH, with the ethnic mix that it had and with rampant Serbian and Croatian nationalism surrounding it, could resist the gravitational pull of the Serbian and Croatian states. The idea of "preventive recognition," admittedly thrust upon the Community by the United States, proved to be wrong from the outset.

It would be difficult to claim that the fighting broke out *because of* recognition. However, it can be said with certainty that the recognition of BiH greatly *contributed* to it. The Community tried to organize a salvage operation in the form of a conference on BiH under the auspices of the general Conference on Yugoslavia. This was the last political attempt the Community made on its own before accepting the role of second fiddle to the UN's first. In March 1992 the Portuguese minister of foreign affairs got the three parties to initial his plan for a cantonization of BiH. The prospects of the Kuthilero Plan lived for about a week until the Muslim president of BiH, under pressure from his own hard-liners, renounced the plan. So this Community child turned out to be just as ineffective as the parent conference had been, precisely because of the premature recognition of BiH.

The situation in BiH, and especially the recognition of it, demonstrated beyond any doubt that the Community was incapable of holding one strategic position and following one line of action in the Yugoslav drama. It accepted the change of the borders of Yugoslavia as a whole even though Yugoslavia had been, after all, a founding member of the UN, a member of the Conference on Security and Co-operation in Europe, and a contractual partner of the Community, believing that this would bring peace and stability in the Balkans. It did not accept the idea of changing the borders of BiH, which was, after all, only one political unit within Yugoslavia and was, from within, subject to the same kind of pressures that blew Yugoslavia apart.

Looking at the same problem from another angle, we see the Community finally accepting the self-determination of the *nations* of Yugoslavia, thus allowing its break-up and the creation of nation-states. In the case of BiH, which was just as much as composite as Yugoslavia and *not* a nation-state, the *ethnic* groups were denied self-determination and were obliged or expected to follow the imposition of a citizens', not an ethnic referendum.

The Community has never come up with a clear and logical explanation for its abandonment or mixing of principles as it found expedient. The overriding concern was the use of force in Yugoslavia, which touched the sensitivity of public opinion in the Community countries. The Community simply *had* to show that it could do something and that it was doing it. Since it was the Serbs and the JNA who were using brute military force more than anybody else, the Community designed its policies around the concept of preventing, less ambitiously containing, and even less ambitiously condemning this use of force. The tragedy of the situation was that the Community's approach did not stop the use of force but made, by its stop-and-go attitude, a lasting and balanced solution more distant and difficult to achieve.

It was and still is true of the Yugoslav drama that there are no clearly good policies towards it, only a choice or selection of difficult, even bad ones.

With hindsight it is easy to see missed opportunities on both sides. Yugoslavia missed its opportunity by declaring its European orientation too late, clinging too long to the totally spent notion of non-alignment. Had Yugoslavia approached Europe with more determination in the mid-eighties, when it became clear that the strategic balance in Europe had changed and that the USSR would not intervene in any way, it probably would have largely avoided or at least reduced internal tensions by hooking up to external, European integration, which at the time offered a positive dynamic.

But even with perfect hindsight it is far from obvious what the European Community should have done. In trying to settle the Yugoslav crisis in a peaceful manner, to mediate conflicting interests and bring about a just, democratic, and peaceful solution, the Community took on an enormous task. In retrospect it is easy to say that the EC bit off more than it could chew. When the choice was made, the Yugoslav problem was regarded by many as smaller and less complex than it was, while the Community seemed stronger, more determined and influential than it actually was.

The Community suffered a great deal of humiliation in the process of "solving" the Yugoslav problem. The lesser embarrassments involved incidents like the harassment of the white-clad Community observers, sarcastically dubbed "ice-cream vendors," and their vehicles. An EC helicopter was shot down in January 1992 and the five men on board killed, and the EC had no adequate response. The Community had progressively to abandon the driver's seat to the UN. Perhaps the biggest humiliation of all was that Yugoslavia, like a mirror of truth, reflected the impotence of the Community as a political power.

The Community chose the wrong time and the wrong foot to step into the Yugoslav drama. It seems to have overlooked the fact that at that moment it was still primarily an economic and not a political power. True, there was not much incentive to step in with economic aid when economic considerations were being ignored internally. But this does not change the fact that the Community had a better chance of solving the complex situation by economic rather than political means, since the Community itself was much stronger in that department. Now we know that it actually should have opted out on the grounds that it simply was not competent to solve this type of problem.

Neither was the Community mature enough to act as a political force in creating the new order on the European continent. It stepped into the Yugoslav jungle armed with a penknife rather than a machete. It was the pressure of Maastricht that made the jungle look smaller and the penknife almost a machete.

The Community cannot, of course, be accused of destroying Yugoslavia. The most that the Community can be accused of is indecision and weakness in the face of aggression and of acting precipitately in its recognition of Croatia and BiH, thus undermining its own conference. It also raised false hopes and expectations whose collapse was not without effect on the conflicting sides in Yugoslavia.

In pushing towards recognition of independent states, the Community was trying to come to terms with two new realities. First, Yugoslavia was disappearing before its eyes and in the worst of all possible ways. Second, Germany was becoming a foreign policy power to be reckoned with. That German pressure forced the Community – against the better judgment of some of its member-states and the advice of the United States and the UN – to agree to recognize any "well-behaved" ex-Yugoslav republic is a fact the Community will have to live with for a long time. In an effort to preserve EC unity the member-countries lost sight of the suffering people of Yugoslavia and the possibility of a long-term stable solution. It has been pointed out that the greatest achievement of the Community is that it did not split up over Yugoslavia, as its member countries had done in the past. This was largely accomplished by compromise and by adopting a policy of appealing to the lowest common denominator, a strategy that the parties in Yugoslavia were also advised to adopt but would not. The Community came through, but the policy that resulted from all the compromise just could not solve a complex problem like the break-up of Yugoslavia.

Europe then had to brace itself for a third reality – the continuation and possible spread of war. "Community action was disappointing in the eyes of those who would have liked to achieve the impossible," said Jacques Delors, the president of the Arbitration Commission. The trouble is that within the Community a majority thought that they could accomplish the impossible; otherwise they would not have acted.

The Community was ill suited for dealing with aggressive nationalism and the use of force within internal boundaries. It can be argued that valuable time, and therefore lives and property, were lost until the Community realized that it could not handle this basic problem of aggression and force but had to turn to the United Nations.

CHAPTER FOURTEEN

A Call for Blue Helmets

Just as the Yugoslav crisis was coming to a head and already turning to violence, the United Nations was at its own peak of political prestige and credibility. It had just come out of the American-inspired and American-led Desert Storm action in the Persian Gulf, which had been carried out under its umbrella. The success of the operation was a boost to the prestige not only of the United States but also of the UN, which had demonstrated a singularity of purpose and political determination quite unknown in recent UN history.

The UN also benefited from the ending of the Cold War and the long-standing confrontation of the US and USSR as permanent members of the Security Council. The UN's time as a victim of ideological and military polarization was over, and a time of genuine joint political action among the different peoples of the world seemed to be in the offing.

So it was more than logical that the UN should become involved in the Yugoslav drama, particularly after it had become obvious that the European Community, the first to try mediation, was unlikely to produce a political solution and a lasting peace.

The first mention of the United Nations in the context of the Yugoslav crisis occurred during August 1991, when the war in Croatia was escalating rapidly. Austria,[1] backed by Britain, Belgium, and France, informed the Security Council that it "reserved the right to initiate informal consultations on the question of Yugoslavia," a beginning that was innocent enough and certainly a long way from the heavy involvement of the UN that subsequently occurred.

The next approach to the UN came in September[2] from the president of the Yugoslav Federal Presidency, Stipe Mesić, who sent a personal letter requesting peace-keeping forces. The other members of the Presidency had not even been aware this letter was being sent, and most of them furiously rejected it when it became public. The response of the UN at the time was twofold. On the one hand the secretary general, Perez de Cuellar, stated that, though the "Yugoslav crisis could seriously endanger international peace and security, the situation in the country was still its internal affair." This was a reflection of the UN's political-diplomatic-bureaucratic reasoning, whereby an "internal" crisis had to "mature politically" for the UN to get involved. On the other hand, that same month the Security Council imposed a "general and complete embargo on all deliveries of weapons and military equipment to Yugoslavia." So the UN was in fact supporting the efforts of the European Community Conference on Yugoslavia, and slowly getting itself involved.

The JNA and Serb pounding of Vukovar changed the situation to "ripe" very shortly thereafter. On 8 October 1991 the secretary general appointed Cyrus Vance, former American secretary of state, to act as his special envoy in the Yugoslav crisis. Not only did this signal that the UN was now ready to become involved; it indicated that UN involvement would again be under the general political guidance of the United States.

Vance's early efforts were hampered by three parallel considerations. First, the Conference on Yugoslavia was under way at the time, and it would not have looked good for Vance and the UN to pull the carpet from under the feet of Lord Carrington and the European Community. So Vance and Carrington announced a joint action in the search for a peaceful solution to the Yugoslav conflict. Secondly, the European Community was trying desperately to breathe life into the Western European Union, which is projected as the defence and security arm of European integration. Talk of sending WEU troops to support the EC political effort turned out to be dangerously empty, also delaying the earliest possible engagement of UN "Blue Helmets."

On the ground, the belligerents in Yugoslavia were still very much at each other, and any desire to honour a genuine cease-fire was still far away. In early November the rump Presidency of Yugoslavia did send a call for Blue Helmets to come to Yugoslavia and maintain peace in exchange for pulling federal troops out of Croatia. But the Presidency that issued this invitation was a political caricature, and its voice meant very little other than a convenient medium through which the Serbian leadership might test new proposals.

Less than two weeks after this invitation Vance met Milošević, Tudjman, and General Kadijević in Geneva. An agreement was reached on an immediate cease-fire. Each of the Yugoslav parties expressed a wish to see the speedy deployment of a UN peace-keeping operation. While progress was made on some other issues, the main one regarding a cease-fire broke down almost immediately.

The Security Council adopted a resolution only a few days later opening the door for the possible use of UN peace-keeping forces but conditional on a positive report of the special envoy. The UN was preparing the ground but being cautious and prudent, using as a possible political lure Vance's anticipated positive assessment. It was made clear that the deployment of peace-keeping forces could only be envisaged with full compliance by all parties with the Geneva Agreement.

Over subsequent weeks of intensive though low-key negotiations, the implementation of the Geneva Agreement was pursued and the general principles defined for a UN peace-keeping operation. In mid-December 1991 the Security Council passed a resolution that, while saying that the time had not yet come to send the peace-keeping force, nevertheless contained a description of a plan for possible involvement. UN involvement was *going to* take place, but the question remained how quickly all sides would run out of the desire to fight and instead allow UN troops to be stationed on the ground.

By this time the European Community had already accepted the German policy of recognizing Croatia and Slovenia as independent and sovereign states. The United Nations and the United States indicated their displeasure. So, as we have seen, did Lord Carrington. But the Germans were adamant and unyielding, and Croatia and Slovenia were thus recognized.

With that act an overall political solution became more distant but a cease-fire became more likely. The Croats with recognition lost their main reason to go on fighting and, despite a considerable loss of territory, were now ready to have UN troops as peace-keepers. The Serbs and the JNA, having also accomplished what they considered their strategic objective, the "liberation" of Serb lands in Croatia, accepted the presence of UN troops.

On 2 January 1992 Vance convened in Sarajevo a meeting between military representatives of Croatia and the JNA at which an accord on a new cease-fire was signed. This one did achieve a drastic reduction in fighting, though there were still occasional skirmishes and mutual provocations. But it allowed the UN to send a group of military liaison officers who had the task of providing good offices to secure the cease-fire and of preparing the ground for the further implementation of the Vance Plan.

The plan called for UN troops to be deployed in troubled areas on the so-called ink-blot principle, meaning that they would not patrol a definite line of cease-fire but would rather have small teams to man twenty-four hour checkpoints scattered throughout the disputed enclaves. This was a wise and necessary compromise, imposed by Vance and the UN because the Croats wanted the UN troops to be stationed on the borders of Croatia, acting as a defensive force for Croatian sovereignty, while the Serbs wanted them to control the actual cease-fire line, acting as a guarantor of their territorial gains in Croatia.

The announcement of the arrival of UN troops gave both sides an opportunity to claim victory. The Croats claimed that this would secure the implementation of their legal system over all Croatia, including the Serb enclaves. The Serbs claimed that in these areas only federal laws would apply, thus ensuring that the Serbs of Croatia would share the same country with other Serbs. In fact and according to the Vance Plan, neither was the case. The territories under the protection of the UN would have local self-rule, with both republican and federal laws suspended until a final solution was found.

The UN was also to disarm the militia and supervise the withdrawal of the JNA. This last objective led to an unpleasant if not entirely unexpected hitch in the operation. The leader of the Serbs in Krajina flatly rejected the deployment of the peace-keeping forces on these territories and in particular the disarmament of the Serb paramilitary units. He also objected to the withdrawal of the JNA and was supported in this by General Mladić, at the time the JNA commander in the area.

This delay caused considerable political embarrassment to Milošević, who until then had been the undisputed leader of Serbs all over Yugoslavia. It forced him to take the unusual step of attacking the Krajina leadership for their insensitivity to the overall Serb cause and for trying to maximize their own local political interests. Eventually Milošević had his way, engineering a vote of no confidence in the rebellious Krajina government and the installation of another, more co-operative one.

With these obstacles out of the way the special envoy and the new secretary general, Boutros Boutros-Ghali, could recommend the establishment of a United Nations Protection Force (UNPROFOR) in Yugoslavia. The UN, under strong pressure from the United States, judged that the time was right. The danger that UN peace-keepers might fail because of a lack of co-operation from any of the Yugoslav parties was seen to be less grave than the possibility that a delay in the dispatch of Blue Helmets would lead to a breakdown of the cease-fire and a new conflagration in Yugoslavia.

The new conflagration that the secretary general and the Security Council had feared was already in the making – not in Croatia, where the UN troops were headed, but in neighbouring BiH. While the UN was preparing to keep the Serbs and Croats apart in Croatia, the Serbs, Croats, and Muslims in Bosnia were on a collision course, disregarding the political solution offered by the peace conference (by now moved to Brussels), and preparing for a new stage in the violent dissolution of Yugoslavia.

The slow realization and "maturing" of political realities and their respective conversion into political and peace-keeping action had once again brought the UN to act on a crisis too late. The troops had a mandate for the Croat-Serb conflict, and it did not include the active prevention of spillovers in BiH. The UN was, of course, fully aware of the possibility of fighting in BiH, but again the situation was not "ripe."

With a thin hope of preventing the outbreak of fighting in BiH by a token gesture, the UN decided to put the headquarters for the UNPROFOR operation in Sarajevo. It was hoped and believed that the presence of the Blue Helmets and the white UN vehicles would act to calm the situation. The supporting tactical reason for the choice of Sarajevo was that this city is centrally located, which would minimize the time and expense for control and logistics. But the good intentions of the UN were not enough to stop the war in BiH. Only a few months after the installation of its headquarters in Sarajevo it was forced to withdraw, leaving, for a while, only a symbolic handful of UN troops.

The areas that were to be protected by the UN were labelled East – which meant eastern Slavonia, best known for the battle for Vukovar – West – meaning the ethnically very mixed western Slavonia – North – the Serb region just south of Zagreb where most of the genocide was committed during the Second World War – and South – the region of Krajina, where the concentration of Serbs is the highest.

By June all the UN forces were in place, taking full command of the terrain and of the process of disarming the paramilitary units. The remnants of the JNA with their heavy artillery also withdrew without incident.

The UN thus embarked on its largest peace-keeping mission in thirty years[3] and the first one ever on the European mainland. It is an extremely delicate mission, involving numerous risks, as the experience of the first eighteen months has shown. The goals of the conflicting sides are not just far apart but diametrically opposed, and the UN is between them, with an explicit mandate "not to prejudge the outcome of political negotiations for a comprehensive settlement of the Yugoslav crisis."

Tudjman and the Croats expected the presence of the UN troops to facilitate the rapid withdrawal of the JNA from Croatia. That has been accomplished. But they also expected the disarming of "Serb bandits," as they like to call the local paramilitary forces, and help in restoring Croatian jurisdiction over Serb-populated territories. All that they expected to be accomplished within a year, or at least as soon as possible.

Milošević and the nationalist Serbs, however, believed that the presence of the UN troops would cement the gains made by the Serbs of Croatia (helped generously by the JNA). The longer the UN stays, Milošević and his allies hope, the more likely it is that Serbs in Krajina will be able, through some profess of self-determination, to leave Croatia and join Serbia.

In Croatia the situation is still a long way from a solution. The UN is offering a framework for political negotiations that has not led very far. The inability of the UN to deliver on the agreement is clearly demonstrated by the practically non-existent return of mainly Croat refugees to the territories under Serb administration. In the first half of 1993, however, Croats did start to return to Sector West, held by the UN, but not to Sector East. More than a consequence of UN mediation, this seems to be a result of a secret agreement between Milõsević and Tudjman to cede to each other the respective territories.

The precarious position of the UN was clearly demonstrated in January 1993, when Croats attacked the southern flank of Krajina. The UN was powerless to stop them, just as it was powerless to stop Serbs from breaking into the depots of heavy artillery under UN control and returning the fire of the Croats. All the UN troops could do was watch from a safe distance and retake their checkpoints once fighting had stopped.

This is clearly a peace-keeping operation as long as there is willingness on all sides to keep the peace. The moment they decide otherwise, the UN can do nothing but watch and offer political mediation. But at least there is consensus among the Security Council powers about the mandate of the UN force. In that sense the involvement of the Blue Helmets in Croatia is made much easier than it eventually became in BiH.

The first appearance of the United Nations in the BiH act of the Yugoslav drama occurred through the imposition of the strictest set

of sanctions, probably, in all UN history. This was a direct consequence of the failed attempt to stop the war by "preventive recognition" of BiH. The United States insisted on this, Secretary of State
James Baker putting his personal prestige behind the concept. All
others, including Russia, supported the United States.

The United States had for a long time stayed on the sidelines,
watching the Yugoslav drama unfold. It strongly supported the idea
of European Community involvement in seeking a political solution
and the Conference on Yugoslavia that this involvement led to. However, the United States made it clear that it was keeping its options
open by not recognizing Slovenia and Croatia when the Community
did. The U.S., much more than the Europeans and certainly more
than Germany, held the Slovenes and Croats co-responsible for the
Yugoslav drama. In March 1992, in a congressional hearing, Baker
said: "Why did the war break out? Because the borders of Yugoslavia
were changed by force!" clearly putting a part of the blame on
Slovenia and Croatia for their initial action.

But the Serb and JNA attitude towards BiH and their clear desire
to repeat in this republic by sword what could not be accomplished
by word enraged the United States and Baker personally, drawing
the U.S. off the fence and into the arena. When it seemed to them
obvious that the war was about to be carried into BiH, the United
States led the Community into "preventive recognition" of BiH and
in return accepted recognition of Slovenia and Croatia. A heavy
wager was placed on this particular card, but it did not win the
desired result. The war in BiH spread like a forest fire.

The Serbs and the JNA were singled out as the main culprits, which
they were, but the sanctions imposed on them would suggest that
they were the only ones, which they were not. Serbia and Montenegro
hastily tried to put up a smokescreen by declaring a new federation
consisting of their two republics and withdrawing from BiH all JNA
personnel from the new federation. This allowed Milošević, or so he
thought, to say that the new Yugoslavia was not involved in the
conflict in BiH.

The world, and especially the United States, could not accept such
an argument. Almost all the JNA equipment remained in Bosnian
Serb hands, and they used it in a most devastating and attention-
grabbing way, almost as if they deliberately wanted to provoke opposition from everyone. And though the Croats were chipping away at
Herzegovina, it was the Serbs who felt the fury of the United States–
led world community reaction through the United Nations.

The sanctions that were imposed on the new Yugoslav federation
included almost every aspect of international relations: a trade and

oil embargo, a freezing of assets and bans on financial transactions and transport, even severing of cultural, sport, and scientific links. Diplomatic relations were also generally scaled down, with most ambassadors withdrawn from Belgrade and many Yugoslav diplomats told to leave their countries of accreditation.

The imposition of the sanctions seemed like a good idea to those proposing them, even though previous experience with sanctions[4] suggested otherwise. There was no serious cost-benefit analysis of their application, and certainly no thought at all about the situation that would develop if they did not work. Western politicians were itching to do something because of increasing media attention and public concern. Something punitive and demonstrably determined had to be done, even if it did not bring the solution closer.

More than a year of sanctions has shown that they have not brought a solution in BiH any closer. In fact there are strong arguments for the reverse, that sanctions have strengthened the hand of aggressive nationalists, and thus the drama on the ground.

As the drama of the war in BiH unfolded, and as the plight of the citizens of Sarajevo became an everyday feature in the media, pressure grew during June 1992, again primarily in and from the United States, to organize humanitarian aid and relief for the besieged city. Again the United Nations was called in to negotiate the handing over of the Sarajevo airport, to provide security for it, and to organize the transportation and delivery of the relief that started arriving on ten to twenty aircraft daily during July. That marked the beginning of the most visible and successful engagement of the UN in the Bosnian war. But even its intervention in its humanitarian, relief capacity was not without substantial problems.

As time passed and the humanitarian problems to be addressed increased, so did the hardships and the temptations of the UN troops performing their mission on the ground within a strictly limited mandate, poorly defined political objectives, and no muscle to defend them and the poorly defined political objectives. In such a situation it was inevitable that the troops would be subjected to some humiliation and the authority of the UN would be undermined.

The UN troops have often been treated as the enemy; they have been accused of taking sides; their vehicles have been stolen; they have been shot at, wounded, and even killed. On a few occasions the warring sides have masqueraded as UN peace-keepers, driving around in white vehicles with UN flags and opening fire on their opponents in order to draw fire against the UN troops. Boutros Boutros-Ghali was heckled by the citizens of Sarajevo during his brief stopover in January of 1993.

The UN suffered an attack on a convoy that was protecting the safe exit of JNA personnel from a Sarajevo barracks. Its officers watched helplessly as the deputy prime minister of the Bosnian government was murdered in cold blood while in a UN vehicle. A group of British soldiers wearing blue helmets were disarmed by Muslim mercenaries. Spanish troops were taken hostage by the Muslim civilian population of Mostar while delivering aid and were not released for several days. The Serbs shelled the French UN positions near Sarajevo for almost an hour, claiming later that a "mistake had occurred."

The United Nations was accused of getting involved in ethnic cleansing when it tried to evacuate the sick, wounded, exhausted, elderly, and children from besieged towns. It was also accused of supporting Serb strangulation of a number of cities when it reacted to the previous accusation and prevented larger-scale movements in order to preserve the ethnic situation as inherited. Not surprisingly, General Lewis MacKenzie, the UN commander from Canada and a veteran of many UN campaigns, declared that this had been by far the most difficult assignment for UN troops to date. And all this from a mandate only to secure and protect the flow of humanitarian aid! There was no peace to keep or to permit the performance of the peace-keeping function, and there was, as developments elsewhere began to show, no serious desire to get involved in peace-making.

On balance, the UN relief and humanitarian efforts will probably be judged as overwhelmingly positive. In the face of many daunting obstacles and problems, some of their own making, the UN officials, officers, and troops performed a gallant mission, saving many, many lives and relieving the suffering of hundreds of thousands of civilians on all sides. They risked and sacrificed their own lives in this bitter territorial dispute and braved unbelievably difficult conditions in order to carry out their mandate. Even when they failed, which was not often, it was not for lack of trying.

The situation is quite different when it comes to assessing the political involvement of the UN in the Bosnian act of the Yugoslav drama. The UN, as we saw, joined the EC in an attempt to find a political framework for a solution while the Conference on Yugoslavia still convened in the Hague. Later the conference moved to Brussels, London, Geneva, New York, and back to Geneva. None of these venues brought more luck or a breakthrough in the political stalemate. As time passed and the impotence of the European Community became more obvious and more embarrassing, the role of the UN gradually increased, and with it the political presence of the U.S. and Russia.

The UN took over the lead foreign political role from the European Community during the London Conference in August 1992.[5] The important political principles set forth at this conference included support for the territorial integrity of BiH; recognition by the international community that territorial gains made by force would not be honoured; and agreement on a plan of action to ensure rigorous application of sanctions against Serbia.

A series of UN Security Council resolutions followed throughout autumn 1992 further specifying the conditions of a resolution of the crisis. But no effective mechanism was developed either to stop the fighting or, more ambitiously, to resolve the crisis. The only measure that was applied was to put more and more public pressure on the rump Yugoslavia as the identified aggressor.

The Geneva Conference, co-chaired by Vance and Owen, was to find mechanisms for the implementation of the London principles. But this was not easy since the Serbs were not responding to the squeeze in the expected and desired way. Nor was there a readiness on the part of the major powers to pressure them by the use of force. The only realistic way forward that Vance and Owen saw was to soften the characterization of the Serbs as aggressors and to put in its stead the formulation "three warring factions."

Learning from the experience of the war in Croatia, Vance and Owen insisted that negotiations must concentrate on reaching a compromise political solution before hostilities could be brought to an end. This meant in effect that any side could continue or start fresh hostilities to pursue its own view of what it wanted or needed before serious talk about peace could start. The negotiations became a hostage of continuing hostilities.

In January 1993 Vance and Owen finally produced a plan that bore their name and offered it to the warring sides and the international community. The Vance-Owen Plan tried to combine the aspirations of the Muslims for a unitary state and the desire of Serbs and Croats to have the ethnic component more pronounced in future relations between the nations of BiH. The result was to be the break-up of BiH into ten units, three groups of three of which would be "dominated" by each of the ethnic groups, with Sarajevo declared an open city. All the prerogatives of the state would be maintained at the level of BiH and would be shared equally by the three communities.

The Serbs immediately rejected the plan, demanding that their war conquests be recognized. The Croats accepted the plan immediately and set out to make the situation on the ground correspond to the plan, since it was particularly generous to them, giving them three units in which they would be the lead ethnic group. The Muslims were unsatisfied, and it took some persuasion to get them to accept the plan. Surprisingly, the Americans were also extremely cool, which was a major handicap to the plan's potential for success.

By April 1993 the international community had managed to organize itself to put final pressure on the Muslims and Milošević to accept the plan. President Clinton threatened military involvement, and Boris Yeltsin, fighting his own battles for survival in Russia, told the Serbs that they could not count on Russia in their further deliberate provocations.

Milošević yielded and accepted the plan, but then the Serbs of Bosnia, led by Karadjić and Mladić, decided to stand firm in spite of pressure from all sides, including Serbia and Milošević.[6] They did not blink in the face of the u.s.-un threat. Obviously, they became heroes in the eyes of most Serbs. The Vance-Owen Plan was dead for all practical purposes. In the meantime, Vance resigned and the former Norwegian minister of foreign affairs, Torval Stoltenberg, was appointed the un's special envoy.

While the new team of mediators went back to the drawing-board, the un Security Council committed itself to the protection of five "safe havens" in BiH. Five countries – the u.s., France, Russia, the uk, and Spain – proposed to put troops on the ground with a mandate to protect these areas with heavy armament and air support. While the merits of this idea were as usual endlessly debated, the mediators came back with a new plan.

The new plan that Owen and Stoltenberg designed and presented in August 1993 resembled the old European Community plan of March 1992, which the Muslims had rejected. It called for the creation of a Union of States in Bosnia, the states being made up along ethnic lines. Sarajevo and Mostar were to be administered by the un and ec respectively for a period of two years. The State of Bosnia would have only symbolic prerogatives, with all real power residing in the ethnic republics composing it. Bosnian Serbs would be given control over 52 per cent of the territory, the Croats over 18 per cent, and the Muslims over the remaining 30 per cent. The plan called for at least fifty thousand un troops to enforce it on the ground. The Muslims rejected the plan again, and the future course of events is unclear.

The failure of both the European Community and the un to mediate a political solution can be traced to a number of internal weaknesses. Paramount among them was the absence of a clear idea of what was to be done, what, other than the defence of principles, was in it for the international community. Principles and moral outrage simply proved insufficient to generate an effective policy.

Though there was no strategic conflict over the territory of former Yugoslavia, there were nevertheless sufficient divergences in the particular interests of certain nations (Germany, the u.s., Greece, Russia,

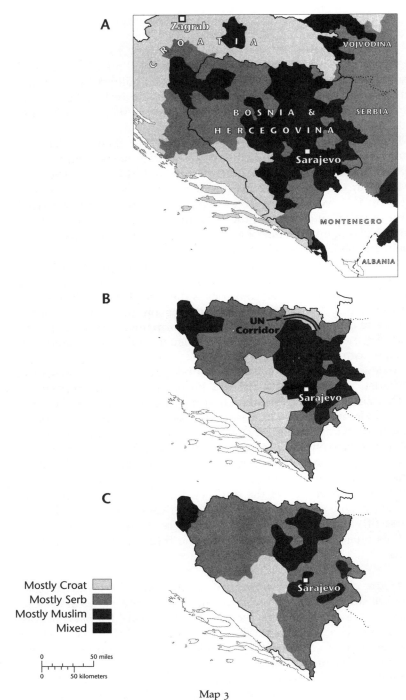

Mostly Croat
Mostly Serb
Mostly Muslim
Mixed

0   50 miles
0   50 kilometers

Map 3
A   the ethnic mix in Bosnia before the war;
B   the division of Bosnia according to the Vance-Owen Plan;
C   the division of Bosnia according to the Owen-Stoltenberg Plan

France, the UK) to prevent a strong common voice and to reduce the UN's scope for action, just as they had previously reduced the scope of the EC, to the least common denominator.

American policy alternated between taking the initiative and following the Europeans. The Americans could not decide whether to take over decisively an issue that was primarily European. Neither could the Europeans. They wanted American muscle, but they also wanted to have the final political say, since this was a European affair. In this tactical waltz of who was to lead and who to follow, both time and valuable initiatives were lost as the situation on the ground rapidly moved from bad to worse. The credibility of the UN, under whose aegis all this was happening, took a pounding.

So did the credibility of NATO, since this Western alliance could not come up with a common strategy that would renew and broaden its mandate, at the same time addressing a burning security issue. And Yugoslavia had long since become such an issue, raising the possibility that two of NATO's southern-flank members – Greece and Turkey – might become embroiled in the spreading violence.

Russia tried to act constructively, at times putting pressure on the Serbs, for whom the Russians were known to have a special understanding. Russian foreign minister Andrej Kozyrev asked that no action be taken without first seeking the approval of the Russians. But this was probably more the reflection of a desire to revive Russia's great-power status than evidence of a special plan or special interests that were opposed to the West. For once in a crisis situation it was not the difference between Russia and the West but difference and confusion in the ranks of the West that lead to the stop-and-go action and a great deal of inaction.

The lack of a clear-cut political goal and objective also meant that there would be confusion over the issue of the use of force in implementing the political solution. From very early in the war there have been calls for the UN to get involved in peace-making, which is to say to use force for a political settlement. This call could most often be heard from the president of BiH, Alija Izetbegović, but not only from him. Tudjman and the Croats called for a UN war against the Serbs. So did the "neutral" Austrians and the Germans, whose constitutions forbade them to send their own soldiers and who were in effect asking others to fight for what they believed was the right way out. Later on and rather ominously the Turks, who have spent centuries fighting in the Balkans, also called for an armed peace-keeping intervention in Bosnia to stop the bleeding of the Muslim population there. They also offered troops.

Gradually the call to resort to arms in imposing a settlement captured the imagination of several well-known commentators and political analysts. By May 1992 the number of voices asking for a "Mountain Storm," suggesting a sequel to the most successful operation of the United Nations (under u.s. leadership) to date, had increased considerably. Bill Clinton, as a candidate in the American presidential elections, also implied that if elected he would not shy away from using some kind of force to help find a political solution.

At the beginning of 1993 Baroness Thatcher, the former British prime minister also known as the "Iron Lady," made the strongest and most passionate plea coming from any acting or retired statesperson. She, of course, pleaded for the use of arms. While her plea went far in demonstrating how irritating and infuriating the situation is, she, like many others, made no suggestion about what the armed intervention should achieve other than the panacea of doing something. Nor did she address the question of how anything achieved could be maintained in the quagmire of aggressive nationalist confrontations.

Dick Cheney, at the time the American secretary of defense, was quoted in December 1992 as saying: "If we had two hundred thousand troops on the ground in Bosnia, I'm not sure what I would tell them to do." Five months later, when the UN was faced with the failure of the Vance-Owen Plan, Field Marshal Sir Richard Vincent of NATO told the political leaders: "For God's sake, decide what you want to achieve before you tell us to go out there and do it."

Western leaders, in public and in private, admit that they have been torn by the dilemma to use force or not. The public pressure to do *something* would suggest the use of their one obvious advantage, overwhelming military power. But given the complexity of the operation, over and above the lack of a clear objective, the size of the operation would be immense if it were to be a true peace-making and then a peace-keeping effort. As is often the case, governments pressed to act by their own constituencies shy away from doing so when the cost becomes clear. Furthermore, there is no guarantee that fighting will not continue and peace-keepers will not be killed in larger numbers. If that happened, the same public opinion that urged that something be done would then rally round the call to bring the boys back home.

Many governments have thus come to the conclusion that making and then keeping peace in BiH would be a tall order with relatively little strategic benefit and full of political risk. They are reluctant to become heavily involved. While there are compelling reasons to step in, they find it difficult to see how they could avoid probable failure, failure being defined as a prolonged and costly presence in Bosnia, combined with the loss of lives of peacemakers and an uncertain impact on the situation.

There has also been talk of a much less costly, limited, "surgical," precisely controlled operation designed to knock out the heavy artillery, tanks, and aircraft. In fact, most advocates of the use of military force actually favour this type of intervention. But here the Europeans (Britain, France, and Spain) and the Americans have been incapable of agreeing. The argument for not using limited military power has been that it would jeopardize the aid and relief efforts of the UN and would put UN troops on the ground in danger of retaliation. An additional argument is that while such a strike would certainly reduce the war toll in Bosnia, it would not stop the war. Efforts have to be directed towards a complete and not a partial solution.

Illustrative of this dilemma over the use of force is the whole debate over the so-called no-fly zone. It took almost two months for the UN to pass a resolution in October 1992 declaring that a no-fly zone was in existence. It took another five months to pass a resolution that gave teeth to this resolution. NATO aircraft started patrolling the skies over BiH only in April 1993. Not that that made much difference, since air-power was never the decisive element in the war. If the no-fly zone was meant to be a message to the Serbs and Croats engaged in partitioning BiH, it was completely lost on them.

But how do you use any kind of force in a situation where the winner is ruthless nationalism on all three sides and the lost are the principles and practices of civilized and democratic conduct, again on all three sides? If a forced substitution of objectives is made and, instead of defending civilized principles of conduct, interventionist forces try to contain the three ethnic groups in their respective territories, this will amount to an open admission that nationalism has won and ethnic cleansing has been legitimized. It is a difficult, no-win situation that can only be solved in the broader context to be discussed in the last chapter.

What seems certain at this time is that the United Nations will indefinitely continue to provide the badly needed humanitarian aid and relief. The Blue Helmets could also come in larger numbers to monitor the Owen-Stoltenberg Plan if it is accepted by all sides, which does not seem very likely at the moment. Though insufficient and frustrating, this seems to be the most that UN troops and personnel can do without a quantum leap in political thinking about collective security. And that does not seem to be quick in coming.

PART FOUR

The Final Curtain

CHAPTER FIFTEEN

Drawing the Threads Together

On 27 April 1992 the Socialist Federative Republic of Yugoslavia, also referred to as the Second Yugoslavia, definitely ceased to exist. One by one the republics had left it. At that moment Slovenia was completely removed, making progress towards economic recovery and consolidating its newly created democracy. Croatia had gained independence but was still waiting for a lasting political solution, with UN troops on its territory monitoring a shaky peace. Bosnia and Herzegovina was being torn apart by a violent war though it had gained international recognition. Macedonia, surrounded by hostile neighbours, was not at war but was unable to overcome Greek objections to the use of its name in its quest for international recognition.

On that day Serbia and Montenegro proclaimed a new Federal Republic of Yugoslavia, hoping that the continued use of the name would place it in the privileged position of natural successor to the previous Yugoslavia in international relations and institutions. Given their implication in the war in BiH, however, that seems doubtful, and these two republics faced an uphill international battle for recognition.

But was that the date of the end of Yugoslavia, or did the end occur much earlier? When does a state stop functioning as such? The conclusion of the Arbitration Commission of the European Community Conference on Yugoslavia that "Yugoslavia as a state is in a state of dissolution" (December 1991) had been true for a long time, long before this pronouncement was made as an answer to the issue of succession of states. Yugoslavia has been in a state of dissolution from the moment aggressive nationalism inherited and revised the Communist legacy. Even before there were cracks appearing that, unattended, slowly spread until the whole structure began to crumble.

It could be argued that Yugoslavia was no longer a state in the real sense of the word at the time the first republics passed constitutions that were not in conformity with the constitution of Yugoslavia. A further blow occurred when the republics started withholding money belonging to the federation and, worse, printing money of their own. The federal state was hollow and helpless when the republics declared boycotts of goods originating in the others and additional taxes on the products, services, or property of citizens from other republics. All this and much more happened before the *de facto* and *de jure* recognition of states that wanted to leave this increasingly unhappy federation.

By a series of mutually reinforcing events the negative spiral of destruction was set in motion, leading finally to the termination of the state, the first such case in modern times in Europe[1] but not the only one. Since then the USSR has dissolved, as has the Czech and Slovak federation.

The first important conclusion to be drawn is that there is no one single cause or explanation for the Yugoslav drama. Some of the explanations that have been offered in this book and elsewhere include the national and other complexities that lie in the foundation of Yugoslavia, Serbian domination of the country in the inter-war period, the traumas of the conflicts during the Second World War, the considerable economic differences among republics, Tito's particular formula for holding the federation together, the new waves of aggressive nationalism led by former Communists like Milošević and Tudjman, and the confused state of collective security after the ending of the Cold War. As in a test with multiple-choice answers, the correct choice is: all of the above.

This analysis has tried to show that dissolution, with its tragic war and massive destruction, happened as a result of a myriad of forces and events as well as mutually linked disruptive moves. The dissolution was a long process leading to a crisis that in turn speeded up the separation. It would be extremely difficult to judge at such close historical quarters, as events are still unfolding, when the point of no return was reached. The choice made in this analysis of the period and events that set in motion the final crisis is, as has been admitted, somewhat arbitrary. Perhaps the inevitable was set in motion before; perhaps Yugoslavia could still have been preserved even later.

This analysis should also show that the destruction of Yugoslavia was not inevitable. To put it a little differently, Yugoslavia was not an artificial creation destined to disintegrate once the authoritarian power that held it together was no longer there.

An important argument for this contention lies in the fact that it was created *twice* and that in both cases the opposition, external and internal, to its creation was symbolic, while the political forces in favour were overwhelming. In spite of the disappointments of the inter-war years and in spite of the tragedy of ethnic confrontations during the Second World War, the nations of Yugoslavia, led by Tito and his partisans, came together again.

Under Tito, Yugoslavia created a unique system, believing it to be a viable alternative. For a long time it not only looked that way but in fact it was. Tito, the subject of enormous criticism and some admiration in the country he left behind, was a masterful politician. He managed to conceal all his personal weaknesses, but even more importantly he managed to conceal the weaknesses of the system he created. His quest for power was stronger than his loyalty or fear of the USSR, and he was clever enough to let the West pay the price. By providing his population with a reasonable standard of living and the possibility of liberal travel, he reduced opposition to the regime to a few intellectuals in permanent protest. The massive social resistance characteristic of other ex-socialist countries never occurred in Yugoslavia.

But there were a number of significant negative elements in the political dynamics Tito promoted. The system, though more open and liberal than the Soviet alternative, was far from democratic. This caused serious problems in the transition to the post-Tito era. Tito personally stopped the economic reforms of the mid-sixties and removed the Serbian liberals in the early seventies, afraid that the Communist hold on power was endangered. That was the first real but lost opportunity to change the course of events. It was also a blow to the Serbs.

He then gave his blessing to the 1974 constitution, which made Yugoslavia a confederal federation. Yugoslavia and the republics were all states at the same time. Which were the citizens to prefer: Yugoslavia or the republics? This arrangement made the separation of the republics, once nationalism started, that much easier. Yugoslavia could not be constructed and held together on the "fear of Yugoslavia." The constitution of 1974 expressed that fear.

Serbia was also reduced in political status to a second-rate republic in Yugoslavia when two of its provinces were promoted to federal units. This was a second blow to the Serbs. It is little wonder then that they wanted to redress the (con)federal political arrangement. They were justified in their grievances, but their objective was set too high and the method they chose was the worst possible.

After Tito, inertia set in. The loss of political dynamics created internal pressures, economic, political, and finally ethnic. An incompetent leadership did not read these pressures as a clear warning for a new round of progressive dynamics but concentrated efforts on small tactical shifts within the existing structure. A second opportunity to move naturally and gradually towards a democratic and economically viable system was lost.

Beneath these small and apparently insignificant changes a dramatic balance of political intentions occurred. Instead of all efforts being directed towards maintaining the viability of Yugoslavia, suddenly the main emphasis was placed on securing a better position *within* Yugoslavia. In the absence of positive and progressive political dynamics, this had to be perceived as a zero-sum game (the gain of one being the loss of the other), and the logic of the situation became increasingly confrontational. The immediately available political tool in this game was to exploit differences. But since the differences in Tito's Yugoslavia had been made smaller not only in propaganda but in fact, now the reverse had to be practised: make the differences stand out, and when that is not enough, blow them up and out of all proportion through aggressive propaganda.

It should be noted that before the crisis broke out, no political force in Yugoslavia, not even the Slovenes, considered the maintenance of Yugoslavia an impossibility. The objective was to change it. This would seem to suggest that integrationist forces within Yugoslavia were indeed strong and a split was not imminent. But these were weakening by the day and with each irresponsible action of the political elite.

Since nobody at that stage challenged Yugoslavia as such, the logical course of action was to proclaim ones's own interpretation of Yugoslavia the only correct one and simultaneously to accuse the other side of being anti-Yugoslav. Tolerance – conceived of as the ability to live with differences – was an early victim. Political actions grew manifestly contrary to the logic of life in a common state. Instead of identifying a commonality of interests, energy was increasingly used to point out, even create differences. The complex Yugoslav state could never be made operational by suppressing or ignoring the differences. But it gradually became totally dysfunctional because the differences were interpreted politically as plots, conspiracies of the "other" side. In the end they were deliberately tied to the national issue, even when there was no cause to do so.

It would be wrong to say that the new nationalist leaders invented the problems that led to the dissolution of Yugoslavia. The raw elements of possible dissolution were there. But they amplified them by their choice of method. As in uncontrolled fusion they brought the elements together, creating a critical mass for the explosion. Unable and unprepared to deal with the issues in a democratic and civilized manner, they resorted to aggressive nationalism. Their personal style, to which unfortunately too few objected and which many applauded, was commanding and arrogant, incompatible with tolerance and negotiation. Given such a style and such an attitude, each and every problem became unsolvable; disagreement turned to conflict and conflict to war.

The new leaders of the republics in Yugoslavia totally disregarded Hume's common-sense principle that the state will be that much more stable and that much closer to its natural equilibrium the more it relies on agreement and the less it uses force. The Yugoslav drama shows, among other things, how easily common sense can break down. In the end, all it took was a few unscrupulous men to stir up hatreds.

Serbian aggressive nationalism bears the greatest, though not exclusive responsibility for the tragic outcome. Serbia needed Yugoslavia the most. It was an arrangement by which all Serbs could live in one country. Therefore, in the long run Yugoslavia's destruction could also mean that Serbs will be the war's biggest losers, in spite of what some, and certainly the nationalist leaders of Serbia, Bosnia, and Krajina, consider a string of victories.

This account has demonstrated that in the historical cycle of Communism the "original sin" was committed *against* the Serbs, not *by* the Serbs. The Serbian leadership, lacking the vision of their liberal predecessors from the sixties, did not choose to correct the wrongs through the democratization of their society. Subsequently the Serbs moved into the role of aggressor, and by any fair measure they have now punished the others many times over for what befell them. They have also severely punished themselves. This, of course, does not excuse what the Serbs have done or what they are doing. It merely suggests that the Serbs had grievances and security worries that had to be taken into account, and still do.

It can be argued convincingly that Serbia had no clear strategy as events unravelled. The strategic aim of the Memorandum of the Serbian Academy was not entirely clear. It was obvious, though, that improvement of the position of the Serbs in the Yugoslav context was the primary objective. There was no specific reference in the Memorandum to the destruction of Yugoslavia, but neither was there insistence that Yugoslavia had to be preserved.

The feeling one gets after reading the Memorandum is that the Serb question is *above* the Yugoslav question and not *a part* of it.

Therefore Yugoslavia, though not necessarily undesirable, was dispensable if it stood in the way. Serbia's implicit fall-back position at the beginning of the crisis was the expectation of making a Greater Serbia on the ruins of Yugoslavia. And if that failed, though few for a second stopped to think that it might, there was still the fall-back position of inheriting a rump Yugoslavia.

In the end, Yugoslavia was destroyed. What the aggressive nationalists now have is a rump, smaller and sometimes labelled "Third Yugoslavia." Greater Serbia has not been created, though it is not entirely out of reach. But already the cost of such a project has become horrendous, and the rump Yugoslavia is faced with many problems from within.

The confusion about goals – if not a whole Yugoslavia, then Greater Serbia, or at least a rump Yugoslavia – was followed by confusion in the choice of means to achieve them. The simplistic logic that these three goals were, like Russian dolls, contained one in the other, proved to be wrong and very costly. These goals were mutually exclusive and each one required a different tactic. Because of this confusion and in the midst of it Serbia found itself in a war, pulling others in as well.

The end result could very well be that, without losing on the battlefield, Serbia could lose practically everything it wanted to achieve by force, gaining in the process only a negative image and making its reintegration into the international community of nations that much more difficult. As a political commentator in Belgrade put it: "From victory to victory to final defeat."

So why did the Serbs act in this way? Earlier on, we saw that the Serbs, unlike some other ethnic groups, had gone through the entire process of national awakening and successfully crowned it with the creation of an independent state. So it was obviously not a case of full-fledged awakening and maturing of national feelings. The Serbs had already accomplished that. Yet the speed with which national sentiment mushroomed does suggest that the maturing of Serbian nationalism was not complete and that in some ways it was provoked by arrangements in the former Yugoslavia.

These issues and aggravations could have been handled differently had the whole political structure in Yugoslavia been more democratic and had they reflected as well as respected the variety of interests. It was and did not. Rather than wait for fuller democratization, which would have brought all the nations of Yugoslavia into a different and democratic political mode, Serbia chose to press the national issue forcefully.

The reading of the Serbian power elite was that it was time, now or never, to take an aggressive stance. The confusion in Yugoslavia and even more the confusion in post–Cold War Europe offered an ideal opportunity. The Serbian leadership felt that an expansionist national ideology similar to those of the nineteenth century would yield the same results they did then. Either Yugoslavia would listen to them, or the country would be broken up and a new one formed that would draw all Serbs into one state by changing the borders.

Milošević himself placed his immense popularity and charisma in the service of this nationalist drive, calculating that it would bring him into a position of power and hold him there. Nationalism for him, like Communism previously, was not an ideological program but an instrument of power. Aggressive nationalism was deliberately whipped up as a way of attaining and keeping power. And Milošević was on top of this process.

An expansionist nationalist platform was combined with unyielding and uncompromising tactics. Milošević led the political battle aggressively, saying, like Pompeii two thousand years before him, that anybody who was not with him was against him. That is why all the republics eventually left Serb-dominated Yugoslavia. Even tiny Montenegro at one point almost joined the ranks of those leaving. It should be recollected that Caesar, in defeating Pompeii, adopted a policy of considering all those who were not against him to be *with* him. A similar attitude from Milošević could have saved Yugoslavia and certainly achieved better results for the Serbs.

Milošević became the undisputed leader of Serbia with a tremendous concentration of power. The opposition was weak and in many ways much closer to Milošević than they would have liked to admit. The common denominator was a national program to save the Serb spirit. Any opposition not containing this position in its platform was easily branded and perceived to be a national traitor. When Milošević reduced the Serbian national question to a question of war and peace, large segments of the opposition helped him, often stepping ahead of his "red nationalism" with their "black nationalism." This created political leaders like "Duke Šešelj," a declared Chetnik. Nobody took him seriously in the beginning. Today he is the most influential politician in Serbia after Milošević.

Milošević had his best chance of going down in history as a saviour of Serbs in 1989. At the pinnacle of his power, having redressed the political balance in Serbia, he had an opportunity to lead the way into a democratic and pluralistic society, at the same time conducting a diplomatic offensive in the world for the cause of Serbs outside of

Serbia. He did neither, but relied instead on the national unity process that he had set in motion. But national unity for the Serbs brought as a consequence the same for the other nations of Yugoslavia, thus making a political solution less possible.

Milošević and his strategists possibly and quite probably factored this into their calculations. It would have been extremely naïve to think that only Serbs were entitled to a national awakening (for a second time) or that only they were capable of it. But what they probably also considered as a decisive element was the *size* of Serbia, the *number* of Serbs, and the fact that they were the first to start the process, thus catching the others unprepared. With some bullying and intimidation, small and frightened opponents would be scared into submission. If war was to break out, Serbs again felt that they would win it. They were sure that the JNA would perform as their striking power, for which the Croats and others were no match.

It has been said that Milošević was the first to discover that Tito was politically dead. That was a necessary but not a sufficient precondition for what followed. The other pre-condition, without which things would not have gone the way they have, was the willingness of the Serbs to be aggressively nationalistic, tough, and unyielding. Serbia as a whole thus deliberately chose to behave in Yugoslavia like a bull in a china shop.

This lack of political vision and of desire to solve problems by compromise was coupled with the fact that Serbia was politically insensitive, very slow to recognize the development of realities, and completely unconcerned about its image. Milošević liked to say: "The truth is on our side, the truth will win, and there is no need to convince anybody that we are right." The Serbs have shown themselves incapable of conveying the reasons for their grievances. Their explanations have been defensive and propagandist. Little wonder that most of the public elsewhere perceive them as vicious and obstinate.

Often at least one step behind, and always acting under pressure, Serbia helped its adversaries by contributing to its own poor image. For example, the Serbs, with their destruction of Vukovar and bombardment of Dubrovnik, actually contributed much more to the recognition of Croatia than the political pressures of German Chancellor Kohl or foreign minister Genscher.

One example will serve to illustrate the slowness with which Serbian political thinking adjusted to political realities: the Serbs accepted the idea of an "asymmetrical federation" in The Hague in October 1991, almost two years after the Slovenes first proposed this idea and the Serbs angrily rejected it. Yet another example: the Serbs were the last to carry out multi-party elections though they were well positioned to be the first and thus gain the image of leaders in a process that was inevitable, instead of the image of latter-day Communists.

The Serbs also turned quickly to force at moments when other methods would have been far more appropriate and fruitful for their cause. When the Slovenes and Croats declared their independence, the international principles of the situation as well as the positions of the main outside actors were still very much in favour of the unity of Yugoslavia. Instead of bringing the attention of Europe and the world to the violation of CSCE principles by Slovenia and Croatia, and especially the human-rights violations of Croatia against its Serb population, Serbia was immediately ready and even eager to take the law into its own hands and defend its brethren from genocide by redrawing borders.

The crucial turning-point that ultimately led to war occurred after the elections in Slovenia, Croatia, and Macedonia, when it became clear that domination was no longer possible in a united Yugoslavia. Thereupon, Serbian nationalism revised its goals. Slovenia was given up. The JNA intervention in Slovenia was led in such a way that this "week-end" war would be lost. The likely aim was to compromise the government of Ante Marković in the eyes of the international public. But a further aim, as later became clear, was to enable the dismissal of the top officer corps in JNA, who still felt themselves to be Yugoslavs and were not sufficiently Serbian.

It was the undeclared war that Serbia waged against the others, always claiming that Serbia was not involved (and that all they were doing was loyally securing the functioning of the federation and the JNA), that ultimately tipped the scales against Serbia. Again Serbia was slow to realize that the war was not only against Croats, or Slovenes, or Muslims, but against the basic principles of modern-day security arrangements in Europe and that Europe, joined by the United States and *even* Russia, would have to act to defend those principles.

However, in one element of their strategic calculation the Serbian leadership has so far been proved right. They calculated that the confusion over security in Europe, the lack of clear leadership, and the lack of precedent in this type of crisis management would give them a free hand to accomplish their aims without severe punitive measures.

The sanctions imposed on Serbia and Montenegro on 30 May 1992 have in the course of the last fifteen months made life in the rump Yugoslavia extremely difficult. Foreign products are in short supply;

hard currency reserves are depleted; many factories have stopped working for lack of raw materials or spare parts; unemployment has more than doubled; inflation at last count was running at about 3 per cent per hour – in short, a total economic disaster. To be sure, not all of these problems are to be attributed to sanctions, but sanctions have played an important part in the economic collapse of Serbia.

However, sanctions did not and in all likelihood will not yield the results at which they aimed. Instead of putting pressure on the regime to adopt more democratic and less aggressive ways, they have actually contributed to Milošević's hold on power. When the sanctions were implemented, no one bothered to explore what would happen if the Serbian economic collapsed without previously generating the desired democratic pressure on Milošević.

In Serbia sanctions are perceived as an unjust and unfair reaction of the world to Serbia's very just demands. In large part this is due to the superior brain-washing capabilities of regime-controlled media. But it is also due to the fact that the world has thus far largely ignored authentic Serbian grievances. The sense of injustice, which Milošević has played on extremely well, gives rise to a peculiarly strong feature of Serbian national spirit. It is called *inat*. It means "stubborn spite," which is connected with disregard for one's own interests. But it also has something to do with pride and dignity.

No serious political opposition to Milošević has resulted from the sanctions and other forms of pressure applied by the international community. For a while it looked as if the Serbian-born American businessman Milan Panić might shake up Milošević, but that did not happen. Milošević invited Panić to be prime minister of the "new Yugoslavia" in June 1992. His aim was to deflect some of the effect of the sanctions through a person who had easy access to power in the West, most notably in the American State Department. From being utterly pliant when he first arrived, Panić turned into Milošević's most formidable challenger. The presidential elections held in December 1992 gave Panić a respectable 36 per cent of the vote.

His program was liberal: he advocated an end to the war in BiH and the return of Yugoslavia to the international community of nations. With more and better support from the West and with the Albanian votes of Kosovo he might have unseated Milošević. It is useless to argue that he would have won more votes in a fair election, since that variable was entirely controlled by Milošević.

At the same time Panić became prime minister, Milošević managed to convince Dobrica Ćosić, the undisputed ideologue and creator of the new wave of Serbian nationalism, to take the office of president of Yugoslavia. That secured Milošević's hold on power even more because Ćosić commanded great respect in the opposition. "Serbian national unity in times of hardship" was his appeal.

A year later, almost to the day, Milošević dismissed Ćosić, engineering a vote of no confidence in the Yugoslav parliament. Ćosić had become too independent, and though a true Serbian nationalist, he had become "soft" and ready to compromise. His ouster in June 1993 gave Milošević the ideal opportunity to jail and for all practical purposes politically liquidate another prominent leader of the Serbian opposition, Vuk Drašković. Acting emotionally and irrationally, Drašković "violated the law" just enough to permit Milošević to have him arrested. The rest of the opposition split over whether to defend Drašković or to blame him for breaking opposition ranks and acting on his own, thus compromising a serious plan to demonstrate against Ćosić's ouster.

At the beginning of autumn 1993 Milošević is very much in command. The only other political figure of any significance in Serbia is the extreme right-wing "Duke Šešelj,"[2] who was instrumental in ousting Ćosić. Sometimes dismissed as a "nut case," he is a hardline radical politician who commands a third of the vote in the Serbian parliament. Initially a creation of Milošević, who wanted Šešelj to split the ranks of the opposition, he now has considerable power and has become an unavoidable factor in Milošević's policy calculations. He applies pressuring towards extremism and radical solutions even when Milošević would take a more moderate course of action. Milošević has effectively become a prisoner of the nationalistic genie that he set loose. Nothing reflects this better than the influence of Šešelj in Serbia and Karadjić in BiH.

The Croatian, and more especially the Slovenian position during the unravelling of the crisis was not to attempt to contain the aggressiveness of Serbian nationalism within the framework of a more democratic Yugoslavia. The lack of democratic institutions, traditions, and an institutionalized plurality of interest was not Serbia's handicap alone. All of former Yugoslavia suffered a democratic deficit.

It cannot be denied that for a time there was a sincere attempt by the Slovenes to open a political dialogue within the Yugoslav framework. But their position was also one of radical expectations and unwillingness to seek a compromise. They scored public-relations points by constantly pretending to be promoting democratic initiatives, at the same time making sure that none of their nationalist aims was in any way compromised.

The best example of this was their constant blocking of free and democratic multi-party elections at the federal level. The Slovenian voters were not to be allowed to create a new multi-party democracy as citizens of Yugoslavia, only as citizens of a national republic. The moment voters cast their votes as citizens of republics and *only* citizens of republics, they objectively, and independently of their will and desire, ceased to be interested citizens of Yugoslavia. This was the Slovenian contribution par excellence to the destruction of Yugoslavia.

They and the Croats decided to gamble even if this meant confronting the aggressive Serbian position. There are good reasons to believe that they actually wished to provoke an armed confrontation, sensing that this would tip the scale of world opinion in their favour, making it easier to reach their objective – independence.

If a Serbian national awakening had born fruit in an independent state in the past, the Slovene and Croats had had no such experience. Therefore, in their case it could be said that an authentic element of national awakening was involved. Prompted by an aggressive Serbian nationalist posture, the Slovenian and Croatian reaction was predictably aggressive also.

The Croatian national leadership was particularly sensitive to the issue of the future of Yugoslavia. A more moderate response to Serbian nationalism and a policy more attuned to the grievances of Serbs in Croatia might have avoided the worst. But the Croatian national awakening also went to extremes, so much so that the republic never bothered to disassociate itself from the Ustashi regime. Even today, well over two years after the birth of the "new and democratic Croatia," this former republic of Yugoslavia has not settled its account with the past. With the Communist past, yes, many times over. But with the dark period of the Ustashi regime, not in the least.

Lately there has been mounting opposition to Tudjman and his nationalistic Croatian Democratic Alliance. Though the opposition largely shares the view of the regime on questions about Croatian sovereignty and territory, they have made clear attempts to embrace democratic values, among other things, by disassociating themselves and breaking away from the notorious war-time regime.

It can be said that the Serbs loaded the gun but the Slovenes and Croats actually fired the first shot at Yugoslavia. And what was the war about? Mostly about *borders*! It was not a war of ideological differences, certainly not a war about the human and civil rights of the oppressed. Initially it was also not a war of national hatred. The Slovenes wanted to redraw the borders of Yugoslavia, breaking away from it unilaterally. The Croats wanted to secure the borders inherited from Tito's Yugoslavia, which included a large Serb minority. The Serbs wanted to change the borders drawn rather arbitrarily and administratively at the end of the Second World War so they could accomplish the Serbian national goal – all Serbs in one country. The Muslims fought to preserve a state for themselves. But so much hatred, such a bloody confrontation, so much destruction? If they could not live together, why did the ethnic groups of Yugoslavia not separate peacefully, as did the constituent groups in the Czech and Slovak republic, which offered a model for peaceful divorce?

They could not separate peacefully because they were not led by democratic ideas, ideals, and institutions. Rather, they were lead by aggressive national-chauvinist "patriots." Their mutually antagonistic national plans had large areas of overlap. The ambitions of one could not be attained in any way except by forcing the other side to submit. This had to lead to conflict and war.

Now that the tensions and war have started, they must be continued. The leaders have built their political supremacy in their respective nations on concern for their own nation and defence against the other, aggressive ones. Abandoning a national-chauvinist platform at this stage would be suicidal since other concerns of citizens could and would emerge, making nationalistic stands redundant.

Hatred was used as an instrument to galvanize the population of respective nations to achieve concrete objectives. Irrational means, such as aggressive and aggrandizing nationalism, were abused to secure very definite and rational ends, no matter how objectionable these ends might be. The results were to be attained even if this meant open confrontation.

And the Yugoslav nations went at each other brutally. The consequences of the first two years of fighting are disastrous and tragic in many ways. There are many victims and many types of victim in this war. Individually, the best-known victim is the state of Yugoslavia, which effectively ceased to exist because of the war. If there is some doubt about the possibility that the Yugoslav republics might have coexisted had the war not taken place, no one inside or outside of Yugoslavia now doubts that the fighting effectively and rapidly brought an end to this country.

Most tragic is the loss of human lives and the injuries sustained by the innocent civilian population caught in the cross-fire and frenzy of nationalist hatreds and the indiscriminate use of heavy weapons. No one knows the precise figures of those killed and wounded to date. The fighting continues. Reports on casualties are unreliable because each side has a desire to conceal the true magnitude of its own losses and exaggerate those of the other. In the short war in Slovenia there were about sixty dead. In Croatia the estimates range between six and thirty thousand dead and between twenty-five and a hundred thousand wounded. In BiH the eighteen months of fighting have caused the deaths of anywhere between a hundred and fifty and two hundred thousand. The number of wounded is in excess of a hundred thousand. The refugees and displaced persons in former Yugoslavia are estimated at two and a half to three million.

Even the lower of these estimates, which are not necessarily more likely to be true, illustrate a vicious and destructive force that was let loose among people who only a decade ago lived in harmony. Now they are involved in a bitter struggle, often descending to bestiality difficult to comprehend and impossible to accept in our times. Yet Serbs, Croats, and Muslims were numbed into acceptance by the massive propaganda effort falling, often, on fertile soil. The insidious design of the nationalist leaders was to draw the average citizen into the web of complicity, and subsequently to enhance his or her dependence on the national leadership by warning that the other side was out to destroy the most important ingredient of a nation – the national spirit. Unfortunately, it worked.

An important victim of the war was the trust that existed among the nationalities of Yugoslavia. Now there is in its place deep mistrust, even hatred. This is particularly true of those parts of Yugoslavia where the ethnic mix pitted neighbour against neighbour in the same village, street, or apartment house.

The infrastructure, the houses, hotels, factories, and bridges, will gradually be rebuilt. Once the fighting stops, people will turn to productive endeavour. The big question remains: will the bridges that have been destroyed between people and nations ever be regenerated? The length of time and type of forces that were necessary ultimately to destroy them prove rather convincingly that Yugoslavia was not, as some would have it, a hodgepodge of nationalities kept together by terror. Terror was the force that did away with Yugoslavia, not the one that held it together.

The tragic and violent internal destruction of Yugoslavia occurred in parallel with the ending of the Cold War and the gains to collective security expected therefrom. In the meantime nations have learned that the post–Cold War world is not as tranquil as expected, and hoped. But the Yugoslav crisis, and then the war, were the first clear indications of possible security problems. They were also a clear indication of the unpreparedness of the West to meet the challenges of post–Cold War and regional crises in Europe.

Yugoslavia thus became a laboratory for new collective security arrangements. There was much experimentation, but nothing seemed to work and some of the unsuccessful tries, such as the premature recognition of Croatia and later Bosnia, brought more harm than good. A paradox of the Yugoslav drama has been that Western governments doing the minimum allowed by the least common denominator actually became more and more deeply involved.

As the fighting progressed from Slovenia to Croatia and then to BiH, it demonstrated with frightening clarity that the world at present has no effective way to stop this kind of war. To stop the fighting would have required a combination of armed force, political authority, and a determination that was just not there. The European Community, which first took charge of the situation, had no armed forces, a political authority that was still in the making, and a determination that was seriously compromised from within by the different interests of its major member-countries.

The determination of the EC was finally enforced by the Germans, with many of the others following more or less reluctantly so as not to disturb the pre-Maastricht atmosphere. It was a desire to achieve a broader compromise that made the Community follow the Germans in dealing with the Yugoslav drama, from which the spirit of compromise was so characteristically absent. But this new determination did not stop the fighting and furthermore contributed to the deterioration of the Community's political authority.

So the United Nations took over as the force that keeps the peace where there is a peace to keep. But the UN is not prepared to fight to impose peace where it is still not wanted. This also is the current position of the United States. The legal and political circumstances of what was Yugoslavia were particularly unfavourable to the usual kinds of international intervention. It was in essence an internal war over the separation of ethnic groups and not an invasion of one country by another. Even the premature recognition of Croatia and Bosnia did not change the essential character of the confrontation.

A major problem was the tendency of a part of the international community to view this conflict as a kind of lingering battle from the Cold War days – namely, the free and democratic Croats struggling against the hard-line Bolshevik Serbs. Whatever the differences between Serbs and Croats, and there are some, this is not one of them. No matter what test we choose for democracy, both the Serbian and the Croatian governments would fail any number of them. But the fixation of the international community, spearheaded by Germany, on this alleged contrast between the disputants has only delayed the process of settling down to a solution.

But what the reaction of the European Community, the UN, the US, NATO, and others has clearly demonstrated is that intervention cannot be engineered on purely humanitarian concerns and moral outrage. All the powers attempting to provide a framework for a solution had also to answer for themselves to their own constituencies: Was it in their interest? Was there a reasonable chance of success? Could the requisite means be mustered? Only the moral outrage and the humanitarian concern were definitely in place. Answers to the other questions were not. As a result the policy of the West has drifted, sometimes showing rather deep divisions within the group, while the fighting continues.

Admittedly, the task to be addressed could hardly have been more complicated, which goes some way towards explaining the inaction of the international community. There is no simple way to settle territorial disputes and border claims. Blame, though it lies heavily on the Serbs and with reason, is actually more widely shared, which makes the situation yet more complicated. How does one impose militarily a lasting solution on a situation like the one in Yugoslavia? Therefore, hopes were and still are pinned on the possibility of finding political solutions though the war goes on. Even worse, there is still the potential for it to spread to other regions of former Yugoslavia.

CHAPTER SIXTEEN

The Balkan Endgame

The two principal territories on to which the war for the dismemberment of Yugoslavia could possibly spread are Kosovo and Macedonia. Kosovo, which acted as a fuse for the violent dissolution of Yugoslavia, has been on the waiting-list for quite some time. The situation there is tense and explosive.

Macedonia, while awaiting international recognition, openly suggested that the war might be carried on to its territory. Even though the country has finally been recognized, it still lies at the crossroads of hostile interests and possible alliances. If fighting were to spread in either or both of these directions, it would tend to carry the conflict even further, beyond the borders of former Yugoslavia. This has clearly become evident to the international community, which, after failing to do so in BiH, has taken some preventative measures, particularly in Macedonia.

The reason for the tension in Kosovo is that both the Serbs, a minority in Kosovo, and the Albanians, a minority in Serbia, believe that the time is approaching to carry out the grand plans of their nationalist leaders. The wars in Croatia and BiH have emboldened both sides to stake out their maximalist positions. As a consequence those positions are diametrically opposed, and the gulf between them could hardly be wider.

The Albanians of Kosovo seek recognition of an independent and sovereign state of Kosovo. They have held a referendum to that effect, elected a parliament and a government, all outside the legal system of Serbia, to which they nominally belong. They refuse to participate in any political process or institution that is related to the state of Serbia, aware that this would unfocus their single-minded objective. Thus, they boycotted the elections held in December 1992, when their million votes could have helped Panić to threaten, perhaps even defeat Milošević and move Serbia towards a more liberal and flexible political structure.

Even the relatively moderate leaders talk about a wide-ranging autonomy for Albanians as only the first step towards a fully independent and sovereign Albanian state in Kosovo. There is no doubt in anybody's mind that the new Albanian state would fuse with Albania proper, thus realizing a part of the dream of a Greater Albania. The other parts of this dream lie in Montenegro and Macedonia.

The Albanians – who started modestly enough with a call for the return of the autonomy specified in the constitution of 1974 – have come a long way, openly proclaiming their desire to secede from Serbia. This has reinforced the official line in Serbia that secession was the Albanian strategy all along but that they used a gradualistic approach so as not to alienate the international community too soon. There is no denying that Albanian appetites have grown considerably. This is illustrated by the fact that they will no longer consider the redrawing of borders that would give Serbia parts of Kosovo containing Orthodox monasteries and other sacred buildings of extreme national and cultural importance. Not that anyone has yet offered such a solution seriously. But it is indicative of the Albanian tactical position that they still feel a need to maximize their demands.

The Serbs consider Kosovo an integral part of their territory and one that, as a whole or in part, can under no condition be separated from it or ceded to another country. They maintain that the autonomy provided by the current Serbian constitution meets all European standards for national minorities and that the Albanians are deliberately rejecting what is offered to provoke tensions and gain the sympathy of the international community. Thus the massive lay-offs of Albanian policemen, doctors, professors, and factory workers are rationalized by the Serbs as a consequence of Albanian defiance of the Serbian legal system. The Albanians, of course, see it as deliberate oppression and a method of ethnic cleansing.

The Serbs insist that they are bringing the "rule of law" to Kosovo. Since that law is resisted by the majority population, it has to be enforced. Serbian order is being offered on a take-it-or-leave-it basis, but the latter choice is implicitly linked to the threat of harsh repression. So far the Albanians have chosen just that.

The leaders of both sides publicly maintain that no solution to Kosovo's accumulated problems can be found without talks and negotiations, but so far they have failed to begin discussions, each side asking for pre-conditions known to be unacceptable to the other. No one has yet offered a platform for negotiations. Although at one point in autumn 1992 education became a negotiable issue, both sides immediately tried manoeuvring for advantage in these talks, and they broke down soon after. The EC and UN conference on Yugoslavia stepped in, trying to revive talks in 1993, but no progress has been recorded.

The war in the rest of what used to be Yugoslavia is in a way reinforcing the aspirations of both sides. The Albanians feel that, should Serbia accomplish its quest to create a Greater Serbia, thus capitalizing on the ethnic principle, their own case would be pressed not against a third party but against a regime in Serbia that is and will remain encouraged by the fact that it accomplished what it did by use of force.

The greatest danger facing Kosovo is not the extremist and unrealistic demands of the Albanian population. These they have no way of enforcing, so their position is much more verbal than real, threatening politically but not physically the precarious peace in the territory. The real danger lies with the nationally agitated Serbs and particularly with Milošević, who might, at a time convenient to him, choose to draw this trump card for a new round of national homogenization.

The precarious balance of high tension and low conflict could be upset easily, if that is needed, to shore up once again the sense of threat to the Serbian national spirit. And what better place to do this than the sacred Kosovo? Most Serbs are still very emotional about Kosovo and would find it unacceptable to have a Serbia without it. Milošević can capitalize on this sentiment at any given moment. The moment he chooses will probably be the moment he feels that he is losing his grip over Serbia and that his popularity is falling. He could then lead a new wave of national homogenization, the weapon he has not hesitated to use in the past, in order to save the situation for him and Serbian nationalists.

The Serbs in Kosovo are among the most radical. In the last elections, the one Albanians boycotted, Željko Ražnjatović-Arkan, the notorious warlord from the Croatian and BiH campaigns, was elected a member of the Serb parliament from Kosovo, though his place of residence is Belgrade – an ominous sign and a clear signal to the local Albanian population.

A war in Kosovo would be particularly bloody. The Albanians, though overwhelming in numbers, have only light arms and would be no match for what the Serbs could bring to the fighting. Open conflict would also, almost inevitably, spill over beyond the boundaries of former Yugoslavia. The Montenegrins, also threatened by the project of a Greater Albania, would not hesitate to side with the

Serbs. They have done that in the past, and on this particular issue there is little doubt that they would do so again.

Macedonia, which would find it impossible either to side with the Albanians against the Serbs or to stay neutral, because of the very large Albanian minority in Macedonia, would involuntarily be drawn into the conflict. The almost 30 per cent of Macedonia's population who are ethnically Albanian have for some time pressed for autonomy, the more radical wing openly asking for an independent Albanian republic in Macedonia, with a view to joining with the Albanians of Kosovo.

Both Montenegro and Macedonia are parts of former Yugoslavia. The internationalization of the conflict would be provided by the involvement of Albania, which would find it impossible to stay aloof from developments concerning their ethnic brethren in Yugoslavia. Though itself very poor and ill armed, Albania would be drawn into any conflict if for no other reason than to draw the attention of Europe and the rest of the world to the plight of the Albanians in Kosovo.

The Greeks, who have a history of strained relations with Albania[1] and who are currently faced with the dual problem of an exodus of Albanian population into Greece and the securing of rights for the Greeks in Albania, would certainly side with Serbia in one way or another. This is not to suggest that Greece would be drawn into an armed alliance but rather that the logic of the situation makes it almost impossible for Greece to sit on the fence in an Albanian-Serbian confrontation.

As for Macedonia, the other potential tinderbox should the flames of war spread across the Balkans, its position is as precarious as one can possibly imagine. It is difficult to think of another country in the world that is surrounded by four hostile neighbours, with no natural allies to count on. As a state it is very young, having been created by Tito in 1944. At the time Serbia, to which this territory had belonged since the Balkan Wars, gave its consent. At the moment the new state, whose recognition the EC's Arbitration Commission recommended before that of Croatia but which still has not gained full acceptance, is a major source of instability in the region. Its neighbours, Europe at large, and the world community might with some justification be alarmed. But the same neighbours who are already alarmed seem also to be interested in maximizing their own national and security interests relative to Macedonia, irrespective of the fact that their actions are contributing to further deterioration.

To the west of Macedonia,[2] Albanians are slowly but surely encroaching, simply by virtue of a higher birth-rate. Some of the *opštinas* in western Macedonia today are solidly Albanian, and others have a majority. Skopje, the capital of Macedonia, is said to have a larger Albanian population than Tirana, the capital of Albania. Though there are no open challenges or territorial demands by Albania, it is clear that the Macedonians view their Albanian population as a potential threat. In that they have common ground with Serbia.

Serbia, which lies to the north of Macedonia, is also perceived as – and in fact is – a possible threat to the independence of Macedonia and the security of the region. The reader should recall from chapter 1 that Skopje was the capital of medieval Serbia when it was at the height of its power. More recently, as explained in chapter 2, Serbia won Macedonia from Turkey and Bulgaria during the Balkan Wars and held on to the territory, though indirectly, until the Second World War. Though at the moment Serbian claims on Macedonia are neither loud nor mainstream, it is not entirely inconceivable that the question of Old Serbia or Southern Serbia, as it used to be called, would be reopened, especially in the context of a conflict with the Albanians of Kosovo and, by implication, those in western Macedonia.

While the idea of three hundred American troops to be stationed as lightly armed observers of the Macedonia-Serbia border was still being contemplated, Milošević paid a hurried visit to Macedonia, trying to dissuade the republic from accepting this plan. He failed, and the Americans came to join the seven hundred UN troops from Scandinavia.

To the east of Macedonia is Bulgaria, which lost Macedonia to the Serbs during the Balkan Wars but still maintains that the Macedonians are actually Bulgars. On linguistic grounds Bulgarians are the closest to the Macedonians. But since the Macedonians themselves largely reject the idea of union, submitting that there are other important elements of ethnicity and statehood, the Bulgar claim fails to bring a solution closer. On the contrary, it adds to the tensions. Bulgaria was among the first to recognize the *state* of Macedonia, angering the Greeks, but at the same time it was careful to specify that there was no such thing as a Macedonian nationality. The expectation on their part would therefore seem to be that the two states with the same nationality would eventually merge, like the two parts of Germany.

Finally, to the south of Macedonia lies Greece, which has played a leading role in preventing the recognition of Macedonia. Though it is generally believed that modern-day Greece has no territorial claims against Macedonia, as it did during the Balkan Wars, it is also clear that the whole idea of a sovereign and independent state of

Macedonia is more than irritating to the Greeks – so much so that they managed to restrain all the major powers of the world from recognizing a state that was desperately seeking such recognition. For over a year the Macedonians struggled diplomatically to be recognized; their request was finally accepted in the UN in May 1993 under the peculiar name of the Former Yugoslav Republic of Macedonia.

The background for this behaviour is just as emotional and potentially irrational as all others in the Yugoslav drama. The Greek Civil War, immediately after the end of the Second World War, had a strong Communist component precisely in those Greek territories also known as Macedonia. These were not part of the Yugoslav republic, though there was active support from Tito and Yugoslavia in the attempt to turn Greece Communist. The Greeks have not forgotten this and are aware that a number of Slav Macedonians, after the defeat of the uprising, fled across the border into the Yugoslav republic of Macedonia, which gave them shelter. This, plus the fact that there has always been a strong Macedonian call either to unify all Macedonians or at least to support their Slav brethren living in Greece in conditions of national deprivation, has made the Greeks extremely suspicious about the whole idea of an independent Macedonian state.

The Macedonians have recently moderated their attitude towards the Slav population in Greece. As a country of two million they cannot behave quite as they did when twenty-two million Yugoslavs stood behind them, giving them the political clout they needed and now no longer have. They have amended their constitution to make clear that they make no territorial claims, but the Greeks were for a long time unyielding: change the name of Macedonia to something else that will not be as suggestive of territorial pretensions. In any event, the attitude of Greece to the new state of Macedonia was for a time the most hostile and unfriendly of all.

This attitude of Greece towards Macedonia has brought it closer to Serbia on questions of regional policy. The two states have a common interest in so far as they regard with horror the prospect of the unification of all Albanians in one state (the horror is shared by most non-Albanian Macedonians). They also shared the desire to postpone the recognition of Macedonia as a sovereign state as far into the future as possible.

Macedonia, sandwiched physically between Greece and Serbia, is suffering from economic strangulation by both. Aside from other regional and security considerations, its deprived population might well contribute to the inherent instability of the region through social unrest.

Farther to the north in the Balkans and central Europe there is a possibly uncomfortable situation developing regarding Hungarian minorities in neighbouring countries. Hungary, on the losing side in both world wars, had its borders determined in such a way that almost two million Hungarians were placed in Romania, more than seven hundred thousand in Slovakia, and almost half a million in the Serb autonomous province of Vojvodina. After the ending of the Cold War and the disappearance of the Warsaw Pact the issue of the Hungarian minority in Romania has once again become a potential crisis point. The Hungarians in Vojvodina, though initially enjoying considerable autonomy, have been used as a political instrument by Hungary to put additional pressure on Yugoslavia and Serbia. Hungary, like Austria, has hardly been neutral in the internal conflicts that destroyed Yugoslavia. This development has, however, brought the already close Serbia and Romania even closer.

Finally, there is the presence of Turkey, which has for centuries been the dominant force in the Balkans. As a regional power also interested in the well-being and security of the Muslims in the region, Turkey is a factor to be considered in any thinking on the Balkan endgame and has not hesitated to reassert its interest in the region. It has also, much to the irritation of Greece, immediately recognized the sovereign state of Macedonia.

There is a sense of *déja vu* about the slide into fragmentation and possible chaos that is now taking place in the Balkans. For generations the verb "to balkanize" – synonymous with splitting into a number of mutually hostile states with ill-defined borders – derived its meaning from the history of the peninsula at the time of the demise of the two great empires, the Austro-Hungarian and, even more so, the Ottoman Empire. Unfortunately for the peoples of the region, disputes over borders and the treatment of national minorities today are just as pressing as they ever were, as is an atmosphere of suspicion and insecurity.

The Balkan nations have responded in a traditional way, by concluding mutual co-operation agreements and seeking alliances to enhance their security. But the formation of alliances, which have in the past tended to square off into hostile blocks, is again leading to the formation of potential rival groups.

It is obvious that a political confrontation over regional matters would pit Serbia and Greece (and possibly Romania), long the arch-enemies of the Ottoman Empire, against Turkey, which would offer support to Albania, Macedonia, and Bulgaria. Though both members of NATO, Greece and Turkey have confronted one another in the recent past over a number of open and unsettled issues, including the question of Cyprus, which makes relations between them tense. The opening of a new question such as Macedonia or Albania could prove to be the straw that breaks the camel's back.

The revival of tensions and the increase in insecurity is occurring at a time when the Balkans in general and Yugoslavia specifically have lost the strategic significance they once had to the great powers of Europe. If in the past the nations and countries of the Balkans reacted to the instigation and prodding of the great powers to behave this way or that, thus provoking incidents and conflicts, today they are very much on their own in trying to settle disputes over boundaries and ethnic minorities that have not been adequately settled in the past.

If anything, the outside world is trying to bring some order and sense of respect for common principles to the region. For the first time in centuries the great powers seem to have a common interest and goal – to bring peace and stability to the region. Though the stop-and-go, patchy, sometimes unprincipled performance of the European Community (and particularly Germany), the United States, Russia, and the United Nations has not yet gone far towards accomplishing this goal, the situation is nevertheless the opposite of the old scenario in which the great powers fought over the region, involving the nations of the Balkans in their larger power struggles.

There are concerns and fears that the Yugoslav crisis cannot be contained within the borders of that troubled and now dissolved country. The history and current state of affairs in the region show that there are a number of flash-points, disputes, and claims that, if compounded, could lead to a major regional confrontation.

As the Yugoslav drama unfolds, threatening to become a broader regional crisis, the need for a new look at the Balkans by the West becomes absolutely essential. The new look would require dropping some of the stereotypes of the old vision of the Balkans. This new look would ideally also be followed by focused, determined, and adequate action to settle the tensions once and for all. The notion that the peoples of the Balkans, like those of Yugoslavia, have been and are embroiled in millennia-old disputes should be dropped. There was a period of time, at the beginning of this century, when the Balkan countries had more than their fair share of wars. But over the long haul the wars among Balkan nations have been no more numerous nor more bloody than the wars fought among the countries that now form the European Community.

It is not only erroneous but also politically stifling to view the situation in the Balkans as destined to remain in a perpetual state of hostilities. The Balkans cannot and should not be viewed as a *specific generator of conflicts*, as opposed to harmonious Western Europe, or as a tribal and somewhat wild region to which different rules apply.

The view that the Balkans are different and that they do not really belong to Europe is not often expressed openly, but the actions of some in the West suggest that it holds considerable sway.[3] This view is both wrong and counter-productive. The processes taking place in the Balkans are those same processes that Western Europe has gone through, mostly in the nineteenth century. They are a syndrome and a virus, admittedly appearing a little late, the open manifestations of the same national, security, and economic considerations and aspirations that Western Europe has resolved. The West, mindful of its own current security, must offer its experience in a more concrete and positive form than just as lessons from history.

The third element in the traditional vision and wisdom concerning the Balkans that should be abandoned is the view that a partial and piecemeal approach is best, that problems should be taken in stride as they pop up, that parties should first be left to work things out among themselves and then, when this does not happen (as it has not and will not), their conflicts contained until the belligerents are exhausted.

If anything, the Yugoslav drama has clearly demonstrated that we are dealing with interrelated phenomena, ethnic, security, and economic considerations that have a significant spill-over effect. The confrontation in Croatia spilled into BiH; it could spill over elsewhere. There are significant advantages of scale in dealing with the problem, that is to say the region, as a whole.

The best way to help the Balkans to subdue its furies is to transform the region in a way that addresses the main issues head-on. First the issue of (in)security. The desire to draw closer to NATO, to benefit from its protective shield, and ideally to become members has been in the minds of many in the Balkan countries, and many have approached the Western security alliance. This clearly demonstrates their concern over security.

NATO is not prepared to extend its membership into this volatile area. But instead of watching the Balkan nations try once more to enhance security by divisive and dangerous alliances, the Western alliance and Russia should offer, in their new spirit of co-operation, an arrangement, a regional security system on which all the countries could rely, one in which NATO and Russia would engage themselves to ensure that obligations are fulfilled. This is not only a question of security in the Balkans. It is also a question of security in Europe as a whole.

The whole region, with the possible exception of Greece, is in desperate need of economic development. Regional co-operation is a necessary element in fostering economic development. The suspicion, the sense of insecurity, and open warfare have either cut economic links or kept them from expanding in a natural way. All countries are now looking outside the area for economic ties, with the EC being the prime target.

The European Community, the United States, the World Bank, the European Bank for Reconstruction and Development, in fact all those who are economically involved in the region should emphasize that ties to the West cannot be a substitute, only a complement to economic co-operation in the region. Incentives should be built into relations with the region to favour projects and affairs that in turn favour the regional approach.

The other side of the same economic coin is to open the doors wider to ongoing European integration for the region as a whole. The Balkan nations should become an integral part of the new European architecture even though there is still no clear picture of what this architecture will produce. They should not be made to wait until the Western European house is fully in order. They should be included while integration is taking place and in spite of the inevitable ups and downs.

They should be looked upon as a whole, not just country by country as is now the case, with the Community and the CSCE maintaining a selective and qualified approach. The total of the Balkans is more than the simple sum of its individual countries, and this specificity must be a factor in the geo-strategic and geo-political equations and considerations of European integration. The region should become a safe and prosperous link between the European Community and the Middle East as well as between Central Europe and the Mediterranean.

The European Community is well placed to wield a strong economic influence on the region. *All* Balkan countries have expressed their wish to link their future to the process of integration in Europe, primarily the European Community. Some have already announced that they will apply for membership in the not-too-distant future. This all-inclusive interest is a powerful possible carrot in the hands of the Community. An additional argument in favour of this approach is to be found in the national interests of EC countries bordering the region, Greece and Italy today, Austria perhaps tomorrow.

There are a number of problems with this integral Balkan approach, and they should be recognized. The changes in a number of Balkan countries towards parliamentary democracy and a market economy are still slow and uncertain. The extremely complex ethnic and political structure of the different countries is insufficiently understood. The region is not a significant trading partner of the EC or any other major power. The region is distant from the leading Community countries, even more so from the United States. All this makes the mobilization of public opinion in favour of deeper involvement difficult.

Above all, there is a war, which makes all kinds of involvement other than military and humanitarian unlikely. Many argue that the war must be stopped before the building of the future can begin. But without an offer of a broader context, a vision of a possible arrangement from which all could profit, chances are that the war will last longer and that it will spread.

Not to try now, at an early stage, when the difficulties and problems are relatively small in the sense that they are localized in one dissolved country, only because it appears complicated or difficult to argue convincingly, is to invite the possibility of larger involvement with higher costs at a later date should a potential regional crisis turn into an actual one. A solution requires knowledge and understanding of the situation, imagination, and bold initiatives. The more developed and stable parts of Europe, with the active involvement of the United States and Russia (for collective security), must show and lead the way towards controlling destructive forces within the region and promoting integration with the rest of Europe.

The question of borders and the human rights of national minorities would not fall into place immediately. They will probably linger as an issue for some time to come. However, these divisive issues would be contained in a framework in which they could not explode in an uncontrollable way. Collective security and gradual economic development would enable the maturing of democracy in the full sense of the word. This would in turn mean that respect for minority rights could be seen more genuinely as respect for civil and human rights, and would make the question of borders less important. The closer we all get to a situation in which borders in the Balkans are less significant, the closer we are to a lasting solution.

CHAPTER SEVENTEEN

Is There a Solution?

The most difficult part of the Yugoslav drama to predict is how and when the final curtain will fall. The war started in Slovenia, moved to Croatia and then to BiH. In Croatia no solution has been reached, nor is there one in sight for BiH, and the war may spread to other regions, primarily to Kosovo. Even worse, there is a possibility, albeit not a strong one, that the war may cross the borders of former Yugoslavia. The negative spiral of events is still not over, and the balance of political forces needed to stop the fighting has not yet been reached.

Even when this balance is reached, the threat to its precarious existence will be there for some time to come. In a context of frenzied nationalism spite and hatred can be stronger than reason. Ignorance can win over wisdom. Irrational behaviour cannot be predicted, so preventive action cannot be taken. Aggressive nationalism is probably the worst type of irrational behaviour, bordering dangerously on collective paranoia.

At one extreme is the obvious position that there *must* be a solution for the simple reason that no crisis, however deep and intricate, has been left without some kind of solution. Given sufficient time, a solution eventually emerges. That, of course, does not say much except that hope must be maintained. In the Yugoslav drama so far fear has been stronger than hope, and not without reason.

At the other extreme would be an attempt to pinpoint and describe a definite solution in terms of a sequence of events, with a definite time-frame, leading to a unique configuration of ethnic and political relations. This type of definite prediction seems out of place given the complexity of the situation, the number of external and internal factors contributing (or not) to a solution, and given the fact that the drama has still not reached its turning-point.

Assuming that the reader, like the author, would like to glance ahead a little, no matter how imprecise and fuzzy the view will be, the only logical approach to adopt is to identify the general characteristics of a solution, to specify some broadly framed pre-conditions for such a solution or solutions, and to trace the reasonably predictable general dynamics of expected events as they relate to the further development and possible resolution of the crisis.

We need first to define a solution. Without going into a deep theoretical elaboration, a solution could be defined as a state in which every antagonist perceives deliberate disturbance for additional gain as more costly than accepting a possible loss in the suggested and accepted compromise – a pragmatic definition, which does not take into account desired and/or accepted principles of conduct.

The evolution of the Yugoslav drama so far unfortunately suggests that upholding principles is only one, and definitely not the most important element for action. Therefore, a formula for a solution must be clinically clean and pragmatic to accommodate a situation in which principles will not play a role at all, or a very minor one. Should the international community decide that upholding and defending principles has a value *in itself*, this will undoubtedly change the character of the solution.

For this reason alone we cannot talk about a *single* solution. But there are a variety of possible scenarios that can help to determine both the time needed to reach a relatively stable point and events on the ground that would provide for stability. Take, for example, the key question of borders, which has earlier been singled out as the key reason for fighting. Will the borders change by force or not? As things stand right now, there are three possible alternatives: border changes by force, negotiated border changes, or no border changes. Or take the corollary of border disputes, which is to say minority rights. Will they be protected by a democratic civil and human code, or will they be protected by force and pressure of the parent nationality and ethnic group?

It has been said many times that the war should stop so that a solution could be sought in peace and by negotiation. Such sound advice typically goes over the heads of excited nationalists. As we have seen, not only those who stand to gain on the ground but those who stand to lose are willing and anxious to continue the fighting, viewing territorial loss as a diplomatic gain. During the war in Croatia thirteen cease-fires were negotiated before the fourteenth held for a while, only to be broken again when it so suited one of the parties. In BiH people have lost count of cease-fires.

Former Yugoslavia offered a unique comparative situation: the fighting in Croatia stopped, yet the cease-fire led nowhere, certainly not closer to a solution. At the same time, in BiH there was continuous fighting in an effort to bring a solution closer. Neither the fighting in BiH nor the cease-fire in Croatia has as yet produced a stable solution.

The moral? National chauvinistic leaderships would rather fight than negotiate. Aggressive nationalism as an ideological and political mode is much more likely to aggravate problems than to solve them. And this type of nationalism has not yet subsided. There is still considerable potential to cause further damage, inflict new wounds, and increase the death toll. Therefore, more fighting seems probable in the future, thus prolonging the time necessary to reach a solution. The next few years could well turn out to be a period of cold peace with sudden blazes of heated fighting.

The essential ingredient of a solution is achieving and maintaining stability in what was Yugoslavia, thus contributing to the stability of the whole Balkan region. Stability can be reached by an agreement of the nations that made up the former Yugoslavia, meaning an agreement between the states that sprang out of its destruction.

But this statement begs the question: Is one key for five or six locks possible? It is indeed difficult to foresee such a development given that there is still a war on and considerable potential for a spread in the fighting. Since the war is about borders and the idea of nation-states, much in the future course of events will depend on the attitude of the international community towards the new wave of creation of nation-states.

For a long while after the Second World War it seemed as if the creation of nation-states, especially if this involved violent changes of borders, was passé. The events in former Yugoslavia and elsewhere in Central and Eastern Europe have demonstrated that the nation-state in Europe has perhaps been written off prematurely. The lax attitude of the West, which has largely solved this problem, has rekindled the hopes of aggressive nationalists in the East. The possibility of creating nation-states prolongs the fighting, since it gives ammunition to those seeking solutions in border changes.

The likely scenario then involves prolonging and renewing the fighting in Croatia and opening the question of Muslim territories in BiH. Since the Muslims there are not a nation, Serbs and Croats would continue the old quarrel over what they were before converting to Islam.

As far as BiH is concerned, there seem to be only two clear options, a reality the international community will have to face. One is based on bringing to BiH the rule of law and civil and human rights, all the while remaining mindful of the ethnic component. This would imply a UN protectorate, since no ethnic group would immediately after the war trust the other or other two to administer it and organize life. The other option is the division of this former Yugoslav republic and, briefly, independent state between the victorious Serbs and Croats. The Muslims could hardly face the second option without a fight, and the Serbs and Croats would fight over the new lines of separation.

The ethnic and administrative borders of Kosovo are another possible flash-point. The creation of ethnic states from former Yugoslavia would give the Albanians new political grounds to continue their struggle for an ethnic state of their own. It is difficult to see this ambition squaring peacefully with the Serbian contention that the "sacred grounds of Kosovo" will be a part of Serbia eternally.

When the war started two years ago, the ethnic mix in Yugoslavia and particularly in BiH was used as a strong argument against the possibility of ethnic nation-states. In the meantime, ethnic cleansing of territories by all sides has made this type of arrangement more likely if not less despicable. Should the final solution involve redrawing borders by recognizing this *fait accompli*, there will still be a problem of residual minorities, which could, with the help of the UN, be resolved through negotiations.

The solution that accepts ethnic borders would therefore certainly prolong the fighting and tensions among the Serbs, Croats, Muslims, and Albanians. Ethnic borders would make the Muslims of BiH a people without a land and the millions who have been forcefully or peacefully resettled a permanent reservoir of anger, frustration, desire for revenge, and irredentism. Co-operation and coexistence between the new ethnically bounded states would be difficult, to say the least. Their behaviour would be out of step with European integrative processes and thus would make participation in those processes strained and halting. Though a solution of sorts, it would be uneasy, strained, and in the long run very costly, and not only for the peoples of former Yugoslavia. The other long-range, which is to say permanent and stable solution, would be based on the concept that human and citizens' rights have *at least* the same value as ethnic or national rights. This solution would be much more attuned to current European political and civili accomplishments.

One can conceive of a situation where the fact of an ethnic mix on the territory of former Yugoslavia simply came to be accepted and, in a way, to reinforce the integration. Logical economic ties, similar and intermingled cultures, intermarriage, and essentially a common language are the possible sources of a genuine integrative tendency among Serbs, Croats, and Muslims, in BiH and elsewhere. Montenegro would certainly join such a grouping and quite possibly Macedonia. The position of the Slovenes is unclear, though they have expressed interest in maintaining economic ties.

This might seem to be coming very close to suggesting that a new, Third or Fourth Yugoslavia could actually be a solution. Very few inside or outside the former republics would contemplate this as a possibility. Those who reject the notion are preoccupied with the visible events of today – that is, the ongoing war. The argument of nationalists inside is based on the premise that if Yugoslavia was good, it would have survived. Fighting and misery, poverty and hatred are to the single-minded nationalists better than the idea of coming together to solve problems. A majority of the population, lead by powerful propaganda, follow this line.

The other argument against the antagonists coming together points to the animosities, scars, killings, rapes, and destruction that have already occurred. The notion that the peoples of Yugoslavia could not live peacefully is in retrospect a self-fulfilling prophecy launched primarily by the aggressive nationalists who sought and are still seeking partition. The common-sense argument is that the ferocity of the confrontation has destroyed Yugoslavia once and for all. That could be true, but it should be left to the peoples of former Yugoslavia to decide in a more stable, democratic, and civil political situation once the worst wave of aggressive nationalism is over, a desirable situation to be discussed a little later.

There is considerable merit in the argument that the need for the republics of ex-Yugoslavia to stay together in some form is *objectively* identifiable. It is not the same for all the states that sprang out of Yugoslavia, but at one level or another it is there. Once the centrifugal forces of destruction have reached their limits, the opposite and integrative forces could and probably will come into play. In other words, the stable point and a final solution need not necessarily be at the farthest extreme brought about by centrifugal forces. Rather, a stable point and therefore a long-run solution could include some measure of the centripetal, integrative forces as well.

The account in this book should have shown that Yugoslavia in its first and second incarnation was indeed a problem. But it was not *only* a problem. It was an attempt at a solution. The problem itself is the coexistence of ethnic groups with recognizable differences. The creation of nation-states inherits the problem; it does not solve it. So a broader, co-operative arrangement does seem necessary to address this fundamental problem.

This is not an argument for the reconstruction of the old Yugo-slavia. It is rather one for keeping our minds and doors open for the possibility of a new entity that would reflect a commonality of inter-ests to the extent that the nations of Yugoslavia perceive one, and to the extent that this perception follows a broader trend of integration on European soil.

The previous two Yugoslavias were born of two world wars. A possible new integrative entity would, in its birth out of and after an internal and divisive war, demonstrate decisively that integrative forces cannot be ignored or bypassed, just as the differences could not be either. The new integrative entity would have difficult obstacles to overcome – difficult, but not entirely impossible, especially with outside encouragement and support, or within the context described in the previous chapter.

It has already been stated earlier that Yugoslavia could *only* be conceived of as a *political* proposition. Yugoslavia was never a nation-state. This made the centre of gravity in Yugoslavia political rather than ethnic. The ethnic conflicts disturbed and then destroyed this centre of gravity, but being political in nature, it does not *remain* destroyed for all time. The three groups of factors mentioned in the introduction as having a decisive influence on the shaping of Yugo-slavia – relations between the nations of Yugoslavia, democratic polit-ical structures, and international influence – could work jointly in the direction of helping and speeding a reintegrative process. It is any-body's guess whether they will, and in what time-frame.

The impact of the international community could prove decisive. The Balkan endgame, and therefore the Yugoslav drama, will depend to a considerable extent on broader developments in Europe, however much the situation seems at the moment to run contrary to the basic and underlying dynamics of integration in the West. Should integra-tive forces in Western Europe in general and in the European Com-munity in particular continue more or less along the path set during the latest phase of Euro-dynamism, bringing the peoples and nations of Europe closer, this cannot but have a positive effect on the speed with which the disintegrative forces now at work in Yugoslavia will change direction.

Should, however, the faltering felt after the signing of the Maastricht Treaty continue or even spread, the effect on the resolution of the Yugoslav drama would be negative, at least in terms of the time needed to reach a solution. Negative would also be a more general yielding to nationalism on the European scene. There are signs that nationalism is on the rise in many countries of Europe, both inside and outside the European Community. But there are no signs as yet that German or French nationalism, for example, will turn into an aggressive and politically dominant force. However, even a moderate rise in nationalism across Europe would make a solution in Yugoslavia that much more difficult to reach.

Adherence to the principles of the UN Charter is another set of codes whose application and observation will have an impact on future scenarios in former Yugoslavia. In addition to humanitarian concern and moral outrage, if the West can conceive of the defence of these principles to be in its vital and strategic interest, just as much as oil, it will be in a position to leave a strong and lasting imprint on the future of the Balkans. Strongly motivated by their commonality of interests, the West and Russia can contribute to peace and a stable solution. That commonality of interests exists, and may be found in concerns for security, stability, and human rights.

It would not help either the stability or the possible new co-operation among the countries emerging from former Yugoslavia if the region were to become a target of spheres of influence. A scenario whereby Slovenia and Croatia rest in the German economic and cultural zone while the others form some kind of Orthodox Balkan federation would reinforce instability. So would the idea of "natural ties" between Slovenia, Croatia, and BiH with countries that were part of the Austro-Hungarian Empire. This notion builds on old links and would be a step backwards into history.

The major question is whether Western Europe is today interested in the same way as it was in the nineteenth century in making a division between the West and the Orthodox Balkans. All the talk about new European architecture would certainly seem to suggest differently. But talk and intentions are one thing, real interests and balances of power something else. A Europe without spheres of influence for particular powers is the best bet for peace and stability in the Balkans and in former Yugoslavia.

All Yugoslav nations have expressed a desire to connect with Europe, meaning primarily the European Community. This ultimate goal and desire is authentic, even though it is well hidden at the moment by behaviour that hardly qualifies the nations of Yugoslavia as good Europeans. But below the thick layers of mutual animosity and antagonism those nations, now with their independent states, do seek an external point of reference in designing their long-run development strategies.

In the context of the general tendency to integrate with the West, Slovenia and Croatia have looked and are looking more closely at Germany. Serbia, by contrast, hopes to capitalize on its traditional relations with France. In order to build bridges rather than make deeper divisions, the external point of reference should be as unified and impartial as possible. The firmer and more solid this point of reference, the more integrative the force it portrays and exhibits, the sooner and stronger will be the influence and the spill-over effect on the Balkans and the states of former Yugoslavia.

The other external influence that the West, and particularly the European Community, could bring to the resolution of the crisis involves the attitude it will have towards the Balkans in general and the countries of ex-Yugoslavia specifically. In principle, the more committed the European Community is towards this region, the closer a solution will be. The problems in the Balkans and in Yugoslavia, are largely of their own making, but the responsibility for finding solutions and, more importantly, the long-term gains in security and stability for Western Europe are also important factors to consider.

This would require a whole new approach towards the new European architecture that the European Community is trying to spearhead. Instead of piecemeal and partial approaches, with a stop-and-go triggering mechanism, a new strategy should be designed and implemented. This strategy should contribute both to the cementing of positive relations in the region and to the inclusion of the region in Europe as a whole. The fact that most Balkan countries are underdeveloped and faced with deep structural changes on their way from socialist to market forms of economic organization indicates that there is a need for the West to establish a complete package of economic assistance.

This argument is mindful of the fact that aggressive nationalism has so far been largely insensitive to economic incentives. But offering an economic framework from the outside, one that would embrace all the antagonistic nationalist aspirations, would seem like a necessary if not sufficient pre-condition to the process of defusing the forces of aggressive nationalism – especially now, when the fighting has taken a heavy toll, when impoverished people are confused and uncertain about whether to follow nationalistic ideologies, and when credible alternatives from constitutional opposition forces in the current regimes need a boost.

Much will depend on the future actions and exposure of the United Nations in what was Yugoslavia. The force immediately recognized as the moving and dominant one behind the UN is the United States. As the sole remaining superpower the U.S. is in a position to influence, more strongly than anybody else, the outcome of this particular crisis. That Yugoslavia has lost the strategic significance it had during the Cold War does not reduce the need to establish and

maintain peace and stability in this region. And it seems that the
u.s. has yet to determine what it considers to be the elements of a
stable solution. The sooner this is defined, the closer we shall be to
a solution.

The second group of factors contributing to a solution is the political and economic structures. Though all new states of ex-Yugoslavia
claim to be democratic, the sad truth is that none of them is as yet,
certainly not the principle antagonists, the Serbs and the Croats.
True, they all have multi-party systems, parliaments, and so on. But
the mechanisms of power are much, much closer to those of one-
party-dominated countries than to the real plurality of interests
expressed in the parliamentary democracies of the West. They are
all to a greater or lesser extent infected by the residues of past
authoritarian regimes. In not one of them, not even Slovenia, though
it is closest to the ideal, can it be said that the leadership and the
political elite truly follow the will and the interests of the people. On
the contrary, through aggressive propaganda and tight control of the
media all are *imposing* their own political preferences. It will take
several years and several consecutive rounds of elections before the
political structures in these states, most notably in Serbia and Croatia,
reach a point of comparison with the Western democracies.

As long as both the public and the parliaments can be manipulated
with the ease with which Milošević and Tudjman have manipulated
theirs, the key to the solution is in their hands rather than in the
hands of the elected representatives.

Democracy, democratic behaviour and tradition, democratic culture
and conduct cannot be imposed, nor can they be transmitted
mechanically. They *must* come from within. There are encouraging
signs of their gradual emergence in the form of stronger opposition
and legitimate pressures on the authoritarian regimes now in power.
Further and more concrete encouragement from the Western democracies would speed up this process and therefore the conditions
required to reach a solution.

Economic structures have also changed very little, and some of the
change has been in the wrong direction. Instead of a drive towards
privatization, for example, *all* Yugoslav republics encouraged, upon
gaining independence, the nationalization of previously socially
owned and self-managed enterprises. Instead of moving towards a
liberal, free-trading, and entrepreneurial economy, Croatia and
Serbia, and to a lesser extent even Slovenia, have drawn much closer
to a command economy than they were at any time in the last three
decades. The war, of course, was used as a convenient excuse.

The economies of the new states will have to undergo the economic reforms initiated by federal Prime Minister Marković, then abandoned by the leaders of the republics in their drive towards independence and statehood. The principles of those reforms were sound, and the leaders of the republics abandoned them for petty nationalistic reasons, not because they had a better way of solving their enormous economic problems. Sooner or later these economic reforms will have to regain centre stage, demonstrating the folly of those who brushed economics aside for national symbols but also highlighting the similarity of problems among the separate states and the advantages of tackling them jointly.

The third and most important group of factors shaping the future of former Yugoslavia is the relations among nations, which have deteriorated over the last few years into nationalistic confrontation and eventually ethnic war. Within this group of factors the most important is aggressive Serbian nationalism. Therefore, any solution will depend more on the future development of this nationalism than on anything else. It all started in Serbia with the whipping up of national sentiments to solve the problem of Kosovo. It will have to end with the fading out or withering away of aggressive Serbian nationalism, again possibly involving the situation in Kosovo.

The Serbs have already lost a great deal in trying to accomplish the goals of their Memorandum. Their choice of methods has been disastrous. Serbs living in one country – Yugoslavia – were whipped into fighting for a Greater Serbia, and as a result Serbs now live in three independent and sovereign states! The accomplishment of a Greater Serbia is still not certain. What is certain is that attaining this goal would involve even more fighting.

The question now is what will happen to Serbia itself if the tendency towards separatism and secession, very much in vogue, is met always and only by force of arms. Serbia has no happy future if it purports to be a nation-state for Serbs only. Unlike the Croatian constitution, which states that "Croatia is the homeland of the Croats," the Serbian constitution states very clearly that "Serbia is the state of all people living in it." But in practise government policy singles out the Serbs as the preferred population.

Serbia cannot be democratic and nationalist at the same time. Had it been democratic enough, co-operative enough, treating the other nations of Yugoslavia in an equal, modern, and emancipated manner, it would have preserved the state of Yugoslavia, and with it the goal of having all Serbs living in one country. In such a democratically structured Yugoslavia the Serbs stood to gain the most, though others would have gained as well. Yugoslavia could not exist in the post-Communist world without a truly democratic foundation. Serbian nationalism, soon to be followed by the reactive nationalism of others, stood in the way.

When we attempt to imagine a new broader entity similar territorially if not politically to the previous Yugoslavia, we return to square one, but with the negative burden of the war. As far as Serbia is concerned, aggressive nationalism threatens the position of Serbs outside of Serbia as well as those within.

The problem with any nationalism, including the Serbian variety, is that it cannot be solved by slamming the door in its face. If anything, experience would suggest the opposite. The more the door is shut, the more defiant and arrogant aggressive nationalists become. This is certainly the situation in Serbia. The political and economic sanctions that were slapped on Serbia over the course of one year have not reduced the ambitions of arrogant nationalists and "patriots," nor have they significantly reduced the support for and popularity of Milošević and his regime.

The opposition to the regime has not been able to profit much from the fact that the outside world also opposes his policies. This is true largely because they were unable to offer a viable and appealing platform as an alternative to Milošević's Serbian national program (as designed in the Memorandum), but also because the West has not reached out to this opposition in any meaningful way.

It is difficult to predict how long it will take Serbia itself to escape from its nationalistic frame of mind and into one that will encourage respect for civil and human rights and for citizens before national passion. The process has started but will probably be very slow. The encouraging fact is that Serbia, though it appears today to be an authoritarian, even brutal state, also has a deeply ingrained liberal democratic tradition, perhaps more of one than have the other nationalities or newly created states of former Yugoslavia.

In several periods of its history Serbia was a leading exponent of democracy and liberalism in the Balkans, certainly among the nations of ex-Yugoslavia. The most recent example springs from the late sixties and early seventies. Had that development matured in an uninterrupted way, Yugoslavia's history might have been quite different and the deep traumatic experience of the early nineties might have been avoided.

Serbia, together with the other nations of Yugoslavia, attempted the utopic road to Communism as a short cut to the future. That route failed, equally for all. Serbia then tried, before other Yugoslav nations, the mythical return to the past and the values of nationalism, resorting at the same time to means that now qualify it as an aggressive state. That has not worked well either. The Serbs are now largely in a state of depression much deeper than the one all this was designed to cure. They are confused and split, the apparant gains in Croatia and Bosnia offset by immense hardships and mounting problems in Serbia itself. Many feel humiliated, and almost all feel totally isolated.

There *are* political forces in Serbia that are capable of contemplating the Serbian national question in a democratic and civilized way. They view with disgust the selection of violence and war as a means to resolve the open issues and the questionable arrangements of the Second Yugoslavia. These political forces do realize that a necessary pre-condition for any movement towards a stable and lasting solution is an inner, radical transformation of the Serbian national spirit. This spirit must address the issue of internal political and economic reforms as well as the question of external relations with the other former Yugoslav republics. Political forces advocating this course of action are still not overwhelming, not even dominant, but their influence is not insignificant and should not be easily discarded in favour of pragmatic contacts with Milŏsević as the key to power.

The danger in Serbia now lies in the type of confrontation that could occur between these agents of progress and moderation and those who have rallied to archaic nationalistic passions and brute force. The latter could become desperate, holding on to power at any cost, shamelessly using nationalist ideology and myths to attain support. The powers of nationalism are hiding behind state structures that they put in place to meet their political needs.

The situation is therefore extremely precarious and explosive, since any attempt to address the political issues of the day outside these structures can easily be characterized as civil disobedience, anarchy, or "mob rule" trying to overcome the "rule of law." Milošević, who was elevated into prominence largely by non-institutional mass rallies, now has no understanding and certainly no desire to share, let alone yield power, under pressures from similar if less well-organized and less well-attended rallies. He is determined to defend the system, *his* system, even if that means using force against his own people and his political opponents, whom he would brand hooligans and anarchists.

Within the institutions of the system there is little chance to generate change, since the Serbian parliament has a majority of members from the Socialist Party and the Serbian Radical Party sticking stubbornly to the nationalist platform.

The economic sanctions imposed by the United Nations have actually increased support for Milošević. But they are also speeding the process of total economic ruin and collapse, which could result in a stage of chaos with political consequences that are difficult to determine. Any confrontation arising from this chaos will not necessarily be a democratic one. So far the workers in Serbia have been unusually quiet, as have most of the managers of enterprises. Their silence was bought by around-the-clock printing of money. But the imminent closure of enterprises, as well as inflation – which is on track to beat the record of the Weimar Republic after the First World War – will shrink the number of those in favour and swell the number of those opposed to the regime.

This would be productive, and exactly what sanctions were introduced for, were it to be articulated through a democratic process, within parliament. A change of people, a change of policies – *without* bloodshed and violent confrontation. This might happen, but the risk is very high that it will not.

Deep polarization in a situation dominated by strong and irrational emotions suggests it is highly likely that Serbian cleansing of their own nationalism will be violent. That will be all the more so because of their need to supply the material and other needs of a larger than necessary army and officer corps springing from the JNA. The inheritance of the JNA by Serbia and Montenegro is already a major financial burden but also a dangerous and limiting factor in international political behaviour. There are also a number of paramilitary formations that are tabling their own claims and seeking "just rewards" for their part in the "war for the liberation of Serbs."

Thus the present political situation in Serbia has a strong militaristic component that the power-hungry nationalist leadership will not hesitate to use in the "defence of the legal state and its institutions" – today, perhaps, against the Albanian population of Kosovo, tomorrow against Serbs who think differently.

Though this worst-case scenario is not in any way imminent, a realistic assessment cannot exclude it. The softer, modern, democratic Serbia that will eventually have to appear is caught in the iron grip of an aggressive nationalism that is not likely to release it without force.

However aggressive Serbian nationalism is supplanted by a democratic and peace-oriented alternative, the next obvious step should be to proclaim a Serbian national state and abandon the name of Yugoslavia. Serbia must make a clean break with the notion that it is the proprietor of the name and the state of Yugoslavia. Milošević's attempt to try to inherit the international position of Yugoslavia for Serbia by clinging on to the name has already proved to be wrong and costly. It should be remembered that Serbian nationalists have declared both the First and the Second Yugoslavia to be a great hallucination of the Serbian nation. The desire to preserve continuity seems cynical in that context.

The future relations of the states deriving from Yugoslavia will, among other things, depend on who carries the name. Should the Serbs insist on continuity and on assuming the caretaker role, the likelihood is very small that others – Macedonians, Muslims, and Croats – would be willing to contemplate closer relations, and certainly not any state-like entity under the old name. Should Serbia abandon the name, however, and allow it to float freely for a while, there is a chance that the other nations could consider re-creating some integrative entity called Yugoslavia, but only if it offered an equal footing for all. This is not to say that the old Yugoslavia could be reconstructed, any more than the old Austro-Hungarian Empire could be. It is only to open the possibility of a renewal of an institutionalized form of integration in the Balkans and in a European context.

The democratic transformation of Serbia would go a long way to ease tensions in Croatia and in BiH. It would be naïve to think that the Croats, Muslims, and Albanians would, with a sigh of relief, immediately adopt a more pragmatic and co-operative posture. But with Serbs taking the lead, moderate forces within non-Serb communities would gradually gain on their respective political landscapes. The ethnic confrontations in Croatia and BiH were largely instigated by aggressive nationalism from Serbia. By the same token and in the opposite direction, a new flow of democratic inspiration from Serbia could not go unheeded elsewhere.

This would be especially true of the Serbs in Croatia and BiH, even though they now, with their victories and conquests, not only have a measure of independence from Belgrade but are also part of the hard-line problem. Though they are justifiably concerned about their human and national rights, especially in Croatia, Serbs in the other republics could gradually be more open to a political settlement of these issues and the necessary guarantees, rather than seeking to ensure their rights by force of arms.

At the same time democratic changes in Serbia would lead to a softening in the negotiating positions and perhaps even the aspirations of Croats and Muslims, in Croatia as well as in BiH. This would be neither quick nor linear, but it would be inevitable. Maintaining a firm and aggressive attitude against Serbs once the policy of Serbia has become open, democratic, and constructive would be counter-productive and self-defeating. For their own sake the Croats and Muslims would need to be more flexible, tolerant, and understanding.

This will bring today's bitter enemies into a situation tomorrow where they will have to look at realistic options in settling outstanding questions. In Croatia the outstanding issue is the status of Serbs in that republic. It is unrealistic to expect a resolution in the direction of the Serbian maximalist claim: total independence and integration of the Krajinas into what is now Yugoslavia but would then become Greater Serbia. It is equally unrealistic to expect a solution along the lines of the Croatian maximalist claim: Serbs will be given guarantees of their human rights but no national recognition.

The most likely solution would have the Serbs in Croatia obtaining special status and a level of national autonomy compatible with modern European standards. Some border corrections should be seriously contemplated. Initially this settlement would have to be guaranteed by the international community, not only politically but by the physical presence of the Blue Helmets.

The political solution in BiH will again have to strike a middle ground between the extreme positions of the warring parties. The Serbs and Croats will have to abandon the idea of partitioning BiH and creating a Greater Serbia and a Greater Croatia. Such concessions could only be made, however, *after* changes in Serbia and Croatia. The Muslims will have to abandon their dream of a unitary BiH in which they have the implicit privilege of the largest ethnic group. This would be and is violently opposed by both Serbs and Croats. Therefore, a solution will have to be sought in the direction of a federal or cantonal BiH. This would preserve the integrity of BiH as a state but would also take account of historical and current reality, which is coloured by deep though artificially induced divisions among ethnic groups.

The way to a co-operative arrangement would require that all former republics, now independent states, recognize each other. So far this has not happened, mostly because of Serbia's position on the succession of Yugoslavia. There has been mutual recognition and establishment of diplomatic relations among Slovenia, Croatia, BiH, and Macedonia. But none of them has established relations with the "rump Yugoslavia" because of the terms of recognition that Serbia is dictating. An early sign that things are moving in a co-operative direction would overcome this obstacle.

Yugoslavia as a state has ceased to exist. But Yugoslavia was never only a state. It has been and remains a geographical region interwoven with numerous geographic, economic, cultural, and family links. It has also been an idea, a vision, and a political objective. Once the bitter feuding is over, the normal course of life will require, even impose, a gradual re-establishment of co-operation, tolerance, and mutual understanding. Yugoslavia will probably never again be a common country of all Yugoslavs, but it can strive to be an association of states with common interests and the capacity to resolve through dialogue and compromise those that conflict.

It is difficult to see such a rational and humane dénouement to the Yugoslav drama at this moment, when the roar of cannon and the flow of blood, the streams of refugees and the destroyed homes bear witness to the hostility and ferocity of this ethnic confrontation. The worst is still possible. We are still in the uncertain phase of the agony. But agony does not always signal imminent death; it is equally the attendant of birth and the renewal of life.

Only if and when a state of mutual respect and co-operation is achieved among the peoples of the region can the final curtain on the Yugoslav drama be said to have fallen.

CHAPTER EIGHTEEN

A Chance for Peace at Last

Four years and six months after tanks first rolled out of Slovenia, and three and a half years after the beginning of war in BiH, the roar of cannons was finally silenced in the fall of 1995 and negotiations to bring peace to BiH and former Yugoslavia started in earnest.

This time, as opposed to the numerous earlier attempts, the efforts of the international community, led decisively by the United States, came to fruition. On 21 November 1995 the so-called Dayton Peace Accord was initialled by President Alija Izetbegović of BiH, President Franjo Tudjman of Croatia, and President Slobodan Milošević of Serbia representing and acting on behalf of rump Yugoslavia and the Bosnian Serbs. On 14 December 1995 the Dayton Peace Accord became an official peace agreement when the same parties signed it at a ceremony held in the Elysée Palace in Paris. The signing was witnessed by all the major players involved in bringing the war to an end, led by President Clinton of the United States and Jacques Chirac of France.

Thus the Yugoslav drama moved to a new stage, one of reconstruction and reconciliation rather than destruction and confrontation. How was this possible? What were the factors and circumstances that finally led the belligerents to sign a peace agreement? The sequence of events that led to the present situation and the present US-led peace initiative includes the following:[1]

In the fall of 1993 the Muslim-dominated Bosnian government rejected the Owen-Stoltenberg Plan, presented in July of that year, which would have maintained the internationally recognized state of BiH but divided it internally along ethnic lines. This was the second time that the Bosnian government had rejected an international proposal, having rejected a similar plan presented by the European Union in March of 1992. In both cases the rejection was made with the tacit agreement and support of the United States. The Bosnian government was at its lowest point at the time of the second rejection. It had just fought a war with Croats, over and above its constant battles with Bosnian Serbs, and the territory it controlled was at a minimum. Most of the international support, however, was on its side and the lifeline provided by American political support kept its hopes alive.

On 6 February 1994 a mortar grenade fell on a busy Sarajevo market, killing sixty-eight people and wounding others. Galvanized by public reactions to this horrendous act, the Western governments created and imposed a 20km exclusion zone and issued an ultimatum to Serbs to withdraw their heavy guns or place them under UN control. The ultimatum was supported by the threat of NATO bombing. The tension was temporarily reduced when the Serbs handed over some of their heavy guns (as did the Bosnian government) and withdrew others. Most importantly, a Russian diplomatic initiative allowed the Serbs to save face, NATO to avoid involvement before it was politically ready, and the Russians to come on board as a partner in the peace-making process.

In March of the same year the so-called Washington agreement was signed. It called for the creation of a Muslim-Croat federal state in BiH confederated with the Republic of Croatia. The agreement had a double purpose: it was intended to peacefully consolidate relations among parties that were amenable, cooperative, and dependent on the United States, thus creating a nucleus for further peace efforts, while also, since it included military cooperation, strengthening the anti-Serb block and redressing the military balance on the ground. Izetbegović called the agreement a "marriage of convenience, not love," but added that sometimes such marriages lasted longer.

It was not until the Dayton Accord in 1995, however, that either the federation or the confederation had any actual effect, with the exception of a joint military action against the Bosnian Serbs. The Croats in BiH, especially those concentrated in Western Herzegovina, feel much closer to their partner in confederation, Croatia, than they do to their federal partners in the country they belong to – BiH, and are in fact much more integrated (through flag, symbols, currency, arms, judiciary, media, etc.) with it. Nor was the military alliance operative during 1994, as the Croats were primarily concerned with their problem at home: the Serb-held Krajina region. Only when they had solved this problem to their liking did the military alliance with the Bosnian government come into full force.

In April of 1994 the first Serb attack on Goražde, a UN-declared safe area, occurred, electrifying the situation once again. In clear defiance of UN resolutions the Serbs attacked – and almost overtook – Goražde in an attempt to shore up morale after they had backed down in the Sarajevo confrontation and to test the resolve of NATO to honour its commitments.

NATO reacted by using its air force, for the first time ever, to knock out targets on the ground. The attack was an exercise in minimal engagement and mattered little militarily. However, it was during this attack that the Serbs first used a weapon that would ultimately hurt them more than their adversaries: they made good on their promise to take hostage if they were bombarded. This gave them a new tactic: take "Blue Helmets" hostage and then negotiate to exchange them for the promise of non-bombardment. NATO failed to follow through on its threat to bomb Serb positions and the Serbs felt stronger than ever. This situation lasted for over a year. During this period NATO worked on strengthening the political will of its members and dealing with a disagreement between countries with troops in the area (France, the UK, and Canada) and the United States over how to redeploy UN troops to make them less vulnerable to hostage-taking.

Perhaps the most important consequence of the Serb's senseless attack on Goražde and their hostage-taking was the loss of Russia's support. The Bosnian Serbs had gambled that Russia would strongly oppose the Western use of arms, thus creating new tensions which they could then exploit to their advantage. Russia, however, felt that it was being manipulated, that its support was being taken for granted, and that the Bosnian Serbs felt it could be used in any way they saw fit. As its great power ambitions were not completely dead (and in fact are reviving), Russia reacted by cutting its links with them.

In May 1994 the major powers formed the so-called Contact Group, essentially an informal Security Council of the UN in which Germany replaced China, to coordinate their efforts and present the belligerants with as unified an international stand as possible under the circumstances. Designed to demonstrate the unity of the international community regarding the main issues and the main approach to be applied in BiH, the Contact Group demonstrated both strength and weakness. It was nominally extremely powerful, yet its lack of a clear leader, as well as the remaining differences among its members despite their acceptance of a common framework, made it ineffective.

In July 1994 the Contact Group offered a new peace proposal with the following main elements:[2] establishment of a cease-fire; partition of a "unified" BiH into two "entities," the already created Bosnian Muslim–Bosnian Croat Federation and an entity for Bosnian Serbs; control by the Croat-Muslims of 51 per cent of Bosnian territory while the Serbs controled the remaining 49 per cent; international guarantees of peace, with troops to monitor the implementation and partition; and international control of Sarajevo and Mostar, the two main divided cities, for two years. No details about the territorial division were provided; Serbs were denied the possibility of a confederational arrangement with Serbia (Yugoslavia) and the plan was offered on a take it or leave it basis, with no information as to what would happen if the plan was rejected. The Croats accepted the proposal outright, the Muslims reluctantly, and the Bosnian Serbs rejected it.

The G-7 Summit in Naples, following in the wake of the Contact Group proposal, confirmed that Russia saw its strategic interests to be in co-operation with the West rather than in support for Milošević or, in particular, Karadjić and Mladić. However, the Russian shift was neither sufficiently clear nor decisive, nor was the unity within NATO ranks sufficient, for the summit to issue a strongly worded statement in full support of the newest Contact Group plan. Thus a golden opportunity to forcefully support the plan was lost.

The Naples Summit, however, more than anything else, convinced Milošević to change his position vis-a-vis the war in BiH. He accepted the Contact Group peace plan, publicly and in principle, as the best way to a stable settlement. Milošević sensed that NATO resolve was gradually strengthening and that internal disagreements within the Western alliance on this question, as well as the political gulf between the Western alliance and Russia, were gradually diminishing and wanted to position himself adequately for the new reality. From that point on his aggressive stance toward Serbian rights to some of the territories of former Yugoslavia changed, becoming less maximalist and more realistic.

The Bosnian Serb's definite rejection of the new peace proposal put them squarely at odds with Milošević's new strategy. Milošević closed the border toward BiH in retaliation, allowing only humanitarian aid through, and took a generally much tougher line toward the Bosnian Serb leadership, at the same time trying to weaken them politically from within by courting the Bosnian Serb constituency directly.

Milošević then allowed UN observers to be stationed along the Drina river, the natural border between BiH and Serbia, and was rewarded by a partial lifting of UN sanctions in sports, culture, and travel restrictions. After this, however, although Serbia continued to ask for a further removal or reduction of sanctions, none occurred until the signing of the Dayton Agreement. The question of sanctions became an important bargaining chip for the West and a very important part of the plan that led to the present political solution of the situation in BiH.

The differing goals of Milošević and Karadjić led to an open split and increased tensions among Serbs everywhere. The radical maximalists in "Serb lands" sided with Karadjić, the "realists" followed Milošević. The army and the police in Serbia, which remained loyal to Milošević, were the deciding factors. But there is no denying that this split damaged Serb unity and led to political deterioration of the Serb position. Milošević continued to hold power and influence over the Bosnian Serbs, since they generally accepted that they could not exist in the long run without Serbia.[3] But the quality of the bond was different and his leadership was no longer undisputed. Karadjić became a legitimate contender as the interpreter of Serb national interests and thus a liability to Milošević.

Milošević tried to turn this situation to his advantage by playing both ends against the middle. He positioned himself to be the peacemaker in former Yugoslavia by suggesting that he and he alone could bring the Bosnian Serbs to the negotiating table at a price acceptable to the West, that of not going to war with the Bosnian Serbs. He sensed that the West would listen because they had no desire to bring Karadjić and Mladić "to order" by military means, but he asked too high a price, one that the West (the United States and Germany in particular) were still not willing to pay. His price was the total removal of sanctions as well as some concessions to Bosnian Serbs. These were stumbling blocks for over a year, until the latest US peace initiative. In the meantime confrontations continued in BiH, particularly around Sarajevo, the UN safe-area of Bihać, and later the UN safe-areas in Eastern BiH.

In December of 1994 former US President Jimmy Carter went to Pale, the headquarters of the Bosnian Serbs, thus breaking their previous total isolation. He managed to broker a cease-fire which was to hold until May 1995, raising hopes in the interim that a political solution could be found. It was not, and in the end this trip created more confusion than clarification about the best way to get peace in BiH.

The Carter cease-fire collapsed before its expiry date and the fighting that followed was some of the most vicious of the whole war. However, it seems that only after this trip was it possible for the United States to officially change its position regarding the ultimate political expectations of the Bosnian Serbs. The collapse of the cease-fire and the United States' first attempt to lead the international community toward a peace settlement in BiH (and Croatia) marked a considerable change in the us position toward the Bosnian Serbs.

In January of 1995 the so called "Z-4" plan[4] for political settlement of the conflict between Croats and Serbs in Croatia was proposed. The plan offered full reintegration of the Serb territories into Croatia with generous provisions for full autonomy and political representation for Serbs. The Serb leader in Croatia, a radical maximalist, rejected even the thought of considering the plan, let alone sitting at a table to negotiate. His argument that it was not offered in good faith since it came at a time when the UN was ready to pull out of Croatia under the threat of Tudjman's withdrawal of mandate was a flimsy cover-up and cost the Croat Serbs dearly in months to come.

The Croats, who, after pressure from the United States, had grudgingly agreed to negotiate the plan, had by now developed a powerful military force. It had been amassed with the tacit agreement of the United States, who were hoping to create a new military balance in former Yugoslavia as the best deterrent to future aggressive action. To that end, retired us military personnel had been employed in Croatia as advisors in training and organizing the Croat army. As well, for three years Croatia had devoted by far the highest percentage of GNP of any country in Europe to military procurement. In spite of the arms embargo imposed on all former republics of Yugoslavia, they had managed to create an army that posed a credible threat to the Serbs in Croatia, provided that Serbia proper stayed out of the war. After the failure of the Carter cease-fire in BiH and the beginning of the offensive by Bosnian Muslim troops, Croatia decided that Serbia's response to an attack was likely to be minimal and mounted a lightning offensive on the territory of Western Slavonia known as the UN Sector West.

The area was overtaken quickly with minimal losses to the Croatian army, the total defeat of Serbian forces and authorities in the region, and a massive exodus of Serbs toward Serbia and BiH, accompanied by the atrocities that have become a hallmark of fighting in former Yugoslavia. The Croats were jubilant, the Serbs downcast. The latter tried to put up a brave front, saying that Knin, the heart of Serb-held territories, would not only fight back but would repel any aggression by Croatia.

Three months later the Croatian army mounted a massive offensive on Knin, which collapsed within a few days without putting up a serious fight. The Serbian army, or what was left of it, together with the great majority of the Serb population in the area, left territory they had inhabited for centuries, significantly reducing the "Serb question" in Croatia.[5] The only remaining Serb-held territory is a narrow sliver of land on the right bank of Danube centred on the now-notorious town of Vukovar. After the Dayton Accord it looks as if this is the only territory previously occupied by the Croatians that will be peacefully reintegrated into Croatia.

In the spring of 1995, after the collapse of the Carter cease-fire, the Muslim-led Bosnian government began an offensive and managed to retake some ground. After three and one-half years of fighting, the largely rag-tag, para-military, and poorly equipped Bosnian army had become a well-organized, better trained, and better equipped fighting force that was more able to counter the Bosnian Serb army. The offensive was a reaction to the lack of progress in finding a political solution and it was intended to either provoke a more sub-stantive and meaningful political effort or else redress the balance militarily.

Though the Bosnian troops did not have the capacity at the time to defeat the Serbs, they did provoke a fierce reaction from the Bosnian Serbs who, during the course of the summer months of 1995, overran two eastern-lying UN safe areas – Srebrenica and Žepa – and critically endangered a third – Goražde. The UN's initial response was weak, largely because of its concern for the hostages that the Serbs had taken by the hundreds as soon as NATO planes started dropping bombs. However public pressure for it to take more decisive action increased as images of tens of thousands of innocent civilians herded away from their homes and stories of rape and maltreatment appeared and horrifying rumours about mass execu-tions of Muslim men of military age began circulating. Once Milošević seemed to have "solved" the hostage problem, NATO finally swung into higher gear. The number of sorties flown by NATO planes was increased to over four hundred a day by September and a number of vitally important Serb military installations as well as ammunition dumps, tanks, and other military equipment were knocked out.

Another reaction to the Serb hostage-taking was the creation of a Rapid Reaction Force, manned mostly by British and French troops but, in contrast to the UN forces with which they were operating in parallel, equipped with offensive weaponry and capable of inflicting serious damage. Ostensibly the purpose of this force was to prevent future hostage-taking, but actually it demonstrated the resolve of France and the United Kingdom not to be humiliated on the ground. It was there either to shore up the UN effort or to facilitate the withdrawal of UN forces and personnel, should that become necessary. At that point which of these would occur depended largely on the reaction of the United States.

Whether prompted by this decisive action of the French and British outside NATO structures or for reasons of their own, such as the need to show leadership before the up-coming presidential elections, the United States finally committed itself fully to a course of action that relied on a heavy stick and a long carrot. The stick was the use of NATO power, the carrot the recognition of the Bosnian Serb state. Together with the previously packaged Bosnian Muslim-Croat alliance, again brokered by Washington, the deterrent of US troops in Macedonia, and the implicit political protection offered to the Albanians in Kosovo, the stage was set for a new attempt to bring peace and stability to the region, this time with the United States clearly in the lead.

During the summer of 1995 the Muslim-Croat military alliance finally came to life in BiH. After having successfully routed the Serbs from the Krajina region, cleansing the area of all but a token number of mostly old and helpless Serbs, Croatia joined with the Muslim-led Bosnian forces as well as the Bosnian Croat units to liberate the Serb-encircled UN safe area of Bihać. With NATO bombardment going on at the same time, the Bosnian Serb military and political leadership locked in quarrels and mutual accusations, and the army on the ground suffering from deep demoralization due to the Serb losses in Croatia, the Croat-Bosnian alliance gained momentum and took over large territories in Western Bosnia, coming close to overtaking Banja Luka, the largest town in Serb possession.

The ease with which the Serbs lost their territories – and the speed with which the Bosnian-Croat alliance was able to take them over – baffled observers previously convinced of Serb invincibility. Not only did Serbs loose the territories that they conquered at the beginning of the war, they also lost some territories that were previously solidly Serb, such as the town of Drvar, which was 97 per cent Serb at the time of the last census in 1991. This offensive was eventually cut short by the United States, who were now preparing to table a new peace proposal, the one which would ultimately hold. The United States put pressure on the Croats and the Bosnian government to cut short their military operation and to refrain from taking Banja Luka. With some grumbling the Croats and Bosnians stopped, feeling that they had been cheated out of a decisive victory.

The total isolation to which the Bosnian Serbs were subjected, as well as the heavy loss of territories held by Serbs in Croatia and later in BiH, brought about a reconciliation between Karadjić and Milo-šević, but clearly under terms dictated by Milošević. Thus, as the interest of the international community in its newest diplomatic effort increased, the belligerence of Bosnian Serbs was significantly moderated, making an agreement that much more likely.

All this took place while the international community continued to condemn the war and its objectives but did far less than was needed, even less than was possible. Its more than four years of mediation had produced almost no results, with the notable exception of the provision of humanitarian aid – though even that was disputed in some quarters.

By seeking a political settlement the international community became part of the problem rather than providing a solution. There was an obvious lack of a clear and unified vision about the conflict itself, a lack of unity in action, and, most importantly, a lack of real interest in resolving the crisis. This led to a problem of leadership and the acceptance of the lowest common denominator as the basis for policy. The policy of the international community had been to undertake as little as possible and still contend that something is being done. There was no willingness to commit what was necessary – economically, politically, and militarily – to resolve the problem.

The local leaders – Milošević, Tudjman, Izetbegović, and Karadjić – exploited differences within the international community with great skill, each pulling in his own direction, making settlement more elusive and dragging the international community deeper and deeper into the conflict. The war dragged on, with untold suffering for the civilian population, because there was always one side (and sometimes more than one since it was a three-way contest) that felt it had more to gain from continued fighting than from a settlement.

Now that the peace agreement has been signed it is being claimed that such a settlement could have been reached more than three years ago. With hindsight this seems true, but one should be cautious with such generalizations. First, we have to see if the current initiative actually leads to a lasting peace and a return of stability in the region. This is not a given, although now that the United States is heavily involved it seems much more likely then at the time when their participation in peace efforts was half-hearted.

Second, given the circumstances prevailing three years ago it was hardly likely that the present "solution" would have occurred. The current position of the international community – which, by the way, is hardly rock-solid – had to "mature." The relative roles of the Europeans and the Americans in the post–Cold War world were not settled, especially when it came to questions of how to deal with regional crises in Europe. Determining their respective position was further complicated for the international players when the Russians, with their differing ideas, views, and policy recommendations, became involved. But if putting together the current effort took time, it is important that it now stay together, as it provides a settlement that opens the way to lasting peace and stability.

Third, the situation on the ground also had to mature. The enormous military advantage that the Serbs had enjoyed since the beginning of the war had to be at least reduced, if not eliminated, before there could be any conceivable reason for them to want to negotiate, rather than continuing to maximize their demands. It seems quite clear that during 1995 the balance of power in former Yugoslavia changed dramatically. Serbia lost a great deal of its power and reduced its strategic ambitions from a maximalist to a "realistic" framework. The Muslims, and especially the Croats, have seen their fortunes grow and their respective position improve.

But Serbia had not lost the war, nor were Croatia and the Muslim-Croat Federation in a position to dictate the terms of peace on their own without intervention from the international community. Wars usually end with winners, which makes it easier to set up post-war arrangements because the looser has little say. In the war(s) in former Yugoslavia this decisive moment was never reached. All sides thus had a bargaining position and some leverage over the outcome. This made the final round of the peace process particularly difficult and delicate.

Notwithstanding the problem of Eastern Slavonia still being in Serb hands, the Gordian knot had been untied in BiH, and that became the focus of the Fraisure/Holbrooke peace initiative.[6] The starting point for the us peace plan was the plan that had been previously suggested by the Contact Group, but with the significant difference that the existence of Republika Srpska (The Republic of Bosnian Serbs) was officially recognized.

The basis of the peace agreement includes the following:

1 Bosnia and Herzegovina (BiH) will continue its legal existence within its present borders and will continue to be recognized internationally and remain a member of the United Nations and other multilateral organizations.

2 BiH will consist of two entities: the Federation of Bosnia and Herzegovina, as established by the Washington Agreements of 1994, and the Republika Srpska. The Federation will have 51 per cent of the territory of BiH while the Serb Republic will have 49 per cent. Neither partner will be allowed to establish controls at the boundaries between the two entities.

3 BiH will be responsible for foreign policy; foreign trade and customs policy; monetary policy; immigration, refugee, and asylum policy and regulation; international and inter-entity criminal law enforcement; and regulation of inter-entity transportation and air traffic control. All governmental functions and powers not expressly assigned in the constitution to the institutions of BiH, which includes most of the functions of a modern state (economic, political, judiciary, policing, etc.) remain the sole responsibility of the two entities within their borders.

4 All refugees and displaced persons have the right to return to their homes of origin and have their property restored or else be compensated for its loss. The early return of refugees is declared to be "an important objective" of the settlement of the conflict in BiH.

5 The parties are committed to "ensure ... the organization of free and fair elections, in particular a politically neutral environment" under the general supervision of the Organization for Security and Cooperation in Europe. Elections are to be held six to nine months after the signing of the agreement, with people expected to vote, in general, in the municipalities they are from originally.

6 The international community will provide military assistance through the Implementation Force (IFOR) led by NATO, assistance in restoration of the functions of state through the Organization for Security and Cooperation in Europe, and financial assistance through the European Union and the World Bank.

There are a host of other provisions in the Agreement[7] that deal with human rights issues, arbitration, policing, civilian implementation, even preservation of national monuments. But the six points given above represent the core of the agreement. It is on the implementation of these points that the future Bosnia and Herzegovina will be made or broken. The areas involved are clearly controversial and highly ambiguous. The agreement attempts to find a workable combination of ethnic-national and civil-liberal principles that will permit a unified BiH state, but it is far from clear whether the present arrangements will be successful. The agreement as accepted has all the markings of an unstable compromise that will allow its signatories to interpret the longer-term prospects as they see fit. No wonder that each side was able to claim "victory" and the accomplishment of its objectives. The Muslim and Bosnian Croat leaders lauded the agreement because, according to them, it spelled the end of the "Greater Serbia" project. The Serb leadership (both in BiH and Serbia) agreed but with a different meaning of the word "end." For them recognition of the Serb Republic has cleared the road toward a "Greater Serbia," albeit smaller then originally envisaged and desired, but now recognized by the international community through recognition of the Serb Republic.

It seems, therefore, that the peace agreement, though an important milestone on the journey to peace, is not a milestone on a short journey but only the beginning of a longer journey that will require persistence and determination to convert the agreed-on principles into a workable political reality. Much will depend on the implementation of point six, which deals with the involvment of the international community. If the implementation of the agreement is adhered to fully, BiH could emerge as a unified state. It could also break up definitely a number of years down the road because ethnic conflict has led to what are effectively ethnically separate entities.

What will lead to permanent peace in BiH? Is it a complete division, as suggested by Henry Kissinger when he held that since BiH has never been a nation, an ethnic group, or a specific cultural identity it cannot function as a modern state? If this is correct, the current agreement would be only a half-way stage to a definite split and the creation of a "Greater Serbia" and "Greater Croatia." In that case the question remaining would be the political fate and the size of a state for the Muslims. Or is peace to be found in restoring some integrity and substance to BiH as a whole – in the revival of multi-ethnic co-existence and the gradual building of a democratic, liberal, and civil society to replace ethno-nationalistic exclusiveness? Again, the current agreement would then be only a stage toward that objective. While it is clear that the current peace agreement is only an interim arrangement, it is not entirely clear which of the two possibilities is more likely to permanently diffuse the tensions that have fed the current conflict and still present a real danger to the peace process in BiH. Furthermore, there is also the question of which of the two directions is less likely to create negative precedents and the possibility of ethnic confrontation elsewhere in the world.

For the second time in this century BiH has become a maelstrom of world politics. Although this time the consequences of events in BiH never came close to the tragic developments that triggered World War I, the shock waves coming from this rugged, mostly mountainous terrain managed to create negative vibrations far and wide. In the past few years BiH has confronted the territorial ambitions of Serbia (or left-over "Yugoslavia") and Croatia, the two adjoining states that have openly claimed areas held by their respective ethic groups in BiH and, a little less conspicuously, the territory and "soul" of the Bosnian Muslim population. It has severely tested the unity of the European Community (later Union) on foreign policy. It has contributed to the tensions and the shift of power in foreign policy matters between the president of the United States and Congress. It has caused trans-Atlantic disagreements between the European Union and the United States on goals and policy. It has brought NATO into "real life action" for the first time ever. It has contributed to the cooling of relations between the United States and Russia, particularly after the NATO bombing of Bosnian Serb positions. The cost of war to the peoples of BiH has been horrendous. About a hundred thousand dead,[8] several hundred thousand wounded or invalided for life, and probably over two and a half million physically displaced from their homes.

Although it had never officially been an independent nation state until recognized as such by the European Community, BiH had developed a core identity and a sense of ethnic tolerance and blending that most probably could have sustained its conversion into a modern, democratic state had it not been for the aggressive and chauvinistic nationalism that spilled over into it, first from Serbia but soon after and with equal measure from Croatia. BiH has thus become, and still is, the target of national-chauvinistic projects that, more or less openly, have in mind the attainment of "Greater Serbia" and "Greater Croatia." The essence of the problem is not that the territory of BiH is subject to aggression from the outside, though that is a part of it. The real problem is that the Serb and Croat ethnic communities in BiH have been the targets of deliberate nationalistic campaigns, the object of which has been to suppress their Bosnian identity and to consolidate and glorify their respective Serb and Croat identities. This could only be accomplished through orchestrated campaigns of "us" against "them" and "hate" instead of "respect and tolerance." The war in BiH was not the inevitable product of centuries of ethnic hatreds, as is often wrongly stated in the West. It was the result of political ambition crystallizing in a nondemocratic, post-Communist atmosphere, of installed fear, and of the mismanagement of the crisis by both domestic and international players. Had the popular misconception that the war in BiH was a consequence of "millennia-old ethic animosities" been true, the war would have broken out in BiH first, rather than in Slovenia and Croatia. Instead, it took a long time and a great deal of concentrated effort by nationalist zealots to create the ethnic division of BiH. It was not easy to persuade the majority of ordinary people that Islam was on an aggressive, fundamentalist march, that all Serbs are cut-throat Chetniks, that Croats are a reincarnation of the dreaded Ustashi. In a great part of BiH it meant "convincing" the people that their trusted friends, good neighbours, even spouses, were actually devilish foes who belonged to "the other side." The propaganda onslaught was so intense, so demanding, and so severe that many have come to regard it as true, seeking comfort in a collective, national identity to ease their consciences in order to hate the other side and take part in an atrocious war.

The campaigns have, tragically, been extremely effective and have produced a tense and seemingly irreversible polarization. The ethnically based ruling political parties have accustomed the people to the belief that there is no possibility of agreement because of the "other side." Since there can be no agreement, war must be fought, territories must be cleansed of the hated enemy, and the blame can conveniently always be placed on "the other side."

The current civil war in BiH is a struggle between peoples with a common Slavic background and a common language. Their primary differences are not ethnic or racial but religious. Indeed, until the national awakening in Serbia and Croatia in the nineteenth century, and again a couple of years ago, the peoples of BiH distinguished among themselves by place of worship, since they had always spoken a single common language. The religions themselves, however, were not the cause of the struggle but a powerful instrument for political manipulation. In the hands of politicians post-Communism led to another, equally totalitarian but this time nationalistic, ideology without ever giving the peoples of BiH a real chance to express their own desires.

The idea of partition, always in the minds of the instigators of the hate campaign, became a self-fulfilling prophecy. To many, both inside and outside BiH, it now seems to be the only available option. The argument goes as follows: even if there was inter-ethnic tolerance in BiH before the war, the war itself has opened so many old wounds and inflicted so many new ones that the status quo is simply unrealistic. The demographic map of BiH has largely been redrawn by the war and national-chauvinism, combat, fear, and terror have displaced close to two and a half million people. Territories have become ethnically homogenized. Ethnic division of BiH is now not only possible, but appears to make sense, to "respect the reality on the ground."

"Respecting the reality on the ground" has become a catch phrase as well as an important basis for the policy implemented in the current peace initiative. While it would be foolish to ignore what is actually happening in designing a strategy and conducting policies, choosing one interpretation of reality among several based on one specific time would be equally unwise. And it could also be dangerous. The reality on the ground is constantly changing and it is difficult to pin down the situation that should serve as the logical start for peace and stability.

The only stable reality is that there are three parties with conflicting interests over how the territory should be divided. The idea that we are dealing with three solid ethnic blocks and therefore with their representative leaders fails to adequately reflect the true situation. In all three ethnic groups there are those who will fight and kill to achieve the final separation of "us" from "them." These people have been in the limelight, because of their acts of war and the power they appear to have within their respective ethnic groups. But there are also large numbers of those for whom a return to a multi-ethnic BiH, organized as a civil and not an ethnic-national society, would be welcome, not to mention the high percentage of those among the more than two and a half million refugees whose "ideology" and political credo is based largely on what will allow them to return to their homes, provided they can feel relatively safe once they get there.

From the prospective of the last four years, and looking ahead as far as the next four, partition may indeed be the only possible solution for BiH, or at least the best available. However, looking at this "solution" from a longer historical perspective and with regard to a broader set of future implications suggests that this method of resolving the current conflict may raise more problems than it has currently "solved."

By reasserting itself simultaneously as the main diplomatic player and the force behind the stick used against the Bosnian Serbs, the United States has taken on a huge responsibility. It has not only mediated the peace but enforced it, first at the negotiating table and then on the ground. Having grumbled about the lack of US participation, European leaders, after having shown that they were incapable of providing leadership, can hardly complain that the United States has finally made its presence felt. The United States peace initiative recognizes the reality of the current ethnic division. Where previously this division was deemed unacceptable on moral considerations and the accepted principles of international conduct, the danger now is that the moral considerations and accepted principles may be overruled in deference to this present reality.

The trick in putting the agreement into effect will be to avoid extreme positions and strike a balance between the reality on the ground and accepted principles of international conduct. The centrepiece of the new peace effort must be to provide a more durable existence for the state of BiH, a state which will of necessity be based on ethnic divisions for some time to come. This idea of a Bosnian state, common to all ethnic groups, should not be abandoned. It must be recognized that the territorial division is only a compromise, since it is obviously purely arbitrary and imposed by international force.

There is no pre-war or post-war criterion, ethnic or otherwise, that makes the 51:49 percent division intrinsically correct and meaningful.

After securing the separation of the armies, the international community should direct its main effort to promoting reconciliation through renewed forms of ethnic cooperation and tolerance in order to restore as quickly as possible some of the pre-war fabric of BiH. This will not be easy, it will not be quick, and it will not be cheap. Events of the last four years have left deep scars and tears in the fabric of all the ethnic groups involved and cooperation will be infinitely more difficult to achieve today than it was at the time of the break-up of Yugoslavia.

The compromise solution for BiH – a common state for the three ethnic groups divided into two entities with substantial autonomy – given the pressures under which it was accomplished, should not be taken as the end but only as a starting point for securing a relative peace and a (precarious) stability in BiH. This peace and stability, supported, secured, and financially aided by the world community, could then serve as the basis for return to the ethnic community structure that characterized BiH before the war – as the basis for the management of ethnic conflict through civil and democratic institutions rather than through violence and ethnic cleansing. In order for real, lasting peace and stability to emerge, the international community will have to maintain a strong presence over a long period of time. This will mean helping financially, in administration, in delivering justice, and in policing the fragile security of a war-torn nation. While peace cannot be made by the international community, its involvement would go a long way toward creating the conditions in which Bosnians of all ethnic origin would eventually overcome hatreds and divisions. This is a long-term project. Perhaps the strongest argument for this arrangement is that the alternative, partition and definite division, is worse and in the long run more costly since it could hardly be accomplished without new fighting.

A simple look at the map and the knowledge that there are over two and a half million refugees should make it clear that division would lead to perpetual fighting, to the sort of situation we see in Lebanon and Ireland, or to the continuation of ethnic cleansing and the ultimate creation of ethnically pure states, and not only in BiH.

Once an ethnically pure "Greater Croatia" and an ethnically pure "Greater Serbia" are created, the contest would move on to who "owns" the Muslims, since, according to both Serbs and Croats, they are not an ethnicity but religiously converted Serbs or Croats. This is a real danger, which is not clearly recognized at this time.

Another danger is that attempting to satisfy the Serbian nationalist beast by feeding it slices of BiH will not quell its appetite and could even increase it. The possibility of the partition of BiH, driven by nationalisms generated in Serbia and Croatia, may also help increase the strength of these nationalisms, thus making the transition to democracy and a civil society in these states that much harder and even further in the future.

Paradoxically, the main difficulty with this long-term approach may not be with the three ethnic communities in BiH but in the will of the principal peace-maker, the United States, to continue its initiative and to follow through on seeing the plan to completion. The United States has a recent history of muscular intervention in complex situations, followed by abrupt withdrawal when an early solution looks impossible. Furthermore the deadline of a year, clearly given because of domestic political pressures during a presidential campaign year, is a sword that cuts two ways. While it puts real pressure on those involved to accomplish as much as possible during that year, there are elements in the settlement that will clearly take much more than a year to accomplish, and attempting to deal with them more quickly could turn out to be counter-productive.

A second concern is that the US leadership will fail to provide a sufficient role for other countries. Because the United States has used its military and political might to broker the peace agreement, they are often seen not as the main but rather as the only credible international player in the Bosnian end-game. This is potentially dangerous since it could lead to a decrease in allied support and an even further increase in Russian displeasure over the way they are being treated with regard to their possible contribution in the Balkans. Disagreement between the allies could quickly lead to a new round of exploitation of differences between the three groups directly involved, making the execution of a peace plan more difficult and reinforcing rather than diminishing ethnic differences.

The third concern is over the substance of the peace plan and the way it evolves from principles into political reality. One aspect that raises potential problems is the finality with which this document is to be treated: nothing that has been agreed upon can be open for renegotiation. In one sense of course, in a situation such as the one which the United States faced in BiH the unyielding character of the document must be viewed as a strength, not a weakness. However, as the situation with the Serbs of Sarajevo clearly shows, there may be unforseen consequences in attempting to implement the agreement.[9]

Another aspect that could create as many problems as it solves is the proposal that elections be held within a year. Elections can, no doubt, be held within a year, but will they be democratic? Will they result in non-ethnic, non-nationalistic leadership for BiH and its two entities, as is clearly the expectation of the peace-makers? This is hardly likely, since a year is much too short a time to sweep away the present strong nationalist sentiments and replace them with a leadership inspired by civil and human rights, the rule of law, and respect for all ethnic groups of BiH. If elections are held before the nationalist euphoria has ebbed, they will only provide unwanted and unwarranted legitimacy for the champions of national division, thus severely compromising the intent of the elections. A better policy would be to work patiently for tactical gains rather than expecting a strategic breakthrough – which will require flexibility in the interpretation of the content of the peace agreement by the international community.

The endgame in BiH will undoubtedly present the outside powers with further agonizing choices. While the consequences of allowing the use of military force to be the final criterion of a political settlement will probably be less dramatic today than they have been in the past (in the eighteenth and nineteenth centuries and World War I and II), the results of such a departure from the accepted norms of international conduct, at least in Europe, will nevertheless be significant not only for Europe but for the world at large. First, there is the risk of an extension of the war in the Balkans. Though this risk may be reduced by establishing a NATO presence in Macedonia, it will not go away. Should the Bosnian state break up through use of military force, the risk of war among peoples further to the south of former Yugoslavia will be considerably increased. Second, it will set a dangerous precedent for the Transcaucasus and other areas where there are ethnic disputes. A logic of territorial division based on military force in the heart of Europe could, and probably will, bring back dangerous beliefs in nationalism and in the idea that interest should be perceived unilaterally and in accord with national-chauvinistic beliefs. Third, in an insidious and indirect way the acceptance of military solutions in general, and the partitioning of BiH in particular, will have a corrosive impact on the Western alliance, on the move toward European unity, on self-respect, and on the established values of democratic societies. All of this, over and above the suffering of the largely innocent population of BiH, should make obvious the need for deep reflection in choosing the direction of the current peace initiative.

True and lasting peace, as stated in the previous chapter, can only come when the force of nationalism is reined in by a respect for civil and human rights, by democracy, and through a willingness to cooperate on an equal footing by all the republics of former Yugoslavia. We are not there yet, and probably will not be in quite a while. But the stage for peace has been set and the final curtain on the bloody Yugoslav drama is slowly setting.

Notes

INTRODUCTION

1 The theoretical discussion of national movements and nationalism is largely based on Miroslav Hroch, "From National Movement to the Fully Formed Nation," *New Left Review* 198 (Mar.–Apr. 1993): 3–20.

CHAPTER ONE

1 An *opština* is a sub-republican administrative unit equivalent to a borough or an arrondissement.
2 Though modern measurements of economic well-being dispute the explanatory power of GNP (gross national product) per capita, for the general public it still remains the simplest and best indicator.
3 As this book goes to press, this strange concoction is actually the official name of the new independent state: the Former Yugoslav Republic of Macedonia!

CHAPTER TWO

1 The discussion of the birth of the Yugoslav idea and its subsequent materialization as a state is based largely on Ivo Banac, *The National Question in Yugoslavia* (Ithaca: Cornell University Press), 1984.
2 Štokavian is one of the three dialects of the Serbo-Croatian language and is by far the most widespread. The other two dialects are Kajkavian and Čakavian, both spoken only in Croatia.
3 Milan Marjanović, *Narod koji nastaje* (The Nation Coming to Existence) (Rijeka 1913).

CHAPTER THREE

1 The name Yugoslavia will be used for simplicity's sake although at this time it was officially called the Kingdom of the Serbs, Croats, and Slovenes and was to change its name only ten years later.
2 Significantly, the Vatican was the very first to recognize the independent states of Slovenia and Croatia formally, in January 1991, a day before Germany and some other states.
3 The monarch of Serbia, King Peter I, who became the first king of the Serbs, Croats, and Slovenes, was aged and ill and effectively abdicated his sovereign powers to the regent, later to become King Alexander I.
4 There were nine of these units bearing the names of rivers (and the coastline) rather than ethnic groups.

CHAPTER FOUR

1 Mihailović was promoted to be minister of war and the commander-in-field of the Royal Yugoslav Army (consisting only of Serbs and Montenegrins). Since the king spent the entire war in London, the British had little choice but to recognize Mihailović as well. As time went by and reports from the field (some sent by Churchill's son Randolph) indicated that Tito, though a Communist, was a better war ally than Mihailović, the British, less than enthusiastically, shifted their support to Tito for purely pragmatic reasons.
2 The first two elite partisan units to be formed, called the "Proletarian Brigades," were more than 80 per cent Serb and Montenegrin, with a Serb and a Montenegrin commanding them.
3 Land in Yugoslavia was never nationalized or fully collectivized as it was in the USSR and some other Communist countries. Throughout the Socialist period over 80 per cent of the land, livestock, and agricultural machinery was privately owned by peasants working on the land.
4 In 1967 Yugoslavia was the first Communist-governed country to introduce a joint-venture law, thus inviting foreign capital. The law, although lacking in substance, was politically important since it indicated a new direction of economic development.
5 The phraseology of this scheme perplexed Yugoslavs as much as it did foreign economic partners.
6 It is still too early to make a definite assessment of the Tito years. The attempt here is neither to glorify nor to satanize Tito's rule but to assess his accomplishments in historical perspective. It is easy, in retrospect, to point out the flaws in his handling of Yugoslavia and the Yugoslavs. All nationalistic leaderships within what used to be Yugoslavia have done so, with the exception of Montenegro and Macedonia.

True, his handling of political opposition left a great deal to be desired. But even with that, he managed to be acceptable to the West (which showered him with financial generosity), tolerated and secretly admired by the East (after Stalin), and largely and genuinely adored in Yugoslavia.

Rather than view Tito and his performance against the background of high human rights and political standards of today, I have tried to portray his performance in historical context and primarily in terms of his success in holding the ethnic groups of Yugoslavia together without much repression.

CHAPTER FIVE

1 A small but very revealing description of the atmosphere comes from a football game between Hajduk and Crvena Zvezda, which was in progress when the speaker announced the news of Tito's death. The game was terminated immediately; the players of both teams (Hajduk from Croatia and Crvena Zvezda from Serbia) left the field crying and hugging each other, while a large part of the stadium sang a well-known loyalty song to Tito. This was *not* stage-managed.
2 For a number of years previous he had been a successful industrial manager, then the prime minister of Croatia and president of the Presidency of that republic.
3 That is why I chose the Fourteenth Congress of the CPY, during which it finally broke up, to be the line of demarcation between the part of the book entitled "Actors" and the one entitled "Plot."

CHAPTER SIX

1 The industry that did develop in Kosovo was very capital intensive (energy, mining, smelting) and was ill suited to the demographic and employment needs.
2 Comintern is the acronym of the Communist International, the organization based in Moscow and heavily influenced by Stalin that gave instructions for the political conduct of Communist parties outside the USSR.
3 Initially this expression covered only the federal units of Yugoslavia. Later, when the number of those in disagreement with Serbian policy came to include the European Community, other European and non-European nations, and finally the UN, this cliché, making headline news in the nationalistic press, included all of them.
4 Milošević himself was the president of the Belgrade CP organization until a year before this confrontation. Many faithful operatives or apparatchiks loyal to him helped enormously in toppling Ivan Stambolić, the previous leader and then president of Serbia.

CHAPTER SEVEN

1 For twenty years before this debate opened there was no such thing as a federal minister of education.
2 An example will illustrate this point well: Priština, the soccer club from the capital of Kosovo, was promoted to the first league. Money, most of it coming from the federal development fund, was immediately poured into modernizing and increasing the capacity of the stadium, even though it was located in a part of town that had no sewage facilities at the time.
3 The name of the copper mine in Kosovo where the strike took place.

CHAPTER EIGHT

1 At the time of the Serbian national awakening he was popularly called "Ayatollah Khomeini" since, like the Iranian spiritual leader, he had no official position in either the party or the state but his word carried a lot of weight.
2 The Belgrade, which is to say Serbian authorities found numerous reasons why the new television station could not transmit from Belgrade.
3 JNA is the acronym for *Jugoslovenska narodna armija*, which means the Yugoslav People's Army. Cynics say that this once formidable fighting force first ceased to be people's, then to be Yugoslav, and was finally no longer an army.
4 At the time of the escalation of the crisis the minister of defence was General Veljko Kadijević, who declared himself a Yugoslav and came from Croatia and a mixed Serb-Croat marriage. His deputy, Admiral Stane Brovert, was a Slovene.
5 Churchill and Stalin are said to have decided, on a paper napkin, to split their influence in post-war Yugoslavia 50:50, while they were negotiating the new spheres of influence in Europe.

CHAPTER NINE

1 Now, after a series of political, economic, and financial shocks, the Community has certainly lost a lot of its previous glamour and appeal. But at the time relevant to our understanding of the crisis in Yugoslavia, it was *the* authority from which to seek political and economic help.
2 I cannot but admit to the same error in judgment. At the time I was Yugoslav ambassador to the European Community, and the reports I sent to my government of conversations with high European officials were typically shaded with uncritical optimism, based objectively on the unfounded optimism and promises of these officials and, subjectively, on a streak of wishful thinking.

CHAPTER TEN

1 Warren Zimmerman, the United States ambassador, and the ambassadors of the European Community were absent, a demonstration of their
dissatisfaction with the way things had been handled in Kosovo. Milošević took offence and would not receive Zimmerman for months,
holding the ambassador responsible for the only blemish on his moment
of total triumph.

2 A senior Serbian Socialist Party official visiting Brussels told me, in the
summer of 1991, that the firm expectation all along had been that the
Muslims of BiH would side with Serbia in a possible showdown with
Croatia. He seemed genuinely bewildered by the fact that this had not
happened.

3 The region in central Croatia comprising a number of *opstinas* with an
overwhelming Serb majority (see map in chapter 1).

4 The Slovenian Communist leader Milan Kucan was elected president of
Slovenia in the first authenthic multi-party elections held in Yugoslavia,
but with a much slimmer margin than Milošević. The Croatian Communist Party candidate lost miserably. A year later Milošević, in new and
this time really multi-party elections, again won easily but with a political image that had in the meantime been tarnished by Serbia's expansionist policy.

5 It later became known that they had planned to do this anyway, regardless of Milošević's tactics, because they were convinced that there could
be no deal in the long run with the Serbs led by Milošević. Milošević's
bullying only made it easier for them, providing a convenient excuse.

6 In Slovenia there were over twenty and in Croatia over thirty parties bid-
ding for votes.

7 A specifically Yugoslav form of ownership whereby the means of production were owned by the whole society and managed, on its behalf,
by the self-managed enterprises using these assets.

8 Not to be confused with Slovenia, Slavonia is a region between Belgrade
and Zagreb, fully in Croatia and north of BiH. While in the Krajina
region Serbs made up a solid majority, Slavonia had a much more balanced ethnic mix, Pakrac included, which was predominantly Croat.

CHAPTER ELEVEN

1 Two days before the proclamation of independence a skirmish in
Maribor in front of the JNA barracks left one person dead. No matter
that he was killed largely by his own fault, falling under an army vehicle
moving *into* the barracks – this aroused the population to a very high
pitch.

2 The destinations were thirty-five land border crossings, one airport near Ljubljana (the capital), and the principal Slovenian maritime port of Koper.

3 In a statement made as late as 9 May 1991.

4 General Hadzić comes from a family that had more than thirty members slaughtered by the Ustashi during the Second World War. It is said that he himself, then a child, witnessed some of the brutal executions, which left a lasting mark on his attitude towards the Croats.

5 An unpleasant expression, to say the least, that has come into current popular use since the fighting began in BiH but that has strong fascist overtones.

6 The town was so thoroughly destroyed that it was compared to Stalingrad during the Second World War. To underline this, a French peace group organized for one day the Metro station "Stalingrad" in Paris to be renamed "Vukovar."

CHAPTER TWELVE

1 The exception being during the Second World War, when some of the most brutal atrocities were committed in Bosnia by all three sides, Muslims and Ustashi Croats against the Serbs, and the Serb Chetniks responding in kind.

2 In secret meetings between Milošević and Tudjman that took place in March and April of the same year the topic of the division of BiH figured prominently, but no conclusion was reached because both sides considered this to be only a sideshow to the question of Serbs in Croatia.

3 Late August 1993, when the international community was attempting to get the three sides to sign a new so-called Owen-Stoltenberg proposal for a peaceful settlement.

4 Americans and Europeans alike were fully aware that regular Croatian troops were fighting in BiH. Since the heavy pounding came from the Serb side, they were chosen to be held singularly responsible.

CHAPTER THIRTEEN

1 At the farewell luncheon I asked President Delors what his strongest impression was after several rounds of talks with the leadership in Yugoslavia. His answer was the lack of interest in the economic aspects of the situation and the overriding importance given the symbols of nationalism.

2 Representatives of the past, present, and future presidency of the Community. This could be at either ministerial or official level.

3 I must honestly confess that, from my vantage point as the Yugoslav ambassador with the Community, I fully shared this view.
4 Declaration on the Situation in Yugoslavia, Extraordinary European Political Co-operation Ministerial Meeting, The Hague, 5 July 1991.
5 British politician who had previously held the posts of minister of foreign affairs and secretary-general of NATO, and had also brought successfully to an end the negotiations on Zimbabwe.
6 Six months later Macedonia had still not been recognized. That prompted Kiro Gligorov, the president of Macedonia, to ask the Community a very relevant question: Does war have to break out in Macedonia for the republic to be recognized? In his view the Community seemed to be favouring recognition of those territories that were violently contested but disregarding those where independence was sought and gained peacefully.

CHAPTER FOURTEEN

1 As a neighbouring country Austria was understandably concerned about events in Yugoslavia. But the course of action this supposedly neutral country took towards the Yugoslav crisis was anything but neutral. It was the first country, even before Germany, to side openly with the territories that in the past had belonged to the Austro-Hungarian Empire, accepting uncritically and advocating loudly the contention that the issue was a confrontation between a democratic Croatia and a Communist Serbia.
2 The same month in which The Hague Conference opened with the expectation of a speedy and fruitful resolution of the political and military confrontation.
3 The only larger operation was in the Belgian Congo in the early sixties. At about the same time as the engagement of UN troops in Yugoslavia, the UN Cambodian operation started, involving an even larger number of troops and more financial resources.
4 Those imposed, for example, on South Africa, Rhodesia, Cuba, Iran, or Iraq.
5 At the same time the UN took over as lead international actor, the European Community accepted Lord Carrington's resignation as chair of The Hague Conference on Yugoslavia and appointed Lord David Owen instead. Cyrus Vance continued on for the UN.
6 There are reports that Milošević was furious at this rejection and read it as an open slap in the face. He spent hours arguing with the Bosnian Serb parliament to accept the plan and came away with only two votes heeding his advice. But as later events have shown, there is no denying that the Bosnian Serb rejection actually suited him.

CHAPTER FIFTEEN

1 The separation of Sweden and Norway and the division of Ireland are probably the only earlier cases.
2 "Duke" is not a hereditary or royal title. It is rather a designation of a high commanding rank in the Chetnik units of yesteryear, the modern version of which Šešelj has revived.

CHAPTER SIXTEEN

1 Greece has territorial claims against Albania, tabled at the Paris Peace Conference in 1946. It is concerned about the life and fate of about 400,000 Greeks living in the south of Albania, a region that Greece refers to as Northern Epyrus. Only in 1987 was a technical state of war between the two countries abandoned.
2 The Macedonians themselves have invented the sarcastic aphorism "Pitiful is the country for which Albania is the West."
3 While in Brussels I have had a number of opportunities to hear "informally," even from very high officials, what a tragic mistake it was to accept Greece into the European Community.

CHAPTER EIGHTEEN

1 Presented here is a selection of important events, not a detailed chronology.
2 The proposal was a slightly modified version of a previous proposal made by the ministers of foreign affairs of France (Juppé) and Germany (Kinkel) that had been widely circulated but never became official. The Contact Group, by taking over the main elements of the proposal, made it more powerful and credible since the group included both the United States and Russia.
3 This was best demonstrated during the hostage crisis in the summer of 1995 when, following a simple order by Milošević, delivered to Karadjić by the chief of Serbia's secret police, Milošević's demand that the hostages be released was immediately met.
4 The Z refers to the first letter of the name of Croatia's capital – Zagreb. The four refers to the four proposers of the plan: representatives of the United States, Russia, UN, and EU, led in this effort by the energetic US ambassador to Croatia Peter Galbraith.
5 There are various stories floating around to explain the phenomenal success of the Croatian army. The Croats, of course, favour the explanation that centres on their military prowess. Others suggest that it was the result of the demoralization of the Serb army and population in Croatia,

drained by four years of tension and suspense about their future. Still others, particularly in Serbia, believe that the easy conquest of Serb-held territories in Croatia can only be explained by a covert or tacit agreement between Milošević and Tudjman. In my view, all three were at work simultaneously. A tacit agreement between leaders is difficult to prove at this time but it seems clear that Tudjman must have been assured of Milošević's inaction before he ordered his troops to attack.

6 Robert Fraisure was the point-man for the United States until his tragic death in a road accident on Mount Igman, on his way to Sarajevo. Richard Holbrooke took over and became involved in an unprecedented shuttle diplomacy, first putting the principles of the accord into place, and then trying to work out the additional details.

7 In fact the document runs to close to 120 pages, which contain the Agreement itself and 12 annexes.

8 No precise figure is available at this time. Sometime in May of 1994 the Western media had somehow "established" that 200,000 people had been killed by that time. That figure has been kept in circulation, though in April of 1995 the Bosnian government revised these figures down to 140,000. My own "guestimate" is based on the following: a) it is reasonably certain that in Sarajevo there have been about 11,000 victims so far; b) Sarajevo constituted about 13 to 14 per cent of the prewar population of BiH; c) Sarajevo took by far the longest and heaviest pounding during the war; individual forays of Serbs into Foča, Bjeljina, Žepa, Srebrnica, etc., notwithstanding, it is unlikely that the rest of BiH took a heavier proportional toll than Sarajevo.

9 The Serbs will not accept easily handing over parts of Sarajevo that they had held throughout the war to the Muslim-Croat entity. They have asked for an extended period of transition, additional security guarantees, or both and say that if these are not provided they will pull out of Sarajevo completely. Should they pull out of Sarajevo, they will have created a situation that the peace-makers certainly did not expect when negotiating the agreement.

A Selected Bibliography of Further Readings

Yugoslavia has always attracted a fair amount of attention and there is a large body of literature covering this subject. Recent events have led to a host of new writings and the field is almost saturated with books and articles, not to mention newspapers and other media. What follows is a highly personal selection of further readings on the subject. The main criteria in suggesting this and not some other assortment of books have been the informative content of the suggested volumes and the author's attempt at an objective, non-partisan attitude toward the various national and nationalist claims on history and current events. Only books have been included, though there are numerous articles that are of high quality, informative, and relevant.

Among the books that take a longer, historical view of the ethnic relations in former Yugoslavia, the classic is Rebecca West's *Black Lamb and Grey Falcon* (New York: Viking Press, 1941). Another forceful account is found in Paul Lendvai, *Eagles in Cobwebs: Nationalism in the Balkans* (New York: Doubleday, 1969). A recent travelogue with numerous astute observations is Brian Hall's *The Impossible Country* (Boston: David Godine, 1994). The account by Ivo Banac, *The National Question in Yugoslavia: Origins, History, Politics* (Ithaca: Cornell University Press, 1984), is generally regarded as the best and most informative when it comes to discussing the creation of the country in 1918 and the immediate aftermath.

There are a number of books that describe and analyse the creation and functioning of the so-called "Second Yugoslavia" that was created during the Second World War. Among these are Leonard Cohen, *The Socialist Pyramid: Elites and Power in Yugoslavia* (Oakville: Mosaic Press, 1989); Bogdan Denitch, *The Legitimation of a Revolution: The Yugoslav Case* (New Haven: Yale University Press, 1979); Harold

Lydall, *Yugoslav Socialism: Theory and Practice* (Oxford/New York: Oxford University Press, 1984); Christopher Prout, *Market Socialism in Yugoslavia* (Oxford/New York: Oxford University Press, 1985); Sabrina Ramet, *Nationalism and Federalism in Yugoslavia*, 2d ed. (Bloomington: Indiana University Press, 1993); Dennison Rusinow, *The Yugoslav Experiment, 1948–1974* (Berkeley: University of California Press, 1977).

Good accounts and analyses of the fateful events and decisions made during the 1960s, when market liberalism was introduced, and the 1970s, when this process was reversed, are offered in Stephen Burg, *Cohesion and Conflict in Socialist Yugoslavia: Political Decisions Making since 1966* (Princeton: Princeton University Press, 1983); and Lenard Cohen and Paul Warwick, *Political Cohesion in a Fragile Mosaic: The Yugoslav Experience* (Boulder: Westview Press, 1983).

The events of the 1980s that led to the final destruction of Yugoslavia are best described and analysed in the following books: Lenard Cohen, *Broken Bonds: The Disintegration of Yugoslavia* (Boulder: Westview Press, 1993); Bogdan Denitch, *Ethnic Nationalism: The Tragic Death of Yugoslavia* (Minneapolis: University of Minnesota Press, 1994); James Gapinski, *Economic Structure and Failure of Yugoslavia* (Westport: Praeger, 1993); Misha Glenny, *The Fall of Yugoslavia* (New York: Penguin, 1992); Vladimir Gligorov, *Why Do Countries Break Up?: The Case of Yugoslavia* (Uppsala, Sweden: Acta Universitatis Upsaliansis, 1994); Branka Magas, *Destruction of Yugoslavia* (London: Verso, 1993); Dennison Rusinow (Ed), *Yugoslavia: A Fractured Federalism* (Washington, D.C.: Wilson Center Press, 1988); Laslo Sekelj, *Yugoslavia: The Process of Disintegration* (Highland Lakes, N.J.: Atlantic Research and Publications, distributed by Columbia University Press, 1993); and Susan Woodword, *The Balkan Tragedy* (Washington, D.C.: Brookings Institute, 1995).

Three books worthy of attention on Bosnia and Hercegovina, which was the center of attention in the last few years, are Razia Ali and Lawrence Lifschultz, eds., *Why Bosnia? The Writings on the Balkan War* (Stony Creek, Conn: Pamphleteer's Press, 1993); Robert Donia and John Fine Jr, *Bosnia and Hercegovina: A Tradition Betrayed* (New York: Columbia University Press, 1994), and Noel Malkolm, *Bosnia: A Short History* (London: Macmillan, 1994).

Finally, a recent collection of reflections on what happened by scholars from the region is offered in Payam Akhavan and Robert Howse, eds, *Yugoslavia – The Former and Future* (Washington, D.C.: The Brookings Institution, 1995).

Index

Adžić, Blagoje, 168
Albania: early history, 21, 34; interest in Macedonia, 242–4, 246; rejects Communism, 139–40; Second World War, 65; Yugoslavia's dissolution, 125
Albanians: in Kosovo, 93, 101–5, 143, 239–42, 273; nationalism, 82–3; not in Tito's forces, 68
Alexander, King of Serbia and Yugoslavia, 48, 55–9, 60
Alexander the Great, 27
Alphabets, 15–17, 28, 30
Arafat, Yasser, 81
Arkan: see Raznjatovic, Zeljko
Atheism, 18
Atrocities: by ultra-nationalists, 169; by Ustashi, 63, 65–6; war in BiH, 182–4, 186, 271
Austria: First World War, 43, 45; Yugoslav history, 29, 33; Yugoslavia's dissolution, 125, 205, 217
Austro-Hungarian Empire, 17, 23, 25–6, 35

Baker, James, 158, 211

Balkans: future, 252, 256–7; today, 135–6, 245–51
Balkan Wars: Macedonia, 27; Serbia, 31
Banja Luka, BiH, 185, 273
Banovina, 60–1
Belgium, 205
Belgrade, Serbia, 74, 105, 157
BiH: see Bosnia and Herzegovina
Bihác, 270, 273
Blue Helmets: see Peacekeepers
Bogumils, 18
Borba (newspaper), 120, 149
Borders: dissolution of Yugoslavia, 234–5; ethnic vs administrative, 10; future, 251–3; history, 35; international recognition, 53; today, 249
Borovo selo, Croatia, 157
Bosanska Krajina, BiH, 181
Bosnia and Herzegovina (BiH): Bosnian Army offensive, 272; compromise solution, 281; division into two entities, 269; economy, 24; elections, 146, 151, 174,

283; escalating tension, 174–8, 209; ethnicity, 22–3; future, 252–4, 263–4, 277–84; intelligentsia, 117; maps, 216; Muslim-Croat federal state, 267, 269; Muslim population, 277; parliamentary reform, 147; political history, 23–4, 68; refugees, 171, 175, 181–2; rejection of peace plans, 266; religions, 18–19; Second World War, 65; target of Serb and Croat nationalism, 278–9; UN peacekeepers, 212–13, 215; Ustashi, 66; war, 173, 178–88, 223
Bosniaks: see Muslim National Party, BiH
Bosnian-Croat military alliance, 267
Bosnians, misnomer, 187
Boutros-Ghali, Boutros, 208, 212
Brezhnev, Leonid, 81
Brezhnev Doctrine, 75
Brioni Agreement, 163
Britain: First World War, 44, 46; peace-keepers, 215; Second World War, 62–3; and Tito, 67; war

in BiH, 217, 219, 268; war in Croatia, 205
Broz, Josip: see Tito
Brussels, Belgium, 209, 213
Bulgaria: First World War, 45; future, 246; interest in Macedonia, 27–8, 33, 243; Second World War, 63
Bush, George, 173

Canada, 268
Carrington, Lord, 194–9, 206, 207
Carter, Jimmy, 270
Carter cease-fire, 270–1
Cheney, Richard, 218
Chetniks, 66–8, 179
China, 268
Chirac, Jacques, 266
Christianity, 17–19, 36–7
Civilians: numbers killed, 235–6; war in BiH, 178–9, 182–6, 212–13; war in Croatia, 169–70, 171
Civil rights, 3
Clerical Party, Slovenia, 47
Clinton, Bill, 215, 218, 266
Cohn-Bendit, Daniel, 74
Cold War: aftermath, 131–7, 205, 236; defence focus, 132; raging, 72
Communism: brought atheism, 18; lack of civil rights, 7; on nationalism, 106
Communist Party of Croatia, 113–14
Communist Party of Serbia, 100, 101
Communist Party of Slovenia, 112–13
Communist Party of Yugoslavia: and JNA, 121; post-unification, 57–8; post-war elections, 68–9; power, 71, 73–6; prepares for war,

67; under Tito, 62, 66; weakens, 91, 110, 143–4, 149
Conference on Security and Co-operation in Europe, 136–7, 139, 231, 248
Constitution: 1920, 55–8; 1931, 60; 1946, 68; 1974, 75–6, 98, 225
Constitution, Serbian, 104, 105–6
Constitutional reform (1990), 146–8
Contact Group, 268; peace proposals, 268–9, 275
Corfu Declaration (1917), 47, 54, 55–6
Ćosić, Dobrica, 108, 116–17, 232–3
Council of Europe, 149
Council of the Anti-Fascist Alliance of Yugoslavia, 68
CPY: see Communist Party of Yugoslavia
Croat banovina, 61
Croatia: authentic nation, 21; backs Kosovo, 94, 97, 103, 114; dissolution of Yugoslavia, 233–5; economy, 26–7, 88; elections, 114, 144–5, 231; escalating tension, 153, 155–9, 165–6; ethnicity, 24–5; future, 256, 263–4; independence, 154, 161, 207, 231, 237; intelligentsia, 117; interest in BiH, 175; and JNA, 122, 123, 152; media, 120; parliamentary reform, 146–8; and peace terms, 275; political history, 25–6, 38–40; Second World War, 63–4, 65; separatist, 59–60; under Tito, 74–5; unification, 47–8; UN peace-keepers, 206–10, 223; US military advi-

sors, 271; Ustashi, 63–8, 151–2, 234; war, 166–73; weaponry, 152, 154, 167
Croatian Democratic Alliance, 145, 234
Croatian National Guard, 156, 165–6
Croatian Party of the Right, 55–6
Croatian Peasant Party, 42, 55–6, 59
Croato-Serbian Coalition, 41–2
Croats: future, 263–4; in BiH, 175, 177–8, 267; military force, 271, 273; national awakening, 38–9; nationalism, 113–14, 145, 151–2, 234, 236; political structure, 53; South Slav unity, 40–3; under Tito, 69; view of Marković, 150; war in BiH, 178–84, 186–8, 214, 219
CSCE: see Conference on Security and Co-operation in Europe
Culture, 3, 108–9
Cyrillic alphabet, 15–17
Czechoslovakia, 75

Dalmatia, 25
Dayton Peace Accord, 266, 267, 274; key provisions, 275–7; putting into effect, 280–4
Delors, Jacques, 158
Democratic Federal Yugoslavia: see Yugoslavia, unification (second)
Democratic Party (1920), 55
DEMOS, 144
Desert Storm: see Gulf War
Djilas, Milovan, 71
Drašković, Vuk, 233
Drina River, 269

Drnovšek, Janez, 141, 149
Drvar, BiH, 273
Dubrovnik, Croatia, 171–2, 230
Dušan, Emperor of Serbia, 27, 30–1
Dutschke, Rudi, 74

Eastern Europe, 132–3, 136
Economy: BiH, 24; Croatia, 26–7; foreign aid, 85–6; future, 258–9; Macedonia, 28, 244–5; Montenegro, 29; Serbia, 32–3; Slovenia, 29–30, 111–12; today, 231–2, 248; under Marković, 89–90, 149–50; under Tito, 71–2, 75–6; weakened after Tito, 83–5, 87–8
Education, centralization, 108–9
Elections: in BiH, 276; post-war, 68; pre-war, 55, 58, 60–1; 1989, 143; 1990, 144–6, 150–1, 174, 231, 233–4; 1992, 232, 239–40
Entente, 44–6, 49
Ethnic fighting: BiH, 178–9, 181, 183, 186; characterizes war, 161; in Croatia, 169–71; see also Chetniks, Ustashi
Ethnicity: at unification, 51–2; banovinas, 61–2; BiH, 22–3, 174–5; Croatia, 24–5; the future, 252–3; JNA, 122; Kosovo, 93; Macedonia, 27; Montenegro, 28; root of war, 160; Serbia, 30; Slovenia, 29
Europe, today, 248
European Bank for Reconstruction and Development, 248

European Community: Brioni Agreement, 163; Conference on Yugoslavia, 206, 223; future, 255–7; and Kosovo, 241; post–Cold War, 133–5, 139; recognizes BiH, 178, 211; recognizes Croatia, 207; recognizes Slovenia, 164, 207; supports unity, 141, 149–50; today, 237–8, 246, 248–9; war in BiH, 176–7, 213, 215, 217, 231
European Community Commission, 158

Federal Presidency: escalating tension, 155, 158; instituted, 76; post-Tito, 81–2; reject peacekeeper request, 205–6; war in Slovenia, 162–3
Federal Republic of Yugoslavia: see Yugoslavia, today
Ferdinand, Archduke of Austria, 23, 32, 43
First World War: begins, 43; BiH, 23; fate of Yugoslavia, 44–7; Montenegro, 28, 51; Serbia, 32, 51
Foreign policy: evolution, 62–3; under Tito, 72–3
France: First World War, 44–5; peace-keepers, 215; Second World War, 62–3; war in BiH, 217, 219, 268; war in Croatia, 205
Future: co-operation, 254–5, 264–5; economy, 258–9; international powers, 255–8; multiple solutions, 251; nationalism, 259–64; political structures, 258; war, 239, 241–2, 245–6, 249, 252

G-7 Summit, 269
Garašanin, Ilija, 37–8, 40, 116
Gazimestan, Serbia, 141
Geneva, Switzerland, 206–7, 213–14
Genscher, Hans-Dietrich, 139
German-Soviet Pact, 66
Germany: attitude to war, 165; First World War, 45; increasing power, 134–5, 139; post-unification, 132, 137; recognizes Croatia, 167, 172, 207; recognizes Slovenia, 207; Second World War, 62–4, 65, 66; and Tito, 67; today, 246; war in BiH, 215, 217; Yugoslav history, 23, 29
Glavaš, Branimir, 170
Goražde, Bosnia, 181, 268, 272
Gorbachev, Mikhail, 173
Governments, unstable, 58–9
"Greater Croatia," 277, 278, 281
"Greater Serbia," 276–7, 278, 281
Greece: and Albania, 242; and Macedonia, 223, 243–4, 245–6; war in BiH, 215, 217; Yugoslav history, 27–8, 33–4
Guerrilla warfare, BiH, 184
Gulf War, 138, 205, 218

Habsburg Empire, 26, 37–9, 44
The Hague, The Netherlands, 213, 230
HDZ (Hrvatska Demokratska Zajednica): see Croatian Democratic Alliance
Helsinki Agreement, 136

Herzeg-Bosna (Croatian
state), 183
Herzegovina: see Bosnia
and Herzegovina
Hitler, Adolf, 62–3
Hostage taking, 268, 272
HRSS Party, Croatia, 54
Hrvatska Demokratska
Zajednica: see Croatian
Democratic Alliance
HSK: see Croato-Serbian
Coalition
HSS Party, 63
Hua Guofeng, 81
Humanitarian aid, 212–13,
219, 238
Human rights, 136, 231,
249
Hungary: Second World
War, 63, 65; today, 245;
Yugoslav history, 25,
33; Yugoslavia's dissolu-
tion, 125

Illyrian movement, 39
Ilok, Croatia, 166
Implementation force
(IFOR), 276
Independence: Croatia,
154, 161, 207, 231, 237;
Slovenia, 154, 161, 164,
207, 231
INL: see Interim National
Legislature
Intelligentsia, 115–18
Interim National Legisla-
ture, 54
International Bank for
Reconstruction and
Development, 141
International Monetary
Fund, 85, 141
International powers:
affect Yugoslavia, 8–9;
bungling in BiH, 274;
economic aid, 85–6;
future of Balkans, 255–
8; recognize Yugoslavia,
53; seek peace, 246–7;
support unity, 149–50;

view of Tito, 70–1, 73,
81; view of Yugoslav
dissolution, 158–9; view
of Yugoslavia post–Cold
War, 137–8; war in BiH,
182–4, 186–8; war in
Croatia, 173; war in Slo-
venia, 163–4; Yugosla-
vian dissolution, 10–11,
124–7, 236–8; see also
specific countries,
United Nations
Islam, 17–19
Italy: First World War, 44,
46, 53; inter-war years,
62–3; Second World
War, 65; and Tito, 67;
Yugoslav history, 23,
29, 33
Ivanić, Momčilo, 57
Izetbegović, Alija: asks for
peace-keepers, 217; and
Dayton Accord, 266;
leads Muslims, 146, 177;
seeks BiH sovereignty,
176–7; seeks compro-
mise, 148, 158, 174–5;
267; war in BiH, 179–80,
186, 187

JNA: see Yugoslav People's
Army
Jović, Bora, 103, 147–8,
155, 157, 158
Jugoslovenska narodna
armija: see Yugoslav
People's Army

Kadijevic, Veljko, 155,
168, 206
Karadjić (Bosnian Serb
leader), 182, 215, 233,
270, 273
Karadjordje (Serbian
leader), 36
Karadžić, Vuk, 37
Kardelj, Edvard, 75, 108
Kingdom of Serbs, Croats,
and Slovenes: see Yugo-
slavia, unification (first)

Kissinger, Henry, 277
Knin, Croatia, 271
Kninska Krajina, Croatia,
142, 152, 156, 170, 208–
10
Koršec, Anton, 44, 47
Kosovo: autonomy, 93–7;
Battle of, 23, 31, 105;
ethnic mix, 31, 142,
143; future, 253; history,
30, 65; relations with
Serbia, 99–100, 101–2,
103–5; student revolt,
82–3, 93; today, 239–
42
Kozyrev, Andrej, 217
Krajina region, 267, 273
Krajišnik, Momčilo, 174
Kreigher, Sergej, 84–5
Kucan, Milan, 144
Kvaternik, Eugen, 39–40

Languages, 19–21, 33, 37,
39
Latin alphabet, 15–17
Ljubljana, Slovenia, 113,
142, 163
Loncar, Budimir, 149
London, England, 213–14
Luxembourg, 158

Maastricht Treaty, 255
Macedonia: authentic
nation, 21; economy, 28;
elections, 145–6, 151,
231; ethnicity, 27; intelligentsia, 117; name
struggles, 223; parlia-
mentary reform, 147;
political history, 27–8;
seeks Yugoslav unity,
174; separatist, 59;
today, 239, 242–5, 246;
US troops in, 273
Macedonians: in Tito's
forces, 68; political
structure, 53
Maček, Vlatko, 63
MacKenzie, Lewis, 213
Magyars, 39

Marković, Ante: attempts orderly dissolution, 154–5; and Milošević, 141; reform strategy, 89–90, 148–50, 153; seeks compromise, 113, 151
Marković, Mirjana, 144
Marković, Svetozar, 38
Maslenica Gorge, 173
Media: role in dissolution, 118–20, 148, 156; under Marković, 149; war in BiH, 182, 187, 212; war in Croatia, 170, 171–2; war in Slovenia, 162
"Memorandum on the Position of Serbia in Yugoslavia," 97–100, 116, 227
Mesić, Stipe, 103, 158, 205
Mihailović, Draža, 66, 67
Milošević, Slobodan: change in strategy, 269; and Ćosić, 116; and Dayton Accord, 266; future, 261–2; and Kosovo, 241; and Macedonia, 243; and media, 118; on economy, 85; on Federal Presidency, 155; on unity, 156; on war, 169; popularity, 92, 270; prepares for war, 156–8; reconciliation with Karadjić, 274; Serbian nationalism, 97, 100–6, 143–4, 229–30, 232–3; sets sights on Yugoslavia, 141–2; and Tudjman, 145; and UN peace-keepers, 206, 208, 210; war in BiH, 175–6, 186, 211, 215; war in Croatia, 114, 173
Mitterrand, François, 173
Mladić, Ratko, 181, 182, 208, 215
Mondale, Walter, 81
Monetary system, Serbian withdrawals, 153–4

Montenegrins: and CPY, 143; in JNA, 122, 178; in Kosovo, 101–2; political structure, 53
Montenegro: considers leaving, 229; disputable nation, 21; economy, 29; ethnicity, 28; First World War, 45–6, 51; and JNA, 122, 123; and Kosovo, 241–2; parliamentary reform, 147; political history, 28–9, 36; Second World War, 65; supports JNA, 169; third Yugoslavia, 223; unification, 48; war in BiH, 211
Mostar, Bosnia, 179, 183, 213, 215, 269
Muslim-Croat federation, in Bosnia, 267, 273, 275
Muslim-Croat military alliance, 267, 273
Muslim National Party, BiH, 176
Muslims: campaign against, 176; future, 263–4, 281; in BiH, 66, 177–8, 277; in Tito's forces, 68; nationalism, 21, 236; support Yugoslav unity, 175; war in BiH, 178–85, 187–8, 213, 214–15

National consciousness, defined, 4
National Council of the Slovenes, Croats, and Serbs, 47–8
National Front, 68
National ideology, defined, 4
Nationalism: aggressive, 4–5, 227, 235, 250, 252, 259–62; Albanian, 82–3; Croatian, 74, 113–14, 151–2, 234; Croato-Serbian, 41; defined, 3–4;

dissolution of Yugoslavia, 6, 7–9, 106, 107, 235–6; future, 259–64, 283; and intelligentsia, 115–18; Serbian, 95–106, 112–13, 227–33; Slovenian, 107–13, 234; smoulders in 1989–90, 90–2; today, 255–6; under Tito, 69, 70
National movements: object of, 5; phases of, 5; Yugoslavia, 3–4
National Radical Party, 55–6
Nations: defined, 6; disputable, 21; Yugoslavia as a whole, 21–2
NATO, 132–3, 136–8, 217–19, 237–8, 266, 268, 278, 283; involvement in bombings, 268, 272–3
Nedić (Serbian General), 65
Nemanja, King of Serbia, 30
The Netherlands, Brioni Agreement, 164
New York, USA, 213
Nikola I, King of Montenegro, 28, 48
North Atlantic Treaty Organization: see NATO

Obrenović, Miloš, 36
October Revolution, Russia, 45, 47
Ohrid, Macedonia, 166
Olympic Games, 1984, 24
Organization for Security and Cooperation in Europe, 276
Osijek, Croatia, 170
Ottoman Empire: brought Islam, 17; military frontier, 26; ruled BiH, 23; ruled east, south, and central, 17, 35–6; ruled Macedonia, 27; ruled Serbia, 31; thrown out

of Balkans, 43; *see also*
Turkey
Owen, Lord David, 199,
214–15, 219
Owen-Stoltenberg Plan,
266

Paganism, 17
Pakrac, Slavonia, 157
Pale, 270
Panić, Milan, 232, 239–40
Parliamentary reform
1990, 146–8
Pašić, Nikola, 44, 46–7
Pavelić, Ante, 59–60, 65
Peace-keepers: in BiH,
212–13, 215; in Croatia,
206–10; large numbers
needed, 184; probable
failure, 217–19; sought
from UN, 176, 205, 206–
7
Pelivan, Jure, 174
Perez de Cuellar, Javier,
206
Perišić (General of JNA),
179
Persian Gulf: *see* Gulf War
Peter I, King of Serbia, 32
Peter II, King of Yugo-
slavia, 61, 63
Plitvice (national park),
157
Poland, 91, 139
Political history: BiH, 23–
4; Croatia, 25–6, 38–40;
Macedonia, 27–8; Mon-
tenegro, 28–9; Serbia,
30–2, 36–8; Slovenia, 29
Political parties: at unification, 55–6; *see also* specific parties
Political structures: after
1990 elections, 146–7;
and dissolution, 6–7;
future, 258; post-unifi-
cation, 52–62; under
Marković, 90–1; under
Tito, 73–5, 225; weak-
ened after Tito, 86–8

Porphyrogenitus (histo-
rian), 40
Privatization, 90, 153
Propaganda, 278–9; *see
also* Media

Radić, Stjepan, 42, 48, 54–
7, 58–9
Radical Party, 38, 44
Rapid Reaction Force, 272
Ražnjatović, Željko, 170,
179, 241
Reform Party, 150–1
Refugees: from BiH, 276;
from Croatia to BiH,
171, 175; numbers, 236;
within BiH, 181–2;
Religions, 17–19, 28, 30,
33
Republic development
fund: and Croatia, 88;
and Serbia, 98–9; and
Slovenia, 88, 111–12
Republika Srpska, 185,
275
River Sava, Bosnia, 181
Romania, 33, 245
Russia: and Bosnian
Serbs, 268; and United
States, 278, 282; future,
256; peace-keepers, 215,
267, 275; sanctions, 211,
231; today, 246–7, 249;
war in BiH, 213, 215,
217; Yugoslav history,
23, 45, 47; *see also*
Soviet Union

Samuel, King of Mace-
donia, 27
Sanctions, 167, 182, 184,
206, 210–12, 214, 231–2,
261, 270
San Stefano Agreement,
23
Santer, Jacques, 158
Sarajevo, Bosnia, 212–13,
214, 266; accord, 207;
assassination of Ferdi-
nand, 23; fighting

begins, 178; interna-
tional control, 269;
Olympic Games 1984,
24; rally for unity, 175;
siege, 181, 182–4, 185–
6
Second World War, 23, 26,
29, 62–3, 65–7
Security Council: *see*
United Nations
Self-administration, 3
Serbia: authentic nation,
21; constitution, 104,
105–6; dissolution of
Yugoslavia, 227–33;
economy, 32–3, 98–9;
elections, 143, 150–1,
231–2, 239–40; esca-
lating tension, 154, 155,
156–9; ethnicity, 30;
First World War, 44–8,
51; future, 256–7; intelligentsia, 116; and JNA,
122, 123, 169; and
Kosovo, 94–7, 99–100,
103–5; and Macedonia,
243; media, 118, 120;
parliamentary reform,
147–8, 153; political history, 28, 30–2, 36–8; and
Romania, 245; Second
World War, 63, 65; third
Yugoslavia, 223; under
Tito, 74–5, 225; unifica-
tion, 48; and UN peace-
keepers, 207–8; and
Vojvodina, 94–7, 103;
war in BiH, 175, 211;
war in Slovenia, 142–3;
weaponry, 180
Serbian Academy of
Sciences and Arts, 97,
116
Serbian militia in Croatia,
152, 165–6, 169
Serbian Radical Party, 261
Serbs: aggressive nation-
alism, 227–33, 282; in
BiH, 96, 142, 175–8;
Chetniks, 66–8; and

Contact Group proposal, 269; and CPY, 143; in Croatia, 96, 100, 114, 142, 145, 151–2, 156, 165–6, 272; and hostage-taking, 268, 272; in JNA, 122, 178; in Kosovo, 101–2, 113, 142, 239–42; in Tito's forces, 68; killed by Ustashi, 65–6; languages, 39; national awakening, 36–7, 104–5; nationalism, 95–106, 112–13, 164, 236, 259–62; political structure, 52–3; rejection of Owen-Stoltenberg plan, 266–7; South Slav unity, 43; split in strategy toward BiH, 270; under Tito, 69, 70; view of Marković, 150–1; war in BiH, 178–88, 213, 214–15, 219; war in Croatia, 168–9, 170–2, 173
Šešelj, "Duke," 229, 233
Skopje, Macedonia, 243
Slavonia, Croatia, 25, 171, 209
Slovakia, 245
Slovenes: in Tito's forces, 68; nationalism, 234; political structure, 53; South Slav unity, 43–4; view of Marković, 150
Slovenia: authentic nation, 21; backs Kosovo, 94, 97, 103, 112; dissolution of Yugoslavia, 233–5; economy, 29–30, 88, 111–12, 223; elections, 144–5, 231, 233–4; escalating tension, 142–4, 153, 156–9; ethnicity, 29; future, 256; independence, 154, 161, 164, 207, 231; intelligentsia, 117; and JNA, 122, 123, 153; media, 119; nationalism,

107–13, 145, 278; parliamentary reform, 146–8; political history, 29; Second World War, 65; under Tito, 74–5; unification, 47; war, 161–3; weaponry, 152
Slovenian army, 156
Socialist Party, Serbia, 261
Social structure, 3
Solution, defined, 250
Soviet Union: collapse, 131, 139, 224; Communist Party, 58; post–Cold Crisis, 138; post–Cold War, 205; Second World War, 62, 66–7; Yugoslavian dissolution, 124; see also Russia
Spain, 215, 219
Split, Croatia, 156
Srebrnica, Bosnia, 181, 272
Stalin, Joseph, 70–1
Starčević, Ante, 39–40
Stoltenberg, Torval, 215, 219
Strossmayer, Josip, 40
Student revolt, Kosovo, 82–3, 93
Supilo, Frane, 46
Šuvar, Stipe, 114

Territorial division, of Bosnia (51:49), 269
Thatcher, Margaret, 218
Tirana, Albania, 243
Tito: characterization, 76–8; death, 76, 81; economic system, 71–2, 75–6; foreign policy, 72–3; and JNA, 121–2; operates from BiH, 23–4; political system, 73–5, 225; post-war, 68–9; schism with Stalin, 70–1; Second World War, 67–8; Slovenes strike at image, 109–10; takes over CPY, 66

Tomislav (Croatian ruler), 25
Treaty of Versailles, 53
Trpimir (Croatian ruler), 25
Trumbić, Ante, 46
Tudjman, Franjo: asks for peace-keepers, 217; and Dayton Accord, 266; elected, 114, 145; escalating tension, 151–2, 156–8; today, 234; and UN peace-keepers, 206, 210; war in BiH, 175, 179–80, 186; war in Croatia, 158, 166, 173
Turkey: today, 245–6; war in BiH, 217; see also Ottoman Empire
Tuzla, Bosnia, 181
Tvrtko I (Bosnian ruler), 23

Unitarism, 41–4
United Kingdom: see Britain
United Nations: arms embargo, 271; Charter, 256; control of heavy guns, 267; efforts to end war, 139, 213–15; future, 257; Gulf War, 139, 205, 218; and Kosovo, 241; peace-keepers in BiH, 176, 212–13, 215, 217–19; peace-keepers in Croatia, 205–10; recognizes Macedonia, 244; sanctions, 167, 182, 184, 206, 210–12, 214, 231–2, 261, 270, 272; today, 126, 237, 246
United Nations Protection Force, 208–9
United States: Cold War, 132; First World War, 44–5; future, 257–8; Gulf War, 138, 205; involvement in Dayton

Accord, 266, 280, 282; peace initiative, 270–1; peace-keepers, 215, 243; presence in Europe, 133–4; recognizes BiH, 178, 211; recognizes Bosnian-Serb state, 273; safe areas, 268, 270, 272; sanctions, 211, 231; supports unity, 141, 150, 158; and Tito, 67; today, 126, 207, 237–8, 246, 248–9; war in BiH, 184, 206, 213–15, 217–19, 268
USSR: *see* Soviet Union
Ustashi: fears of revival, 151–2; ruled Croatia, 63, 65–6; still remembered, 234; and Tito, 67–8

Vance, Cyrus, 167, 206–8, 214–15
Vatican, 53
Vidovdan Constitution: *see* Constitution 1920
Vincent, Richard, 218
Vitezović, Pavao, 38
Vlassi, Azem, 104
Vojvodina, Serbia, 93–7, 103, 245
von Ribbentrop, Joachim, 63
Vrhovec, Josip, 86–7, 94, 108
Vukovar, Croatia, 25, 157, 166, 171, 206, 230, 272

War: begins, 161; character of, 160; future, 239, 241–2, 245–6, 249, 252, 283; in BiH, 173, 178–88; in Croatia, 166–73; in Slovenia, 161–3; preparations for, 156–7, 165–6
War-lords, 169–70
Warsaw Pact, 132, 133, 136, 137
Washington Agreements, 1994, 275
Weaponry: Croatia, 152, 154, 167; Serbs in BiH, 180; taken by JNA, 152; UN embargo, 167, 182, 184, 206
Western Europe: conditions of aid, 133, 136; future, 255–7; poor economies, 133
Western European Union (WEU), 138, 206
Western Herzegovina, 267
Wilson, Woodrow, 45
World Bank, 85, 248, 276

Yeltsin, Boris, 215
Youth, Slovenia, 109–10, 111
Yugoslav Academy of Sciences, Zagreb, 40
Yugoslav Committee, 44, 46–7, 54
Yugoslavia: dissolution, 223–4, 226–38; escalating tension, 141–59; fall of Communism, 140; forces of creation, 48–50; future, 254–5, 264–5; inter-war years, 53–62; maps 1945–92, 16; maps, impact of empires on, 18; post–Cold War, 137–8; post-Tito, 91–2; Second World War, 62–4, 65; size, 15; today, 223, 228; under Tito, 225; unification (first), 44, 48, 51–3, 60; unification (second), 68; unitarism, 36, 41–2, 44–8
Yugoslav National Party, 60
Yugoslav People's Army (JNA): BiH, 175, 177, 178–80, 185, 211, 213; Croatia, 152–3, 165, 166–9, 171–2; future, 262; and Jović, 155; led by Tito, 82; and Marković, 155; Serbia, 153–4; Slovenia, 109, 110–11, 153, 162–3, 231; and UN peace-keepers, 207–8; Yugoslavian dissolution, 121–4, 156–7, 160–1
YUTEL (television station), 120, 149

Z-4 plan, 271
Zagreb, Croatia, 74, 209
Žepa, Bosnia, 181, 272
ZNG: *see* Croatian National Guard